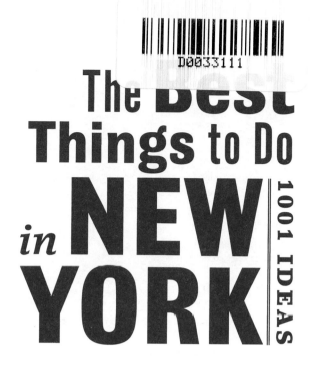

# The Best Things to Do in *NEW YORK*

## 1001 IDEAS

By Caitlin Leffel and Jacob Lehman

UNIVERSE PUBLISHING
A Division of Rizzoli International Publications

First published in the United States of America in 2006
by Universe Publishing
A Division of Rizzoli International Publications, Inc.
300 Park Avenue South
New York, NY 10010
www.rizzoliusa.com

2007 2008 2009 / 10 9 8 7 6 5 4 3 2

Distributed in the U.S. trade by Random House, New York

Designed by Susan Van Horn for Headcase Design
Printed in the United States of America

ISBN-13: 978-0-7893-1398-0
Library of Congress Catalog Control Number: 2006906702

# DEDICATION

*CL*

To my dad, who's been showing me great things about New York all my life; Alex, the best thing I found in New York; and in memory of my mom, who New York will always miss.

*JL*

To David and Melanie, Michael and Rosa, and Maryana, all of whom have made New York my second home.

# A note about maps and subways:

A good map and a MetroCard can get you pretty much anywhere you need to go in this city.

For each entry, we've listed the closest subway stations and lines that stop at them, but keep in mind that the subway that is most convenient can depend on your starting location and route, and that some trains run only on certain days or hours. Also, train lines are subject to service changes and suspensions on evenings and weekends. A full system map is available online at www.mta.info, and information on service changes are listed there as well. The MTA website also has maps and information about buses in the five boroughs.

The best maps we've found are published by Streetwise. They have over a dozen maps for New York City, including maps for Manhattan, Brooklyn, the Bronx, and Queens, plus several detailed neighborhood maps, maps focused on cultural activities, bus and subway maps, and address finders. Streetwise maps are available at bookstores and travel stores allover, or you can order online at www.streetwisemaps. N.B. They do not currently offer a map for Staten Island.

# TABLE OF CONTENTS

# ACKNOWLEDGMENTS

Whatever the body of work, acknowledgments often begin from the premise that it would not have been possible to create it without the people named. This book is no different, except that in this case, it's true in more ways than one.

The first thanks goes to the people at Universe who trusted us with this book in the first place—Charles Miers, Ellen Nidy, and Kathleen Jayes. Another thanks to Kathleen, our editor, for helping us persevere through this wonderful but unwieldy project with her hard work, patience and encouragement. Also thanks to Nancy King, our copyeditor, and Tricia Levi, whose contributions included a mastery of the subway system for which we are extremely grateful.

We would especially like to thank our expert contributors— Rick Bell, Joseph O. Holmes, Bret Watson, David Masello, Andrea Strong, Francisco Liuzzi, Laura Dave, Pavia Rosati, Wendy Mitchell and A.J. Jacobs—for their expertise, generosity, and enthusiasm when we contacted them (or, in one case, accosted them at the gym) about contributing to this book. We'd also like to thank Alison Lowenstein, who also generously shared her NYC expertise with us, and Allan Ishac, whose ideas for great things to do in New York are limitless.

Finally, we would like to thank all of the people—friends, family members, acquaintances, and a few that we never even met—who shared their personal lists of bests with us over the last year and a half. Your tips were invaluable, and through them we discovered many, many wonderful things about New York. There are too many of you to name, but you know who you are, and you can find your suggestions all over the book.

# INTRODUCTION

**N**ew York is the ultimate metropolis, a true melting pot, a city with an ocean, rivers, lakes, islands, and the sound; home to some of the world's premier art and culture, the restaurant capital of the world, and the city that never sleeps. Yes, there's a lot you can do here. But with so many activities, across so many areas, all the time, it is no small task to wrap your head around the infinite number of offerings, and to uncover all the treats hidden in the city's nooks and crannies. Plus, among all the possible things that one can do, there are some that are better than others, and more than a few (1,001, as we found out) that are truly, unequivocally great. In *The Best Things to Do in New York*, we have crossed genres and boroughs to find the city's best offerings. A city guide like no other, we have gone beyond locations and events to tap into the variety of experiences in this city, from $10 manicures to $700 dinners; subterranean wonders to views from staggering heights; edifying classes and offbeat activities to classic haunts and historic landmarks—and everything in between.

When Jacob and I were first approached about doing this book, I remember thinking "One thousand and one—how are we ever going to come up with that many really good things to do?" Having grown up in New York, I was acutely aware of the city's riches—world-class museums, historic sites, glamorous shops, restaurants of every shape, size, and taste—and I certainly appreciated my proximity to such largesse. But despite their elite status in guidebooks and tour itineraries, great treasures alone do not best things make. As anyone who has fought crowds, stood in interminable lines, or borne unsubstantiated attitude can tell you, it is the quality of the overall experience that catapults an activity over the bar of the simply impressive and into the realm of the supremely special and indisputably enjoyable. As I happily discovered, there are plenty of the latter type of experiences to be had here, things that are wonderful, incredible, and exceptional in more ways than I could have imagined. In this book, we have drawn from months of research and hundreds of visits to select what we believe are the best experiences of this city, and laid them out as specifically as possible. Visiting the Met, for instance, *can* be a wonderful experience—but, frankly, it can also be frightfully overwhelming. So instead of simply telling you to visit, we've suggested taking a museum highlights tour, and making an appointment for a private viewing of the drawings collections, a special amenity offered by the museum that is easily overlooked in the shadow of its grandeur. We also aimed to be both open-minded and critical, which meant trying things that may not have been to our particular taste, and not including entries for stock New York activities unless they satisfied our exacting criteria for a "best thing." Certain things, which will remain nameless, did not make the cut because—despite their fame or reputation or longevity—they were not exceedingly pleasant experiences when viewed objectively. In other cities, fame or longevity might have carried more weight, but in New York, the competition is stiff.

Also contributing to my initial feeling of being daunted by the scope of the project was that, in my adult life, I confess, I had become lazy. My New York was a city within the city, existing inside a ten-block radius from my apartment in Manhattan to my office, both downtown, with occasional, activity-specific forays uptown and to Brooklyn—plus vivid memories of certain things that I loved as a kid. But when we started this project, I began carting out those memories—like watching chess at Washington Square Park with my dad, and being excited and intimidated by those fast-handed renegades; or standing transfixed for as long as my mom would let me in front of the marbles at the Forbes Gallery; or school field trips to the Queens Hall of Science—and I was eager to see whether they were still as magical as I remembered (they all were, only more so). Then I realized that there were dozens of things that I did daily, weekly, or in season—bike rides along the Hudson River, literary readings at bars and bookstores, great meals at all sorts of different places, walks around new neighborhoods—that, while not necessarily standard guidebook fare, were special, often idiosyncratic experiences, each terrific in its own right. And from there, I started to think about all the things that I had wanted to do, was curious about trying, or that I had heard about but had never gotten around to, like taking a continuing-education class at New York University or the New School, visiting the Lower East Side Tenement Museum, or going to that Bohemian beer garden in Queens that people kept telling me about. At that point, I was convinced that not only were there 1,001 really, really great things to do here, but that there was also a need for someone to pluck them out from the rest of the city's offerings. Jacob and I accepted the challenge.

Of course, that was only the beginning. Many of the entries we ended up with are things that a year ago, I hadn't even heard of. That is in large part thanks to Jacob's pioneering spirit and infectious enthusiasm about the city. A relatively recent transplant to New York, Jacob awed me with his breadth of knowledge about my hometown (you can touch Cole Porter's piano in the Waldorf lobby? Who knew?), and earned his stripes many times over with his remarkable eagerness to explore (you have him to thank for all of the entries on City Island). We also hunted down treasures through research and tips from friends and family (so as not to confine readers to the range of our tastes). I can't tell you how surprised I was to learn that there is a real, working farm in Queens, or how often I used Hop-stop.com to plan a fact-finding excursion, and one of the nicest evenings I spent all year was the class I took at the Miette Culinary Studio with my cousins.

Ultimately, this book changed from being a seemingly insurmountable task to a true labor of love, stoking my fascination with New York anew with every chapter. I have deepened my affection for this city, and my appreciation for its unique character and multitude of amazing and unexpected facets. Throughout the process, Jacob and I were wowed again and again by new discoveries and the delectable treats we unearthed from place to place. We hope that you will have as much fun as we did.

*—Caitlin Leffel*

# HOW TO USE THIS BOOK

O ur book is intended to be inspirational and informative, livelier than a regular guidebook but with the same practical information that will allow you, our readers, to get up and go. Our only base requirement for consideration was that something be a legitimately great thing to do, regardless of reputation, sentimental value, or location. For our research, we scoured New York City to its farthest reaches for its best offerings, and then tried to pare these down to only the truly, indisputably wonderful. Our primary goal (and challenge) was to inspire without overwhelming, and rouse readers from their homes, hotel rooms, or subway cars to partake of New York's most special offerings.

In keeping with this "inspirational" objective, we have divided the book by theme rather than by specific activity or location. We chose not to rank entries, because after narrowing down all of the best things to do, it seemed beside the point to compare whether the view from the top of the Empire State Building was better than, say, a meal at one of the city's best restaurants. The themes of the chapters are what we deemed to be, broadly speaking, the ten best categories of things to do in New York, including one for all of the idiosyncratic features that can't quite be categorized as anything but "Only in New York." We have delved into every place, site, activity, and service listed in each of these chapters—large and small, famous and unknown—to find the things that make each one particularly great. Most of the time, we centered the entries around a special facet of the place or activity, but occasionally, for certain large entities (the Empire State Building, Grand Central Terminal, Central and Prospect Parks, for example), we divided the sites into different entries according to features that we felt were special and distinct enough to stand on their own. We have tried our best to keep our delineations clear, and not subdivide specific places too much, but to help you, our readers, we've meticulously cross-referenced the book, so if you are reading about, for instance, the New Year's Eve run at Central or Prospect Parks in the "24-Hour Fun" chapter, you'll be able to easily find the main entry for each park in "The Great Outdoors." In the back, we've also included indexes that will make it easier to find activities in certain locations or categories. Also, to bridge the gap between a printed book and the constantly changing city, we've included our favorite Web sites for local information and services. We would also like to note that the Internet is a perfect chronicler for the city that never sleeps, and we strongly recommend using it as much as possible when planning outings and events. Although we have included the most up-to-date information for every entry, providing phone numbers, subway directions and more, details on prices, hours, and other specifics are always subject to change. Not only do Web sites reliably deliver the most current information (and as we found out, usually more efficiently than a phone call), they also provide updates on new features, exhibits, and offerings.

The best way to use this book is to read it. Sure, you could just use it to look things up, and yes, if you check the index, you will be able to find the page where we list, for instance, the opening hours for MoMA. But if you merely glance at the main entry for the museum, you'd miss what a local art critic considers his favorite painting there, a tip about the view from the fifth-floor café, and reading about the museum's incredible film program. Instead, we suggest that you spend some time with this book—read entire chapters, flip through different sections, follow our cross-references. There's a lot more in here than just general overviews and practical information, and so much to discover about places you are thinking of going—as well as places you've already been. In addition to the entries themselves, we've also included little-known facts we discovered called "Did you knows?," historical notes about famous people and places, and a section in each chapter in which local experts share "five bests" in their area of expertise.

Several times during the process, we were asked who the book was for— tourists or residents. The answer is both—really. Even if you are a New Yorker who can remember when riding the subway cost a dime, you'll find plenty of things to take advantage of in these pages, including special delivery services, continuing education classes, and all-night gyms. And for those of you who are visiting, there is a wealth of activities to enjoy, many not covered by other guidebooks and all with the logistical information you need to enjoy them. Both groups of readers will, we hope, relish discovering, remembering, and experiencing the city's finest treasures.

CHAPTER 1:

# The Classics

**W**hen thinking about the best things to do anywhere, it's easy to ignore the obvious and hunt for the obscure. This is even easier in a place with the diverse character and the trendsetting inclinations of New York. With so much that's new, unusual, and ephemeral, there is a tendency to seek out the cutting edge and to discount anything that might be on the itinerary of a high school field trip. Yet, though they're well known, easy to spot, and often very crowded, places like the Statue of Liberty, the Empire State Building, and the Brooklyn Bridge are undeniably among New York's greatest assets. They are symbols of the city, representing the magnificence, the power, and the imagination for which New York prides itself.

But, of course, it's not only the celebrated sites across the city skyline that have made New York what it is today. There are shops, hotels, bars and restaurants, sporting events, and even grocery stores with influential provenances, each full of treasured relics and forgotten secrets that point to the rich and eclectic history of the tastes, fashions, lifestyles, and achievements of New Yorkers through the ages. What makes a place or an experience "a classic" has to do more with its history than its fame or age. Sites of memorable events, yearly rituals, or remnants of bygone eras also symbolize significant facets of New York, from the historic to the idiosyncratic. Moreover, these iconic tidbits come from many periods of the city's history, both recent and long-gone—from the colonial years, through the Roaring Twenties and Prohibition, to the high-rolling eighties and then on into their current incarnations. In this chapter, you'll find places of all kinds that have figured prominently in the development of the city's character, from the sites of famous events to legendary old haunts and some good, old-fashioned New York activities worth waiting in line for.

Sadly, some of these spots have surely seen better days. Places like the Ziegfeld Theater or Café des Artistes are not what they once were, but because of their colorful history we feel that they still merit an entry. The fact that something is still standing is not necessarily enough to make it a "best," but since so many legendary places are gone without a trace (Max's Kansas City, the famous '60s hangout, is a deli; both Ebbets Field and the Polo Grounds are now the sites of apartment complexes), any place that was a stomping ground for so many New York characters in its heyday—and hasn't been turned into a luxury condo development or a Starbucks—deserves a salute.

## 1. Climb (almost) to the top of the **Statue of Liberty.**

Consider this: it took France twenty years, 450,000 pounds of steel and copper, multiple national fundraising campaigns, and 214 shipping crates to get the Statue of Liberty to her home in Manhattan harbor—all as a gift to us. It is no wonder then that the Statue of Liberty is such an inspiring landmark. The enormity of the project aside (including the extra year, additional 27,000 tons of concrete for the pedestal, and exhaustive fundraising efforts it took on our shores before she was presented to the public), Lady Liberty has stood sentry before the city of New York since 1886, and she has become a symbol of both the city and the nation, of freedom and friendship. Viewing her from across the Hudson River, you can appreciate how she watches over the city with a strong, unwavering gaze; viewing her from up close and inside, you can appreciate the magnificent feat of engineering, cooperation, and patriotism that brought her here. For security reasons, you can no longer climb to the top, but a glass ceiling has been constructed at the top of the pedestal, which gives an excellent view of her interior. (And as anyone who did it can vouch, the walk up those narrow stairs isn't actually such a great thing to do, anyway.) Also in the pedestal is the Statue of Liberty Museum, which includes the statue's original torch. Afterward, you can continue on to **Ellis Island** (see below) on the same ferry that you arrived on.
*Subway: 4,5 to Bowling Green; 1 to South Ferry. Open daily, except Christmas Day. Admission to the statue is free, but timed reservations are required. Reservations can be made by calling 1-866-STATUE4 or online at www.statuereservations.com. A limited number of same-day reservations are also available at the ferries on a first-come/first-served basis. Ferries depart from Battery Park in lower Manhattan and from Liberty State Park in New Jersey; for more information on the ferries, schedules, and ticket prices, visit www.circlelinedown-town.com. For more information on the statue, call 212-363-3200 or visit www.nps.gov/stli.*

## 2. Look for your ancestors at **Ellis Island.**

Almost half of all Americans can trace their roots through the doors of Ellis Island. Ellis Island was designated as the national immigration station at the end of the nineteenth century, when control of immigration was taken over by the federal government. Some 2 million people passed through it on their way to becoming Americans between its opening in 1892 and its closing in 1954, sometimes thousands a day.

(And despite its reputation as the "Island of Tears," most immigrants made it through in a couple of hours, and only 2 percent were sent back.) The Ellis Island Museum is located in a beautifully restored Beaux-Arts–style building, where the immigrants were processed and examined before being given permission to enter the country. There are exhibits, artifacts, documents, and oral histories about Ellis Island and the immigration experience, plus many resources for tracing your genealogy. You can browse through the immigration records at the American Family Immigration history center, and then go outside to see the Wall of Honor, on which are inscribed the names of more than 600,000 courageous immigrants.

*Open daily, except Christmas Day. Admission is free. Ellis Island is accessible by the same ferries that serve the Statue of Liberty; see previous page for details. For more information on the museum, call 212-363-3206 or visit www.ellisisland.com.*

## 3. Go (almost) to the top of the Empire State Building.

The Empire State building is *the* quintessential skyscraper, and its illuminated figure is the centerpiece of the Manhattan skyline. Constructed in the early 1930s as part of a contest to build the world's tallest building, the Empire State Building eclipsed the Chrysler Building by a few hundred feet. (And, perhaps more impressive to New Yorkers, was completed ahead of schedule, in just one year and forty-five days.) After the Depression, the Empire State Building came to define Midtown Manhattan as modern, exciting, and full of promise, inspiring the building of other skyscrapers around town. It remained the tallest building in the world for more than four decades, until the World Trade Center towers were built in the mid-1970s. Between its grand Art Deco style and its astonishing size, the ESB (as it's sometimes known) is an incredible site, both to behold and to look down from. Though the top observatory (on the 102nd floor) is open only sporadically, the view from the eighty-sixth floor is still spectacular.

*350 FIFTH AVENUE BETWEEN 33RD AND 34TH STREETS IN MANHATTAN. Subway: 6 to 33rd Street, D, D, F, V, N, R, Q, W to 34th Street-Herald Square. Eighty-sixth-floor observatory open daily (see page 79); the 102nd-floor observatory is open on a limited basis. For more information on hours and ticket prices, visit www.esbnyc.com.*

*For Empire State Building lights, see page 316.*

*For Empire State Building Run, see page 360.*

## 4. Take a trip to a foreign land at the United Nations.

The eighteen-acre UN complex along the East River is designated international territory, outside of the jurisdiction of the city and the state (though we don't advise trying to hide out there to evade a parking violation). On the tour, which is offered, not surprisingly, in dozens of different languages, you'll see the chambers of the Security Council and the General Assembly Hall, as well as special exhibits and a collection of art and artifacts from member nations. Afterward, you can sample the local cuisine in the **Delegates Dining Room** (see page 202), and then send a postcard from the UN post office, with a special United Nations stamp from its land of origin.

*FIRST AVENUE BETWEEN 42ND AND 48TH STREETS IN MANHATTAN. Subway: 4, 5, 6, 7 to Grand Central-42nd Street. Tours offered daily, about every half hour. For more information, schedules, and ticket prices, call 212-963-TOUR or visit www.un.org/tours.*

→ **DID YOU KNOW?** *When New York City was chosen to host the early Security Council meetings of the United Nations, it was in far less formal surroundings than the UN complex: the swimming pool of the Bronx campus of Hunter College served as a postwar assembly hall for the young diplomatic organization, and is responsible for bringing Winston Churchill to the Bronx for the first time.*

## 5. Walk (or bike) across the **Brooklyn Bridge**.

For a real treat, time your trip so that you can see the sunset. When you make it to (or back to) the Brooklyn side, stop in for some coal-oven pizza at **Grimaldi's** (a Sinatra favorite—see page 203).

*Subway: (for Manhattan) 2, 3, J, M, Z to Fulton Street, 4, 5, 6 to Brooklyn Bridge-City Hall, A, C to Broadway-Nassau Street; (for Brooklyn) A, C to High Street.*

## 6. Pretend to be a World War II flying ace at the **Intrepid**.

If you think the skyscrapers make you feel puny, try looking up at the Intrepid from the pier below. Commissioned for action during World War II, the aircraft carrier also served during the Vietnam and Cold Wars, and later was used by NASA as a recovery vehicle. Inside, the museum has some great interactive exhibits (such as flight simulators and naval navigation demonstrations), but to really feel like you're part of the crew, head to the hangar and flight decks. There, you can see and explore the museum's collection of vintage and modern aircraft, from actual fighter planes that landed on the carrier during World War II to a retired British Airways Concorde jet. Particularly, well, intrepid couples can even have their weddings on board.

*PIER 86 BY 46TH STREET AND THE HUDSON RIVER IN MANHATTAN. Subway: A, C, E to 42nd Street-Port Authority Bus Terminal. For more information, ticket prices, and operating hours, call 877-957-SHIP or visit www.intrepidmuseum.org.*

## 7. Take refuge in **Saint Patrick's Cathedral** . . .

Part of this church's spiritual majesty comes from its location: it's right in the middle of one of the most famous shopping strips in the world, its great Gothic spires towering above Fifth Avenue. The contrast between its architectural magnificence and the surrounding retail extravagance is stark, and rather awe-inspiring. Mass is held every day of the week (the church seats a congregation of 2,200), but you can come in between masses to explore the church's many fine details, such as the great rose stained-glass window and, fittingly, an altar designed by Tiffany & Co. Even when the cathedral is as crowded as the department stores across the street, there's a solemnity that takes you away from the earthly chaos outside.

*14 EAST 51ST STREET AT FIFTH AVENUE IN MANHATTAN. Subway: B, D, F, V to 47th-50th Streets-Rockefeller Center. 212-753-2261. www.ny-archdiocese.org.*

→ **DID YOU KNOW?** *The first televised midnight mass was broadcast from Saint Patrick's Cathedral on Christmas Eve, 1948. Today, televised masses at Saint Patrick's are broadcast daily on local channels.*

## 8. . . . or be humbled at the **Cathedral of Saint John the Divine**.

Saint John the Divine is considered the largest cathedral in the world and is one of the most infamously drawn-out construction projects in the country. The cathedral has been under construction on and off since the cornerstone was laid in 1892, and it's still not quite "finished." However, despite the ongoing work, it remains one of the city's most remarkable sites, as well as a powerful and moving spiritual center. In addition to the grand, Gothic-style features, such as the famous nave, which is the size of two football fields, what is particularly uplifting about the cathedral is its unmistakably ecumenical spirit. The Chapel of the Seven Tongues, for instance, is an homage to New York's diversity, made up of special chapels dedicated to seven saints, each chapel representing a country or ethnicity of the people that helped build the church. Saint John's also glorifies the arts; it is home to a gold triptych by the artist Keith Haring (his only religious work) as well as numerous concerts, performances, and literary events. Visiting Saint John's is a stirring experience no matter what your faith, and its glorious, unfinished state is a poignant metaphor for our own lives.

*1047 AMSTERDAM AVENUE NEAR 110TH STREET IN MANHATTAN. Subway: 1 to 110th Street (Cathedral Parkway); B, C to Cathedral Parkway (110th Street). 212-316-7490. www.stjohndivine.org.*

## 9. Check out the tombstones in the churchyard at **Trinity Church** . . .

Alexander Hamilton and Robert Fulton are among the notable early Americans buried in the churchyard of this historic neo-Gothic church. One of the oldest churches in the country, it was built in 1697 as an Anglican church chartered by the king of England. During the period of the Revolution, some of the parishioners took part in the Continental Congresses, while the clergy remained with the crown, and Trinity's destiny mirrored that of the country as a whole. After the war, the church's charter was ratified by the newly independent state of New York, freeing it from paying dues and declaring loyalty to the British monarchy, and in 1789, its rector was appointed the first bishop of the new diocese of New York. The church building, having burned down in 1776, was rebuilt and reopened in 1788. (This second structure was destroyed in 1839 and rebuilt for a third time.) In between the construction of the first church and the second, services were held at nearby Saint Paul's Chapel, part of the Trinity parish, including a thanksgiving service for George Washington after his inauguration as president.

*Open daily. 74 BROADWAY AT WALL STREET IN MANHATTAN. Subway: 1, N, R, W to Rector Street; 4, 5 to Wall Street. 212-602-0800. www.trinitywallstreet.org.*

→ **DID YOU KNOW?** *Saint Paul's Chapel, located at Broadway and Fulton, is the oldest public building in continuous use in New York City.*

## 10. . . . and at **Trinity Cemetery**.

Confusingly, the main burial ground of Trinity Church is located all the way uptown, on a plot of land that was part of the former Audubon estate. (Trinity parish bought the land from the family in 1842, when an ordinance was passed prohibiting burials in lower Manhattan.) It is the only active burial ground in the borough of Manhattan, although burials are now restricted to direct descendants of those already interred there. In addition to John James Audubon, the naturalist, the cemetery contains the graves of John Jacob Astor and Clement Clarke Moore (author of the poem "A Visit from Saint Nicholas"), as well as beautiful and elaborate mausoleums, vaults, and tombs of many one-time prominent and affluent New Yorkers.

*Open daily. 770 RIVERSIDE DRIVE IN MANHATTAN. Subway: 1 to 157th Street; C to 155th Street. 212-368-1600.*

## 11. See the Rockettes at **Radio City Music Hall**.

Originally a dance troupe from St. Louis called the "Missouri Rockets," the Rockettes captivated audiences with their flying kicks when they performed at Radio City Music Hall's opening night in 1932, and they have been dancing there ever since. If you

think that what today's pop stars do on stage is dancing, then you're in for a treat. Performing in the traditional *Radio City Christmas Spectacular*, as well as other events during the year, their acts consist of intricately choreographed routines of eye-high kicks performed in perfect tandem. The costumes are more beautiful than ever, and thanks to modern technologies like Lycra and spandex, have only gotten shorter and tighter. This is one of the few venues where it's entirely appropriate (and practically inevitable) to ogle the girls' legs.

SIXTH AVENUE, BETWEEN 50TH AND 51ST STREETS IN MANHATTAN. Subway: B, D, F, V to 47th-50th Streets-Rockefeller Center; N, R, W to 49th Street. 212-307-7171. www.radiocity.com.

12. See the city from the **Circle Line**.

Of all the traditional tourist attractions, this is one that plenty of New Yorkers agree is a pretty great thing to do, and unlike some other famous activities, is something that many have actually done themselves. The three-hour Full Island cruise gets you a view of all five boroughs, plus three rivers, seven bridges, and two dozen major landmarks; the two-hour Harbor Lights cruise does a semicircle around Manhattan in the evening. You can sit and listen to the jaunty commentary, or get some wine, and toast the city from the deck.

Sightseeing cruises leave from PIER 83, 42ND STREET AND THE HUDSON RIVER IN MANHATTAN. Subway: A, C, E to 42nd Street-Port Authority Bus Terminal. For information, schedules, and prices, call 212-563-3200 or visit www.circleline42.com.

Grand Central

Grand Central Terminal has stood in the heart of New York City for nearly a century, and its presence and influence have shaped the development of the city's Midtown area. Constructed over a decade between 1903 and 1913 through the combined efforts of two architecture firms (Reed and Stern, and Warren and Wetmore), the terminal came to embody the dashing, cosmopolitan lifestyle of the city as much as the Empire State Building, the Chrysler Building, the Waldorf-Astoria, and the other buildings that grew up around it.

Though nominally a train station, anyone who's ever been to Grand Central knows that it is so much more. Over the course of its existence, Grand Central has been home not only to trains but also to a host of other distractions: an art gallery, an art school, various exhibitions, a newsreel movie theater, a rail history museum, bars, restaurants, stores, and shoeshine stands. On top of this, the building itself is full of secrets and stories that will forever be part of New York legend (Franklin Delano

Roosevelt's secret passage from the station to the Waldorf-Astoria, for one). Declared a National Historic Landmark in 1978, and beautifully restored to its original glory in 1998, the terminal is both a mine of New York history and a very real part of New York life today.

*42ND STREET BETWEEN LEXINGTON AVENUE AND PARK AVENUE IN MANHATTAN. Subway: 4, 5, 6, 7, S to Grand Central-42nd Street.*

**13. *Find your way to the Campbell Apartment,*** the "secret" bar upstairs at Grand Central Terminal. This warm, oak-paneled, stone hall was formerly the property of John W. Campbell, the fabulously wealthy business tycoon who bought the corner of the railway station in the 1920s and transformed the space into a distinguished Renaissance-style apartment, which served as his office by day and a club for private parties by night. The bar is grand, old-fashioned, and cozy, and the bartenders know how to mix a very strong martini. There is an entrance to the bar from Vanderbilt Avenue, but the real aficionado will seek out the elegant Art Deco elevator down in the station concourse.

*15 VANDERBILT AVENUE AT GRAND CENTRAL TERMINAL. 212-953-0409. www.hospitalityholdings.com.*

**14. *Tell a secret to someone on the other side of the room at the whispering gallery.*** Standing in opposite corners of the concourse, you can face the wall and have your voice travel across the curve of the domed roof. The faintest whisper will sound on the other side as if you were only a foot away.

*WHISPERING GALLERY, DINING CONCOURSE.*

**15. *Get your shoes shined outside Grand Central.*** You can't get into **Campbell Apartment** without good, shiny shoes. Take a chair outside the main entrances on 42nd Street and enjoy people-watching in one of the busiest parts of Midtown.

**16. *Have an old-fashioned lunch at the Oyster Bar.*** This landmark restaurant has been located "below sea level" in Grand Central since 1913, the year the terminal opened. Today, the Oyster Bar is a bastion of lunchtime civility, surrounded as it is by an entire dining concourse of fast-food options. So when "working lunches" and toss-your-own salads get you down, retreat to the Oyster Bar, and enjoy some of New York's best seafood (including nearly thirty kinds of oysters)—and maybe a martini or two—before heading back to the office.

*LOWER LEVEL. 212-490-6650. www.oysterbarny.com.*

**17. *Tell a story to StoryCorps, and be a part of American history!***
StoryCorps is a program aiming to record a people's history of the United States, voice by voice, from city to city. For $10, anyone can sit in front of a microphone in a booth with a sound engineer and just talk—the tapes will be saved in the Library of Congress, and the most intriguing tales will be played on NPR. The program set up its very first booth in Grand Central, where it will remain for the foreseeable future. Because of the popularity of the project, reservations are now required. (There is another booth in lower Manhattan, in the concourse of the World Trade Center PATH station. Priority at this booth is given to people involved in the relief efforts for 9/11, local residents and business owners, and friends and family members of people who perished in the World Trade Center attacks.)
*STORYCORPS BOOTH, BILTMORE ROOM IN GRAND CENTRAL TERMINAL BETWEEN TRACKS 41 AND 42. Reservations can be made by phone at 800-850-4406 or online at www.storycorps.net.*

## 18. Bounce on the keyboard at **FAO Schwarz**.
It was a nightmare right out of the Brothers Grimm when FAO Schwarz buckled to the pressure of the toy chain behemoths and closed its beloved Fifth Avenue playground, to the horror of kids, New Yorkers, and doll collectors and Lego fans around the world. But there's a happy ending, at least for now: in December 2004, the struggling company reopened the Fifth Avenue store, and it's grander than ever, with plenty of new, over-the-top tricks up its sleeve, including an old-fashioned soda parlor that sells $100 drinks, $10,000 stuffed animals, and mini-Ferraris (they also hold extravagant children's sleepover birthday parties; for more details, see page 341). But as big kids know, a trip to FAO Schwarz is more about the experience than what you bring home, and they will be happy to hear that FAO hasn't dispensed with the old favorites—you can still dance on the electric keyboard just like Tom Hanks did in *Big*.
*767 FIFTH AVENUE AT 58TH STREET IN MANHATTAN. Subway: F to 57th Street; N, R, W to Fifth Avenue/59th Street. 212-644-9400 ext. 4242. www.fao.com.*

## 19. Go ring shopping (or pretend to) at **Tiffany**.
Between the little blue box, the diamond setting that bears its name, and the ubiquitous image of Holly Golightly eating a pastry in front of its Fifth Avenue window, Tiffany is one of the most well-recognized stores in the world. It is a grand old establishment whose rarified status has perhaps been taken down a notch by an influx of tourists buying $100 signature key chains, but this increased popularity has in fact

only enhanced its image as *the* New York jewelry store. And though there are now outlets in shopping malls all over the world, that hasn't stopped thousands of couples from making the trip to the original Fifth Avenue location to buy their engagement rings. (Not to mention the ones who come in asking for Cracker Jack rings to be engraved.)

*FIFTH AVENUE AT 57TH STREET IN MANHATTAN. Subway: E, V to Fifth Avenue/53rd Street; N, R, W to Fifth Avenue/59th Street. 212-755-8000. www.tiffany.com. For more on jewelry stores, see chapter 7.*

## Watch the Macy's Fourth of July Fireworks

This is the biggest fireworks show in the country; it uses more than fifty times the number of fireworks than the average American display. Each year, tens of thousands of fireworks are set off from barges in three different locations (in the East River by 34th Street, off the southern tip of Manhattan by the South Street Seaport, and by the Statue of Liberty and Liberty State Park) in a spectacularly choreographed show. They're hard to miss—pretty much anywhere above street level in Manhattan, Brooklyn, or Queens will give you some kind of view. But the closer (and higher up from the ground) you are to the East River or South Street Seaport, the better. If you don't have any friends living on high floors in the East 30s—and don't feel comfortable sneaking into a party at a stranger's apartment—here are the public places with the best views.

*Macy's Fourth of July Fireworks show starts at 9:00 p.m. on July 4. For specific information on the show, check newspapers or visit www.macys.com.*

**20. *The FDR Drive:*** The traditional Manhattan viewing point is on the FDR drive, between 14th and 42nd Streets. If you want a good seat, you'll have to get there a few hours before the fireworks start, and be prepared for crowds, security checks, and a lot of sitting around (use the bathroom before you go). However, this is the best view you can get of the fireworks; they go off right above your head.

*The fireworks can be viewed from the southbound lane of the FDR Drive between 14th and 42nd Streets. Accessible by taking the ramp at 23rd, 38th, and 42nd Streets, starting at 7:00 p.m. Subway: 6 to 23rd Street, 33rd Street, and 4, 5, 6 to Grand Central-42nd Street.*

>>> TIP: *If you can't (or don't want to) get to the FDR Drive early enough to get a seat, try heading to Midtown around when the fireworks begin and*

*walk east. You can get a good view of the show overhead from anywhere east of First Avenue from the 20s through the 40s.*

**21. *Gantry Plaza State Park*:** At this new waterfront park, you can get a clear, unobstructed view of the fireworks that are sent off the barges on the East River, set against the Manhattan skyline.
*474 FORTY-EIGHTH AVENUE ALONG THE EAST RIVER IN QUEENS. Subway: 7 to Vernon Boulevard-Jackson Avenue; E, V to 23rd Street-Ely Avenue.*

**22. *Brooklyn Heights Promenade*:** This is a cool place to watch the fireworks because you can see the displays in the East River and off of South Street Seaport with the Manhattan skyline underneath. Crowds are sizable but not unmanageable. If you're lucky enough to be on top of a building, depending on where you are in the area, you can even see the display coming from Liberty State Park, too.
*BETWEEN MONTAGUE AND MIDDAGH STREETS ALONG THE EAST RIVER IN BROOKLYN. Subway: 2, 3 to Clark Street; A, C to High Street; M to Court Street; N, R to Court Street-Borough Hall.*

**23. *Hudson River Park*:** Though this park doesn't offer as clear or close up a view as some of the others, the lower portion of Hudson River Park is a good place to watch the fireworks, particularly if you don't want to spend your entire day finding a seat and waiting for them to start. From here, you get a good view of the fireworks by Liberty State Park, as they go off above the Statue of Liberty. And depending on how far down you are in the park, you may also be able to see the ones coming from the southern tip of Manhattan. It tends to be less crowded and more comfortable than most of the other places (including Battery Park, a little further south), so even if you show up at 8:50 p.m., you can probably still get a nice spot on the grass with a decent view.
*WEST SIDE OF MANHATTAN ALONG THE HUDSON RIVER. For fireworks viewing, go below 14th Street. Subway: A, C, E to 14th Street; L to Eighth Avenue.*

## 24. Take a carriage ride in **Central Park.**

Though plenty of New Yorkers wouldn't be caught dead in one of these, millions of happy couples have made this tourist-heavy attraction a bona fide classic. It's no secret that riding through Central Park in a horse-drawn carriage is one of the most romantic things you can do in the city, and if statistics were kept on the city's most popular spots for a proposal, these buggies might easily top the list. The prices for rides aren't exorbitant (between $35 and $75, depending on length of ride), and it's not hard to do: the carriages are usually lined up on the south end of the park, waiting for customers. The ride is even more romantic in the winter, when you can cuddle under blankets with your beloved. Just be sure you like your companion, and the cold.

*NORTH SIDE OF 59TH STREET BETWEEN FIFTH AND SIXTH AVENUES IN MANHATTAN. Subway: 1, A, C, B, D to 59th Street-Columbus Circle; F to 57th Street; N, R, W to Fifth Avenue/59th Street; Q to Midtown-57th Street.*

## 25. See a **Broadway show**.

Not sure what's playing? *Playbill's* **official Web site** has synopses, performances times, and theater locations for all Broadway shows. Also on the Web site is information about and listings for shows with standing room or lottery policies. These are special tickets available at the box office on the day of the performance, from the time the box office opens until it sells out. The policies vary from show to show (some give preference to students; some give only one ticket per person; many are cash only), the availability is completely unpredictable, and waits are inevitable—however, if you have time to wait in line and don't mind standing, this is a great way to see a sold-out show that you wouldn't be able to catch otherwise.

If you don't have your heart set on a certain show and have some time, you can also try your luck at one of two **TKTS booths**. There you can buy tickets for shows on the same day (at the South Street Seaport booth, you can purchase matinee tickets the day before). The tickets are 20 to 50 percent less than at the box office, but be prepared—they only take cash or travelers' checks.

For a completely authentic Broadway experience, pair your evening with a meal at one of the joints on "Restaurant Row," the famous strip of restaurants lining 46th Street between Eighth and Ninth Avenues. **Joe Allen** is a reliable place to see the stars when they're not on stage—and the food is good, too. (Tip: Go after the shows let out.) *Playbill's official Web site is www.playbill.com. For information on the TKTS booths, visit the Theater Development Fund's Web site, www.tdf.org. Joe Allen is at 326 West 46th Street between Eighth and Ninth Avenues. 212-581-6464. www.joeallenrestaurant.com. Subway (for both): 1, 2, 3, 7, N, Q, R, W, S to Times Square-42nd Street; A, C, E to 42nd Street-Port Authority Bus Terminal.*

→ **DID YOU KNOW?** *Many Broadway shows adopted lottery policies after the '90s hit musical* Rent *started reserving the first two rows of the orchestra for $20 day-of tickets to accommodate students and other young people who made up a big part of the show's fan base.*

## 26. Watch the **New York City Marathon**.

The New York City Marathon has grown from a modest, low-budget race around Central Park to the premier long-distance running event in the country. For the first incarnation, in 1970, only a small crowd of people showed up to watch 127 runners compete for old bowling trophies (the marathon's entire budget was $1,000). Today the race attracts thousands of runners—who compete for more than $500,000 in prize money—as well as millions of spectators. And the competition begins long before race day: nearly 100,000 athletes from around the world vie for 35,000 spots that are selected by lottery. The course was expanded in 1976 and now travels through all five boroughs, starting from the Staten Island side of the **Verrazano-Narrows Bridge** (see page 67), then passing through Brooklyn, Queens, across Manhattan to the Bronx, and back into Manhattan to finish in Central Park. The marathon has been the site of record-setting victories, stunning accomplishments and upsets, and even played a part in the most infamous episode in the history of modern footraces. Rosie Ruiz, who received a respectable finish time of 2:56:29 in the 1979 marathon, was later revealed to have traveled part of the course on the subway. (The hoax was uncovered six months later, when she completed the Boston Marathon in record time, after jumping into the race from the crowd a few miles before the finish line.)

Since we're not in good enough shape to attempt it ourselves, we can't vouch for how great running the marathon actually is. Watching it in person, however, is an exciting way to soak up New York spirit. Seeing this great spectacle from the street is exhilarating and breeds heartwarming camaraderie, as everyone cheers the athletes as they go by. Check the map—you can pick any spot along the route and cheer for free. For the best view of the finish line, you can purchase tickets for bleacher seats adjacent to it, which also have a view of a big-screen broadcast of the runners as they approach.

*First Sunday in November. VIP seating (bleacher seats) costs $55; members of New York Road Runners are eligible for a discount. For more information, call 212-423-2249 or visit www.ingnycmarathon.org.*

## 27. Watch the **U.S. Open**.

In 2005, the U.S. Open celebrated its 125th anniversary with two glorious weeks of tennis. The Open has grown from its humble beginnings as an amateur singles championship in 1881 into the biggest grand slam event on the tennis world circuit. It is to New York what Wimbledon is to London, capturing the character of its locale, enjoyed by tennis fans and non-tennis fans alike. Watched by millions around the world on television, it is a great event to see up close. The USTA's magnificent National Tennis Center is in Flushing Meadows, the large and beautiful park in Queens that has hosted two World's Fairs (1939 and 1964) and is home to the Unisphere, the globe sculpture from the 1964 fair, and **Shea Stadium** (see below). Whether you have seats in the Arthur Ashe Stadium for the final, or you're strolling around the park watching the games on giant TV screens outside the grounds, the U.S. Open is as much a New York event as a sporting one.

*USTA NATIONAL TENNIS CENTER, FLUSHING MEADOWS-CORONA PARK IN QUEENS. Subway: 7 to Willets Point-Shea Stadium. www.usopen.org.*

---

## 28. Get to a Yankee game early, and visit **Monument Park.**

Even the most rabid Boston fan will grudgingly admit that the Yankees have a monumental history. Since 1932, the team has honored its many greats at Monument Park. Here you can see tributes to Yankee heroes like Babe Ruth, Lou Gehrig, Mickey Mantle, and Joe DiMaggio, along with plaques honoring other great figures in Yankee history, like Yogi Berra, Phil Rizzuto, and longtime Yankee broadcaster, Mel Allen. Before the game, you can also watch batting practice, and then try to get autographs from current players as they leave for the dugout.

*161ST STREET AT RIVER AVENUE IN THE BRONX. Monument Park is open to ticket holders on game days, from the time gates open until forty-five minutes before the game starts. N.B.: Bleacher-seat ticket holders cannot access the park. Subway: 4, B, D to 161 Street-Yankee Stadium. For more information on batting practice, directions, and hours, call 718-293-4300 or visit newyork.yankees.mlb.com.*

---

## 29. Enjoy the quirks of **Shea Stadium.**

Shea Stadium has been home to the New York Mets since they left the **Polo Grounds** (see page 50) at the beginning of their third season. When the stadium opened in 1964, it boasted state-of-the-art features like an escalator system and a capability to convert from baseball diamond to football field. Forty years later, Shea is not exactly in the forefront of stadium innovation, but it still has a few idiosyncratic quirks that Mets fans love and Yankee fans love to mock. It is the noisiest ballpark in the major leagues, thanks to the planes from nearby LaGuardia airport; and it also has the kitschy Mets Magic Hat, an oversize top hat that sits in center field. Every time a Mets player hits a home run, an apple with the Mets logo on it pops out of the hat. And though there are no historic monuments to visit like there are at Yankee Stadium (the Mets have only been around since the early '60s), you can watch batting practice before the game.

*Batting practice is open for viewing by ticket holders. 123-01 ROOSEVELT AVENUE IN QUEENS. Subway: 7 to Willets Point-Shea Stadium. For more information, directions, and practice schedule, call 718-507-TIXX or visit newyork.mets.mlb.com.*

## 30. Watch the New York Knicks play at **Madison Square Garden**.

This may be one of the more difficult things to do in New York: however well (or poorly) the Knicks are doing, tickets to games are always in great demand, and with good reason. The Garden is New York's most famous arena, and the Knicks have played basketball there since its opening in 1968; its status in basketball and city history was cemented when the team won its very first championship there in 1970. If you do manage to get seats, you can expect to rub shoulders with the cream of New York celebrity. Of course, the Knicks aren't the only game in town—the Garden is also the home stadium to the Rangers and the WNBA team, the New York Liberty, as well as serving as the premier rock concert site in Manhattan, a legendary boxing venue, and the place to see the circus when it comes to town.
*SEVENTH AVENUE BETWEEN 31ST AND 33RD STREETS IN MANHATTAN. Subway: 1, 2, 3, A, C, E to 34th Street-Penn Station. 212-465-MSG1. www.thegarden.com/sports_knicks.jsp.*

## 31. Hear tonight's jokes before anyone else at a **late night talk show**.

New York has been home to the nation's sharpest bedtime storytellers since Steve Allen charmed the nation with the first *Tonight Show* in 1954, a late-night companion to one of the longest-running television shows in history, NBC's *Today Show*. Since then, New York's evening *comperes* have been the best loved in the business, with legendary hosts like Ed Sullivan and Johnny Carson bringing the biggest stars to the city, launching the careers of countless actors and comics, and cementing the city's reputation as the cultural mouthpiece of the nation. While Johnny, Jay, and others have been lured out west to Hollywood, New York City still boasts the hosts with the most—Dave, Conan, and Jon.
*N.B.: Age restrictions apply to all three, so bring your ID and don't get your hopes up if you're under eighteen—they make no exceptions.* **LATE SHOW WITH DAVID LETTERMAN:** *1697 BROADWAY BETWEEN WEST 53RD AND WEST 54TH STREETS. Subway: B, D, E to Seventh Avenue. www.cbs.com.* **LATE NIGHT WITH CONAN O'BRIEN:** *30 ROCKEFELLER PLAZA, 49TH STREET BETWEEN FIFTH AND SIXTH AVENUES. Subway: D, D, F, V to 47th 50th Streets Rockefeller Center. www.nbc.com.* **THE DAILY SHOW WITH JON STEWART:** *733 ELEVENTH AVENUE BETWEEN 51ST AND 52ND STREETS. Subway: C, E to 50th Street; 1, A, C, B, D to 59th Street-Columbus Circle. www.comedycentral.com.*

## 32. Check out the **Christmas windows**.

It's a grand old New York tradition, and each store has its own look, so visit them all for the full seasonal effect. (Tip: escape the crowds by going at night, after the stores have closed.)

Start downtown with Macy's. The annual window displays aren't as lavish as those at some of the other stores, but the annual *Miracle on 34th Street* windows that line 34th Street are nice to stop by after a visit to **Santaland** (see page 346).

Then move over to Fifth Avenue to Lord & Taylor. Lord & Taylor was the first of the department stores to do themed Christmas windows, a legacy that they take very seriously. Their windows are poised on freight elevators, so they can be lowered and assembled in the basement (as opposed to the other stores, who must cover their windows while they are being dressed). The most traditional of all the holiday displays, their windows use elaborate décor and intricate details, usually to tell an explicitly Christmas-themed story.

From there, it's a few blocks up to Saks Fifth Avenue, whose windows are often just as packed as those at Lord & Taylor. Their windows also tend toward popular classic Christmas themes, and their location just across from the Christmas tree at Rockefeller Center (see below) doesn't hurt.

Then wander up to **Bergdorf Goodman** (see page 240) for the elegant and fashion-forward creations overseen by window-dresser extraordinaire, Linda Fargo.

Finally, head over to Madison Avenue for Simon Doonan's whimsical display at **Barneys** (see page 241). Always the cheekiest of the bunch, Doonan's windows are naughty and nice, and he often uses celebrity caricatures in satirical PG-13–rated scenes. Doonan's windows are crowd-pleasers all year round and always worth checking out.

*Christmas windows are usually unveiled in November and stay up until just after New Year's. All of the following locations are in Manhattan:*

**Macy's:** *151 WEST 34TH STREET BETWEEN BROADWAY AND SEVENTH AVENUE. Subway: 1, 2, 3, A, C, E to 34th Street-Penn Station; B, D, F, V, N, Q, R, W to 34th Street-Herald Square.*

**Lord & Taylor:** *424 FIFTH AVENUE AT 39TH STREET. Subway: B, D, F, V to 42nd Street-Bryant Park; 7 to Fifth Avenue-Bryant Park.*

**Saks Fifth Avenue:** *611 FIFTH AVENUE AT 50TH STREET. Subway: B, D, F, V to 47th-50th Streets-Rockefeller Center.*

**Bergdorf Goodman:** *754 FIFTH AVENUE AT 57TH STREET. Subway: F to 57th Street.*

**Barneys:** *660 MADISON AVENUE AT 60TH STREET. Subway: N, R, W to Fifth Avenue-59th Street.*

## 33. Visit the Christmas tree in **Rockefeller Center** . . .

For the most pleasant visit, try going at night. There'll still be plenty of tree-viewers around (unless there's a blizzard!), but at least you won't have to contend with the regular daytime pedestrians. Plus, the tree is that much more dazzling against the night sky.

*The tree is up from the end of November through New Year's and is lit from 5:30 a.m. to 11:30 p.m. Best viewing is from Fifth Avenue between 47th and 50th Streets. Subway: B, D, F, V to 47th-50th Streets-Rockefeller Center. For more information, visit www.rockefellercenter.com.*

## 34. . . . or go skating underneath it.

There's no need to visit this tiny rink (it can accommodate only 150 skaters at a time) except at Christmastime, when you can skate right up close to the famous Rockefeller Center Christmas tree. It's almost always maddeningly crowded, so again, going late at night is a good idea (the rink is open until midnight during the holiday season—for more information, see page 333). But twirling around underneath a nearly 100-foot-tall Christmas tree is worth the effort.

*The rink is open daily, October through April, and is located in the middle of Rockefeller Center. Subway: B, D, F, V to 47th–50th Streets-Rockefeller Center. Call 212-332-7654 for information, prices, and schedules. www.therinkatrockcenter.com.*

## 35. Learn about Revolutionary War—era history at **Fraunces Tavern**.

Though there's no plaque, it's very possible that at some point George Washington slept here. He certainly did plenty of other things here, including, most famously, giving his troops a farewell address after the Revolutionary War before returning to Mount Vernon. But the modest three-story building on Pearl Street is much more than just the place where the founding fathers came to drink. Founded as the Queen's Head by Samuel Fraunces in 1762 (the name was changed after the Revolution), this tavern played many parts during the nation's formative years. The New York Chamber of Commerce was founded here in 1768, and after the Revolution it was used as the offices for the Departments of Treasury, War, and Foreign Affairs. Operated by the fraternal organization Sons of the Revolution, the museum displays a collection of American art and artifacts from colonial, revolutionary, and early federal years, such as paintings, furniture, weapons, documents, personal artifacts, and flags. You can also visit the Long Room, where Washington delivered his farewell address. Downstairs, have a bite or a drink at the colonial-themed bar and restaurant.

*54 PEARL STREET AT BROAD STREET IN MANHATTAN. Subway: 2, 3 to Wall Street; 4, 5 to Bowling Green; J, M, Z to Broad Street. For more information, hours, schedules, and prices, call 212-425-1778 or visit www.frauncestavernmuseum.org.*

→ **DID YOU KNOW?** *Before the building that became the tavern was erected, this was the site of the city's first landfill.*

## 36. Get a custom-flavored prescription filled at **C.O. Bigelow**.

Bigelow, the oldest apothecary in the country—Mark Twain used to fill his prescriptions here—is a New York institution *par excellence*. (Mr. Bigelow, the store cat, had his obituary in the *New York Times*.) Shopping at Bigelow feels like an experience out of another, chain-free world, not only because of the old-fashioned wooden counters

from which chemists fetch the products you want, but also because of the eclectic selection of goods. In addition to the staples available at mainstream drugstores, you'll find homeopathic products, lots of hard-to-find and high-end international brands, and all sorts of gorgeous accessories, particularly for hair. At the pharmacy, you can get your medicine custom flavored and then delivered to your door.
*414 SIXTH AVENUE, BETWEEN 8TH AND 9TH STREETS IN MANHATTAN. Subway: A, C, E, B, D, F, V to West 4th Street. 212-533-2700. www.bigelowchemists.com.*

## 37. Get a straight-razor shave at the **Paul Molé Barber Shop**.

A proper straight-razor shave is a dying art—and a luxurious treat. Paul Molé has been in business in the same narrow barbershop on the Upper East Side for close to a century, and getting a shave here hasn't changed much since then. An authentic experience from the warm, steamed towels down to the sharp silver blade, the barbers are reassuringly experienced and deliver the best shave in the city. You'll leave looking and feeling a better man.
*1031 LEXINGTON AVENUE BETWEEN 73RD AND 74TH STREETS IN MANHATTAN. Subway: 6 to 77th Street. 212-535-8461.*

## 38. Look for famous faces (part 1) at **Elaine's**.

Celebrity is never far from this legendary Upper East Side restaurant, where the imperious Elaine Kaufman has been shielding the likes of Woody Allen, Michael Caine, Candace Bushnell, and other famous New Yorkers from oglers since its opening in 1963. Elaine's reputation as a legendary hostess has grown from her generosity toward irregularly paying writer friends and from her ruthless efforts to keep out the riffraff—she has been known to have fistfights with unwanted diners and to eject more common customers in favor of a big name or two. While other restaurants run hot and cold like a bad brownstone faucet, Elaine's has remained a refuge for a certain veteran celebrity set, who've been going there since before anyone knew their names.
*1703 SECOND AVENUE BETWEEN 88TH AND 89TH STREETS IN MANHATTAN. Subway: 4, 5, 6 to 86th Street. 212-534-8114.*

## 39. Look for famous faces (part 2) at **Sardi's**.

Plenty of theater-district restaurants have a regular roster of famous patrons, but the only one that can truly guarantee that you'll see stars is Sardi's. Started in 1921 as The Little Restaurant by Vincent Sardi, it quickly became a clubhouse for Broadway stars. At the first Tony Awards in 1947, Sardi was honored for "providing a…home and comfort for the theater folk at Sardi's for twenty years." The restaurant's claim to fame is the collection of caricatures, an idea that Sardi got from a well-known restaurant in Paris. Some 1,200 portraits line the wall, drawn in a harsh, exaggerated caricature style that has famously angered some of the models. (Maureen Stapleton allegedly stole her portrait and burned it and didn't come back to the restaurant until Vincent Sardi Jr. took it over and wrote her a note saying that all was forgiven. She returned, and a new portrait of her was done in 1996.) The current caricaturist-in-residence, Richard Baratz, does around twenty new portraits each year, which are formally unveiled at an annual ceremony with the "honorees."

*234 WEST 44TH STREET, BETWEEN BROADWAY AND EIGHTH AVENUE IN MANHATTAN. Subway: 1, 2, 3, 7, N, Q, R, W, S to Times Square-42nd Street; A, C, E to 42nd Street-Port Authority Bus Terminal. 212-221-8440. www.sardis.com.*

→ **DID YOU KNOW?** *Sardi hired an artist named Alex Gard to draw the portraits of the stars who frequented the restaurant, in exchange for one free meal a day. To maintain a good working relationship, Sardi couldn't criticize the portraits, and Gard couldn't criticize the food.*

## 40. Visit **Tavern on the Green**.

Tavern on the Green, the ornate glittering palace in Central Park, has perhaps the most humble provenance of any restaurant in New York: it originally housed the sheep that grazed on Sheep Meadow. Now a solid fixture of New York history, the tavern's unpretentious start in the late nineteenth century was just the beginning of its long and bumpy journey to becoming one of the most well-known restaurants in the world. It has opened, shut down, and reopened, always to much fanfare; it has been used for movie scenes, hosted premiere parties, and is *the* New York wedding cliché; and its illuminated façade peeking out of the park is one of the most familiar images of New York. A $10 million renovation in the mid-1970s turned it into the over-the-top wonderland that it is today, full of the decorative features that New Yorkers love to hate. The crystal chandeliers, hand-painted murals, abundant floral bouquets, carved mirrors, and copper and gold-leaf weather vanes give it an opulent it slightly anachronistic feel, kind of like a Mad Hatter's tea party on an unlimited budget. The food is, well, what you might expect from a lavishly themed attraction, but going to Tavern on the Green for the food is like walking to the top of the Eiffel Tower for exercise—theoretically possible, but entirely beside the point.

*CENTRAL PARK WEST AT 67TH STREET IN MANHATTAN. Subway: B, C to 72nd Street; 1 to 66th Street-Lincoln Center; A, C, B, D to 59th Street-Columbus Circle. 212-873-3200. www.tavernonthegreen.com.*

→ **DID YOU KNOW?** *In 1934, when the legendary New York Parks Commissioner Robert Moses decided that the old sheepfold should be turned into a restaurant, he shipped the sheep out to **Prospect Park** (see page 219), and reassigned their shepherd to the lion house in the Central Park Zoo.*

## 41. Have a "Red Snapper" at the St. Regis Hotel's **King Cole Bar.**

Named for the Maxfield Parrish mural depicting the Mother Goose character that graces the wall, this bar occupies an important part of cocktail history: it claims to be the birthplace of the Bloody Mary—though here they still call it by its "real" name, the Red Snapper. (The bartender who invented the drink also worked at a bar in Paris; "Bloody Mary" was what they called it there.) Order a Red Snapper, and then hunker down in one of the leather club chairs with a fancy tray of nuts and bar snacks, and you'll feel classy and authentically big-time.

*2 EAST 55TH STREET AT FIFTH AVENUE IN MANHATTAN. Subway: E, V to Fifth Avenue/53rd Street. 212-753-4500. www.stregis.com.*

→ **DID YOU KNOW?** *The bar's namesake mural was actually made for another hotel, the Knickerbocker, on Broadway and 42nd Street, where it originally hung after it was completed in 1906. When the Knickerbocker closed during Prohibition, the mural was saved and eventually relocated to the St. Regis in 1935.*

## Make time for tea

For a glimpse into the civilized city of yesteryear, there's no more effective way to do it than with afternoon tea. Though not the institution that it is in London, afternoon tea here is an uncommonly decadent pleasure, a vestige of an old-fashioned, high-class world where people with the means didn't think twice about pausing to enjoy an extra meal. In addition, tea is a fitting way to take in the legendary grandeur of some of the city's longstanding bastions of high society. The following hotels are themselves classic New York haunts from this lost era of leisure and refinement, and enjoying an authentic, well-appointed afternoon tea at one of them is the best way we can think of to appreciate their legacy and be transported back to their glory days.

### 42. *The Rotunda in the Pierre Hotel:*

For years, the Pierre and the Plaza engaged in a subtle rivalry across Fifth Avenue, each proudly standing as its own version of the grand New York hotel. The Plaza was the showier of the two, but now that that hotel has closed, the subdued grandeur of the Pierre, which exudes a more discreet kind of charm, shines a little brighter.

If you can summon up the courage to penetrate the hotel's forbiddingly posh exterior (Tip: the main entrance is on 60th Street, not under the canopy on Fifth Avenue), tea in the Rotunda is a nice reward. Everything else on the ground floor—the main lobby, the restaurant, the bar—is the picture of patrician refinement, with subdued lighting, tame furniture, and low ceilings. The Rotunda, in contrast, is a visual feast of romance and sumptuous color, with its whimsical shape (a rotunda on the ground floor?), plush couches, and lavish *trompe l'oeil* murals depicting gods and goddesses along a perfect blue sky. It's as if all of the splendor, the decadence, and the extravagance of the hotel were reserved for this single room. Tea, served daily from 3:00 p.m. to 5:30 p.m., is a fitting activity for this special, splendid space. Some of the figures in the murals depict the hotel's former patrons; as you nibble on your sandwiches, see if you can find Jackie O.

*FIFTH AVENUE AT 61ST STREET IN MANHATTAN. Subway: N, R, W to Fifth Avenue/59th Street. 212-838-8000. www.tajhotels.com.*

---

**43.** *Astor Court at the St. Regis Hotel:* Right across from **King Cole Bar** (see opposite) is the posh Astor Court restaurant. Afternoon tea at Astor Court (served daily from 3:15 p.m. to 5:30 p.m.) is more elegant than decadent, with abundant flowers, the requisite *trompe l'oeil* ceiling, and first-class table settings. The harpist that often plays during teatime adds an additional touch of refinement.

*2 EAST 55TH STREET AT FIFTH AVENUE IN MANHATTAN. Subway: E, V to Fifth Avenue/53rd Street. 212-753-4500. www.stregis.com.*

---

**44.** *The Cocktail Terrace at the Waldorf-Astoria:* Since its inception, many famous figures have resided at this grand Art Deco hotel, among them Cole Porter, who immortalized one of the hotel's other well-known features, the Waldorf salad, in his song "You're the Top," from the musical *Anything Goes.* Porter wrote many of his most famous lyrics at the Waldorf Towers, where he lived in style for a quarter of a century, from the late 1930s until near his death in 1964.

Porter's light-colored Steinway—covered in his own coffee cup circles and cigarette burns—still sits in a balcony lounge called the Cocktail Terrace. They won't let you play it, but they do have someone playing when the lounge is open (Wednesday through Sunday), and during breaks, you can go up and inspect it. You can have a drink here in the early evenings, as the name implies, but they'll send you across the lobby to Sir Harry's Bar when they start to close up around 8:00 p.m., so afternoon tea is the way to go. Served until 5:30 p.m., tea at the Cocktail Terrace is light, gay, and relatively laid-back as teatime goes. Instead of sitting up straight at well-appointed tables, you can languish in plush sofas or sink into easy chairs and, shielded from onlookers, dip your scones to your heart's content.

*WALDORF-ASTORIA HOTEL, PARK AVENUE LOBBY, 301 PARK AVENUE BETWEEN 49TH AND 50TH STREETS IN MANHATTAN. Subway: 6 to 51st Street; E, V to Lexington Avenue/53rd Street. 212-872-4818. www.waldorfastoria.com.*

→ **DON'T MISS:** The Wheel of Life, *the enormous mosaic on the floor of the lobby, just inside the Park Avenue entrance, below the cocktail terrace. The mosaic depicts six stages in the life of man in colorful, stunning detail.*

**45. *Lady Mendl's Tea Salon*** at the Inn on Irving Place: Though not technically a classic spot (the inn has been open only since 1994), this exquisite salon exudes a formal air that recalls another time and comes with an excellent provenance. The inn is housed in two connected nineteenth-century townhouses, whose original architectural details have been preserved. As befitting its namesake (Lady Mendl was the title acquired by the turn-of-the-century decorator Elsie de Wolfe when she married), the salon is resplendent and impeccably furnished with Victorian *accoutrements*. Lady Mendl's serves a proper high tea (Wednesday through Sunday, in two sittings, reservations required): a dainty feast comprises five courses of salads, sandwiches, scones, and sweets.

*56 IRVING PLACE, BETWEEN 17TH AND 18TH STREETS IN MANHATTAN. Subway: 4, 5, 6, L, N, Q, R, W to 14th Street-Union Square. For reservations, call 212-533-4466. www.innatirving.com.*

## 46. Hobnob with the jet set at **Harry Cipriani**.

Opened in 1985 by the son of Giuseppe Cipriani, a Venetian restaurateur from the early-to-mid-twentieth century, Harry Cipriani is a duplicate of Harry's Bar Venice, the famous ex-pat hangout patronized by Ernest Hemingway, Orson Welles, the Aga Kahn, and Peggy Guggenheim. The list of regulars at the New York restaurant is nearly as luminous (though it would be uncivilized to name names). The restaurant is physically connected to the **Sherry-Netherland** (see page 102), the exquisite residential hotel, and shares with it the same charmed and clubby atmosphere. It's the kind of place where people have regular tables, a meeting ground of the well known and the well-to-do. **Cipriani Downtown** is a less formal version of Harry Cipriani and a perpetual socialite hangout. It's where young heirs and heiresses go after they've fine-tuned their social skills at the Fifth Avenue location.

*718 FIFTH AVENUE AT 59TH STREET IN MANHATTAN. Subway: N, R, W to Fifth Avenue/59th Street. 212-753-5566. Cipriani Downtown, 376 WEST BROADWAY AT BROOME STREET IN MANHATTAN. Subway: C, E to Spring Street. 212-343-0999. www.cipriani.com.*

## 47. See Woody Allen play at the **Carlyle Hotel**.

Many people come to the Carlyle to see **Ludwig Bemelman's Madeline murals** (see page 134) in the bar that bears his name. But a slightly less well-known feature of the Carlyle is the fact that Woody Allen has a regular Monday night gig from early fall through late spring at the Café Carlyle supper club. For an $85 cover, you can see New York's most famous living native son pick up the clarinet and perform with the Eddie Davis New Orleans Jazz Band.

*35 EAST 76TH STREET AT MADISON AVENUE IN MANHATTAN. Subway: 6 to 77th Street. 212-744-1600. www.thecarlyle.com.*

## 48. Dine among the murals at **Café des Artistes**.

One of the oldest restaurants in Manhattan, Café des Artistes has been serving the well-heeled and *bon vivants* since 1917. Once frequented by artists and creatives like Marcel Duchamp and Isadora Duncan, the café has resisted the temptation to innovate, and the old New York feeling has been preserved perfectly, right down to the deliberately classic French cuisine (no tofu or lemongrass here). Just after the turn of the century, the neighborhood was populated largely by artists, and the café was opened to serve the residents of the **Hotel des Artistes** in the building above it. (The rooms had only basic kitchens, so tenants sent down ingredients and cooking instructions to the kitchen by dumbwaiter.) Though the hotel is no longer open, the café still has a bit of an insider feel (especially in the parlor, the new, casual walk-in area), but the artists you're likely to see will be more along the lines of Paul Newman or Itzhak Perlman, since the struggling ones have long since been priced out of the neighborhood. The atmosphere, however, is largely unchanged; the dining rooms remain cradled by Howard Chandler Christy's murals of frolicking nymphs, which nearly a century later, still seem a little risqué. Even the old-fashioned menu can be a bit enchanting—a relic from this gay, more carefree time.

*1 WEST 67TH STREET BETWEEN COLUMBUS AND CENTRAL PARK WEST IN MANHATTAN. Subway: 1 to 66th Street-Lincoln Center. 212-877-3500. www.cafenyc.com.*

→ **DID YOU KNOW?** *On February 1, 1919, the first Miss America was crowned at the Chu Chin Chow Ball at the Hotel des Artistes. (Unfortunately, the winner turned out not to be much of a "Miss"—she was married with two children.)*

## 49. Hang out in the lobby of the **Chelsea Hotel**.

If New York City is a place where the unconventional retreat from all corners of the world, then the Chelsea Hotel is their temple. This bastion of eccentricity on West 23rd Street has a long and checkered history as a home, hangout, and refuge for some of the most radical artists of the past century. This is where Sid killed Nancy (and then himself), where Dylan Thomas lived out his last booze-filled year, where William Burroughs wrote *Naked Lunch*, and where Andy Warhol filmed *Chelsea Girls*. Built in 1883 in what was then the city's burgeoning theater district, it was New York's first cooperative apartment complex and was the tallest building in the city until 1902. After the theater district migrated uptown around the turn of the century, 23rd Street quickly became commercialized, the residential building folded, and in 1905, it was turned into a hotel. Mark Twain and members of the Ashcan School were among the early guests and tenants who established the Chelsea's reputation as a haven for artists. These days, it still attracts an offbeat and arty crowd, both in the guest rooms and the apartments. Evidence of the hotel's illustrious past can be seen in the lobby, which displays an art collection that rivals those of the **galleries** (see page 141) that have cropped up a few blocks west. *222 WEST 23RD STREET BETWEEN SEVENTH AND EIGHTH AVENUES IN MANHATTAN. Subway: C, E to 23rd Street. 212-243-3700. www.hotelchelsea.com.*

## 50. See an arty movie at the **Paris Theater**.

Sandwiched between Bergdorf Goodman and the Plaza stands this little one-screen movie theater. Before the **Angelika**, the **Sunshine**, and **Film Forum** (see pages 157-159), the Paris was showing foreign and other outside-of-Hollywood movies, many of them the films that we consider classics today. The Paris has the nebulous distinction of being considered the oldest continually running "art-house" theater in the United States (it opened in 1948), but more precisely, it is known for its unusual programming (including some famous long runs—Franco Zeffirelli's *Romeo and Juliet* played here for over a year) and old-fashioned movie theater sensibility (one screen, no concession stand, no waiting area). Yet despite its anachronisms, and the fact that plenty of "arty" movies can now be seen at other forward-thinking multiplexes, the Paris still attracts a crowd. No matter what the season, people who don't look like they've ever been below 59th Street patiently wait in line for showings of first-run movies like Kenneth Branagh's four-hour *Hamlet* or Merchant Ivory's *Howard's End*. The Paris occasionally does revivals, and though known for its long runs, the theater now holds Saturday **midnight shows** (see page 343) of classic films. *4 WEST 58TH STREET BETWEEN FIFTH AND SIXTH AVENUES IN MANHATTAN. Subway: N, R, W to Fifth Avenue/59th Street. 212-688-3800.*

## 51. See an epic movie at the **Ziegfeld**.

Though it doesn't have the same intense nostalgia as the **Paris** (see opposite), seeing a movie at the Ziegfeld still feels special. There's nothing small or independent about it—it's currently operated by Clearview Cinemas—but this 1,131-seat theater is New York's last remaining movie palace. The current theater was built in the 1960s on the site of Florenz Ziegfeld's original Ziegfeld Theater. Though the red carpet lining the interior is not as plush as it once was, the theater itself still exudes majesty and large stature. Intimate it's not, but it's a grand old place for a spectacle movie.

*141 WEST 54TH STREET BETWEEN SIXTH AND SEVENTH AVENUES IN MANHATTAN. Subway: E, V to Fifth Avenue/53rd Street; F to 57th Street; N, Q, R, W to 57th Street. 212-777-FILM. www.clearviewcinemas.com.*

## Shop like they did in the old days.

How—and where—New Yorkers shop for food is both a relic of old-fashioned urban ways and a facet of our intensely pedestrian and cosmopolitan lifestyle. Unlike most of the rest of the country, many New Yorkers still do at least part of their food shopping in family-owned groceries, specialty stores, and local markets. It is an experience broadened by the number of places one passes on a given day and limited only by what can be carried in two hands while walking.

This way of shopping was also perpetuated by the assumption that these types of stores had fresher and more interesting products than the bigger supermarkets. This conviction has been challenged by the arrival of Whole Foods, Trader Joe's and other specialty food chains—places that most New Yorkers have ambivalent feelings about. Still, even if the stock at places like the stores below is no longer as unusual as it once was, people still seek them out for their reliable quality, knowledgeable proprietors, and idiosyncratic specialties.

The stores below have all achieved unofficial landmark status for their contributions to the city's food shopping. Today, in an increasingly homogenized retail landscape, they are monuments to a unique feature of the New York lifestyle, and something to savor as much as the food they sell. (For more gourmet food markets, see page 175.)

**52. *Dean & DeLuca:*** The products may not seem particularly exotic today, but before Dean & DeLuca, most New Yorkers wouldn't have known a loaf of artisan bread if it hit them on the head. This SoHo fine-food emporium pioneered the idea of a gourmet grocery store and introduced the city to sun-dried tomatoes, truffles, and extra-virgin olive oil. Those who shopped at Dean & DeLuca during its early years in the '70s and '80s may fondly remember the generous samples of imported cheeses, decadent pastries, and flavored breads, which previously were attainable only by flying to Europe. (It's also a great place to pick up a delectable free nibble; for more, see page 285.) Today, it is still one of the best sources in the city for imported and domestic fine foods and ingredients, and it carries products from other countries that are hard to find elsewhere. It is not an exaggeration to say that Dean & DeLuca has played a significant role in shaping the palate of Americans in recent years (as well as defining the neighborhood of SoHo as a cool and cosmopolitan place to be). So take a trip downtown and have an espresso toast to this prominent place in New York's gastronomic development.

*560 BROADWAY AT PRINCE STREET IN MANHATTAN. Subway: N, R, W to Prince Street. 212-226-6800. www.deananddeluca.com.*

**53. *Zabar's:*** Zabar's is the granddad of the big Upper West Side food markets. The 80th Street behemoth was born out of a single smoked fish counter operated by Louis and Lillian Zabar in 1934. Their reputation for high-quality fish at reasonable prices earned them a strong following, and eventually the Zabars took over the entire market. Today, you can buy everything from caviar to coffee appliances here. It's not always the most pleasant place to shop, but consider the crowds and commotion positive signs that it's not going to be turned into a Best Buy anytime soon. Grab some sandwiches and salads to go, and take them over to nearby Riverside Park for a picnic.

*2245 BROADWAY AT 80TH STREET IN MANHATTAN. Subway: 1 to 79th Street. 212-787-2000. www.zabars.com.*

**54. *Russ & Daughters:*** Another family-owned business that started out as a smoked meat operation is Russ & Daughters. Instead of expanding into other foods and commodities as **Zabar's** did, this beloved Lower East Side institution has largely stuck to fish. You can buy breads, salads, and cookies as well, but it's the herrings, caviar, and smoked and cured meats that have kept people coming for four generations.

*179 EAST HOUSTON STREET BETWEEN ORCHARD AND ALLEN STREETS IN MANHATTAN. Subway: F, V to Lower East Side-Second Avenue. 212-475-4880. www.russanddaughters.com.*

**55. *Faicco's Pork Butcher:*** Situated on the quiet, western end of Bleecker Street, Faicco's has been serving wonderful Italian meats to its Greenwich Village neighbors for nearly 110 years. Treats made from delicious, fresh cuts of pork fill every counter: there are meatballs, cutlets, cured meats, casseroles, pasta sauces, sausages, and special delicacies like the *arancini*— crispy breaded rice balls stuffed with prosciutto and cheese. The place is always busy and retains a real neighborhood feel: crowds of old Italian women come in for the pastas, meats, and other Italian groceries, while working lunchers stop in to order a sandwich made with Faicco's amazing pork loin. Faicco's makes its own sausage and mozzarella daily and will cut any kind of pork any way you choose.

*260 BLEECKER STREET BETWEEN MORTON STREET AND LEROY STREET IN MANHATTAN. Subway: 1 to Christopher Street-Sheridan Square; A, C, E, B, D, F, V to West 4th Street. 212-243-1974.*

## 56. Have seafood at **Lundy Brothers**.

For more than seventy years, this enormous restaurant has served what just might be the most delicious seafood in New York. Lundy Brothers is right in the heart of Sheepshead Bay, Brooklyn's biggest fishing spot, so the fish is as fresh as it gets. Ever since it opened in 1934, Lundy Brothers has been the traditional way to end a day by the sea in Brooklyn. These days the reputation of its seafood—the clam chowders, the seafood pastas, and the incredible shellfish samplers, decadent tiers of crab, lobster, clams, mussels, shrimp, and oysters—draws people in from all over the world. Ask for a window seat and you can look out across the busy street at the brightly lit boats in the bay—the only view that can rival the lively atmosphere inside.

*1901 EMMONS AVENUE IN BROOKLYN. Subway: B, Q to Sheepshead Bay. 718-743-0022. www.lundysrestaurant.com.*

## 57. Grumble about gentrification at **Pete's Tavern**.

"The tavern that O. Henry made famous" also claims to hold the designation of New York City's longest continuously operating bar. They started serving in 1864 and haven't stopped since, not even during Prohibition, when disguised as a flower shop Pete's served as a popular speakeasy. O. Henry famously wrote "The Gift of the Magi" seated at one of the booths up front, and despite the fanfare for Ludwig Bemelmans at the **Carlyle Hotel** (see page 134), it was at Pete's that Bemelmans allegedly wrote the first *Madeline* book. But Pete's greatest accomplishment is that nearly 150 years after it opened, it is still a popular neighborhood watering hole.

*129 EAST 18TH STREET AT IRVING PLACE IN MANHATTAN. Subway: 4, 5, 6, L, N, Q, R, W to 14th Street-Union Square. 212-473-7676. www.petestavern.com.*

## 58. Get the giggles at **Caroline's**.

Though it's only a quarter of a century old, Caroline's has quickly become Manhattan's busiest and most famous comedy club, hosting new and famous stand-up comics seven nights a week. In 1989, a whole night at the club was filmed for posterity and released as the movie *Caroline's Comedy Hour*, which was turned into a hit series on the A&E network. Now in its third locale in Times Square (featuring a décor that earned an award from the American Institute of Architecture), Caroline's attracts the biggest names in today's comedy world, from Jerry Seinfeld to Rosie O'Donnell and Dave Chappelle—and serves a good supper, too.

*1626 BROADWAY BETWEEN 49TH AND 50TH STREETS IN MANHATTAN. Subway: 1 to 50th Street; N, R, W to 49th Street. 212-757-4100. www.carolines.com.*

## See a set at a famous jazz club.

Jazz and New York have gone hand in hand since Duke Ellington, Count Basie, and Billie Holiday lit up the clubs during the Harlem Renaissance of the 1920s and 1930s. As the popularity and reputation of jazz grew through the twentieth century, and as tastes and styles came to shape the districts of the city, jazz venues became beloved fixtures of New York, and the Big Apple became the beloved home of jazz musicians from across the world. Although many of the older establishments are long gone, there still remains a thriving jazz circuit in New York, in the grand revue halls of Harlem, the sophisticated supper clubs of Midtown west and the smoky underground bars of Greenwich Village. If you stick to these three neighborhoods, good jazz and the remnants of a golden musical age will never be far away. Below are some of our favorites, but it's also a good idea to keep an eye on the local listings for performers, concerts, and new venues.

**59. *The Lenox Lounge*** has been a pillar of Harlem's musical community for almost seventy years. As one of the finer bars and restaurants in the neighborhood it has always attracted locals and tourists alike, and as one of the city's most prestigious venues it has hosted all the legends of jazz through the decades, from Billie Holiday and John Coltrane to Roy Meriwether and Jimmy McGriff. When there isn't a big-name performer onstage, the house bands keep the place jumping with Latin, big band, and jam nights.

*288 MALCOLM X BOULEVARD BETWEEN 124TH AND 125TH STREETS IN MANHATTAN. Subway: 2, 3 to 125th Street. 212-427-0253. www.lenoxlounge.com.*

**60. *Birdland:*** Named for Charlie Parker, who called the original club the "jazz corner of the world," Birdland remains an institution of the Midtown jazz scene that lit up Manhattan in the 1950s and 1960s. Every big name in the history of jazz has played here, and the club's walls are covered in memorabilia of everyone from Duke Ellington to John Coltrane.
*315 WEST 44TH STREET BETWEEN EIGHTH AND NINTH AVENUES IN MANHATTAN. Subway: A, C, E to 42nd Street-Port Authority Bus Terminal. 212-581-3080. www.birdlandjazz.com.*

**61. *Village Vanguard:*** On Valentine's Day 2005, this West Village jazz mecca celebrated its seventieth year at the forefront of the New York scene. Since its inception in 1935, the club has hosted some of the all-time greats, from Pete Seeger and the prewar crooners to Miles Davis, Thelonius Monk, and the masters of modern jazz. Today, the Vanguard still books the best players around, and its acoustics are so revered by the musicians who play here that many have recorded albums on its stage. Go on a Monday night to hear the renowned Vanguard Jazz Orchestra, the house band that has played here for nearly 35 years. Note: downtown jazz fans should also have a drink and a listen at **55**, a classic jazz dive that has featured great musicians onstage—and retained a Prohibition-era feel—since 1919.
*VILLAGE VANGUARD: 178 SEVENTH AVENUE AT WEST 11TH STREET IN MANHATTAN. Subway: 1, 2, 3 to 14th Street. 212-255-4037. www.villagevanguard.com.*
*55: 55 CHRISTOPHER STREET BETWEEN SEVENTH AVENUE AND WAVERLY PLACE IN MANHATTAN. Subway: 1 to Christopher Street-Sheridan Square. 212-929-9883.*

**62. *St. Nick's Pub*** is probably the most authentic—and unpretentious—jazz club in the city. Located deep in Harlem's Sugar Hill district, the club is friendly and cheap and the music is always great. Choose the long bar for free over a table on the floor ($20), and you can enjoy simple drinks and great music for old–New York prices. There are live jazz musicians on the stage every night but Tuesday, and local artists frequently come to sit in on a session. Even Stevie Wonder has been known to drop in.
*773 SAINT NICHOLAS AVENUE BETWEEN 146TH AND 148TH STREETS IN MANHATTAN. Subway: A, C, B, D to 145th Street. 212-283-9728.*

**63. *Vote for the winner at Amateur Night at the Apollo Theater*,** the night that helped launch the careers of Ella Fitzgerald, James Brown, and Lauryn Hill. On Wednesday nights, the most famous soul and Motown theater in the world offers its stage to new musicians who might one day become legends—just like the ones you see on the walls of the Walk of Fame, the photographic exhibit of the theater's history set in the hallways backstage. *253 WEST 125TH STREET BETWEEN FREDERICK DOUGLASS BOULEVARD AND MANHATTAN AVENUE IN MANHATTAN. Subway: A, C, B, D to 125th Street. 212-531-5300. www.apollotheater.com.*

## 64. Feast on design at **Lever House Restaurant**.

Now more than fifty years old, this Park Avenue monument to modern architecture appropriately houses one of the most interesting-looking contemporary restaurants in the city. When it was built in 1952, Lever House was Park Avenue's first glass-covered office high-rise; half a century later, acclaimed designer Mark Newson's modish interior ensures the restaurant's singularity among Midtown's working-lunch spots. Set in a cool, airy room whose décor is at once retro and modern, with a bright bar at one end and booths along one wall, the restaurant's ambience is uniquely quiet and laid-back. The menu is a mix of French and American cuisine, and the fish and poultry dishes are always good. While this is a great (and unusually relaxed) place for an evening meal, Lever House livens up on weekday afternoons, when Midtown hotshots descend in droves for its lunchtime menu.
*390 PARK AVENUE AT 53RD STREET IN MANHATTAN. Subway: 6 to 51st Street; E, V to Lexington Avenue/53rd Street. 212-888-2700. www.leverhouse.com.*

## 65. Toast Dylan Thomas at the **White Horse Tavern**.

This village pub is New York's quintessential literary haunt—in addition to Thomas, Norman Mailer, James Baldwin, Allen Ginsberg, and Jack Kerouac all drank here. It's a nice old-fashioned place to have a drink, no matter what your passion, but all aspiring writers and poets should make the pilgrimage. If the portraits of Thomas don't get your creative juices flowing, then perhaps the whiskey will.
*567 HUDSON STREET BETWEEN PERRY STREET AND WEST 11TH STREET IN MANHATTAN. Subway: A, C, E to 14th Street; L to Eighth Avenue. 212-243-9260.*

## 66. Pass up Pastis for **Odeon**.

Many of today's cool, celebrity-packed restaurants pay homage to Odeon, the Tribeca pioneer immortalized in *Bright Lights, Big City*. This is perhaps because, unlikely as it is, Odeon has managed an enviable feat in the world of New York dining and nightlife: going from hot spot to classic. (The original owner was **Keith McNally**, a restaurateur famously adept at creating sought-after spots, including **Pastis**. For more on McNally, see page 163.) The transition hasn't been seamless, but as many once impenetrable destinations have come and gone, Odeon has hung on by its legendary reputation— and it helps that good bistro food never goes out of style.

*145 WEST BROADWAY AT THOMAS STREET IN MANHATTAN. Subway: 1, 2, 3, A, C to Chambers Street. 212-233-0507. www.odeonrestaurant.com.*

## 67. Dinner and dancing at the **Rainbow Room**.

New York's original supper club is the perfect place to sip a dry cocktail and look out over the city. The biggest names in showbiz have climbed to the sixty-fifth floor of 30 Rock since its aristocratic origins in the 1930s, and it's still a good place to spot the city's glitterati in full swing. On Fridays and Saturdays, you can go for old-fashioned dinner and dancing, with live music, of course. Just remember: the dress code is formal.

*30 ROCKEFELLER PLAZA, 65TH FLOOR. 49TH STREET BETWEEN FIFTH AND SIXTH AVENUES IN MANHATTAN. Subway: B, D, F, V to 47th-50th Streets-Rockefeller Center. 212-632-5100. www.rainbowroom.com.*

## 68. Drink at the Round Table at the **Algonquin Hotel**.

The Algonquin has long been a celebrated haunt of New York literary types, from the Round Table's origins as a meeting place for such figures as Dorothy Parker and George Kaufman. Since the 1930s, the hotel has allowed a cat free run of the place: look out for the current resident feline at your feet in the Oak Room.

*59 WEST 44TH STREET BETWEEN FIFTH AND SIXTH AVENUES IN MANHATTAN. Subway: 7 to Fifth Avenue-Bryant Park; B, D, F, V to 42nd Street-Bryant Park. 212-840-6800. www.algonquinhotel.com.*

## 69. Ogle the interior at the **Four Seasons**.

You may never lead the kind of life where you have a regular lunch table at the Four Seasons, but that shouldn't stop you from eating there on a special occasion. This restaurant defines timeless style. Opened in 1950, the Four Seasons is the only archi tecturally landmarked interior in New York, but Philip Johnson's modernist design still looks cutting-edge. For lunch, the famed Grill Room is the place to be seated to see the crème de la crème of Midtown working society, but at night, when the movers and shakers have cleared out, the exquisite Pool Room, with its eponymous marble pool and color-changing trees, is the apex of elegant dining.

*99 EAST 52ND STREET BETWEEN LEXINGTON AND PARK AVENUES IN MANHATTAN. Subway: 6 to 51st Street; E, V to Lexington Avenue/53rd Street. 212-754-9494. www.fourseasonsrestaurant.com.*

## 70. Eat pizza at **Lombardi's** in Little Italy, America's very first pizzeria.

Many pizza joints in this town boast that they are "original," but after one hundred years on Spring Street, Lombardi's, New York's true original pizzeria, still serves up some of the most delicious pies in the city. Founded in 1905 by Gennaro Lombardi, the restaurant plays the part perfectly: red-and-white checked tablecloths, giant pizzas on silver pedestals, and stuffed calzones—all the good stuff. The lines that run outside the restaurant most nights of the week testify to its enduring popularity. Although it faces stiff competition from the other **great pizzerias** of the city (see page 203 for a rundown of the best pizza places), Lombardi's remains a favorite, with a warm and lively atmosphere and a menu that defines the American pizza joint. The food here hasn't changed much over the course of a century—the toppings are traditional, the sauces are simple, and the mozzarella is thick and fresh—but why should it? This is pizza the way it is supposed to be.

*32 SPRING STREET BETWEEN MOTT AND MULBERRY STREETS IN MANHATTAN. Subway: 6 to Spring Street. 212-941-7994. www.lombardisoriginalpizza.com.*

## 71. Order a frrrozen hot chocolate at **Serendipity**.

Despite woefully tongue-in-cheek touches like "Catcher in the Rye" sandwiches and Andy Warhol look-alike contests (he was once a regular), this eccentric New York institution still charms, a legendary eatery that has hosted celebrities, tourists, families, and sweet-toothed New Yorkers ever since it opened half a century ago. Although you could eat a whole meal here, Serendipity is better known as the home of some of the most delicious and indulgent desserts in the city—enormous chocolate fudge cake sundaes, peanut butter and chocolate ice creams, and banana splits like you wouldn't believe. The trademark dish is the frrrozen hot chocolate, a giant bowl of sweetness that seems bottomless until you finish it and wish you had another. Try sipping one of these from two straws with a sweetheart—it's like being at a classic American soda fountain dreamed up by Warhol.

*225 EAST 60TH STREET BETWEEN SECOND AND THIRD AVENUES IN MANHATTAN. Subway: 4, 5, 6 to 59th Street; N, R, W, to Lexington Avenue/59th Street. 212-838-3531. www.serendipity3.com.*

## 72. Have a cannoli (or two) at **Veniero's**.

For more than a century, this has been the place for Italian sweets in the East Village. Opened in 1894 as a pool hall with pastries, the shop and café still has many of its original architectural details, and a dizzying amount of good old fashioned calorie- and cream-laden treats to enjoy. Get a cappuccino and a cannoli (regular or chocolate-dipped), and relax in the cozy café, where you can admire the etched glass doors, exquisite marble floors, and the old-fashioned décor. Then take a number at the counter and get another cannoli to take home for later.

*342 EAST 11ᵀᴴ STREET, BETWEEN FIRST AND SECOND AVENUES IN MANHATTAN. Subway: L to First Avenue. 212-674-7070. www.venierospastry.com.*

## 73. Get a table at **Rao's**.

With a long-standing reputation as one of the hardest restaurants in the city to get into, Rao's is a quaint and authentic little Italian restaurant hidden away in East Harlem. A century ago, Rao's was the neighborhood favorite for the local Italian community, and it has since found favor with celebrities, in-the-know uptowners, and lovers of authentic southern Italian cooking all over the city. Call early to reserve a table, or else prop up the bar until there's one available—it can be done.

*455 EAST 114ᵀᴴ STREET AT PLEASANT AVENUE IN MANHATTAN. N.B.: Open Monday through Friday for dinner only. Subway: 6 to 116ᵗʰ Street. 212-722-6709. www.raos.com.*

## 74. Power breakfast at **Michael's**.

For a trip back to the glamorous, high-rolling times of the late twentieth century, have breakfast at Michael's. When it opened it the mid-'80s, Michael's was known for its then-exotic California cuisine, stylish contemporary art, and the business breakfast scene. Aside from the hairstyles and shoulder pads, not too much has changed, and you can still see executives hashing out deals over egg-white omelets.

*24 WEST 55ᵀᴴ STREET, BETWEEN FIFTH AND SIXTH AVENUES IN MANHATTAN. Subway: E, V to Fifth Avenue/53ʳᵈ Street. 212-767-0555. www.michaelsnewyork.com.*

## 75. Power lunch at the **Palm**.

Though you can now go to the Palm in Los Angeles, Miami, and Mexico City, the original Second Avenue location has classic New York written all over it—literally. Considered the country's oldest family owned sit down restaurant chain, the Palm was opened in 1926 by two Italian immigrants from Parma—which was the restaurant's intended name. However, a language barrier between the owners and the city register resulted in its being known as "the Palm." The cuisine was originally Italian, too, but they started serving steaks at the request of the executives, newsmen, and journalists who worked in the neighborhood. Those steaks—originally purchased from a butcher a few blocks up and carried to the kitchen by hand—garnered a large and loyal following. Eventually they made it onto the menu, and the rest is history. Back when lunch meant sirloins and stiff drinks, and businessmen meant, well, men, the Palm was the place to go. As the rest of Midtown popped up around it, the

Second Avenue stalwart held its own for almost fifty years until 1972, when at the behest of then-ambassador to the UN, George Bush, they opened their first branch in Washington, D.C. Today, there are more than twenty-five branches, but aside from the addition of lobster to the menu in 1965, nothing much has changed at the New York location.

*837 SECOND AVENUE, BETWEEN 44TH AND 45TH STREETS IN MANHATTAN. Subway: 4, 5, 6, 7 to Grand Central-42nd Street. 212-687-2953. www.thepalm.com.*

→ **DID YOU KNOW?** *Because they had no money to decorate, the original owners struck a deal with the newspaper artists and cartoonists who frequented the Palm: they could draw on the walls in exchange for a plate of spaghetti. Today, you can see cartoons of Batman, Popeye, and Beetle Bailey by their original artists, and regulars such as Yogi Berra, Francis Ford Coppola, Hugh Hefner, and J. Edgar Hoover immortalized on the walls.*

## 76. Get a bottle from the wine cellar at **One if by Land, Two if by Sea**.

This cozy West Village restaurant has been a favorite spot for lovebirds and Casanovas for more than thirty years—which in this city of rapid turnover is a feat of longevity in itself. The building's history, however, really dates back another two hundred years. Originally part of Richmond Hill, George Washington's headquarters, the building was first used as a carriage house during the defense of Manhattan in the mid-1700s; after the war, it was purchased by Aaron Burr as his private carriage house. Underneath the restaurant, where the wine cellar is now located, is a series of tunnels that once led all the way to the Hudson River. These tunnels are believed to have been used to smuggle in contraband during the Revolutionary War and were later part of the Underground Railroad.

*17 BARROW STREET BETWEEN BLEECKER AND WEST 4TH STREETS IN MANHATTAN. Subway: A, C, E, B, D, F, V to West 4th Street. 212-255-8649. www.oneifbyland.com.*

## 77. Warm up on a cold night by the fireplace with an ale and some fries at **Chumley's**.

This signless, sawdust-covered dive is also a great place for drinking on the sly any time of the year: there are two entrances (or exits) so people could escape police raids back in the days of Prohibition. They also have a fine selection of beers, excellent pub grub, and an impressive collection of literary memorabilia from some famous former patrons.

*86 BEDFORD STREET BETWEEN BARROW AND GROVE STREETS IN MANHATTAN. Subway: 1 to Christopher Street-Sheridan Square; A, C, E, B, D, F, V to West 4th Street.*

→ **DID YOU KNOW?** *The phrase "86 it" comes from Chumley's: during Prohibition, patrons were told to "86 it" before a raid, meaning to leave by the front entrance because it was unmarked.*

## 78. Choose between light and dark at **McSorley's Old Ale House**.

Opened in 1854, McSorley's is one of the oldest bars in New York, and it's defiantly old-fashioned. They started letting in women in the '70s; aside from that, everything else is pretty much the same as it was 150 years ago. Drinking at McSorley's is a good antidote to the city's high-pressure, cutting-edge, here-today-gone-tomorrow bar culture. Just don't expect a fancy beer menu: they brew only two types of ale, and you have to buy your drinks in pairs.

*15 EAST 7TH STREET BETWEEN BOWERY AND SECOND AVENUE IN MANHATTAN. Subway: F, V to Lower East Side-Second Avenue. 212-473-9148.*

## 79. Drink to New York under the shadow of the Brooklyn Bridge at the **Bridge Café**,

the oldest business in New York. (The restaurant eclipses Chase Manhattan, the runner-up, by five years.) The Bridge Café has been operating out of a beautiful old building on Water Street since 1794, when the area around the South Street Seaport was altogether unsavory. These days, the building is much the same and you can still get a rum if you'd like, but the clientele is more city than sailor, and a good wine might go better with the excellent seafood-focused menu.

*279 WATER STREET BETWEEN DOVER STREET AND PECK SLIP IN MANHATTAN. Subway: 6 to Brooklyn Bridge-City Hall. 212-227-3344.*

## Lament a legendary New York landmark that's passed.

Sadly, not every great spot in the city has made it to the present. Gentrifying neighborhoods, skyrocketing rents, changing tastes, and just plain time has brought on the demise of some truly great New York places. Here, we take a moment to remember some of the city's beloved institutions that are no longer with us (and one that's teetering on death's door...):

**80.** *The Plaza:* This eminent hotel (the only hotel in New York City to be designated a National Historic Landmark) figures prominently in the collective memory of New Yorkers and people from around the world. This is where Eloise played, Macauley Culkin hid out, and Cary Grant was kidnapped. The Plaza took its final reservation on April 29, 2005, and since then has been shuttered, its conspicuous façade surrounded by gates and barriers. At press time, a revamped Plaza was slated to reopen in 2007, with private residences and luxury shops.

*Located at 59TH STREET AND FIFTH AVENUE IN MANHATTAN. Subway: N, R, W to Fifth Avenue/59th Street.*

**81. *The Polo Grounds:*** Technically, there were four incarnations of the Polo Grounds, the historic baseball field that was home at different points to three New York baseball teams. The first one, where the New York Giants played between 1883 and 1888, was located at the northern tip of Central Park, so called because it had been converted from a polo ground to a baseball field. Polo Grounds II, III, and IV were all located around 155th Street and Frederick Douglass Boulevard, on a site overlooking Coogan's Bluff that is now a housing project. Although Polo Grounds IV is the only one anyone living today might have been to, collectively, the Polo Grounds are a local legend of glory and rebuff. The Polo Grounds are where "the greatest game ever played" was played on October 2, 1951, and where "the shot heard round the world" was hit (ending that same game). It was the longtime home of the Giants, before they left for San Francisco, and it was the first home of the Mets during their first two seasons, before they left for **Shea Stadium** and the rejected field was laid to rest in 1964. Still, the Polo Grounds may have gotten the last laugh. Who knows what kind of glorious future these two teams might've had if they hadn't left?

*Formerly located at 155TH STREET AND FREDERICK DOUGLASS BOULEVARD IN MANHATTAN.*

**82. *Ebbets Field:*** No other lost landmark in the city can more easily bring tears to a grown man's eyes than Ebbets Field, and plenty of baseball fans and longtime New Yorkers are still hurt by the demise of that stadium and the way their team left them. Opened in 1913, the stadium was home to the beloved Brooklyn Dodgers until 1957, when the team's owner made good on a threat to move them out West. The stadium was demolished in 1960 and now is the site of a group of apartment buildings known as the Jackie Robinson Apartments, after the Dodger great.

*Formerly located at 55 SULLIVAN PLACE IN BROOKLYN.*

**83. *CBGB:*** This shabby club on the Bowery is a rock-and-roll legend. CBGB is responsible for bringing punk music to the forefront of the music scene in the 1970s, and it was home to some of the best and most influential bands of that generation. Opened in 1973 by country-music obsessive Hilly Kristal, the club was originally intended to be a bluegrass venue, until the prevailing tastes of the Lower East Side took the music and CBGB in a new direction. Everyone from East Coast favorites like the Ramones, the Modern Lovers, and the Cars, to Television, Patti Smith, Deborah Harry, the Stilettos, and the Sex Pistols has graced (and disgraced) its stages, and it boasts the most notoriously abused bathrooms in the city. For now, at least, the Country BlueGrass Blues club still attracts amazing acts and dedicated crowds. With the future of this New York institution under threat (see page 325), our advice is to go see a show, check out the bathrooms, and spend a few minutes in the gallery next door to get a feel of what CBGB is and has always been about.

*315 BOWERY BETWEEN 1ST AND 2ND STREETS IN MANHATTAN. Subway: 6 to Bleecker Street; F, V to Lower East Side-Second Avenue. 212-982-4052. www.cbgb.com.*

**84. *Max's Kansas City:*** This legendary hangout frequented by artists and performers was a cauldron of creativity which churned some of the late-twentieth century's great artistic figures. Max's was where everyone came—when everyone was Andy Warhol, Roy Lichtenstein, Patti Smith, Bob Dylan, Bruce Springsteen, and Abbie Hoffman. Deborah Harry waited tables there; the Velvet Underground produced a live album there; both the B-52s and Bob Marley and the Wailers made their New York debuts there. Owner Mickey Ruskin offered advice, fostered creativity, and championed future stars for a few magical years until the '70s, when the magic faded, and Max's disappeared.

*Formerly located at 213 PARK AVENUE SOUTH BETWEEN 17TH AND 18TH STREETS IN MANHATTAN.*

**85. *Pips Comedy Club:*** Considered America's first comedy club, Pips was an unofficial comedian's hall of fame. It was where Rodney Dangerfield first complained about getting "no respect"; and the last place where Lenny Bruce was scheduled to perform (though he didn't make it). Woody Allen was once passed up for the house MC position here, and Jerry Seinfeld used to perform here for $35 a weekend. In more recent years, the big headliners were few and far between, but the restaurant still did its best to keep this cultural landmark alive. The menu featured the Andy Kaufman "All You Can Eat Ice Cream Sundae," in honor of the eccentric comic who loved the ice cream at Pips so much that he asked to be paid in it.

*Formerly located at 2005 EMMONS AVENUE BY OCEAN AVENUE IN BROOKLYN. www.pipscomedy.com.*

# Expert Contributor: Ric Bell

Ric Bell, FAIA, is the Executive Director of the New York chapter of the American Institute of Architects, housed in the **Center for Architecture** (see page 302).

## MY FIVE FAVORITE CLASSIC BUILDINGS IN NEW YORK

### 86. *McGraw-Hill Building*

When completed in 1931, Raymond Hood's horizontally banded McGraw-Hill Building towered over 42nd Street between Eighth and Ninth Avenues and the adjacent elevated subway. I worked for fifteen years here, in an open studio with views to the horizon in four directions. A block west of "America's crossroads" at Times Square, its location was linked to New York's zoning regulations—the mixed-use of printing presses and editorial offices was tolerated in Hell's Kitchen. At thirty-three stories tall, it stood alone as Midtown expanded east and north. The distinctive green terracotta sign-band top proclaiming the publishing house's name was illuminated for one night only in the early 1990s.

*330 WEST 42ND STREET BETWEEN EIGHTH AND NINTH AVENUES IN MANHATTAN. Subway: 1, 2, 3, 7, N, Q, R, S to Times Square-42nd Street; A, C, E to 42nd Street-Port Authority Bus Terminal.*

### 87. *Municipal Building*

For fifteen months I worked as an architectural bureaucrat in Manhattan's Municipal Building, across the street from City Hall Park. Completed in 1913, the building is the beautiful result of a competition won by McKim Mead & White; seeing photographs and film of "Civic Fame" being reinstalled atop its peak is as close to Fellini as one gets in Manhattan. With over a million square feet of office space for administrators and elected officials, the Municipal Building allowed the diminutive 1812 City Hall to remain the ceremonial center of political power. And with wedding-cake frills and operable windows, the building from the start was a combination of excess and practicality. Straddling Chambers Street, its monumental arch stands as a portal between Manhattan and Brooklyn.

*1 CENTRE STREET AT CHAMBERS STREET IN MANHATTAN. Subway: 4, 5, 6 to Brooklyn Bridge-City Hall; J, M to Chambers Street; N, R, W to City Hall.*

### 88. *Lever House*

Seen as a fraternal twin tower to the Seagram Building, Lever House, by Gordon Bunshaft of Skidmore Owings & Merrill, shook up stodgy Park Avenue in ways that the more sober Seagram did not. Lever House is excruciatingly beautiful, elegant in the way that the Rat Pack was elegant and refined in the way that cars of the period are in your face. The now-classic use of green glass and the animated creation of an elevated garden and asymmetric open plaza expressed an openness of spirit, an urbanistic clarity befitting the Liverpudlian soap conglomerates' headquarters. With a narrow floorplate assuring that almost every occupant of the building would be near a window and have a view, Lever House expressed premature ambitions toward green architecture; that expression continues with a recent head-to-toe renovation by the Polshek Partnership.

*390 PARK AVENUE AT 53ᴿᴰ STREET IN MANHATTAN. Subway: 6 to 51ˢᵗ Street; E, V to Lexington Avenue/53rd Street.*

## 89. *Lipstick Building*

John Burgee and Philip Johnson—with help from high-fashion architect Ronnette Riley—took chances at Third Avenue and 43rd Street that they could not take on Fifth Avenue. They created the most feminine of skyscrapers, the so-called Lipstick Building—given its natty nickname for reasons that go beyond its purple-brown urban lipshade. The slender and curving shape of each office floor evokes the form of a cosmetic department purchase, a visible lipstick that you might find hidden among the miniature model towers in Riley's collection. The Lipstick Building—more than 2 Columbus Circle, AT&T, or any other pretender—points out that modernism in New York is skin-deep, and has fun doing so.

*885 THIRD AVENUE BETWEEN 53ᴿᴰ AND 54ᵀᴴ STREETS IN MANHATTAN. Subway: 6 to 51ˢᵗ Street; E, V to Lexington Avenue/53rd Street.*

## 90. *7WTC*

The new 7WTC tower by David Childs of Skidmore Owings & Merrill (opened in May 2006) replaces its namesake, destroyed on September 11, 2001. It is a superb building that reminds me of Danny DeVito in *Twins*—all dressed up, and waiting for the bigger sibling. Where previously there was a roadblock, the new building permits a Greenwich Street view corridor to the World Trade Center site. Reconstructed elements at the building's base are masked by the twinkling exterior wall art of James Carpenter, and the words of Jenny Holzer's moving installation in the lobby keep visitors thinking. Innovative stairway design assures that building safety is taken very seriously in the first new building to be completed in lower Manhattan since the 2001 terrorist attack. One of the wisest urban planners in the history of New York has called it "the first building of the twenty-first century."

*250 GREENWICH STREET AT MURRAY STREET IN MANHATTAN. Subway: 2, 3 to Park Place; E to World Trade Center.*

CHAPTER 2:

# Views & Sights

**L**ook up, look down, look around—no matter where you look in this city, you're guaranteed to see something remarkable. On the streets, there's always something new to gaze upon—a restaurant that has suddenly opened in a spot that was long vacant, a movie shoot, a street performer attracting a crowd. The constantly changing and unpredictable nature of the city gives every outing the potential for unexpected excitement. But there are also plenty of places—obvious and unlikely—with reliably spectacular views. This chapter has the best sites worth seeking out.

The panorama of the city seen from the top of a building is the quintessential New York view. The top of the Empire State Building is the city's signature vantage point, but it's not only the skyscrapers that have stellar views. The top of every building offers its own special glimpse of the city, revealing a perspective visible only from overhead. Of course, many of these buildings are private residences, so only occupants and their invitees are privy to them, but plenty are open to the public—including a whole host of rooftop bars and lounges, where you can comfortably drink in the view for as long as you please (as long as you keep drinking).

Then there are the waterfronts and all the glorious vistas they afford—river views, ocean views from boardwalks and beaches, island views, and of course the sunrises and sunsets over the water. Here, the transit department has helped us quite a bit, offering some of the city's best water views courtesy of its bridges, subways, ferries, and the Roosevelt Island Tram.

Of course, the best views aren't always of the city's natural or man-made landscapes. Watching human dramas unfold in some of New York's colorful locales can be fascinating and surprising, whether for the pleasurable juxtaposition of so many different people at a single crossroads or the uniformity of a specific milieu so complete, you'd think you were in a different country (or world). And don't forget the buildings themselves—feats of architecture and engineering are yours to admire and wonder at, as long as you keep your eyes open.

Enjoy the views!

# Rooftop Bars

Though they used to be as subtle as speakeasies, over the past couple of years, rooftop bars have gone mainstream, and nowadays they seem to be cropping up faster than ATMs. Hotels are one of the few kinds of buildings with an incentive to turn their roofs into lively public spaces, so that's where most rooftop bars are located. Some have been around for ages but were traditionally frequented only by hotel guests and not really thought of as a destination for anyone not staying there. However, with the advent of the hip luxury and boutique hotels came a new spate of rooftops with high profiles, built-in caché, and excellent views. Note: Except for two (which we've specified), all of these bars are open to the public; however, some of them are open only during the warmer months, so it's best to call before heading out.

## 91. Immerse yourself in silence and a martini at the **Pen-Top Bar and Terrace,** the rooftop of the recently renovated Peninsula Hotel. For the $20 price of a cocktail ($80 if you choose the one with Cristal—see page 288 for more details), you also get quite a view. From here you can see up the length of Central Park all the way to Harlem and down below to the throngs of tourists on Fifth Avenue, who seem very, very far away…

*700 FIFTH AVENUE AT 55TH STREET IN MANHATTAN. Subway: E, V to Fifth Avenue/53rd Street. F to 57th Street. 212-956-2888. www.newyork.peninsula.com.*

## 92. Vertigo, voyeurism, or both will keep you glued to the railing at the **Top of the Tower,** the discreet Art Deco bar on the roof of the Beekman Tower Hotel in Midtown. The wall around this penthouse bar is so low you can lean over and look straight down First Avenue. To the west is New Jersey, and to the east you can see Roosevelt Island and the neon lights of the Long Island and Pepsi-Cola signs. Voyeurs take note: you can easily pass many hours staring through a martini into the well-lit rooms of several neighboring apartment buildings.

*FIRST AVENUE AND 49TH STREET IN MANHATTAN. Subway: 6 to 51st Street; E, V to Lexington Avenue/53rd Street. 212-355-7300. For more information, see the listing for Beekman Tower Hotel at www.affiniahotels.com.*

## 93. Look up at the two most impressive buildings of Midtown—the Empire State Building and the Chrysler Building—from the **Rare View**.

This aptly named bar and restaurant ("rare" is a play on the view and the burgers they serve) on top of the sixteen-floor Shelburne Hotel puts you face to midsection with the Midtown skyscrapers. The tropical-looking trees and lounge chairs make it feel like an elevated beach in the middle of the city.

*303 LEXINGTON AVENUE AT 37TH STREET IN MANHATTAN. Subway: 6 to 33rd Street. 212-481-1999. www.rarebarandgrill.com.*

## 94. Bask in the shadow of the Empire State Building at the Hotel Metro Rooftop Bar.

This small, humble roof deck has an exclusive yet amateurish feel—drinks are served in plastic glasses full of ice from a small cart—and offers an excellent close-up of the city's tallest building.

*45 WEST 35TH STREET BETWEEN FIFTH AND SIXTH AVENUES IN MANHATTAN. Subway: B, D, F, V, N, Q, R, W to 34th Street-Herald Square. 212-947-2500. www.hotelmetronyc.com.*

## 95. It's not part of a hotel, but one of the city's best rooftop treats is to drink champagne on the rooftop terrace of the Metropolitan Museum.

There's a new sculpture installed here each year, but the real thing to admire is the incredible view of Central Park—the same one that people living on Fifth Avenue pay millions for. (The views of those buildings are great to look at as well— try to find some of the lovely private gardens on the rooftops.)

*1000 FIFTH AVENUE AT 82ND STREET IN MANHATTAN. Subway: 4, 5, 6 to 86th Street. 212-535-7710. www.met.org. See page 118 for more information on the museum.*

## 96. Look down on Soho House members–literally–from the top of the Hotel Gansevoort.

The spectacular lounge on top of this chic Meatpacking District hotel lets you gaze out from all four sides of the building. You can see the towers of Midtown facing the Hudson River, and in the right light, the New Jersey coast looks positively sun-kissed. You can also watch the hammock swing by the pool on the famously lavish roof of the elite private club, Soho House, a few floors lower down. The Gansevoort has a rooftop pool, too, and one-ups the rival Soho House's with an underwater music system. But this pool's just for hotel guests, so lest you forget your place in the social pecking order and try to take a dip, the friendly hotel enforcers will escort you back to the lounge.

*18 NINTH AVENUE AT 13TH STREET IN MANHATTAN. Subway: A, C, E to 14th Street; L to Eighth Avenue. 212-206-6700. www.hotelgansevoort.com.*

## 97. See the city in a 360-degree panorama at the **View Lounge**.

It's worth the trip to the top of the Marriott Marquis in Times Square to experience New York's only revolving restaurant and bar. A recent overhaul has improved the food and drink—and removed the dance floor—but the view is as stellar as it has always been. The clientele hasn't changed much either, so you'll be admiring the skyline with business travelers and couples in town for the evening to celebrate an anniversary or a birthday.
*1535 BROADWAY BETWEEN 45TH AND 46TH STREETS, 48TH FLOOR, IN MANHATTAN. Subway: 1, 2, 3, 7, N, Q, R, W, S to Times Square-42nd Street. 212-398-1900. www.nymarriottmarquis.com.*

## 98. Another place with a great Times Square view is Ava Lounge on top of the **Dream Hotel**.

The crazy décor inside the bar is hard to ignore, but don't let it distract you from going to the windows to look Times Square straight in the eye (the hotel is only fifteen stories high, which makes for an almost eerie close-up of the neon billboards). For a more panoramic view, go out to the impeccably manicured garden terrace (open spring through fall, weather permitting), and try to make out the Hudson River behind the steely buildings and the pulsating lights. More surreal views can be found in the hotel's lobby—there's a wild copper statue of Catherine the Great, and a 4,000-gallon fish tank, the largest indoor aquarium in North America.
*210 WEST 55TH STREET BETWEEN BROADWAY AND SEVENTH AVENUE IN MANHATTAN. Subway: 1 to 50th Street; E, V to Fifth Avenue/53rd Street. 212-956-7020. www.avaloungenyc.com.*

N.B.: The following two bars are technically reserved for hotel guests and not open to the public. But the views are so lovely, we couldn't resist including them. Either splurge and make an overnight of it, or pose as guests who have lost their key (at your own risk).

**99. Hudson Hotel Sky Terrace:** Jersey's not quite Monaco, but this beachy rooftop bar feels just like an elevated café on the Riviera.
*356 WEST 58TH STREET BETWEEN EIGHTH AND NINTH AVENUES IN MANHATTAN. Subway: 1, A, C, B, D to 59th Street-Columbus Circle. 212-554-6000. www.morganshotelgroup.com.*

**100. A60 at 60 Thompson Hotel:** A great cityscape view from an unusual vantage point, right in the middle of SoHo.
*60 THOMPSON STREET BETWEEN SPRING AND BROOME STREETS IN MANHATTAN. Subway: C, E to Spring Street. 877-431-0400. www.60thompson.com.*

# More rooms with a view

A restaurant is a trickier venture to pull off on a roof (though there are some—see below), but that doesn't mean that the city lacks for restaurants with impressive views. Whether high up, on the water, or right in the middle of a bustling locale, the following restaurants offer built-in ambience that equals (or exceeds) the quality of the food they serve.

### 101. Check out northern Manhattan at **Terrace in the Sky**.

Nestled on the sixteenth floor of a building by Columbia University, this indoor/outdoor rooftop restaurant is like dining in a bird's nest with very fancy food.
*400 WEST 119TH STREET BETWEEN AMSTERDAM AVENUE AND MORNINGSIDE DRIVE IN MANHATTAN. Subway: 1 to 116th Street-Columbia University. 212-666-9490. www.terraceinthesky.com.*

### 102. Check out lower Manhattan at **Alma**.

You wouldn't know it from its modest brick exterior, but this Mexican joint in Brooklyn has a rooftop deck (open in season) with glorious views of the lower Manhattan skyline. After your meal, head downstairs to B61, the bar on the ground floor—the river views from the bay windows aren't bad either.
*187 COLUMBIA STREET AT DEGRAW STREET IN BROOKLYN. Subway: F, G to Carroll Street. 718-643-5400. www.almarestaurant.com. N.B.: Alma and B61 share an address but have different hours.*

### 103. Sneak into the ballroom at the **Rainbow Room** on a weeknight for one of the best views of the city.

The Rainbow Room is famed for its spectacular views, as well as its legendary Big Band–era ballroom, which is used only for dinner and dancing on Friday and Saturday nights. Come by the restaurant for dinner or drinks on any other night of the week, and you can see the glittering panorama of city lights flickering in the nighttime through the three walls of windows that enclose the dining room. Then, when no one's looking, you can slip through a door in the back to see the Rainbow Room's other great site. There, you'll find the grand Art Deco ballroom under wraps, and you can peek through the curtains for a private viewing of the scene from 30 Rock. There's even an upright piano in a corridor if the views inspire you ....
*30 ROCKEFELLER PLAZA, 65TH FLOOR, IN MANHATTAN. 212-632-5100. www.rainbowroom.com. For full entry, see page 47.*

## 104. View MoMA's sculpture garden from above at **Terrace 5**.

If you make it all the way to Museum of Modern Art's top floor, you'll be rewarded by this lovely (and relatively calm) seasonal café. You'll need to pay admission to the museum, but the view and the treats—snacks and desserts from **Danny Meyer**'s hospitality group (see page 163)—are worth it.

*11 WEST 53RD STREET, FIFTH FLOOR, BETWEEN FIFTH AND SIXTH AVENUES IN MANHATTAN. Subway: E, V to Fifth Avenue/53rd Street. 212-708-9400. www.moma.org. For more information on the museum, see page 121.*

## 105. See Manhattan in a different way at the **River Café**.

When you see the view, it's hard to believe that this restaurant hasn't been around forever. But when founder Michael "Buzzy" O'Keefe decided in the late '70s to open a restaurant under the Brooklyn Bridge, everyone thought he was crazy to consider such a desolate area. How times have changed. Go to this Brooklyn waterfront pioneer for dinner, lunch, brunch, whatever—just don't forget to look out the window.

*1 WATER STREET IN BROOKLYN. Subway: 2, 3 to Clark Street; A, C to High Street. 718-522-5200. www.rivercafe.com.*

## 106. Get ferried to the **Water's Edge**.

The comparisons are inevitable: they're both in boroughs, both on barges, and both boast exquisite waterfront views of Manhattan. But this Long Island City restaurant overlooking the East River has one feature that the River Café lacks: it offers free ferry service from Manhattan.

*EAST RIVER AT 44TH DRIVE IN QUEENS. Ferry service available nightly from 34th Street pier in Manhattan; ferries depart from Manhattan on the hour between 6:00 p.m. and 10:00 p.m. and return at a quarter to, until 10:45 p.m. 718-482-0033.*
*www.watersedgenyc.com.*

## 107. Pretend you're on a (semi-) private yacht at the **Water Club**.

Manhattan's answer to Brooklyn's River Café and Queen's Water's Edge is this fancy barge-top restaurant in the East River. Looking out from the enclosed dining room or the seasonal Crow's Nest bar on the upper deck, you can gaze across the river to Queens and at the sparkling lights of Midtown Manhattan right in front of you.

*EAST RIVER NEAR 32ND STREET IN MANHATTAN. For more information and directions, call 212-683-3333 or visit www.thewaterclub.com.*

### 108. See the sun set over New Jersey from the **Boat Basin Café**.

Though it hasn't been around as long as some, this seasonal riverside bar and restaurant fits right in on the Upper West Side and is something of a warm-weather institution. Located above the 79th Street Boat Basin in Riverside Park, in a series of stone structures that look like Roman ruins, the café has endeared itself to its notoriously opinionated neighbors with excellent burgers, a baby- and dog-friendly attitude, and the breathtaking river views.

*WEST 79TH STREET AND THE HUDSON RIVER IN MANHATTAN. Open April through October, weather permitting. Subway: 1 to 79th Street. 212-496-5542. www.boatbasincafe.com.*

### 109. See Manhattan in panorama from **Giando on the Water**.

Located near the Brooklyn foot of the Williamsburg Bridge, Giando is an extravagant Italian restaurant with a lavish dining room and walls of floor-to-ceiling windows facing the East River. Its location affords one of the broadest panoramas of the city, looking south beyond the Manhattan Bridge to downtown Manhattan and north beyond the Williamsburg Bridge to Midtown. In warmer months, you can have dessert or drinks on the terrace, without any glass coming between you and the view.

*400 KENT AVENUE BETWEEN BROADWAY AND SOUTH 8TH STREET IN BROOKLYN. www.giandoonthewater.com.*

### 110. Watch the action at Grand Central at **Metrazur** or **Cipriani Dolce**.

Both of these restaurants—which face each other from balconies across the terminal—are like indoor urban terraces. They overlook Grand Central's famous main hall, with its lovely, recently restored ceiling shining above, and some of the most dynamic people-watching in the city just below. Come for drinks in the late afternoon and watch commuters of all shapes and sizes scurry to make their trains.

*GRAND CENTRAL TERMINAL. 42ND STREET BETWEEN LEXINGTON AND MADISON AVENUES IN MANHATTAN. Subway: 4, 5, 6, 7, S to Grand Central-42nd Street. Metrazur is on the east balcony; Cipriani Dolce is on the west.*

**Metrazur:** *212-687-4600. www.charliepalmer.com/metrazur.*

**Cipriani Dolce:** *212-973-0999. www.cipriani.com. See page 77 for more information.*

*For more on Cipriani, see entry on page 38.*

*For full entry on Grand Central Terminal, see page 23.*

# Time Warner Center

This enormous complex boasts more vistas from a single site than any-where else in the city. Located right on Columbus Circle, at the foot of Central Park, pretty much everywhere in the two-building glass-fronted complex has a good view of something. (Except for the **Whole Foods** in the basement—see page 69 for a Whole Foods with a view.)
*10 COLUMBUS CIRCLE AT 59TH STREET IN MANHATTAN. Subway: 1, A, C, B, D to 59th Street-Columbus Circle.*

Starting from the top . . .

**111. *Asiate:*** At this Franco-Japanese restaurant in the Mandarin Oriental Hotel, the main decorative element is the spectacular Central Park panorama presented through sixteen-foot-tall windows. The wall of wine—their 1,300-bottle collection displayed by the entryway—is also an impressive sight.
*Mandarin Oriental Hotel, Thirty-fifth floor. 212-805-8881.*

**112. *Lobby Lounge.*** Clever name. Yes, it's adjacent to the Mandarin Orien-tal's lobby—but that lobby is 280 feet above street level! Enjoy the view of Broadway over drinks, snacks, or afternoon tea.
*Mandarin Oriental Hotel, Thirty-fifth floor. 212-805-8881.*

**113.** A little further down, ***Dizzy's Jazz Club Coca-Cola*** on the fifth floor offers great close-ups of Central Park—as well as the street performers.
*Dizzy's is part of Jazz at Lincoln Center; for more information, see page 147, call 212-258-9595, or visit www.jalc.org.*

**114. *The dining rooms in the fourth-floor "restaurant collection"*—** which include **Per Se** and **Masa** (for full entries, see pages 166-7) all have excellent views. But take note: these are some of the most expensive (and exclusive) restaurants in the city, so advance planning is advised.
*Fourth floor.*

## 115. Ride the Wonder Wheel at **Coney Island**.

Sit in one of the cars that don't swing and you'll be able to take in breathtaking views of the Atlantic Ocean in one direction and the Manhattan skyline in another.
*ASTROLAND, 1000 SURF AVENUE AT WEST 10TH STREET IN BROOKLYN. Open March through Octo-ber. Subway: D, F, N, Q to Coney Island-Stillwell Avenue. www.astroland.com. See also page 348.*

### 116. Watch the sun set from the roof deck of the arch in **Wagner Park**.

Watching the sun go down from anywhere along the boardwalk of Battery Park is beautiful, but the unobstructed views of Lady Liberty and the small islands below Manhattan from Wagner Park are amazing.

*OFF BATTERY PLACE, JUST NORTH OF BATTERY PARK IN MANHATTAN. Subway: 1 to South Ferry.*

### 117. See the stars (the real ones) at Columbia University's **Rutherford Observatory**.

Seeing the constellations with the naked eye is one of the few things you can't do in New York. But Columbia University's observatory periodically opens its doors to the public for stargazing, usually one Friday a month. Under the guidance of a professor or grad student, you can use the observatory's equipment to break through the city's "light pollution" and admire the vast night sky.

*PUPIN HALL, COLUMBIA UNIVERSITY. 120TH STREET BETWEEN BROADWAY AND AMSTER-DAM AVENUE IN MANHATTAN. (The public must enter through the Columbia campus.) Sub-way: 1 to 116th Street. Schedule and frequency of open nights vary; call 212-854-3278 or visit www.astro.columbia.edu/~observe/ for current information.*

→ **DID YOU KNOW?** *Pupin Hall is where the first atomic bomb was developed, hence the name "Manhattan Project."*

### 118. Make your way to the tip of **Far Rockaway** and stand on the beach at nightfall.

The coasts of Brooklyn, Queens, and New Jersey light up like a long, drawn out fireworks display.

*FAR ROCKAWAY IN QUEENS. Subway: A to Rockaway Park/Beach 116th Street or Far Rockaway-Mott Avenue.*

## Esplanades & Promenades

The city's waterfront walkways offer lovely views of different parts of the city from afar, and a stroll along one of them is a pleasant reminder that no matter where you are in the concrete jungle, you're never landlocked.

**119.** *Brooklyn Heights Promenade:* A walk along the esplanade in one of Brooklyn's oldest neighborhoods is impressive and romantic, any time of day or night. On one side are views of lower Manhattan, and on the other, complementary views of tranquil streets lined with beautiful brownstones.

*BETWEEN MONTAGUE STREET AND MIDDAGH STREET AT THE WATER'S EDGE IN BROOK-LYN. Subway: 2, 3 to Clark Street.*

**120. *Battery Park Promenade:*** From here, at the southern tip of Manhattan, you have an unobstructed view of the waters in front of you—a good way to pass the time while waiting in line for the ferry to the **Statue of Liberty** and **Ellis Island** (see page 18).

*BATTERY PARK, NEAR THE CASTLE CLINTON MONUMENT IN MANHATTAN. Subway: 1 to South Ferry; 4, 5 to Bowling Green.*

**121. *Coney Island/Brighton Beach Boardwalks:*** Walk off your **Nathan's Famous hot dog** (see page 349) by strolling from the vendors at Coney Island to the Russian cafés of Brighton Beach on the huge, wooden boardwalk by the sea.

*FROM SURF AVENUE TO BRIGHTON BEACH AVENUE AND THE OCEAN IN BROOKLYN. Subway: B, Q to Brighton Beach; D, F, N, Q to Coney Island-Stillwell Avenue.*

**122. *FDR Boardwalk:***

This beach, and the two-and-a-half-mile boardwalk (the fourth largest in the world) that runs along it, look out toward the Atlantic on one side and toward lower Manhattan and Liberty, Governor, and Ellis Islands from the other. Come at sunset and watch the city turn pink and orange as the sun drops behind it. During the day, the boardwalk is surprisingly pleasant to bike along, because while it's still not quite as smooth as a paved road, it's generally not as clogged with pedestrians as some of the city's other boardwalks, and cyclists are well tolerated. You can also enjoy ocean breezes and a killer view of the Verrazano-Narrows Bridge.

*SOUTH BEACH IN STATEN ISLAND. Staten Island Ferry to St. George; then bus S51 to Father Capodanno Boulevard.*

**123. *Bobby Wagner Walkway at Carl Schurz Park:***

The West Side doesn't have a monopoly on the best waterfront views in Manhattan. Bobby Wagner Walk is the three-mile esplanade that extends from 63rd to 125th Street along the East River. Between 81st and 90th Streets, there is an elevated portion (also known as John Finley walk) adjacent to Carl Schurz Park that offers a wonderful uninterrupted panorama of the East River and its landmarks. True, it's not as pastoral as, say, the Palisades across the Hudson, but you get a good urban mix of islands (Randall's, Ward's, and Roosevelt), bridges (the Triborough and the Hells Gate), the lighthouse at the tip of **Roosevelt Island** (see page 234), and usually a tugboat or two. The park itself is uncommonly pretty, with winding pathways overlooking idyllic clearings

dotted with benches and fountains, an unusually pleasant dog run with a river view, and hidden among the trees, Gracie Mansion.
*BETWEEN 84TH AND 90TH STREETS ALONG THE EAST RIVER IN MANHATTAN. Subway: 4, 5, 6 to 86th Street.*

# Bridges & Tunnels

Thank goodness for the water. Without it, the dramatic scenery that separates different pieces of the city would be gone, and interborough transportation would be limited to views of streets and the insides of dark tunnels. Fortunately, geography and the transit department have blessed us with some incredible vistas at various crossings. Try some of these great transportation options, and enjoy the views that those lucky enough to commute that way get to experience every day.

## BRIDGES

Many of the bridges that connect the boroughs of New York to each other and to their neighboring state, New Jersey, are not only feats of modern engineering in their own right (the Verrazano-Narrows Bridge, to give one example, was until recently the longest suspension bridge in the world) but also offer some of the most spectacular views of the city. From the right vantage point—whether it's from the window of a moving train, through the rear windshield of a speeding cab, or from a bench in the middle of the bridge itself—looking at New York from its bridges can be one of the most revealing, exciting, and romantic things to do.

### 124. *The Brooklyn Bridge:*

Stretching across the East River between City Hall in lower Manhattan and Brooklyn Heights, the Brooklyn Bridge is the most famous of the city's bridges and by far the most beautiful. Walk across at dawn or at dusk and stop at one of the benches along the way for a breathtaking sunrise or sunset view. Look north toward the skyscrapers of Midtown or gaze south across the water toward the Atlantic Ocean and the Statue of Liberty.

### 125. *Manhattan Bridge:*

Reaching from the easternmost end of Canal Street in Manhattan to DUMBO in west Brooklyn, the best thing to see from the Manhattan Bridge is its neighbor, the Brooklyn Bridge. There are cutaways in the structure of the bridge that let pedestrians look out over the water at the lower tips of Brooklyn and Manhattan, and north toward the Williamsburg Bridge and the towers of Midtown. The views can be enjoyed in both directions by riding one of the subways (B, D, N, Q—see opposite for more information) that use the bridge to travel between the boroughs.

### 126. *George Washington Bridge:*
Although crossing the George Washington Bridge means stepping out of New York—it runs from 178ᵗʰ Street in Manhattan over the Hudson River to Fort Lee in New Jersey—a walk over the southern side of this mighty suspension bridge offers unbeatable views of Manhattan.

### 127. *Verrazano-Narrows Bridge:*
Connecting the boroughs of Brooklyn and Staten Island by stretching across the Narrows from Bay Ridge to the Staten Island Expressway, the Verrazano-Narrows Bridge is now the second longest suspension bridge in the world and an amazing sight to see. Although plans have been in the works since the bridge's construction in 1964, there is still no pedestrian walkway, so you have to drive across to see the glittering lights of the outer boroughs. But if that's not an option, the bridge is an equally impressive site from the ground, so it's worth finding a spot on the coast of Brooklyn or Staten Island from which to take it in.

## TRAINS
Subways are well known as efficient and convenient ways to get from point A to point B, but often overlooked (or unknown) is the fact that certain train rides are scenic as well. At different points along the subway system, the trains emerge from underground and cross bridges, climb elevated tracks, or ride alongside the ocean, routinely treating passengers to a picturesque diversion on top of the transportation they paid for.
*(For information on individual subway lines and locations, visit www.mta.info.)*

### 128. *7 train into Queens:*
as you enter the borough, the train curves and gives you amazing views of the Manhattan skyline and an aerial tour of the graffiti art at **5Pointz** (see page 137).

### 129. *4 train into the Bronx:*
Don't blink! For a split second, you can see inside **Yankee Stadium** (see page 30).

### 130. *Q train in Brooklyn:*
Survey the beach scene before you plop your blanket down. For a quick tour of the Brooklyn beaches, let the Q train take you from Sheepshead Bay and Brighton Beach all the way around to **Coney Island** (see page 348) and the **Aquarium** (see page 224).

### 131. *F train to Brooklyn:*
A few stops into Brooklyn, the F train emerges from its tunnel into the picturesque neighborhood of Carroll Gardens, where it rises and runs elevated over Park Slope.

Get out at Smith-9th Streets and enjoy the views across Brooklyn to Manhattan and the Statue of Liberty from the platform—the highest elevated point of New York's train system.

### 132. *B, D, N, Q train over the Manhattan Bridge:*
Whichever direction you travel, you get an exquisite view of the Brooklyn Bridge, suspended between the water and the sky.

### 133. Look at the fall foliage in Central Park from BG at **Bergdorf Goodman**.
If you can't make it upstate, the view from the store's seventh-floor café can satisfy yearnings for autumnal beauty. (The Kelly Wearstler décor inside isn't bad to look at, either.)
*754 FIFTH AVENUE AT 57TH STREET IN MANHATTAN. Subway: N, R, W to Fifth Avenue/59th Street. 212-753-7300. www.bergdorfgoodman.com. See full entry page 240.*

### 134. Take the ferry to **Staten Island**
and enjoy a twenty-five-minute tour of great New York vistas. On the way over, you'll roll by the Statue of Liberty, Ellis Island, and Governors Island; on the way back, you'll get a glorious view of the Manhattan skyline—all for free.
*The Staten Island ferry runs between Whitehall Terminal in Manhattan and St. George Terminal on Staten Island. For more information and ferry schedules, visit www.nyc.gov/html/-dot/html/masstran/ferries/statfery.html#info.*

### 135. Ride the tram to **Roosevelt Island**
and back, and catch a tantalizing glimpse up and down the East River and over Manhattan, Brooklyn, and Queens while you glide through the air.
*59TH STREET AND SECOND AVENUE IN MANHATTAN. Subway: 4, 5, 6 to 59th Street; N, R, W to Lexington Avenue/59th Street. N.B.: At press time, the tram was closed for repairs and scheduled to reopen in fall 2006. For more information, visit www.rioc.com.*

136. Stretching from Manhattan to the **Verrazano-Narrows Bridge** (see page 67), **the view of New York harbor from the grounds of the Alice Austen House** is an unexpected treat at this spectacular historic house (once lived in by the nineteenth-century photographer) and museum. In addition to the breathtaking panorama, you can also enjoy Austen's lovely gardens and a collection of her photographs that document the social history of her time.

*2 HYLAN BOULEVARD IN STATEN ISLAND. Grounds open daily until dusk; museum open daily from noon to 5:00 p.m., except January and February and major holidays. Staten Island Ferry to St. George Terminal; then S51 bus to Hylan Boulevard. For more information, call 718-816-4506 or visit www.aliceausten.org.*

**137.** Although it's not completed yet, **the views at Empire-Fulton Ferry State Park (also known as Brooklyn Bridge Park)** are already some of the most incredible vantages in the city. The combination of the distant buildings of lower Manhattan across the water and the Brooklyn Bridge looming overhead makes for an unusual and exquisite mix of urban architecture and natural beauty. With plans for piers, floating bridges, and restored marshlands, it will only become more extraordinary as the development progresses. FYI: There are also plans for housing, so start saving your pennies.

*EAST RIVER BETWEEN THE BROOKLYN AND MANHATTAN BRIDGES. Subway: 2, 3 to Clark Street; A, C to High Street; F to York Street. For more information on the park and development project, call 718-802-0603 or visit www.bbpc.net. For information on outdoor programs in the park, see chapter 6, "The Great Outdoors."*

**138.** Check out the Bronx, the aqueducts, and the oldest interborough bridge from the top of the **High Bridge Water Tower.**
OK, we'll slow down. First, the High Bridge Water Tower is that scary-looking tower that stands all by itself in upper Manhattan—the one you see on the way to Yankee Stadium. Second, yes, those stone arches really are aqueducts, and yes, they really were once used to bring water into the city. Third, the bridge—built to bring water to the city from the aqueducts—is older than the Brooklyn Bridge by a good forty years. The water tower, located in what is now known as Highbridge Park, is not regularly open to the public but can be climbed and toured on various dates throughout the year (One of which is **OpenHouseNewYork**; see page 71.)

*HIGHBRIDGE PARK, WEST 155TH AND DYCKMAN STREETS BETWEEN EDGECOMBE AND AMSTERDAM AVENUES IN MANHATTAN. Subway: 1 to 157th Street; C to 155th Street. For more information and scheduled visiting days, visit www.nycgovparks.org.*

**139.** The view of Union Square from the local **Whole Foods'** sit-down café upstairs is the *only* reason we'd recommend visiting this store. The upstairs seating area has perfect views of the plaza on the 14th Street side of the park and whatever happens to be going on on there: protests, demonstrations, skaters doing tricks, or temporary art displays. But checkout lines on the first floor frequently snake around the entire take-out area, creating gourmet urban chaos. Our advice: skip the maddening crowds below and eat before you come.

*4 UNION SQUARE BETWEEN BROADWAY AND UNIVERSITY PLACE IN MANHATTAN. Subway: 4, 5, 6, L, N, Q, R, W to 14th Street-Union Square. 212-673-5388. www.wholefoods.com.*

### 140. Stop for a look at the Cloisters from **Margaret Corbin Drive**.

One of the most pleasurable things about visiting the **Cloisters** (see page 120) is the walk along Margaret Corbin Drive to the museum's entrance, high up in Fort Tryon Park. The walkway leads straight through one of the city's most beautifully land-scaped flower gardens, beyond which lies the Hudson River and magnificent views of the valley extending north toward the Bronx and south toward the distant Mid-town skyline. And once you reach the Cloisters, the views from all sides of the museum are astonishing.

*FORT TRYON PARK IN MANHATTAN. Subway: A to 190th Street. 212-923-3700. For more information on the museum, see entry on page 120.*

### 141. The view of Manhattan, Brooklyn, Ellis Island, the Statue of Liberty and more...from **Governors Island**.

More than two centuries after we gave Governors Island to the government to use as a military training ground, it was finally returned to us in 2003. Since then, the city and the park service have been in the process of converting its grounds and historic structures (including two massive nineteenth-century fortifications) for public access. Visiting hours are limited and vary, but when you can get there (by ferry, a ten-minute ride from lower Manhattan), you'll be treated to striking views of the city all around you.

*The Governors Island ferry departs from the Battery Maritime Building at 10 SOUTH STREET IN MANHATTAN. Subway: 1 to South Ferry; 4, 5 to Bowling Green; R, W to Whitehall Street-South Ferry. For current visiting hours, call 212-825-3045 or visit www.nps.gov.*

### 142. We don't know where the idea came from, but the **Water Taxi Beach** in **Long Island City** is an excellent new vantage point for the New York area. New York Water Taxi carted in 400 tons of sand and a couple of picnic tables and turned the Hunter's Point ferry stop into a beach. The spectacular built-in waterfront views of Midtown are best enjoyed from a beach chair (bring your own) with a tropical drink from the tiki-themed concession shack. The beach is easily accessible by subway, bus, car, and, of course, water taxi.

*Hunter's Point Pier, 2 BORDEN STREET AND THE EAST RIVER IN QUEENS. Subway: 7 to Vernon Boulevard-Jackson Avenue; G to 21st Street. Water Taxi Beach is open from summer through early October, weather permitting. For more information, visit www.watertaxibeach.com.*

## 143. Peek into other people's houses during **OpenHouseNewYork**.

One weekend a year, nearly 200 private buildings and structures around the five boroughs open their doors to the public. Most offer free guided tours highlighting each site's history or notable features. The roster includes a variety of monuments, historic buildings, parks, and even private homes (it also includes several places listed in this chapter, such as **High Bridge Tower**, the **Highline**, and **Governors Island**), many of which are seldom or never open at any other time of the year. Our suggestion: browse the schedule online around the time of the festival, then try to check out as many as you can.

*OpenHouseNewYork is held annually for one weekend in early October. For more information, call 917-583-2398 or visit www.ohny.org.*

## 144. Get a bird's-eye view of the city on a **helicopter tour**.

Nervous? The tours last between two and seventeen minutes, so by the time you actually remember to be scared, you'll already be on your way down.

*Liberty Helicopters operates one heliport in Manhattan: PIER 6 ON THE EAST RIVER. For information on tours, schedules, and prices, call 212-967-6464 or visit www.libertyhelicopters.com.*

## 145. Enjoy medieval views of Central Park from the highest points of **Belvedere Castle**, a fantastical folly from whose towers and balconies visitors can gaze down upon Turtle Pond, the Great Lawn, and into the Delacorte Theater, where **Shakespeare in the Park** (see page 153) takes place every summer.

*MID-PARK AT 81ST STREET IN MANHATTAN. For more information on Central Park, see entry on page 218. Subway: 6 to 77th Street; B, C to 81st Street-Museum of Natural History.*

## 146. Time your climb up the bell tower at **Riverside Church** so that you arrive on the hour.

Then look out across the whole city as some of the largest (and loudest) bells in the world ring out.

*490 RIVERSIDE DRIVE AT CLAREMONT AVENUE IN MANHATTAN. Subway: 1 to 116th Street-Columbia University. www.theriversidechurchny.org.*

### 147. Sit on a bench below Pier 17 at **South Street Seaport**

and look across the river. You can while away an afternoon watching the busy waters between you and the borough of Brooklyn, which looks close enough to swim to (not something we'd recommend).

*SOUTH STREET AND WATER STREET IN MANHATTAN. Subway: 1 to South Ferry; 2, 3 to Wall Street; 4, 5 to Bowling Green; J, M, Z to Broad Street; R, W to Whitehall Street-South Ferry.*

### 148. See Manhattan from the **Shearwater.**

The traditional way to see the island in detail is the **Circle Line** (see page 23), but a classy alternative is this elegant, vintage, 82-foot, 49-person schooner that gives water tours. You'll cruise by the sites of New York harbor, including the Statue of Liberty, Ellis and Governors Islands, and the Brooklyn and Manhattan Bridges. When you dock next to the other yachts at the Battery Park marina, who will know that it's not yours?

*The Shearwater sails from April through October. NORTH COVE YACHT HARBOR (HUDSON RIVER, IN FRONT OF THE WORLD FINANCIAL CENTER) IN MANHATTAN. Subway: 1 to Rector Street; E to World Trade Center; R, W to Cortlandt Street. Public sails are offered daily. For more information, schedules, and prices, call 212-619-0885 or visit www.shearwatersailing.com.*

### 149. Watch a ball game from the highest tier of **Yankee Stadium**.

You'll be right behind home plate, so not only will you get an amazing view of what's going on inside the stadium, but you can also see all the way across the river to where the fans are cheering in Manhattan.

*161ST STREET AT RIVER AVENUE IN THE BRONX. Subway: 4, B, D to 161st Street-Yankee Stadium. http://newyork.yankees.mlb.com. For full entry on the Yankees, see page 30.*

### 150. Watch the sun set behind the **Colgate clock**, an often-overlooked New

Jersey attraction that you get a great view of from Hudson River Park. Pick a spot on a grassy pier and watch the sun go down behind the clock's giant octagonal face. Try Pier 45 by Perry Street.

*HUDSON RIVER PARK IN MANHATTAN. Subway: 1 to Rector Street.*

### 151. Stand by the lighthouse at the northern tip of **Roosevelt Island**

for a breathtaking view of Midtown and uptown Manhattan.

*LIGHTHOUSE PARK ON ROOSEVELT ISLAND. Subway: F to Roosevelt Island; Roosevelt Island Tram.*

## 152. Find the lighthouse under the **George Washington Bridge**.

From next to the forty-foot-high Little Red Lighthouse, you can see all the way up the Hudson River to the north, the Palisades to the west, and the bridge directly overhead. *178TH STREET AND THE HUDSON RIVER IN MANHATTAN. Subway: A to 175th Street.*

→ **DID YOU KNOW?** *This lighthouse (whose official name is the Jeffrey's Hook Lighthouse) was the subject of a popular 1942 children's book by Hildegarde H. Smith called* The Little Red Lighthouse and the Great Gray Bridge. *When the lighthouse was decommissioned in 1947, it was supposed to be torn down, but outcry from fans of the book prevented it, and it was turned into a National Historic Landmark.*

## 153. Enjoy the picture-perfect view of Central Park from **Bow Bridge**.

This low-lying cast-iron bridge delicately meanders across the lake, offering a scenic view of Manhattan's bucolic center. You'll see rowboaters bobbing along between the flowering fields of Cherry Hills and the wild green landscape of the Ramble. *WEST OF BETHESDA TERRACE BY 74TH STREET IN MANHATTAN'S CENTRAL PARK. Subway: B, C to 72nd Street. For more information on the park, see entry on page 216.*
*N.B.: There are thirty-six bridges and arches all over Central Park, many of which offer unusual views of particular areas. Check out a map before you visit the park.*

## 154. See across state lines from **Lafayette's feet**.

At the 9th Street entrance to Prospect Park, a monument commemorates New York's favorite Frenchman. Follow his gaze down 9th Street and you'll see all the way to the edge of Brooklyn, across lower Manhattan to the Jersey hills on the horizon. Go on a pleasant day and you might understand why Jack Kerouac said, "Whenever spring comes to New York, I can't stand the suggestion of the land that comes blowing over the river from New Jersey, and I've got to go."
*PROSPECT PARK WEST AND 9TH STREET IN BROOKLYN. For more information on the park, see entry on page 219. Subway: F to 15th Street-Prospect Park or Seventh Avenue.*

## 155. See where Manhattan ends and the Bronx begins at the **Half Moon Overlook**.

At the southwesternmost tip of the Bronx, the hillside neighborhood of Marble Hill ascends to a natural vantage point known as **Spuyten Duyvil**, whose views of the Hudson River and upper Manhattan are unrivalled. Named for the creek that used to run into the mainland from the Hudson, Spuyten Duyvil is the meeting point of the two boroughs, offering dramatic scenery that makes it a wonderful place to walk. Start

from the Spuyten Duyvil Metro-North rail station and walk south along the shorefront park. Just south of Palisade Avenue, the path takes you up to the Half Moon Overlook, a quiet semicircular viewing point with the perfect perspective over the river.
*SPUYTEN DUYVIL SHOREFRONT PARK IN MANHATTAN. Subway: 1 to Marble Hill-225th Street or Metro-North Railroad (Hudson Link) to Spuyten Duyvil.*

→ **DID YOU KNOW (PART 1)?** *Spuyten Duyvil takes its name from the Dutch-American folk legend of Anthony Van Corlaer, the loyal trumpeter of Peter Stuyvesant (a Dutchman who was mayor of New York in the early seventeenth century) who drowned swimming across the creek to warn his countrymen of attack from the British. With no ferry to take him across, Van Corlaer tried to swim "en spijt den Duyvil" (in spite of the Devil). Locals still say you can hear his trumpet sounding out across the water on windy nights.*

→ **DID YOU KNOW (PART 2)?** *The neighborhood of Marble Hill is the only part of the borough of Manhattan physically connected to the mainland. It was originally the northernmost tip of Manhattan, but the construction of the Harlem River Ship Canal in 1895 severed it from the island. For the next twenty years, Marble Hill was an island until the small creek that separated it from the mainland was filled. Despite being geographically joined to the Bronx, however, Marble Hill is still considered part of Manhattan.*

## 156. Sit on **Grant's Tomb**.

The impressive memorial for General Grant (it contains the tombs of both him and his wife) is situated in the middle of a stretch of park that offers some of the prettiest views of the Hudson River and the old stone buildings along Riverside Drive. Sit on the wall and look down over Riverside Park to the water, or walk north behind the memorial to the road bridge that extends into Harlem, where semicircular viewing points are built into the stonework so you can look across Harlem and the Hudson.
*RIVERSIDE DRIVE AT 122ND STREET IN MANHATTAN. Subway: 1, A, C, B, D to 125th Street.*

## 157. Take a trip back in time at the **Red Hook waterfront**.

Walking along the docks and back streets at the port of Red Hook is like stepping back in time. One hundred and fifty years ago, before the construction of the Brooklyn-Queens Expressway overwhelmed the neighborhood, Red Hook was one of the busiest ports in the world. Today, the quaint waterfront is quiet and often overlooked, but it still boasts wonderful views across the East River to Governors Island and to the Atlantic.

*CONOVER STREET AND BEARD STREET, RED HOOK IN BROOKLYN. Subway: F to Smith-9th Streets.*

---

## 158. Go to the top of the **Rock**.

After nearly twenty years and a $75 million renovation, the spectacular roof on the seventieth floor of Rockefeller Center reopened in 2005. Though a good deal shorter than the **Empire State Building** (see page 19), the roof of the Rock has one great advantage: it doesn't have a spire, so there's no structure in the middle blocking your view from one side to another. This means that the top of this mighty Midtown skyscraper offers the clearest north-south views of New York by a long shot. The Rock is right in the middle of Manhattan, ten blocks south of Central Park and pretty much in the center of the island. You can look south and see straight down over Liberty Island, and turn around to see past Central Park all the way to Harlem. Make reservations in advance, and you won't have to wait in line for hours like at the Empire State Building.

*30 ROCKEFELLER PLAZA, 49TH STREET BETWEEN FIFTH AND SIXTH AVENUES IN MANHATTAN. Subway: B, D, F, V to 47th-50th Streets-Rockefeller Center.*

---

## 159. Rise above the city on the **Chelsea Highline**.

Proof that in New York, everything old becomes new again: the dilapidated remains of the Chelsea Highline, an elevated Depression-era transport system that runs along Tenth Avenue, is in the process of being turned into an elevated park. Inspired by Paris's Promenade Plantée, a three-mile stretch of elevated viaducts that was converted into a planted pedestrian walkway in the 1990s, the Chelsea Highline will be a unique public space that is removed from the city streets and full of plantings, terraces, gardens, and sitting areas. Because the highline runs over the middle of blocks (instead of directly over the avenue), in addition to exquisite views of the Hudson River to the west and the Manhattan skyline to the east, you will also be privy to a bird's eye view of passages, gardens, and other secret spaces. The highline runs for twenty-two blocks, between Gansevoort and West 34th Streets, but the first section (between Gansevoort and 15th Streets) is scheduled to open in fall 2007. Until then, however, it's considered private property, so if you want a view, you'll have to wait until **OpenHouseNewYork** (see page 71).

*TENTH AVENUE BETWEEN GANSEVOORT AND WEST 34TH STREETS IN MANHATTAN. Subway: for southern end, A, C, E to 14th Street; L to Eighth Avenue; for northern end, 1, 2, 3, A, C, E to 34th Street–Penn Station. For more information on the highline and the restoration project, visit www.thehighline.org.*

## 160. Get an aerial view of New York without leaving the ground at the **New York Panorama**.

This permanent exhibit at the Queens Museum of Art is a popular destination for school groups, but it's guaranteed to knock the socks off visitors of all ages. This 9,335-square-foot bird's-eye model of New York City lays out 320 miles of terrain, including 850,000 buildings, and accurately depicts the topography to scale (1 inch = 100 feet). A longtime favorite attraction, the panorama was built for the 1964 World's Fair. Between 1992 and 1994, it was closed and updated to reflect the changes in landscape during the three decades since its construction. (Also under construction is a version of the Tribute in Light, the light memorials to the Twin Towers, which will be added to the panorama.) It's quite a sight to behold, both for the view of the land and the mind-boggling detail in which it is depicted. The most shocking feature: how diminutive Manhattan is compared to the other boroughs.

*QUEENS MUSEUM OF ART, NEW YORK CITY BUILDING, FLUSHING MEADOWS CORONA PARK IN QUEENS. Subway: 7 to Willets Point-Shea Stadium. The museum is open Wednesday through Sunday; free guided tours of the panorama are offered on Saturday at 3:30 p.m. For more information on hours, directions, and exhibits, call 718-592-9700 or visit www.queensmuseum.org.*

## 161. Stand at the top of **Park Avenue** and look downtown.

Flanked on either side by distinguished buildings like the Armory and the Waldorf-Astoria, as well as some of the city's most exclusive addresses, the view down Park Avenue is the ultimate cosmopolitan vista. The planted gardens on the mall lead the way down to 42nd Street, where the graceful Helmsley Building straddles the avenue and sucks the traffic away.

*PARK AVENUE BETWEEN 42ND AND 96TH STREETS IN MANHATTAN. Best places to stand are in the 70s and 80s. Subway: 4, 5, 6 to 86th Street; 6 to 77th Street.*

## 162. Look down on Amsterdam Avenue from the **overpass**.

Crossing Amsterdam Avenue at 117th Street, this landscaped extension of Columbia University's main campus is a delightful little perch from which to gaze at the city. Manhattan is laid out in front of you, from the beautiful university buildings and the nearby **Cathedral of Saint John the Divine** (see page 21) all the way downtown. Also on the overpass is Henry Moore's famous ***Three Way Piece*** sculpture, which spins when you push it (see page 142).

*ACROSS AMSTERDAM AVENUE, ACCESSIBLE BETWEEN 116TH AND 118TH STREETS IN MANHATTAN. Subway: 1 to 116th Street-Columbia University.*

# People-watching

People are among the most prominent features in the city—and can be some of the most interesting things to look at. In addition to **Metrazur** and **Cipriani Dolce** in Grand Central (see page 77), here are some particularly good vantage points for human sightseeing of all genres:

**163.** *For a mix:* Large enough that you can relax but well-trafficked enough to make it interesting, the *stairs in front of the Metropolitan Museum of Art* is the best place to see a wide variety of people all at once. While most of the other places listed here are good for niche sightings, the steps in front of the Met are the crossroads of so many different kinds of people—foreign tourists, tony art patrons, prep-school kids hanging out during free periods—that the possibilities are limitless.

*1000 FIFTH AVENUE BETWEEN 82ND AND 84TH STREETS IN MANHATTAN. Subway: 4, 5, 6 to 86th Street.*

**164.** *For celebrities: Pastis* has the optimal conditions for celebrity sighting: it draws a collection of famous people at pretty much every meal, and it's big enough and has been open long enough that you actually have a chance of getting in. (Most of the time. If you wait long enough.) Though most celebrity hot spots are tepid long before regular people can get in the door, Pastis's relative longevity (it opened in 2000) and its provenance (it was opened by **Keith McNally**, the city's most trusted scene-maker in the restaurant business; see page 163) have established for Pastis the unlikely dual identity of celebrity clubhouse and neighborhood institution. At breakfast, lunch, and dinner (and brunch), this is the place to go to see the somebodies off-screen.

*9 NINTH AVENUE AT LITTLE WEST 12TH STREET IN MANHATTAN. Subway: A, C, E to 14th Street; L to Eighth Avenue. 212-929-4844. www.pastisny.com.*

**165.** *For athletes:* From near-professional cyclists to souped-up weekend warriors, *Central Park Drive* is ideal for active-people watching. The benches along the drive are great places to take a break from whatever you're doing and watch the people whiz by on foot, bike, rollerblade, unicycle, or what have you. Some benches are established hangouts for different recreational communities, so novices should look before they sit.

*Central Park Drive is closed to traffic on weekends and on weekdays between 7:00 p.m. and 10:00 p.m.; much of it is also closed between 10 a.m. and 3 p.m. For more information on Central Park, see entry on page 216.*

**166. *For a picture-perfect ethnic enclave: The Brighton Beach boardwalk*** is a people-watching dream: a comfortable public place where you can watch endless scenes from another world play out without anyone taking notice of you. From the boardwalk, you have front-row seats of the main set of Little Odessa—the beach, the restaurants, the nightclubs—and all of its vivid characters.
*BRIDGEWATER AVENUE IN BROOKLYN. Subway: B, Q to Brighton Beach.*

**167. *For wild costumes:*** Nothing beats the ***Eighth Avenue "catwalk"*** post-Gay Pride Parade. Typically, warm weather plus flamboyant dressers turn the strip between 14th and 23rd Streets into a veritable costume parade of its own, where you can see cowboys chatting up fairy princesses and much more. Actually, it's pretty much a block party all weekend long, so any time you go should be quite a display. (Just don't try to camp out at one of the open-front bars unless you really want to party. The window seats at Better Burger on the corner of 19th and the bench in front of the Tasti D-Lite between 21st and 22nd are good alternative viewing locations.)
*Last Sunday in June. EIGHTH AVENUE BETWEEN 14TH AND 23RD STREETS IN MAN-HATTAN. Subway: A, C, E to 14th Street; L to Eighth Avenue; C, E to 23rd Street.* *For more information on the parade, see entry on page 90.*

**168. *For the unemployed and aspiring (uptown):*** Once the preserve of aristocrats and the literati, reading and writing over innumerable cappuccinos is how many New Yorkers now spend their days. Certain coffee shops and cafés attract a steady crowd during traditional working hours—they toil away on their laptops, working on their next novel, screenplay, or business plan. The ***Hungarian Pastry Shop*** is a long-standing favorite of the Upper West Side intelligentsia—its walls are plastered with the jackets of the many successful books that have been penned here over the years. It is the perfect place to see writers (professional or otherwise) and Columbia University students having impassioned discussions about existentialism.
*1030 AMSTERDAM AVENUE BETWEEN 110TH AND 111TH STREETS IN MANHATTAN. Subway: 1, B, C to 110th Street (Cathedral Parkway).*

**169. *For the unemployed and aspiring (downtown): Café Doma*** on Perry Street is the place to be. Everybody is writing, reading, or mouthing words from a script, and if the customers aren't enough to keep you entertained, the endless stream of West Village characters strolling by the corner windows should do it.

*17 PERRY STREET AT SEVENTH AVENUE IN MANHATTAN. Subway: 1 to Christopher Street-Sheridan Square; A, C, E, B, D, F, V to West 4th Street.*

**170. *For shoppers (uptown):*** Find a seat around the fountains at **Columbus Circle** and watch the teeming crowds of uptown shoppers converge from all sides on this popular resting place. Everyone from museum-going tourists to upscale Fifth Avenue department store regulars schlep their bags to the bottom of the park for a breather.
*COLUMBUS CIRCLE AT THE SOUTHWEST CORNER OF CENTRAL PARK IN MANHATTAN. Subway: 1, A, C, B, D to 59th Street-Columbus Circle.*

**171. *For shoppers (downtown):*** Take a seat on one of the benches that line the **playground on Thompson Street** (at Spring Street) and educate yourself about the different Greenwich Village and SoHo boutiques by observing who's carrying which shopping bag.
*Thompson Street at Spring Street in Manhattan. Subway: C, E to Spring Street.*

**172. *For high fashion (sometimes to a ridiculous degree):*** Hang out by the tents in **Bryant Park** during Fashion Week. You'll see editors, models, stylists, and celebrities all dolled up in the season's best, plus a press stunt here and there. If you can manage to get an invite to a show (or offer your services to a PR company as an usher), you'll be privy to some front-row voyeurism inside the tents, and you can partake in the abundant swag that sponsors generously dole out to those cool enough to make it in. Fashion Week is held in September and February, but unless you really want to see cranky fashionistas in heels slip on the ice, September is the more pleasant option.
*TENT ENTRANCE ON SIXTH AVENUE BY 41ST STREET IN MANHATTAN. Subway: 7 to Fifth Avenue-Bryant Park; B, D, F, V to 42nd Street–Bryant Park.*

And of course, for the grand finale, no list of New York's best views would be complete without a mention of...

## 173. ...a trip to the top of the **Empire State Building**.

Pay the entry fee, take the elevator to the eighty-sixth-floor observation deck, and look around. That's New York for you.
*350 FIFTH AVENUE BETWEEN 33RD AND 34TH STREETS IN MANHATTAN. www.esbnyc.org. For more information on the building and its history, see entry on page 19.*

# Expert contributor: Joseph O. Holmes

Joseph O. Holmes is a fine-art photographer based in Brooklyn. He teaches photography at New York University and exhibits his photos in New York and
around the United States. He posts a new photo of New York City every day at
http://joesnyc.com.

## MY FIVE FAVORITE SPOTS TO PHOTOGRAPH — AND
## PHOTOGRAPH FROM — IN NEW YORK

### 174. *The walkway of the Manhattan Bridge:*

The Brooklyn Bridge may be more popular with pedestrians, but the best view of the
bridge itself is from up the East River a bit, from the less well-known walkway of the
Manhattan Bridge. Accessible from DUMBO in Brooklyn and Chinatown in Manhattan, the walkway has spectacular views south. The best views are on the Manhattan
end, where you can look down toward Chinatown and the Lower East Side. (The
Brooklyn end looks down into the streets of DUMBO.) Every now and then, a subway
train will rumble by, just a few feet from the walkway. Photo tip: use your widest-angle
lens to capture the vistas.

*ENTER FROM CANAL STREET AT BOWERY IN MANHATTAN, OR AT JAY STREET NEAR SANDS
STREET IN BROOKLYN. Subway (Manhattan): J, M, Z to Essex Street or F to Delancey Street;
(Brooklyn) A, C to High Street or F to York Street.*

### 175. *The Brooklyn Botanic Garden:*

I visit the BBG all year, and there's never a time when I don't come home with stunning photos. The Japanese Garden is serene after a snowfall, and gorgeous daffodils
cover entire hillsides in the spring. The lily ponds are home to dragonflies and huge
orange koi (a type of carp). Late in the day is the best time for gorgeous light and
beautiful shadows. Photo tip: use a macro lens to shoot the inside of a backlit flower
for magnificent color images.

*1000 WASHINGTON AVENUE IN BROOKLYN. Subway: B, Q to Prospect Park; 2, 3 to Eastern
Parkway-Brooklyn Museum. 718-623-7200. www.bbg.org.*

### 176. *DUMBO:*

The neighborhood under the Manhattan Bridge (the acronym stands for Down
Under the Manhattan Bridge Overpass) on the Brooklyn waterfront is slowly being
gentrified, but it's still a fabulous spot to find some of the city's best examples of serious graffiti and street art along Water Street between the Manhattan and Brooklyn
Bridges, as well as picturesque warehouses and abandoned industrial buildings.

There are also some incredible views looking up at the bridges from the Empire-Fulton Ferry State Park, and it's all just a short walk south to the Brooklyn Heights Promenade, with the city's most famous views of the Manhattan skyline. Photo tip: with the sun setting toward the southwest, dusk often brings breathtaking sunset views of the Manhattan skyline; take a tripod to the promenade and shoot until dark.

*Subway: A, C to High Street; F to York Street, and then a short walk toward the water.*

### 177. *Times Square:*

It's been photographed so many times that it's nearly impossible to get a fresh shot of the signs and buildings of Times Square, but that's not why I head there on a regular basis with my camera. Times Square turns out to be a terrific place to photograph people: tourists, of course, but also street musicians, office workers, occasional con artists, and the crowds that gather outside the upstairs MTV studios or the ground-level *Good Morning America* studio, both near 44th Street and Broadway. Photo tip: find whatever attraction is drawing a crowd—then turn around and snap the people watching it.

*42ND STREET BETWEEN SIXTH AND NINTH AVENUES IN MANHATTAN. Subway: 1, 2, 3, 7, A, C, E, N, Q, R, W, S to 42nd Street-Times Square.*

### 178. *The subway:*

Contrary to popular belief, it's perfectly legal to take photos in the New York City subway. As a street photographer, I love to get candid shots of train riders, including the street **musicians and performers who sometimes pass through the cars** (see page 369). But check out the Times Square station—particularly the tunnels connecting the A, C, and E lines with the 1, 2, and 3—for the best variety of street performers and artists. Photo tip: always, always tip the performers at least a dollar before shooting.

*For subway maps and route information, visit www.mta.info.*

CHAPTER 3:

# On the Street & Underground

This chapter is devoted to one of New York's unique, idiosyncratic treasures: its streets (and what's underneath them). Difficult to quantify but precious to many inhabitants, New York's street culture is varied, vibrant, and full of possibility—a cherished feature that the city both flaunts and guards, and that is truly accessible only by foot. To its pedestrians, New York offers secret gardens off the driven path, glorious displays of art and architecture, spontaneous entertainment, and edible treasures galore—and it punishes motorists with one-way streets, Byzantine parking restrictions, and uncooperative traffic lights. While in most other places—even major metropolitan areas—walking has gone the way of shoeshines and telephone booths, in New York (thanks to active community groups and falling crime rates), the streets are better than ever.

This chapter also celebrates the city's wonderful subterranean culture. With roughly seven million regular riders spread across 468 stations, the subway system is its own underground neighborhood, one that unites New Yorkers from all boroughs, who are as familiar with the twists and turns of their home stations and regular routes as they are with their apartments. And just like every New York neighborhood, the subway system has its own quirks and character, with historic sites, glorious architecture, and more than 150 works of original art.

Perhaps more than any other chapter in the book, this one encourages you to explore, and to be excited by the possibility of discovery. In this chapter, you'll find plenty of things worth seeking out—street festivals, parades, flea markets, and famous movie sites—but many of the entries are for curiosities or charming details that you may have passed many times without knowing where to look or what is special about them. Wonderful things to see and do abound, so keep your eyes open and your feet on the ground.

# Street Fairs & Festivals

## 179. Bump into a **street fair**.

Although there are no official rules distinguishing them, street fairs differ from flea markets in that they move from place to place, and most of the merchandise is new and manufactured rather than secondhand, antique, or handmade crafts. The street fair "season" runs from April to Thanksgiving, and there's at least one (often more), rain or shine, every weekend during that period. Although each street fair is ostensibly different and tied to a particular neighborhood group or organization, the merchandise and food at most fairs are pretty much the same because almost every fair is produced by the same company that lines up the vendors. (The fairs also all have the same hours: Saturday or Sunday, 10:00 a.m. to 6:00 p.m.) While some of the offerings do change from year to year, you can count on finding discontinued Gap clothing, socks, ties and scarves, cheap sunglasses, jewelry, cosmetics, handbags (mostly designer knock-offs), other cheap clothing, incense and spices, a couple of gadgets that look like they'd be sold on an infomercial, quickie back rubs, and, for food, crepes, kebabs, grilled corn, fruit shakes, and kettle corn. We recommend them as a diversion, rather than as a destination: a trip to a street fair probably won't have the same sense of discovery as a planned outing to a flea market, but if you happen to bump into one, it can give a little variety to a regular walk and is a dependable source for **cheap back rubs** (see page 283) and free samples of kettle corn.

*For list of upcoming fairs, visit www.nycstreetfairs.com/sched.html.*

## 180. Feast at **San Gennaro,**

New York's oldest and biggest street festival. Each fall, the streets of Little Italy host a lively eleven-day block party to salute the patron saint of Naples. People of all ethnicities come to partake in the festivities, which include live concerts, several parades, religious processions, and the International Cannoli Eating Championship (the record in 2005: twenty-six cannolis in six minutes).

*September. THE FEAST RUNS ALONG MULBERRY STREET BETWEEN CANAL STREET AND HOUSTON STREET, AND ON GRAND STREET AND HESTER STREET BETWEEN MOTT STREET AND BAXTER STREET IN MANHATTAN. Subway: 6, N, Q, R, W, J, M, Z to Canal Street; B, D to Grand Street. For dates and a schedule of events, visit www.sangennaro.org.*

### 181. Celebrate Brooklyn at the **Atlantic Antic**.

On one Sunday in September, there is a 1$^1/_2$-mile outpouring of Brooklyn pride called the Atlantic Antic, which is one of the best street fairs of the year, in any borough. The thirty-two-year-old fair is produced by the Atlantic Avenue Local Development Corporation and very unlike the street fairs described above; you'll find that the majority of the booths are hosted by local businesses. Instead of crepes, kettle corn, and cheap sunglasses, there's food from **Sahadi's** (see page 176) and neighborhood restaurants, plus books, jewelry boutiques, live music, martial arts demonstrations, a bounce castle, and pony rides. There's definitely a heavy local flavor to this fair and the neighborhood spirit is contagious; it's a lot of fun no matter what borough (or state) you're from.

*September. ATLANTIC AVENUE BETWEEN FOURTH AVENUE AND HICKS STREET IN BROOK-LYN. Subway: 2, 3, 4, 5, B, Q to Atlantic Avenue; A, C, G to Hoyt-Schermerhorn Street; D, M, R to Atlantic Avenue-Pacific Street; N to Pacific Street. For more information, the date of this year's fair, and an event schedule, visit www.atlanticave.org.*

### 182. Pig out at the **Big Apple Barbeque Block Party**.

At this two-day urban cookout, award-winning pit masters from all over the country fire up their barbeques in Madison Square Park. You can feast on brisket, ribs, and pork barbequed to perfection while enjoying musical performances, book signings, and other events throughout the day. The 2005 event featured a "Wine for Swine" tasting with **Danny Meyer** (see page 163) and a screening of the documentary *Barbecue: A Texas Love Story*. It's a block party, so admission is free, but you have to buy the food ($7 per plate, with one side). For $100, you can buy a "Bubba Fast Pass," which lets you bypass the lines at the pit masters' tents. Proceeds benefit the Madison Park Conservancy, which oversees the maintenance and programming of the park.

*June. MADISON SQUARE PARK, 23RD TO 26TH STREETS BETWEEN FIFTH AND MADISON AVENUES IN MANHATTAN. Subway: 6 to 23rd Street; N, R, W to 23rd Street. www.bigapplebbq.org.*

### 183. Visit—for free!—the nine museums that call Fifth Avenue home during the **Museum Mile Festival**.

This annual high-culture block party, held on a Tuesday evening each June, celebrates New York's historic "museum mile," a consortium of the museums that line upper Fifth Avenue. For more than twenty-five years, some of New York's finest museums—including the Met, the Neue Galerie, El Museo del Barrio, the Cooper-Hewitt, the Guggenheim, and the Museum of the City of New York (for more information, see chapter 4)—have opened their doors to the public and brought together uptown, downtown, and out-of-town for an evening of art and revelry. In addition to access to the museums, there are also free performances, music, and displays all along Fifth Avenue between 82nd and 105th Streets, which is closed to traffic during the festival. *June. FIFTH AVENUE BETWEEN 82ND AND 105TH STREETS IN MANHATTAN. Subway: 4, 5, 6 to 86th Street; 6 to 77th or 96th Streets. For a schedule of events and a list of participating museums, visit www.museummilefestival.org.*

## 184. Listen to your favorite authors tell stories at the **Great Read in the Park**.

Plenty of New Yorkers (your authors included) mourned the loss of "New York Is Book Country," an annual street fair where starstruck readers could meet their favorite authors and take home publishing freebies like calendars, promotional posters, and buttons. Sadly, the fair was suspended in 2005, but on its regular weekend, the *New York Times* and Bryant Park stepped in with the "Great Read in the Park," an event launched to celebrate the seventieth anniversary of the *New York Times Book Review* and expected to continue as an annual festival. Unlike NYIBC, where booths lined Fifth Avenue, street fair–style, the Great Read is contained in Bryant Park, and, as the name implies, is centered around scheduled readings, book signings, panel discussions, and other organized events. (There was even a book appraisal table, where you could bring in old books to be assessed by a rare book dealer.)

*October. BRYANT PARK, 40TH TO 42ND STREETS BETWEEN FIFTH AND SIXTH AVENUES IN MANHATTAN. Subway: B, D, F, V to 42nd Street-Bryant Park; 7 to Fifth Avenue-Bryant Park. For more information, visit www.greatreadinthepark.com.*

## 185. Enjoy the East Village during the **Howl! Festival**.

For one week toward the end of summer, the bars, clubs, cafés, bookstores, and parks of the East Village turn themselves over to the countercultural legacies that have colored their streets since the 1950s. Named for the seminal poem by Allen Ginsberg, the festival preserves the spirit of the Beat Generation that did so much to define the reputation of New York's Lower East Side. Poetry readings, jazz performances, avant-garde dramatics, political debates, and screenings of independent movies spring up on every corner and in every dingy basement, and the whole neighborhood buzzes with its biggest crowds of the year. The highlights of the week are invariably the free events in Tompkins Square Park, the heart of the East Village, where live music, readings, and dance performances take place throughout each day, and where festival-goers can join impromptu classes in art, sculpture, or writing. There are always appearances, scheduled or otherwise, by indie stalwarts such as Steve Buscemi and John Waters, but it's the spirit of the week and the energy of the artists, performers, and visitors that make the Howl! Festival so special.

*Late summer/early fall. TOMPKINS SQUARE PARK IN MANHATTAN. Subway: F, V to Lower East Side-Second Avenue; L to First Avenue. For dates and a schedule of events, check local papers or www.howlfestival.com.*

## 186. Enjoy Indian food, dancing, and fireworks at the South Street Seaport Deepvali Celebration.

For one day each fall, South Street Seaport lights up with the vibrant colors of saris and fireworks for an annual Deepvali celebration (also known as Diwali), the Hindu festival signifying the triumph of good over evil. The event usually takes place a few weeks before Deepvali, so that it's still warm enough for an outdoor party. The all-day event includes performances, storytelling, a food fair, and a shopping bazaar. Deepvali actually means "festival of lights," and the event concludes with a fireworks display over the East River. People of all religions and ethnicities are welcome at the party, and it's a great one for enjoying the last dose of outdoor holiday fun before the cold sets in.

*Early October. SOUTH STREET SEAPORT IN MANHATTAN. Subway: 2, 3, 4, 5, J, M, Z to Fulton Street; A, C to Broadway-Nassau Street. For more information on program and schedule, visit the Web site for the New York chapter of the Association of Indians in America: www.aianewyork.org.*

## 187. Go back in time at the Cloisters' Medieval Festival.

What more fitting setting for a Renaissance festival than the **Cloisters** (see page 120)? This annual event, held each autumn, has all of the requisite Renaissance-fair trappings: lavish costumes, minstrels, jugglers, jesters, and, of course, a joust.

*Fall. FORT TRYON PARK IN MANHATTAN. Subway: A to 190th Street. 212-923-3700. www.metmuseum.org.*

## 188. Celebrate Bastille Day (part 1).

The annual Bastille Day Festival held by the **Alliance Française** (see page 300), the most well-established of the city's Bastille Day celebrations, features music, dancing, performances, and plenty of food.

*Sunday near Bastille Day (July 14th). 60TH STREET BETWEEN FIFTH AND LEXINGTON AVENUES IN MANHATTAN. Subway: 4, 5, 6 to 59th Street; N, R, W to Fifth Avenue/59th Street or Lexington Avenue/59th Street. For more information and the date of next year's festival, visit www.fiaf.org or call 212-355-6100.*

## 189. Celebrate **Bastille Day** (part 2): the Waiter's Race.

Downtown, the lower Manhattan branch of Brasserie Les Halles holds a ten-day bi-national Independence Day celebration between July 4 and 14, with special menus and events throughout the week, culminating with an outdoor block party on Bastille Day. The main event is the "Waiter's Race," a traditional Bastille Day competition in which waiters must race across the street carrying full trays without spilling a drop. The contest at Les Halles is so popular that teams of waiters have flown in from other countries to participate, and they now hold special races for customers, children, and chefs.

*July 4 to 14; Bastille Day block party is held July 14. 15 JOHN STREET BETWEEN BROADWAY AND NASSAU STREET IN MANHATTAN. Subway: 2, 3 4, 5, J, M, Z to Fulton Street; A, C to Broadway-Nassau Street. 212-285-8585. www.leshalles.net.*

## 190. Celebrate **Bastille Day** (part 3): Petanque.

Thought bocce was the only kind of lawn bowling around? Brooklyn boasts an emerging French quartier of restaurants and bars, and at this annual Bastille Day celebration on Smith Street, you can try your hand at the quintessential French street sport, petanque. For the event, temporary courts are set up and filled with the traditional mounds of sand to prevent anyone from confusing it with that other European street game. Local stores and restaurants join in the celebration, and the street is filled with stalls selling food, drink, and other treats.

*Sunday near Bastille Day, 9:00 a.m. to 8:00 p.m. SMITH STREET BETWEEN PACIFIC AND BERGEN STREETS IN BROOKLYN. Subway: F, G to Bergen Street.*

## 191. Take a kid on the haunted carousel at the **Prospect Park Halloween Carnival**.

Walking through the ravine of Prospect Park on a windy fall day can be scary even without the monsters, witches, skeletons, and ghosts that populate its woods on Halloween. But every year, local volunteers transform the park into a great Halloween party, with walks through the decorated woods, events, rides, games, and frights spread out across the park. Kids can enhance their costumes with an expert face-painter or help carve spectacular pumpkins on the grass in Nethermead. Fair games are flavored with a ghoulish twist—here you throw balls at skulls, not cans—and the snacks are warm and seasonal, from spicy pumpkin pie to mulled wine for the grown-ups. Gather round for scary stories of the ghosts of Brooklyn past at the Lefferts Homestead or walk through the creepy haunted barn at the zoo. The highlight of the day is a frightening ride on the haunted carousel: the lights go down and evil laughter booms out as bats, spiders, and ghosts drift around the spinning children's heads. *Saturday before Halloween, usually from noon to 3:00 p.m. PROSPECT PARK IN BROOKLYN. Subway: 2, 3 to Grand Army Plaza or Eastern Parkway-Brooklyn Museum; F to Seventh Avenue or 15th Street-Prospect Park; B, Q to Prospect Park. For details, visit www.prospect-park.org.*

## 192. Paint your face and samba down Sixth Avenue at the
# Brazil Day Festival.

On September 7, 1822, Brazil won independence from Portugal, and on the first Sunday in September, New York celebrates this victory. The northern end of Sixth Avenue, from 43rd Street up to Central Park, is lined with stages, stalls, and bandstands. The Brazil Day Festival is one of the most colorful, sexy, and lively of the city's street fairs: teams of footballers in the patriotic yellow and green stripes play games in the street; troupes of amazing dancers perform up and down the avenue; and Brazilian restaurants and food stores sell delicious snacks and exotic fruit juices.

*First Sunday in September, 10:00 a.m. to 7:00 p.m. SIXTH AVENUE BETWEEN 42ND AND 56TH STREETS IN MANHATTAN. Subway: B, D, F, V to 47th-50th Streets-Rockefeller Center. Check local listings for festival details.*

## 193. Sing the "Dachs Song" along with the dogs at the
# Washington Square Park Dachshund Festival.

On the first Saturday in October ("Dachtober Fest") and the last Saturday in April ("the Dachshund Spring Fiesta"), proud dachshund owners (don't call them hot dogs!) congregate under the arch in Washington Square Park for the singing of the "Dach Song." Many of the dogs come in costume, although the festival coordinators stress that fancy dress isn't mandatory, and they welcome those outside the dachshund family to join them as well. The song is pretty much it for organized activities—the "festival" is intended as a social event for dogs and their owners—but the spectacle of dozens of tiny pups all dressed up as their glowing parents show them off is too precious to miss. As a bulldog-owning passerby once lamented, "You don't get that kind of camaraderie among bulldog owners."

*First Saturday in October and last Saturday in April. Meet under the arch in Washington Square Park; singing starts at noon. FIFTH AVENUE AT WASHINGTON SQUARE NORTH IN MANHATTAN. Subway: A, C, E, B, D, F, V to West 4th Street.*

# Parades

## 194. Sit on the street and watch the **Macy's Thanksgiving Day Parade . . .**

Yes, it's early in the morning, and yes, it's usually pretty cold (it might even snow), but watching the Macy's Thanksgiving Day Parade is something that everyone should do at least once, preferably with (or as) a kid. Even if you've watched it on TV every year, the enormous balloons, the elaborate floats, and the choreography of the marching bands are truly exciting to see in person, and it feels a lot more like a parade without the commentary or commercial breaks. Go early (i.e., well before 9:00 a.m., when the parade starts) and grab a spot on the street. Our favorite viewing spots are on Central Park West, where the streets are a bit wider (the parade starts at 77th Street). Wherever you go, the crowd is pretty deep, but if you've got little kids, they can sit underneath the police barriers and have a front-row view of the parade going by. You can't bring folding chairs, but hot chocolate is a must.

*Thanksgiving morning at 9:00 a.m. THE PARADE STARTS AT 77TH STREET AND CENTRAL PARK WEST, CROSSES TO BROADWAY AT COLUMBUS CIRCLE, AND THEN PROCEEDS DOWN BROADWAY TO MACY'S AT 34TH STREET IN MANHATTAN. Subways: 1, A, C, B, D to 59th Street-Columbus Circle; B, C to 72nd Street or 81st Street-Museum of Natural History; N, R, W to 49th Street or 57th Street. For more information and a map of the parade route, visit www.macy.com.*

→ **DID YOU KNOW?** *The parade was started in 1924 and has been held every year since (except between 1942 and 1944 when Macy's donated the balloons to the war effort).*

## 195. . . . but first, watch the **balloons being inflated** the night before.

The night before Thanksgiving, you can watch the balloons being blown up between 77th and 81st streets by the American Museum of Natural History. The view is best from above, but if you can't snag one of the luxury apartments in the vicinity (or don't have a friend who lives in one), you can watch the annual spectacle for free on the street below.

*Balloons are inflated outside the Museum of Natural History on the Wednesday before Thanksgiving Day from 3:00 p.m. to 10:00 p.m. 77TH TO 81ST STREETS BETWEEN CENTRAL PARK WEST AND COLUMBUS AVENUE IN MANHATTAN. Subway: B, C to 81st Street-Museum of Natural History.*

### 196. Celebrate the beginning of summer at the **Mermaid Parade**.

The Mermaid Parade has the festive spirit of the Macy's Thanksgiving Day Parade, the flamboyant style of the Halloween Parade, and exudes New York pride like none other. Every year, to mark the beginning of beach season, a King Neptune and Queen Mermaid lead a dazzling, vaguely maritime-themed costume parade along Coney Island's Surf Avenue, with elaborate floats, swimsuit-clad marchers, and assorted sea creatures waving to bystanders from the top of antique cars. If you've got a gorgeous costume, you can march, but you must register in advance on the Coney Island Web site (see below) and pay a small fee. Watching is free, however, and the experience is priceless. This is truly New York at its best—an event where people of different types and ages come together just to have fun. It's a spectacle like none other and should not be missed.

*First Saturday after the summer solstice. CONEY ISLAND BOARDWALK IN BROOKLYN. Subway: F, D, N, Q to Coney Island-Stillwell Avenue. For more information and the date of this year's parade, visit www.coneyisland.com/mermaid. For more information on Coney Island and its attractions, see page 348.*

### 197. Spend the last day of the summer at the **West Indian-American Day Parade & Carnival**.

For most of the country, the first Monday in September is Labor Day, a bittersweet national holiday signaling the end of summer and a day off from work. Here, it's West Indian-American Day, the day of the city's biggest parade. The parade, which travels down Eastern Parkway to Grand Army Plaza, tops off a four-day celebration of West Indian and Caribbean culture. The parade itself is an all-day affair, drawing more than three million people who come to see the elaborate floats and masquerade performers, listen to steel drums and calypso music, and gorge on food from all different parts of the Caribbean.

*Labor Day, 11:00 a.m. to 6:00 p.m. EASTERN PARKWAY FROM ROCHESTER STREET TO GRAND ARMY PLAZA IN BROOKLYN. Subway: 2, 3 to Grand Army Plaza or 3, 4 to Utica Avenue. For more information, visit www.wiadca.org.*

### 198. Check out **PrideFest** and the **Gay Pride Parade**.

The Lesbian, Gay, Bisexual, and Transgender (LGBT) Pride March (commonly known as the Gay Pride Parade) tops off a weeklong commemoration of the historic Stonewall raid in 1969, the event that set off a nationwide gay rights movement. The parade, held the last Sunday in June, starts at 52nd Street and goes down Fifth Avenue, then Sixth, then over to Christopher Street, ending by the Stonewall Bar, where it feeds into an enormous block party called PrideFest that lasts into the wee hours of the night. There is a moment of silence at 2:00 p.m. to honor those who have died of AIDS, but otherwise, the parade and PrideFest are upbeat, inspiring festivals that, in the spirit of inclusion, welcome anyone and everyone to celebrate. If you're anywhere in the area, the parade is hard to miss—and it's nearly impossible not to get swept up in its lively, good-humored spirit—but it's from Union Square south that is the most fun to watch from.

*Last Sunday in June. Parade starts at noon; PrideFest starts at 11:00 a.m. and continues until 10:00 p.m. FIFTH AVENUE FROM 52ND STREET TO 8TH STREET, ACROSS 8TH STREET TO CHRISTOPHER STREET, CHRISTOPHER STREET TO GREENWICH STREET IN MANHATTAN. Subway: 4, 5, 6, L, N, Q, R, W to 14th Street-Union Square; 1 to Christopher Street-Sheridan Square (for PrideFest). For more information and to view schedules and exact parade route, visit www.hopinc.org.*

## 199. Show off your costume at the **Village Halloween Parade**.

In most places, there aren't many good things to do on Halloween once you've aged out of trick-or-treating. But in New York, you can march in the Village Halloween Parade, the nation's largest and most famous Halloween celebration and the city's most inclusive parade. No need to be a member of a certain group or organization or to apply far in advance—all you have to do is show up at the starting point, pick a spot, and march! (If you like, you can let the parade organizers know beforehand what you'll be dressing as through their Web site.) If you don't want to come in costume, you can also volunteer to man one of the many elaborate puppets that are made for the parade each year. You can watch it from the streets, but because most of the action is pretty low to the ground (there are no big floats or balloons), it can be hard to get a good view from behind the crowds—and besides, once the music gets going and the costumes start rolling out, we bet you'll be sorry if you've left yours at home.

*Halloween. The line to march begins at 6:30 p.m. (and accepts marchers until 8:30 p.m.) at the HERE Art Center (Sixth Avenue between Spring and Canal Streets). The parade starts at 7:00 p.m. UP SIXTH AVENUE FROM SPRING STREET TO 23RD STREET IN MANHATTAN. Subways: C, E to Spring Street; A, C, E, B, D, F, V to West 4th Streets; F, V to 14th Street; L to Sixth Avenue. For more information, visit www.halloween-nyc.com.*

→ **DID YOU KNOW?** *The Village Halloween Parade—now the largest organized Halloween celebration in the country—was started by one man in 1973. A puppeteer and mask-maker, he started doing it as a walk with his own and other neighborhood children.*

## 200. Watch the Lion Dance at the **Chinese New Year** celebration.

The traditional Chinese New Year celebration begins on the first day of the new lunar year and lasts for two weeks until the full moon. During this time, hundreds of people brave the cold for days and come out to Chinatown for performances, ceremonial dances, firecracker displays, and a big parade. See the troupes of dancers perform traditional Lion Dances, where several members join to form a lion's body and dance through the streets.

*Chinese New Year occurs in January or February; the parade in Chinatown is usually held on a Sunday during the New Year celebration. CHINATOWN AROUND MOTT, CANAL, AND BAYARD STREETS IN MANHATTAN. Subway: 6, N, Q, R, W, J, M, Z to Canal. Check local listings for parade date.*

## 201. Watch (or march in) the **Art Parade**.

To kick off the simultaneous start of the art season and New York Fashion Week, the fun-loving SoHo gallery Deitch Projects started an annual Art Parade in 2005. The inaugural event was a celebration of creative spirit and a wake-up call to the city after the lazy month of August, as artists, fashion designers, and other imaginative participants strolled along Grand Street with wild floats, beautifully painted banners, and crazy costumes. If you want to see creativity in action—or if you just can't wait for Halloween—mark your calendar.

*Early September. Deitch Projects is located at 76 GRAND STREET BETWEEN WOOSTER AND GREENE STREETS IN MANHATTAN. Subway: 1, 6, A, C, E, N, R, W to Canal Street. If you would like to march in the parade, send your proposal to info@deitchprojects.com. For more information, call 212-343-7300 or visit www.Deitch.com.*

## Give your debit card a break and shop at a **flea market.**

Like many cities, New York has a vibrant flea-market culture, with a ceaseless supply of crafts and antiques and a continuous demand of dedicated shoppers. But unlike the never-ending bazaars of Portobello Road or Camden Town in London, or Clignancourt in Paris, most of the flea markets here are the more manageable "boutique-style." They are relatively small, with a comparatively well-edited selection of vendors, and though the merchandise doesn't vary that much from market to market (i.e., clothes, jewelry, collectibles, furniture), each has its own devoted clientele. All of the following markets are easy to navigate and can be visited in a morning or an afternoon. And most are open year-round—a testament both to the appeal of the goods as well as to the devotion of the people who operate and frequent them.

**202. Annex/Hell's Kitchen:** Formerly known as the 26th Street Market, the Annex was long the most popular flea market in the city, and most weekends you were likely to see as many celebrities as antique clocks (the Web page even has a "VIP shopper list" that names all the celebrities who have been spotted there). Recently, it merged with the Hell's Kitchen flea market, a fashion-focused Annex spin-off with designers and craft makers. Now the markets share HK's space in a closed-to-traffic area on 39th Street between Tenth and Eleventh Avenues. Annex devotees may at first feel disoriented with the new layout, which looks more like a street fair than the traditional flea market square, but they will quickly feel at home when they see their beloved antique vendors of Annex hocking their vintage wares, next to the jewelry, clothing, and craft makers. N.B.: The market has launched another spin-off in Brooklyn on the corner of Smith and Union Streets.

*Saturday and Sunday, year-round. 39TH STREET BETWEEN NINTH AND TENTH AVENUES IN MANHATTAN. Subway: 1, 2, 3, 7, N, Q, R, W, S to Times Square-42nd Street; A, C, E to 42nd Street-Port Authority Bus Terminal. 212-243-5343. www.hellskitchenfleamarket.com.*

**203. Greenflea Market:** The Upper West Side's answer to the Annex is Greenflea, an indoor/outdoor market held every Sunday at MS 44, a middle school near the Museum of Natural History. Outside in the playground, the vendors are a mix of secondhand vendors selling crafts, jewelry, and clothing, and a small Greenmarket (see page 169) on the northern end. Inside, mostly antiques, vintage clothing, and collectibles are sold. Greenflea is operated by the parent's association of two neighborhood public schools, and the money it generates goes toward enrichment programs at the two schools. There is also a sister location in the West Village on Saturdays at PS 41.

*Uptown: Sundays. COLUMBUS AVENUE BETWEEN 76TH AND 77TH STREETS IN MANHATTAN. Subway: 1 to 79th Street or B, C to 81st Street-Museum of Natural History.*
*Downtown: Saturdays. GREENWICH AVENUE AT CHARLES STREET IN MANHATTAN. Subway: 1, 2, 3 to 14th Street; A,C, E, B, D, F, V to West 4th Street. 212-239-3025. www.greenfleamarkets.com.*

**204. PS 321:** The parent's association of PS 321 in Brooklyn's Park Slope operates a flea market in the school's playground every Saturday and Sunday. The vendors sell antique, vintage, and homemade wares, and like Greenflea, the proceeds fund enrichment programs at the school.

*Saturdays and Sundays. 180 SEVENTH AVENUE BETWEEN 1ST AND 2ND STREETS IN BROOKLYN. Subway: F to Seventh Avenue. 718-330-9395. www.ps321.org.*

**205. NoHo:** This daily flea market in an old parking lot next to the Tower Records on Broadway sells mostly funky clothing, slogan T-shirts, cheap jewelry, trinkets, and sunglasses, plus some music and posters. You won't find precious antiques or vintage treasures, but if you get a craving for some authentic street fair–style apparel off-season (or in the middle of the week—it's one of the few flea markets open on weekdays), this is the place to go.

*Daily, year-round. BROADWAY BETWEEN EAST 4TH STREET AND GREAT JONES STREETS IN MANHATTAN. Subway: 6 to Astor Place; N, R, W to 8th Street-New York University.*

*Note: There is another daily flea market nearby, ON THE CORNER OF SPRING AND WOOSTER STREETS IN MANHATTAN. This one is quite small—less than ten vendors—and like NoHo doesn't have antiques, but there is some great clothing here, particularly the brightly printed styles of BeeBop and Wally. (Subway: C,E to Spring Street.)*

**206. *Saint Patrick's Old Cathedral Outdoor Market:*** There's no used merchandise at this NoLita market held at New York's first cathedral church (it became Saint Patrick's Old Cathedral when the new Saint Patrick's Cathedral opened in 1879—see page 21), so the selection is a little more upscale than most. Instead of antique and secondhand vendors, artists and craftspeople sell original art, jewelry, and accessories similar to what is sold at the boutiques in the surrounding area.

*Friday through Sunday, April through December. PRINCE STREET BETWEEN MOTT AND MULBERRY STREETS IN MANHATTAN. Subway: 6 to Spring Street; B, D, F, V to Broadway-Lafayette Street; N, R, W to Prince Street. www.oldstpatricksmarket.com.*

**207. *Union Square Holiday Market:*** Just after Thanksgiving, when the fall harvest of the Greenmarket is over and winter is approaching, the lower plaza in front of Union Square turns into a holiday bazaar, with dozens of craftspeople and artists hawking their wares. The goods are on the crafty and creative side—carved wooden boxes, jewelry, woven scarves—and not all of them are as cheap as you might think. However, it is a convenient place to find a holiday gift, and though it gets packed on weekends, it's a nice place to walk around on weekdays if the weather isn't too harsh (the stalls provide cover from the elements but little warmth).

*Late November through Christmas. UNION SQUARE AND 14TH STREET IN MANHATTAN. Subway: 4, 5, 6, L, N, Q, R, W to 14th Street-Union Square.*

## 208. Check out stoop sales in Brooklyn.

The Big Apple version of the yard sale is the seasonal stoop sales that happen along the quiet, brownstone-lined streets in the neighborhoods of Brooklyn. On weekends, you can usually count on seeing several on residential streets in neighborhoods like Brooklyn Heights, Carroll Gardens, Cobble Hill, and Park Slope. People usually advertise by putting up flyers around the neighborhoods, and directions can be found inscribed on the sidewalks in chalk.

*Various locations, Brooklyn.*

# Go on a **walking tour**....

Whether you've been here a few hours or forty years, a walking tour can be an edifying way to see the city. There are literally hundreds to choose from, and they run the gamut from historical sightseeing excursions, to the urbane Brooklyn house tours, to more specialized jaunts focused on gastronomy, art, and architecture. Here are some suggestions:

**209. *Big Onion Walking Tours:*** Now in their fifteenth year of operation, the Big Onion tours are considered the most comprehensive and intelligent tours in the city. The vast range of outings on offer includes expeditions through ethnic neighborhoods like Chinatown and Little Italy, walks through celebrated artistic communities such as Greenwich Village and SoHo, treks through the oldest parts of the city from Harlem through Central Park to the South Street Seaport, and much, much more. Led by doctoral students, historians, and longtime local residents—people who know their stuff—the tours are well thought-out and extremely informative, encompassing all that's of interest in each district and sometimes focusing on one aspect in particular. A tour might, for instance, highlight the unique architecture of old Brooklyn brownstones in Park Slope, the history of the New York intelligentsia on the Upper West Side, or the visible legacies of immigrant communities on the Lower East Side. Tours almost always start at 1:00 p.m., but check the Web site or call the tour hotline for up-to-date schedules and information.

*Big Onion Walking Tours, 212-439-1090, www.bigonion.com.*

**210. *Eat your way through the city on a food-focused walking tour.*** Any notions you may have of walking tours as hokey field trips will disappear when you experience the gourmet expeditions offered by the **Institute of Culinary Education** (see page 296). Each season, they offer more than a dozen different tours, including ethnic explorations of enclaves such as Chinatown, Curry Hill, the Lower East Side, and, via the 7 train, the many ex-pat cuisines of Queens; specialty- and ingredient-focused tours on wine or chocolate, or a carnivore tour led by Mr. Cutlets (aka "the Maharajah of Meat"); tours of markets; and even a gastronomic scavenger hunt held in conjunction with **Watson Adventures** (see page 104). The schedule changes each season, so check online to see what's currently on offer. Reservations are required, and these tours do fill up, so it's a good idea to reserve early.

*Tour times and departure points vary; see online schedule for specifics. Tours are held on weekends and cost between $60 and $100 per person. To register, call 212-847-0757 or e-mail RecreationalDivision@iceculinary.com. For more information, visit www.iceculinary.com/recreational/walking_tours.shtml. For address and additional information about*

*ICE, see page 296.*

**211. Flushing Jazz Trail:** Queens is the unofficial capital of jazz and was the home of America's most famous jazz musicians. The Flushing Council for Culture and the Arts offers a monthly "Queens Jazz Trail," which features the homes and hangouts of greats such as Dizzy Gillespie, Ella Fitzgerald, Count Basie, Billie Holiday, and John Coltrane, and includes a stop at the Louis Armstrong House Museum (for details, see expert contributor sidebar below).

*First Saturday of every month from 1:00 p.m. to 4:00 p.m. FLUSHING TOWN HALL. 137-35 NORTHERN BOULEVARD IN QUEENS. Subway: 7 to Flushing-Main Street. 718-463-7700. www.flushingtownhall.org.*

**212. Talking Street Walking Tours:** How would you like to have Jerry Stiller take you through the sweatshops in the Garment District? Or Sigourney Weaver tell you about the Fed and the New York Stock Exchange? A company called Street Talk offers cell-phone walking tours of a dozen significant sites in these two history-rich neighborhoods, led by the above-mentioned New Yorkers, respectively. (They plan to add more tours in the future.) The tours work like an audio guide in a museum, except that it comes through your cell phone. You call the number for the tour when you get to the first stop, listen to the commentary, then hang up when it's over. Then you call the number again when you move to the next site, and the commentary will resume at that point. (The maps of the tours are available on their Web site, and you can print them out to take with you.) The appeal of these (besides getting a tour by a celebrity, of course) is that you can enjoy them at your own pace, any time you want, and they benefit neighborhood charities. A portion of the proceeds from the Lower East Side walking tour goes to the Henry Street Settlement, and a portion from the lower Manhattan tour goes to the World Trade Center Memorial Foundation.

*Tours are $5.95 each, payable by credit card at the time of call, plus whatever usage or roaming charges may apply on your cell phone plan. The commentary in total lasts about thirty minutes for the Lower East Side tour and forty minutes for the lower Manhattan tour. Tours are available 24 hours a day, 7 days a week. Lower East Side tour: 212-262-TOUR (8687); lower Manhattan tour: 212-586-TOUR (8687). For details and maps of tour routes, visit www.talkingstreet.com.*

**213. Municipal Art Society Walking Tours:** The Municipal Art Society of New York, a formidably accomplished civic group dedicated to the instigation and preservation of creative, useful, and beautiful works of public art in the city, has been sponsoring architectural tours of the five boroughs for fifty years. Led by a mix of architectural historians, urban planners, geographers, and writers, the walking tours are organized around districts whose streets and buildings reflect periods of particular political, artistic, or social interest, so there is a real coherence to the walk and the tour guide's patter. Subjects include "Art Deco Midtown," which takes in the Waldorf-Astoria and

Rockefeller Center, among other examples of the period; a tour chronicling the history of the New York skyscraper; and an exploration of the architectural remnants of old middle-European communities on the Upper East Side. The MAS now offers bus tours, too, including a drive around the historic north shore of Staten Island. The tours are popular, so check their Web site or hotline for schedules and tour details ahead of time. *Walking tours are $12; bus tours $15. 212-935-3960. www.mas.org.*

**214. *Brooklyn House Tours.*** Brooklyn residents never tire of regaling people with the residential beauty of their borough, and they've got good reason to be so house-proud. Brooklyn has many enclaves with grand, notable, and interesting houses and brownstones, and the natural curiosity about what lies inside these private treasures has evolved into a rigorous enterprise of house tours. In the spring and fall, many neighborhood organizations (Brooklyn is nothing if not neighborhood-oriented) offer inside-and-outside tours of some of the area's prominent private homes and gardens. The Brooklyn Heights Association Landmarks House and Garden Tour (in early May) is among the most popular, which takes pie-eyed visitors through differ-ent homes in the historic district, showing off the neighborhood's celebrated and diverse nineteenth- and early-twentieth-century architecture. Other areas that can be explored on tours are Clinton Hill, with its glorious turn-of-the-century mansions; Cobble Hill and Prospect Heights, otherwise known as "Brownstone Brooklyn," with their exquisite private gardens; and Flatbush, which has a stunning array of Victorian-era houses. Even those familiar with Brooklyn may be shocked by the grandeur of the houses in certain areas, and it's interesting to see how the current owners co-exist within their exalted habitats. Of course, the voyeuristic pleasure of nosing around a stranger's house goes without saying.

*For more information and a list of annual tours with descriptions and dates, call 718-855-7882 or visit the Brooklyn Information and Culture Web site at www.brooklynx.org.*

## . . . or take **your own walking tour,** guided by one of these two excel-lent city chroniclers:

**215: *Songlines.*** Jim Naureckas's "virtual walking tour" of Manhattan is truly one of the city's greatest treasures, and using his online street map is one of the best things to do in New York. Go to his modest, unflashy Web site, and you will find a meticulous point-by-point history of New York City streets, with an entry for nearly every address (yes, you read that right). On the homepage, he explains his inspiration for the site, and then pro-vides a list of streets and avenues to view. Choose one, and you'll be taken to a page where you can cruise from one end to the other (west to east for streets; north to south for avenues), reading the eclectic histories of each block, both real (historic and current) and imagined (from literature, movies, and comic books). As of this writing, he's mapped from the Village up through 44th Street, and from Avenue D to Eleventh Avenue (including entries on Hudson River piers). But what is perhaps even more impressive than the fact that Naureckas took the time to put this together is that he's still working—not only are new streets added regularly but existing streets are updated and expanded upon. *www.nysonglines.com.*

**216. *Forgotten NY:*** Kevin Walsh, a Brooklyn native who's been around long enough to have witnessed the construction of the Verrazano-Narrows Bridge as a child, created and maintains a wonderful Web site devoted to the exploration of New York past and present. With amazing patience, a keen eye for detail, and an unrivalled passion for the secrets of the city, Walsh continues to scour the five boroughs for forgotten points of historical interest that range from little-known lighthouses to ancient Indian trading sites, from buried landmarks to rooftop views, and from overlooked garden spots to rusted-over signposts. The Web site is updated regularly and is illustrated with hundreds of photographs that reveal a city within a city, the remains of a metropolis hidden by the New York we know today. Sign up for a Forgotten NY tour, and you can join a gang of intrepid explorers on their next journey—keep an eye on the Web site to see when the next tour is announced, and experience one of the Web's best New York resources in action. *www.forgotten-ny.com.*

## Interesting Houses & Beautiful Blocks

### 217. Walk down the "**Block Beautiful ...**"

Aka 19th Street between Third Avenue and Irving Place. The name comes from an issue of *House Beautiful* from the turn of the twentieth century, praising Frederick J. Sterner's remodeling of the block's nineteenth-century row houses. Ironically, the name stuck and refers today to those same well-preserved early-twentieth-century houses Sterner praised then for their modernity. The buildings on this quiet block are truly interesting; even architecture neophytes will delight in the eclectic and colorful houses and brownstones. Look out for the four figurines of jockeys in front of no. 139, the lion gargoyles in front of no. 145, the surprising brick exterior of no. 130, and the beautiful gable on top of no. 124. Famous past residents of the block include George Bellows, Ethel Barrymore, and the painter Cecilia Beaux; the ivy-covered four-story mansion on the northeast corner (80 Irving Place) was also used as the home of Sigourney Weaver's character in *Working Girl*.
*19TH STREET BETWEEN THIRD AVENUE AND IRVING PLACE IN MANHATTAN. Subway: 4, 5, 6,*

*L, N, Q, R, W to 14th Street-Union Square.*
## ...or walk down a **beautiful block**.

Though they don't boast 19th Street's official title, the following blocks and areas are all lovely to wander:

**218. *The Village:*** Bohemian history and celebrated residents aside, the parts of the West Village that lie between the Hudson River and Seventh Avenue South, where the streets break the mold of Manhattan's grid system, are among the most charming in the city. Spend an afternoon walking along Bank, Commerce, Perry, Gay, Barrow, Charles, and Morton Streets, and you will find not only some of the most beautiful and eccentric houses in New York but also some pleasant surprises in hidden bookshops, bars, restaurants, and alleyways. Can you find Bookleaves, the Village's beloved used bookstore? And can you discover all the entrances to **Chumley's** (see page 50)? In spring, the blossoming trees that line the blocks are stunning; in winter, it is one of the few neighborhoods where the smell of woodburning stoves still fills the evening air. *MANHATTAN. Subway: 1 to Christopher Street-Sheridan Square; A, C, E, B, D, F, V to West 4th Street.*

**219. *Brooklyn Heights:*** Although much of Brooklyn Heights can be admired for its architecture and for its value as a historic district of old Brooklyn, there are a few blocks that stand out as some of the prettiest and most romantic streets in New York. Build up to a stroll along the **Promenade** (see page 64) by walking around Willow Street, Love Lane, Joralemon Street, Pierrepont Place, and the "fruit" streets (Cranberry Street, Orange Street, and Pineapple Street)—all roads that extend into Brooklyn Heights between the Promenade, Atlantic Avenue, and Cadman Plaza. Be sure to find Grace Court Alley and Hunt's Lane, two of the smallest streets in the neighborhood whose buildings were formerly stables for Brooklyn's more well-to-do residents. At night, the light drifting over the East River and flickering from the gas lamps outside the houses makes you feel like you've stepped into another time. *BROOKLYN. Subway: 2, 3 to Clark Street; M, R to Court Street-Borough Hall.*

**220. *Central Park West:*** The Upper East Side may have been considered New York's "Gold Coast," but for the city's best urban castles, you've got to head across the park. Central Park West boasts several palatial apartment buildings, the grandeur of which will be striking to even the most jaded New Yorker. Highlights include the Beresford (211 CPW at 81st Street), a majestic building that wraps around to 81st Street and over-looks the Museum of Natural History, affording its residents the Holy Grail of New York real estate: green exposure on both sides (it's also the best place from which to watch the balloons being blown up for the **Macy's Thanksgiving Day Parade**; see page 89); the Kenilworth (151 CPW), distinguished by its ornate two-tone brick and limestone façade; the San Remo (145 CPW between 74th and 75th Streets), a twin-towered Art Deco masterpiece that has been home to Rita Hayworth, Dustin Hoffman, and Diane Keaton; the handsome Langham, with its pyramids and elegant entry marquee (135 CPW between 73rd and 74th Streets), and of course, the Dakota (1 West 72nd Street at CPW). Further north is the El Dorado (300 CPW between 90th and 91st), another twin-towered behemoth designed by the same architect who made the San Remo.

*MANHATTAN. Subway: 1, A, C, B, D to 59th Street-Columbus Circle; B, C to 72nd Street, 81st Street- Museum of Natural History, 86th or 96th Streets.*

**221. *Washington Square North:*** This well-preserved stretch of townhouses, known as "the Row," looks like it hasn't changed since Henry James was around. But unless you're thinking of going into academia, you'll have to content yourself with admiring the buildings from the park. Like many pieces of desirable downtown real estate, these houses are owned by New York University and are mostly inhabited by deans and professors. Speaking of the NYU monopoly, just around the corner from the Row is **Washington Mews**, a quaint cobblestone street between University Place and Fifth Avenue just north of the park. Although it is officially a private street, nobody will notice if you walk through it, provided you keep your mouth shut—the Mews is home to NYU's La Maison Française, and French is the *lingua franca* here.

*BETWEEN UNIVERSITY PLACE AND FIFTH AVENUE IN MANHATTAN, ONE BLOCK NORTH OF WASHINGTON SQUARE PARK. Subway: A, C, E, B, D, F, V to West 4th Street.*

**222. *Historic Park Slope:*** The part of Park Slope that runs from Prospect Park to Seventh Avenue between Grand Army Plaza and 3rd Street is among the more austere and beautiful parts of Brooklyn. Walk the "extra block" (a small block that disrupts the otherwise meticulously gridded area) that runs between Garfield Place, Polhemus Place, Carroll Street, and Fiske Place, for a true sense of the history of the neighborhood's buildings; and 3rd Street, one of the widest and prettiest blocks in the neighborhood and the epitome of quiet, tree-lined Brooklyn.

*BETWEEN GRAND ARMY PLAZA, PROSPECT PARK, AND THIRD STREET IN BROOKLYN. Subway: 2, 3 to Grand Army Plaza; D, M, N, R to Union Street or 9th Street; F to Seventh Avenue.*

# While you're walking the streets, check out a house of distinction.

Whether for their history, their tenants, or their architecture, the following houses and buildings are all worth seeking out if you find yourself in the neighborhood. (Note: These are some of our favorites, but New York is filled with interesting buildings. A good way to find out about them is by looking at Songlines—see page 97. If you happen to see a remarkable house, note its address, and then check the site and read the entry that accompanies it.)

## 223. Find the plaque for **Bela Bartók**.

For the last five years of his life—1940 to 1945, the happiest period of his self-imposed exile in the United States—influential composer Bela Bartók lived with his pianist wife in relative poverty on West 57th Street. A plaque commemorates his time at the building.

*309 WEST 57TH STREET BETWEEN FIFTH AND SIXTH AVENUES IN MANHATTAN. Subway: F, V to 57th Street; N, Q, R, W to 57th Street.*

## 224. Don't blink or you'll miss the **narrowest house** in the city.

This little house is quite distinguished despite its size. Built in 1873, it was originally used as the carriage entrance for the house next door, no. 77, also known as the Isaacs-Hendricks House, which is the oldest house in the Village (it was built in 1799). At just 9½ feet wide, no. 75½ is now considered the narrowest house in the city. But its diminutive size hasn't prevented it from attracting some big-name tenants: John Barrymore once lived there, as did the poet Edna St. Vincent Millay.

*75½ BEDFORD STREET BETWEEN COMMERCE AND MORTON STREETS IN MANHATTAN. Subway: 1 to Christopher Street-Sheridan Square.*

## 225. Stand on **Allen Ginsberg's stoop**.

From the mid-1950s until shortly before his death in 1997, legendary Beat poet and hero of the East Village Allen Ginsberg lived in a humble apartment at 206 East 7th Street. His rooms were the meeting place of many influential poets and musicians, and everyone acquainted with Ginsberg from Bob Dylan to Jack Kerouac visited him here.

*206 EAST 7TH STREET BETWEEN AVENUES B AND C IN MANHATTAN. Subway: L to First Avenue; F, V to Lower East Side-Second Avenue.*

## 226. Look up at the **Sherry-Netherland**.

When it opened in 1927, the impressive, state-of-the-art Sherry-Netherland promised to be "a smart address for years to come." Catering to the pre-jet jet set, it offered luxurious pieds-à-terre with all the amenities of a hotel suite, in what was then the tallest apartment building in the world. Though other skyscrapers now dwarf it along the Manhattan skyline, the Sherry-Netherland still holds its own, inside and out. From the dramatic Gothic minaret to the famous clock just outside on the sidewalk, the façade exudes stature and majesty. Inside, the lobby, which is based on the Vatican library, is decorated with crystal chandeliers, hand-loomed French carpets, and classical friezes rescued from the Vanderbilt mansion that used to stand on 57th Street. It's still primarily a residential hotel, but if the architecture isn't enough to draw you there, there's also **Harry Cipriani** (see page 38) in the lobby.

*781 FIFTH AVENUE BETWEEN 59TH AND 60TH STREETS IN MANHATTAN. Subway: N, R, W to Fifth Avenue/59th Street. www.sherrynetherland.com.*

## 227. Find country in the city at the **Mount Vernon Hotel Museum and Garden**.

The appearance of this nineteenth-century mansion hidden smack in the middle of the city is a sight in itself. Originally built as a retreat for New Yorkers when this part of the city was rural, the mansion has been preserved, and despite the changes that have taken place around it, it remains pretty much as it was two centuries ago. Stand at the foot of the quaint little path and look up through the pretty flower garden to its front door. You'll enjoy the rare site of a country cottage in Midtown (and film buffs will recognize it as one of the treats of Manhattan that Sam Waterston's character shows off in Woody Allen's *Hannah and Her Sisters*).

*421 EAST 61ST STREET BETWEEN FIRST AND YORK AVENUES IN MANHATTAN. Subway: 4, 5, 6 to 59th Street; N, R, W to Lexington Avenue/59th Street. www.mvhm.org.*

# Subways & Subway Stations

→ **DID YOU KNOW?** *The number of subway stations within the New York City transit system (468) is only 35 fewer than the number of stations of all other subway systems in the country combined.*

## 228. Visit the **subterranean art gallery**.

If you think that the New York City subway system isn't much to look at, think again. Our subway stations boast many interesting temporary and permanent works of art, nearly 150 in all, including some by renowned artists such as Roy Lichtenstein, Romare Bearden, and Elizabeth Murray. These works take different forms and ornament everything from the tiles on the walls to the benches on the platform. Keep your eyes open on your next trip to see what you pass by, or plan a route to see specific works using www.NYCSubway.org, which keeps a running list of artwork in the stations.

## 229. Hide or bribe a train conductor to let you stay on the 6 train and see the abandoned **City Hall Station**.

This one is a bit of a cheat, since we're sure our readers are upstanding citizens who wouldn't dream of flouting the MTA. However, we thought this was just too cool to leave out. If you stay on the 6 train going downtown after Brooklyn Bridge/City Hall— the last stop—you'll get to loop around through the original, abandoned City Hall station (it was closed in 1945 because it was structurally unable to accommodate newer, longer trains) as the train returns to the uptown platform. The station has been preserved architecturally and is surprisingly elegant, with beautiful tiled arches and chandeliers. If you don't want to tempt the law, the **New York Transit Museum** occasionally conducts tours of the station (see following entry, and page 133).

*BROOKLYN BRIDGE/CITY HALL STATION IN MANHATTAN. Subway: 6 train to Brooklyn Bridge-City Hall.*

## 230. Take a ride with the **Transit Museum**.

You can explore hidden parts of the subway system with one of the many excellent subway tours led by the **Transit Museum** (see full entry on page 133). During the tours, which are offered regularly throughout the year, you'll learn about the transit system history and operation, and see things like abandoned stations (see above), decommissioned subway cars, power stations, and control centers.

*Reservations required. Note: Tours require MetroCard fare in addition to the tour price. For a list of upcoming programs, call 718-694-1600 or visit www.mta.nyc.ny.us/mta/museum.*

## 231. Plan your route with **www.hopstop.com**.

Even (or especially) the most intrepid travelers can be stymied by an obscure location, and while MapQuest may be the navigational tool of choice for the rest of the

country, without listing subway stations and bus routes, its driver-oriented directions make New Yorkers feel like second-class citizens. Hopstop.com has jumped in to fill this gap. It works just like MapQuest, where you fill in your departure and arrival locations and borough, but instead of driving directions, you get a door-to-door route, with walking and subway directions, maps, and approximate travel times. You can customize your route depending on whether or not you want to include buses (you can also choose to get a bus-only itinerary), and if you'd prefer more walking/less transfers or less walking/more transfers. You can also put in your approximate travel day and time, and it will calculate the length of the trip based on the train schedule, and will tell you, say, how long you're likely to wait for the G train on a Sunday afternoon. (It does not, unfortunately, account for service changes on evenings and weekends.) In addition, it offers features like a mobile service, where you can register to receive the same direction services on your phone or PDA, and space on the Web site where you can rate and read ratings of individual subway lines.
*www.hopstop.com*

## 232. Use solar power in the **Coney Island-Stillwell Avenue Terminal**.

The train ride to Coney Island's Stillwell Avenue station, the terminus of the D, F, N, and Q lines, used to be known as "the scariest ride at Coney Island," a reference to the station's dilapidated and seedy state by the second half of the twentieth century. In May 2005—after two years of construction and service changes—the MTA unveiled a brand-new, European-style (think Germany's *bahnhofs*) terminal, a handsome glass-and-steel structure that is the city's largest aboveground subway station. But the design isn't just for looks—the glass canopy takes in sunlight that is used to provide power for the station and connected stores and businesses (though not the subway itself). It is the only subway terminal in the system that uses solar power—which is fitting, considering the station's proximity to the beach.
*D, F, N, Q to Coney Island-Stillwell Avenue in Brooklyn.*

## 233. Go on an **urban scavenger hunt**.

You'll see the city in a new way when you're scouring streets, parks, and even museums for answers to cryptic riddles on a Watson Adventures scavenger hunt. Teams of up to six people (you can participate as a group or be assigned to one) compete against one another to come up with answers to riddles, trivia, and arcane New York knowledge as they travel from site to site. Clues are cryptic and humorous and ask players to find things like a saint who looks like Mick Jagger in the Metropolitan Museum. They offer hunts in more than a dozen historic areas and neighborhoods, including Central Park, the Bronx Zoo, Lower Manhattan, Chinatown, and Little Italy, as well as indoor hunts at the Met, the Museum of Natural History, MoMA, and the Cloisters. Pick an area or place that you're interested in learning more about (or one you know well, if you want to test your knowledge), and put on your thinking cap!

*Hunts are held on weekends, year-round, and last between two and three hours. Prices vary. To sign up, call 877-946-4868 or e-mail rsvp@watsonadventures.com. For more information and a schedule, visit www.watsonadventures.com.*

## 234. Play **capture the flag** on the city streets . . .

In 2005, an enterprising college student and Long Island native brought the public games he'd started in Toronto to the streets of New York. By the end of the summer, NYGames was running weekly group games of capture the flag, each time within different designated streets. The rules of the game are too complicated to review here, but suffice it to say, it's a lot different than the game you played at summer camp. Because it's played on the streets (and not in parks), the whole thing has a bit of an underground, vaguely subversive feel, but it is (as far as we know) perfectly legal. The best way to find out about the games is to go to the Web site and check the schedule or sign up for the newsletter. Then all you have to do is show up, and you'll be assigned to a team. It's the best alternative use of the streets we can think of.

*For more information, visit www.nygames.net.*

## 235. . . . or be an **Assassin**.

Is New York feeling a little too safe to you these days? Then sign up for StreetWars, a three-week water gun Assassin tournament that takes place on the city streets each summer, where the object is to "shoot" as many living targets as you can without getting shot yourself. Each participant is provided with the name and picture of their initial target, plus the target's home and work addresses. Once you shoot your target, you take on their target, and keep going until you are either shot by your killer or are the last one standing. (The winner gets a cash prize.) The game is run by a mysterious "Shadow Government" that invisibly oversees the entire campaign.

*For more information, visit www.streetwars.net.*

## 236. Step on private property on **Christopher Street**.

In front of the Village Cigar Shop, there is a small plaque in the sidewalk, which, if you look very closely, says "Property of the Hess Estate Which has Never been Designated for Public Purpose." According to **Forgotten NY** (see page 98), the plaque came from

a former owner of the property, who was forced to give up his building to accommodate the Seventh Avenue subway in the early twentieth century. He held on to this
small parcel of land—how, we're not sure—and marked it with this plaque when they
laid the new sidewalk.
*CHRISTOPHER STREET AND SEVENTH AVENUE SOUTH IN MANHATTAN. Subway: 1 to
Christopher Street-Sheridan Square.*

## 237. Look up at the Lenin statue on the roof of the **Red Square building**.

Built during a period of Soviet nostalgia in the late 1980s, this large bronze statue of
Vladimir Ilyich Ulyanov Lenin is easy to miss if you don't know it's there, but strangely
reassuring to see once you know it is.
*250 EAST HOUSTON STREET BETWEEN AVENUES A AND B IN MANHATTAN. Subway: F, V to
Lower East Side-Second Avenue.*

## 238. Follow the names in the **"Canyon of Heroes"** downtown.

Set into the sidewalk on Broadway, from Bowling Green up to Park Place by City Hall,
are a series of granite plaques that commemorate all the heroes—politicians, singers,
astronauts, actors, diplomats, and baseball players—who have been honored with
ticker-tape parades down Broadway. "Canyon" is the name given to the stretch of
Broadway overshadowed by the early skyscrapers of the financial district. The
plaques mark the dates of each of the nearly two hundred historic parades that have
taken place here, from the dedication of the Statue of Liberty in 1886 to the Yankees'
World Series celebration in 2000, and they touch on everyone from Charles Lind-
bergh to President John F. Kennedy and Pope John Paul II.
*BROADWAY FROM BOWLING GREEN TO PARK PLACE IN MANHATTAN. Subway: 4, 5, 6 to
Brooklyn Bridge-City Hall; J, M, Z to Chambers Street.*

## 239. Keep your eye on the street at the **Library Walk.**

On 41st Street between Madison and Fifth Avenues, there is a line of plaques in the sidewalk honoring literature. Each plaque bears a quote from an author or historic figure on
the pleasure of reading and has its own design motif (a quote comparing reading to a
good drink, for instance, is in the shape of a martini glass). Not all of the authors or works
immortalized are well known, but the path leads up to the entrance of the **New York
Public Library** (see page 291), where you can do further research, if you like.
*41ST STREET BETWEEN FIFTH AND MADISON AVENUES IN MANHATTAN. Subway: 7 to Fifth
Avenue-Bryant Park; B, D, F, V to 42nd Street-Bryant Park.*

## 240. Discover the **African Burial Ground.**

In 1991, the construction of a federal office building on the cusp of the financial district downtown unearthed boxes containing the remains of more than four hundred Africans. The five- to six-acre burial ground is thought to be the only pre-Revolutionary African cemetery in the country and was in use during the eighteenth century. In the 1700s, after **Trinity Church** (see page 22) banned Africans from its cemetery, the African community was forced to move south, to the land we know now as lower Manhattan, to bury their dead. The site of the African Burial Ground has become a designated landmark frequented by many with an interest in or a link to New York's ancestry. On display inside the federal office building built above the site are several artifacts recovered from the burial ground—a carved wooden African coffin, some skeletal remains, and photographs and illustrations depicting the burial site as it might have looked centuries ago—and a permanent monument designed by Rodney Léon is under construction and will be open to the public in late fall 2006. The African Burial Ground Association conducts lectures and events, held at various locations across the city, designed to educate and to improve public awareness in collaboration with its Office of Public Education and Interpretation.

*DUANE STREET AND ELK STREET IN MANHATTAN. Subway: 2, 3 to Park Place; 4, 5, 6 to Brooklyn Bridge-City Hall; J, M, Z to Chambers Street. www.africanburialground.com.*

## 241. Remember John Lennon at **Strawberry Fields.**

Just inside Central Park, across from his erstwhile home at the Dakota, a memorial plaque is set into the pathway honoring John Lennon. The spot is said to have been a favorite of John and Yoko Ono, who lived in New York for several years before John's death in 1980. Almost every day you'll find devoted fans sitting around the plaque, singing Lennon songs, or leaving wreaths, cards, and flowers in his memory. If you're in New York on December 8, you can join the crowds that gather here to mark the anniversary of his assassination, which took place just yards away across Central Park West.

*CENTRAL PARK BY THE 72ND STREET ENTRANCE IN MANHATTAN. Subway: 1, 2, 3, B, C to 72nd Street.*

## 242. Look down on the city's **biggest subway map in SoHo.**

Laid into the sidewalk on Greene Street, outside the SoHo building, is Belgian artist Françoise Schein's interpretation of the city's transportation system. Created in 1986, *Subway Map Floating on a New York Sidewalk* uses stainless steel rods for tracks and small lights for the SoHo stations and won the City Art Commission for the best piece of work that year. Stretching the length of the block between Prince and Spring Streets, the map covers only trains in Manhattan because the sidewalk width wasn't able to accommodate the other boroughs. Dulled over time and worn under foot, it's not easy to recognize that you're walking on a map in the bustle of SoHo, but finding it will make you think of the MTA in a whole new way.

*GREENE STREET BETWEEN PRINCE AND SPRING STREETS IN MANHATTAN. Subway: 6 to Spring Street; B, D, F, V to Broadway-Lafayette Street.*

## Time to look at the street

The furniture of New York streets—its benches, subway entrances, street lamps, and signposts—is as much a part of the city's character as its skyline. From the 1860s on, oversize cast-iron clocks were a ubiquitous feature of the streets, manufactured by the great clockmakers of the East Coast and often endorsed by the stores they stood in front of. But, like checkered taxicabs and "WALK/DON'T WALK" pedestrian crossing signs, over time they have been phased out, and now only a few remain. Below is a list of some of the city's remaining public timepieces, both new and old, that are worth taking the time to notice.

**243. Metronome:** High on a building wall at the south side of Union Square, this work of art by Kristin Jones tells the time to the second in fifteen brightly lit numbers. Read the numbers from left to right to see the time as it ticks toward midnight; read from right to left to see the time count down to midnight.

*14TH STREET BETWEEN FOURTH AVENUE AND BROADWAY IN MANHATTAN. Subway: 4, 5, 6, L, N, Q, R, W to 14th Street-Union Square.*

**244. The sidewalk clock:** Buried in the sidewalk at the intersection of Broadway and Maiden Lane is a clock that has told the right time since 1899—the only clock of its kind in the country.

*BROADWAY AT MAIDEN LANE IN MANHATTAN. Subway: 4, 5, A, C to Broadway-Nassau Street.*

**245. The Yorkville Clock** on Third Avenue at 85th Street is a designated landmark, a classic street clock designed to resemble a giant pocket watch right down to the fob ring.

*THIRD AVENUE AT 85TH STREET IN MANHATTAN. Subway: 4, 5, 6 to 86th Street.*

**246. *The New York Sun Clock*** at Broadway and Chambers Street is the last surviving piece from the building that once housed the newspaper.
*BROADWAY AT CHAMBERS STREET IN MANHATTAN. Subway: 1, 2, 3, A, C to Chambers Street.*

**247. *The Tribeca Grand Clock*,** outside the hotel on Sixth Avenue and Church Street, is a recent revival of the cast-iron timepiece.
**TRIBECA GRAND HOTEL,** *SIXTH AVENUE AT CHURCH STREET IN MANHATTAN. Subway: 1 to Franklin Street; A, C, E to Canal Street.*

**248. *The Seth Thomas Clock*** at Fifth Avenue and 44th Street is a grand street clock, made by the manufacturer of the Grand Central ceiling clock.
*FIFTH AVENUE AT 44TH STREET IN MANHATTAN. Subway: 7 to Fifth Avenue-Bryant Park; B, D, F, V to 42nd Street-Bryant Park.*

**249. *The Golden Clock*** on Fifth Avenue at Madison Square Park is one of the most picturesque, set in the sidewalk in line with the Flatiron building.
*FIFTH AVENUE AT 23RD STREET IN MANHATTAN. Subway: F, V, N, R, W to 23rd Street.*

**250. *The Williamsburg Bank building*'s** giant four-faced clock, on Atlantic Avenue and Fourth Avenue, was the largest clock in the world until 1929 and is big enough to see from all over downtown Brooklyn.
*ATLANTIC AVENUE AT FOURTH AVENUE IN BROOKLYN. Subway: 2, 3, 4, 5, B, N, Q to Atlantic Avenue; D, M, R to Atlantic Avenue-Pacific Street; N to Pacific Street.*

**251.** The clock on the ***Schwarzenbach building*** on Park Avenue South has two little mechanical gnomes who signal the turning of the hour by what looks like one beating the other with a stick.
*470 PARK AVENUE SOUTH BETWEEN 30TH AND 31ST STREETS IN MANHATTAN. Subway: 6 to 28th Street.*

## 252. Cruise the **vendors at Union Square**.

As former Mayor Rudolph Giuliani no doubt found out in his efforts to sweep the streets clean, street vendors are an inextricable part of the city's landscape. From Canal Street to Harlem, Brooklyn, the Bronx and beyond, there is no shortage of places to buy knock-off purses, cheap sunglasses, incense, jewelry, and books and DVDs of dubious provenance, and though they're spread around the city, many of the offerings seem to come from the same place. That's not the case in Union Square, where most of the vendors are craftsmen selling their own works. The offerings in this area (roughly the southwest end of the park, including Union Square West between 14th and 16th Streets) range from Xeroxed movie scripts and mediocre paintings to beautiful handmade jewelry and clothing, fairly accomplished paintings and photographs, really interesting magnets, and one guy who'll do pushups with you standing on top of him. Our favorite "vendors" here are the Mighty Mutts volunteers, who stand at the south end of the park on weekends (by the Ghandi statue). You can buy T-shirts and tank tops with the adorable "Mighty Mutts" logo to benefit this no-kill animal shelter and volunteer rescue organization, or perhaps take home one of the adorable rescued cats or dogs that they have with them. The vendors are in the park every day, even when the **Greenmarket** (see page 169) is in session (Monday, Wednesday, Friday, and Saturday), but on those days they all cluster by 14th Street.

*UNION SQUARE BY 14TH STREET IN MANHATTAN. Subway: 4, 5, 6, L, N, Q, R, W to 14th Street-Union Square.*

*For more information on Mighty Mutts, visit http://members.tripod.com/-~MightyMutts.*

### 253. Go to the **Park Avenue Christmas Tree Lighting Ceremony**.

On the first Sunday in December, a ceremony is held on Park Avenue at 91st Street for the lighting of the trees that line the 2½ miles of the avenue's mall (from 97th Street to 48th Street). There are carols and choir performances, followed by a moment of silence before all of the trees are simultaneously illuminated.

*First Sunday in December. PARK AVENUE AT 91ST STREET IN MANHATTAN. Subway: 4, 5, 6 to 86th Street. For more information, contact the Brick Church, www.brickchurch.org.*

### 254. Dare to go in **Billy's Antiques & Props**.

"We buy apartment contents" proclaims the sign on the front. Inside this dark, covered eyesore on Houston Street, you'll find all sorts of unusual things, like old carnival games and science class–style skeletons, along with secondhand furniture and paintings.

*76 EAST HOUSTON STREET BETWEEN ELIZABETH STREET AND THE BOWERY IN MANHATTAN. Subway: F, V to Lower East Side-Second Avenue.*

# Eat on the Street!

Eating street food is one of life's most delectable guilty pleasures. It's usually messy, often unhealthy, and you don't really know where it's been. As the most pedestrian city in the country (and arguably the world), New York has the best and most varied street food selection, from the traditional hot dog to a darn good dosa. Here are our favorites. (Vendors can be found throughout the city, unless otherwise noted.)

**255. *Hot dogs:*** Always a classic. Best topped with sauerkraut, then doused with mustard.

**256. *Pretzels:*** The hot dog cart's vegetarian alternative. Best with mustard.

**257. *Knishes:*** Good when you need something dense and starchy to fill you up. Also excellent with mustard.

**258. *Roasted nuts:*** The smell alone is one of the best things about New York.

**259. *Coffee from the Mud Trucks:*** How do they get such good coffee from those little trucks? *(Check the Web site for times and locations: www.the-mudtruck.com)*

**260. *Exotic fruit:*** Look for mangoes, lychees, and rambutans from the vendors on the southeast corner of Mulberry and Canal Streets.

**261. *Carved mango flowers:*** Refreshing, and a fresh alternative to ice cream or smoothies. *(By Union Square, often by the northeast corner of 14th Street and University Place.)*

**262. *Gelato from the Otto gelato cart in Washington Square Park:*** Try the olive oil flavor.

**263. *Dosas from New York Dosa:*** Like a crepe, only better. *(Washington Square Park.)*

**264. *Mister Softee ice cream cone:*** Check the name on the truck before you buy. There are plenty of Softee imposters, but the real Mister Softee has them all beat.

# Expert Contributor: Bret Watson of Watson Adventures

Bret Watson is the founder and president of Watson Adventures Scavenger Hunts, which stages fun, informative hunts for the public every weekend. He also puts out a monthly e-newsletter called the "Culture Vulture" filled with New York trivia, quotes, and more. You can find out about the hunts and see the newsletter at www.watsonadventures.com.

## MY FIVE FAVORITE PLACES TO VISIT IN NEW YORK

**265. *Satchmo's "office" in the Louis Armstrong House:*** Step into this time machine and set the dial for 1971, the year Armstrong died. His homey second-floor "office" looks untouched since he departed, but there's one special addition: the docent can touch a button and trigger a recording of the gravel-voiced great chatting in this very room. You'll feel like you have a personal audience with the king of jazz. *34-56 107TH STREET AT 37TH AVENUE IN QUEENS. Subway: 7 to 111th Street. 718-478-8274. www.satchmo.net.*

**266. *Dyker Heights, Brooklyn:*** The most lavish, outrageous Christmas-light extravaganzas can be found on the miniature *palazzi* crammed into this largely Italian neighborhood. Sign up for the walking tour led by tour guide *nonpareil* Justin Ferate. The highlight: a house so decked out that the explosion of lights and characters continues up the front steps and into the living room—go ahead, have a look inside. Ferate will also show you the best place for pastry and hot chocolate along the way. *82ND TO 84TH STREETS BETWEEN TENTH AND ELEVENTH AVENUES IN BROOKLYN. Subway: D to 79th Street. For more information about Justin Ferate and his tours, visit www.justinsnewyork.com.*

**267. *That dark patch on the ceiling of Grand Central:*** Stand in the main hall of the terminal, facing the track entrances. Look up at the ceiling constellation, with its parade of Zodiac figures. Over by the crab, straddling the ceiling and the molding along the edge, find a dark rectangle that seems about the size of an envelope. During the 1990s cleaning, this patch was left untouched to show how dingy the ceiling used to be. *For more information on Grand Central and other things to do there, see entry on page 23. 42ND STREET BETWEEN LEXINGTON AND MADISON AVENUES IN MANHATTAN. Subway: 4, 5, 6, 7, S to Grand Central-42nd Street.*

**268. *Congo Gorilla Forest at the Bronx Zoo:*** This time *you* are the caged animal, gazing through large, panoramic windows at a forest glade populated with gorillas great and small. Unlike a lot of zoo exhibits, these primates stay close to the windows, and you can watch simian soap operas playing out in grimaces, grooming, games, and wild tussles. The newer Tiger Mountain exhibit follows the same idea, offering a close-up view of feline muscles rippling under sleek pelts. However, the tigers often don't come quite as close; leave it to cats to act aloof.

*FORDHAM ROAD AT THE BRONX RIVER PARKWAY IN THE BRONX. Subway: 2, 5 to West Farms Square-East Tremont Avenue; 2 to Pelham Parkway. 718-367-1010. www.bronxzoo.com.*

**269. *Staten Island Yankees game:*** Here's the perfect place to be on a summer night: the third base–side stands in the smaller Yankee stadium, with a beer and a hot dog, watching a ball game played before the backdrop of New York harbor and the lighted spires of Manhattan glistening like Oz in the distance. The seats are cheap and usually still available at game time, and the stadium is steps away from the ferry, so you can bookend the game with free cruises. Sweet as the summer breeze.

*75 RICHMOND TERRACE AT ST. GEORGE IN STATEN ISLAND. Take the Staten Island ferry and follow signs from the ferry to the ballpark. 718-720-9265. www.siyanks.com.*

## The Best Famous Movie Sites

Some of the most iconic moments in American cinema have taken place on our streets, and many filmmakers have cast the city as their backdrop over and over again (we could easily have given Woody Allen's movies an entire chapter). From gritty to romantic, colossal to comedic, New York has played a wide range of parts. Here are our favorites of the city's starring roles:

**270. *Strut down Brooklyn's 86th Street just like John Travolta did in Saturday Night Fever.*** The dance club used in the movie, called "The Spectrum" is still there, too—it's a popular gay disco.

*802 64TH STREET AT EIGHTH AVENUE IN BROOKLYN. Subway: N to Eighth Avenue.*

**271. *Have a treat at the bakery where Cher was* Moonstruck.** Its current incarnation, an off-shoot of the Park Slope café Naidre's, has treats as good as the Cammareri's brothers used to make.

*502 HENRY STREET AT SACKETT STREET IN BROOKLYN. Subway: F to Carroll Street.*

**272. Stand over the subway grate that made Marilyn famous.** From *The Seven Year Itch*, the image that launched a million tchotchkes.
*52ND STREET AND LEXINGTON AVENUE IN MANHATTAN. Subway: 6 to 51st Street; E, V to Lexington Avenue/53rd Street.*

**273. Look for love at the "MacDowell's" on Queens Boulevard in Elmhurst.** It's a Wendy's now but otherwise pretty much the same as when Eddie Murphy worked there in *Coming to America*.
*85-07 QUEENS BOULEVARD IN QUEENS. Subway: R to Grand Avenue/Newtown.*

**274. Speak in funny voices at the Temple of Dendur like in When Harry Met Sally.** The most famous scene from this movie takes place in **Katz's** (see page 169), but the sounds the actors make at the temple are a little easier for most people to pull off.
**Metropolitan Museum of Art.** *1000 FIFTH AVENUE AT 82ND STREET IN MANHATTAN. Subway: 4, 5, 6 to 86th Street. 212-535-7710. www.met.org. See entry on page 118 for more information on the museum.*

**275. Check out the goods at Love Saves the Day**, the vintage store where Madonna traded in her infamous jacket in *Desperately Seeking Susan*.
*119 SECOND AVENUE AT 7TH STREET IN MANHATTAN. Subway: 6 to Astor Place.*

**276. Check your patriotism at Bloomingdale's** right where Robin Williams defects from the Soviet Union in *Moscow on the Hudson*.
*LEXINGTON AVENUE BETWEEN 59TH AND 60TH STREETS IN MANHATTAN. Subway: 4, 5, 6 to 59th Street; N, R, W to Lexington Avenue/59th Street.*

**277. Visit the fire station from Ghostbusters.** On display are photos of the cast taken during the shoot.
*14 NORTH MOORE STREET AT VARICK STREET IN MANHATTAN. Subway: 1 to Franklin Street.*

**278. Get a pickle from the shop in Crossing Delancey.** Though it was called "Posner's Pickles" in the movie, after Peter Riegert's character, Sam Posner, the storefront used was actually that of the famous **Guss's Pickles** (see page 168). You can still visit Guss's, although it has moved from the original location used in the movie around the corner to Orchard Street.
*85/87 ORCHARD STREET BETWEEN GRAND STREET AND BROOME STREET IN MANHATTAN. Subway: F to Delancey Street; J, M, Z to Essex Street.*

**279.** *Run around the reservoir as fast as Dustin Hoffman did in* **Marathon Man** *(or walk slowly around the wrong way as* **Woody Allen** *did in* **Hannah and Her Sisters***).*
*CENTRAL PARK NEAR 91ST STREET IN MANHATTAN. Subway: 6 to 96th Street; B, C to 96th Street.*

**280.** *Take in an art movie at the Thalia.* They've shown Woody Allen's own movies at the theater where he took Diane Keaton in *Annie Hall* to see *The Sorrow and the Pity.*
*2537 BROADWAY AT 95TH STREET IN MANHATTAN. Subway: 1, 2, 3 to 96th Street. 212-864-5400. www.symphonyspace.org.*

**281.** *Break into song at Harry Winston, just like Edward Norton in* **Everyone Says I Love You.**
*718 FIFTH AVENUE AT 56TH STREET IN MANHATTAN. Subway: E, V to Fifth Avenue/53rd Street; N, R, W to Fifth Avenue/59th Street. 212-245-2006. www.harrywinston.com.*

**282.** *Impress a girl (or two) with Sam Waterston's architectural tour of New York from* **Hannah and Her Sisters.** With Carrie Fisher in the front seat and a fuming Dianne Wiest in the back, Waterston's character, an architect, takes them on a late-night drive past his favorite buildings in Manhattan, including the Dakota and the **Mount Vernon Hotel Museum and Garden** (see page 102).
**Dakota:** *1 WEST 72ND STREET AT CPW IN MANHATTAN. Subway: B,C to 72nd Street.*
**Mount Vernon Hotel Museum and Garden:** *421 EAST 61ST STREET BETWEEN FIRST AND YORK AVENUES IN MANHATTAN. Subway: 4, 5, 6, N, R, W to Lexington Avenue/51st Street. www.mvhm.org.*

**283.** *Check for highjackers on the 28th Street subway platform as in* **The Taking of the Pelham One Two Three.** Also, stick around until the end of the film, when the last highjacker climbs out of the manhole, and you'll see what Union Square looked like pre-gentrification.
*28TH STREET AND LEXINGTON AVENUE (6 subway station); and UNION SQUARE IN MANHATTAN.*

**284.** *Watch out for witches in the courtyard of the Dakota.* Along with Mia Farrow and John Cassavetes, the Dakota stars in the 1968 occult classic, *Rosemary's Baby.* Only a handful of scenes occur outside of its famous walls, and though the building has been home to many celebrities, this is one of the very few movies actually shot here.

*1 WEST 72ND STREET AT CPW IN MANHATTAN. Subway: B,C to 72nd Street.*

**285. Whisper conspiratorially over breakfast at the Clinton Diner in Maspeth.** This is where Robert De Niro smashes up a phone booth and Henry says, "That's when I knew Jimmy was gonna get whacked" in *Goodfellas*.

*56-26 MASPETH AVENUE AT 56TH ROAD IN QUEENS. Call restaurant for directions by MTA bus. 718-894-1566.*

**286. Wait for a date at Café Lalo** like Meg Ryan did in *You've Got Mail*. There are more than one hundred different pies, cakes, and other desserts, so unless you're really indecisive, it's a better choice than Starbucks, where "people with no decision-making ability whatsoever make six decisions to get one cup of coffee," as Tom Hank's character says in the same movie.

*201 WEST 83RD STREET BETWEEN BROADWAY AND AMSTERDAM AVENUE IN MANHATTAN. Subway: 1 to 79th Street or 86th Street. 212-496-6031.*

**287. Walk around the childhood haunts of Noodles, Max, Cockeye, and Dominic** from *Once Upon a Time in America* in Williamsburg and DUMBO, Brooklyn. The westernmost stretch of 8th Street South leading up to the Williamsburg Bridge is where Max and Noodles meet, and the junction of Water Street and Washington Street beneath the Manhattan Bridge is the iconic location where Dominic "slipped" and was shot by Bugsy.

*Both locations in Brooklyn. 8TH STREET SOUTH. Subway: L to Bedford Avenue. WATER STREET AND WASHINGTON STREET. Subway: A, C to Jay Street-Borough Hall; F to York Street.*

CHAPTER 4:

# Arts & Culture

There are cities that are older, bigger, and more populated, but none surpass New York in terms of art and culture. From world-class museums to outdoor art shows; from glorious Broadway theaters to hole-in-the-wall performance spaces; from classical ballet and opera as grand as can be to movie theaters showing classic, independent, and limited-release features that are nearly impossible to find elsewhere—New York has superior art and creative performances of every size, shape, and genre. With so much that's beautiful, entertaining, and worthwhile happening all over—from venerable institutions famed for their first-class offerings to experimental ventures that challenge patrons with innovative art forms—we've tried (with great difficulty) to narrow them down a little, and give you only the best of the best for museums, visual art, music, dance, theater, and film. In the process, we discovered how much wonderful, rewarding art there really is here, in both the established venues and outside the mainstream. This discovery proves the point that New York is the ultimate crucible for the arts, as it can produce both the classic and the new in inspired ways, and it always delivers a hungry yet critical audience. If you explore the following offerings, you will be pleased to see how thoroughly the city's cultural institutions excel at presenting arts in all mediums, and at nurturing those yet to be discovered.

## Museums

Note: Many of the museums listed here that charge admission have designated free or pay-what-you-wish hours or days, some of which feature special programs and performances. For more information, please see page 284 or contact the museums directly.

### 288. Face the T-rex and the big blue whale at the
## American Museum of Natural History . . .

One of New York's best-loved museums, the American Museum of Natural History is the most impressive museum of its kind in the world, and one of the most enjoyable. Installed in a mammoth complex along Central Park West that includes both the distinguished old halls and the spectacular new Rose Center, the museum's world-renowned permanent collections are exhibited in beautiful spaces with cutting-edge media. In the fossil halls, the famous Tyrannosaurus rex crouches aggressively over the largest single collection of dinosaur fossils in the world. In the recently renovated Milstein Hall of Ocean Life, the popular 94-foot model of a blue whale hangs suspended over a room of amazing exhibits about the history of aquatic evolution and the technology used in marine biology today. The mammal, bird, and culture halls are filled with so many eye-catching dioramas and artifacts that everyone learns something new with each trip to the museum, and the traveling exhibits—which recently included a room of beautiful tropical butterflies and a collection of fossils representing the very latest in paleontology—are always amazing.

### 289. . . . and make sure to leave time to visit the Rose
## Center for Earth and Space,

the stunning glass structure that houses the new Hayden Planetarium. The awesome collection of photographs, displays, and interactive exhibits reveals as much as we know of the history and beauty of the universe. Go in the afternoon for one of the space shows—either *The Search for Life*, narrated by Harrison Ford, or *Passport to the Universe*, narrated by Tom Hanks—or on Friday evenings for Starry Nights, when the Rose Center's spectacular ceiling lights provide the perfect setting for live jazz and light refreshments.

**American Museum of Natural History & Rose Center for Earth and Space.** *79TH STREET AND CENTRAL PARK WEST IN MANHATTAN. (Rose Center entrance is at 81st Street between Central Park West and Columbus Avenue.) Subway: 1, 9 to 79th Street; B, C to 81st Street-Museum of Natural History. Open daily, 10:00 a.m. to 5:45 p.m. (Rose Center remains open until 8:45 p.m. on Friday). Admission to both (suggested): $14 for adults, $8 for children. Additional fees may apply for space shows and other presentations. 212-769-5100. www.amnh.org.*

### 290. Take the "museum highlights tour" at the Met (or use ours).

The city's most prestigious museum suffers from what you might call an embarrassment of riches: it's simply too much, too many, too good. From ancient Egyptian, Islamic, Asian, Oceanic, Greek, and Roman art and artifacts, to European painting and sculpture, modern art, furniture, decorative arts, and costumes and textiles, the Metropolitan

Museum of Art is an inexhaustible repository of incredible, original, must-see treasures, displayed in a seemingly infinite number of exquisite galleries. It's more than anyone—tourist or native—could see in a week, and the overwhelming number of masterpieces would intimidate any visitor. Of course, there may be a single gallery, collection, period or show that draws you, so by all means, go on in. But if not, the hour-long **museum highlights tour** (free with admission) is a wonderful way to get an overview of the Met's many treasures. However, we could not resist putting in some of our personal highlights, so if guided tours aren't your thing, here are our picks:

**Egyptian Galleries** (first floor): A large and exciting collection of Egyptian art and artifacts includes hieroglyphics and paintings on papyrus, sphinxes, jewelry, and tombs. The centerpiece is the Temple of Dendur, an enormous Nubian sandstone temple from 15 B.C. that stands in a glass-enclosed room.

**Arms & Armor** (first floor): The Met's collection of suits of armor, weapons, firearms, and other military paraphernalia dates from 400 B.C. through the nineteenth century. There are pieces from Europe, Asia, the Middle East, India, and North America, including the largest collection of Japanese arms outside of Japan.

**European & American Paintings** (first and second floors): The Met's painting galleries present the *crème de la crème* of European painting, from works by the Old Masters through the nineteenth century. And though it's thought of as a more historic and classical museum, the Met also has a nice collection of modern works, with paintings by Picasso, Matisse, Miro, and Balthus's incredible *The Mountain*.

**Drawings Collection:** This is a really neat one. Because of their fragility, only a small fraction of the museum's collection of drawings and prints are on display at any one time, either in the rotating selection displayed in the department's gallery, or as part of other exhibitions. However, you can view the collection—an incredible holding of 11,000 drawings and 1.5 million prints focused on West European and American works on paper made after the fifteenth century—privately, by appointment, Tuesday through Friday. During the appointment, you'll browse through the catalog of holdings and select the works you want to see, which are then brought out for you to view up close by the museum staff.

*Appointments are scheduled Tuesday through Friday, from 10:00 a.m. to 12:30 p.m., and 2:00 p.m. to 4:30 p.m. Call the museum for more information:* *see details page 120.*

*The rooftop sculpture garden:* See page 58 for information.
*1000 FIFTH AVENUE AT 82ND STREET IN MANHATTAN. Open Tuesday through Sunday, 9:30 a.m. to 5:30 p.m. (until 9:00 p.m. on Friday and Saturday). Admission (suggested): $15 for adults, $10 for seniors, $7 for students, free for children under 12. Subway: 4, 5, 6 to 86th Street. 212-535-7710. www.metmuseum.org.*

## 291. See the unicorn tapestries at **the Cloisters**.

Set deep in Fort Tryon Park, surrounded by beautiful landscaped gardens overlooking the Hudson, the Cloisters, part of the Metropolitan Museum, is a glittering treasury of European medieval art. The stunning permanent collection of paintings, triptychs, sculptures, armor, furniture, stained glass, and other artifacts is housed in a building made up of original stonework from medieval French cloisters. Perhaps the most impressive objects in the whole collection are the seven "Unicorn Tapestries," a series of fifteenth-century Netherlandish masterpieces of woven wool and silk and among the most beautiful and complex medieval tapestries that survive today. Make sure to leave enough time to enjoy the walk along Margaret Corbin Drive through Fort Tryon Park and up the ancient stone steps to the museum.
*FORT TRYON PARK IN MANHATTAN. Open (November to February) Tuesday through Sunday, 9:30 a.m. to 4:45 p.m.; (March to October) Tuesday through Sunday, 9:30 a.m. to 5:15 p.m. Admission (suggested): $15. Subway: A to 190th Street. Bus: M4 bus to Fort Tryon Park/The Cloisters. 212-923-3700. www.metmuseum.org.*

## 292. Relax and recharge at the **Brooklyn Museum**.

Now nearly eighty years old, the Brooklyn Museum is the second largest museum in New York and something of a buried treasure among the city's cultural institutions. Located far from the boisterous activity of Fifth Avenue's Museum Mile and beside the Brooklyn Botanic Garden at the eastern side of Prospect Park, this grand museum is home to world-renowned permanent collections of Egyptian, Asian, and Islamic art and artifacts, as well as changing exhibits of acclaimed contemporary art, photography, and historic pieces from every culture in the world. Spacious, comfortable, and always quieter than the major museums in Manhattan (except during First Saturdays, the museum's monthly party and program of free events), the Brooklyn Museum makes a noticeable effort to enhance the pleasure of the museum visit—an experience that in other esteemed institutions often suffers from disagreeable atmospheric conditions. In the galleries, there are comfortable, movable chairs for visitors to place in front of pieces they wish to linger over, and the easily negotiable layout encourages visitors to explore without feeling overwhelmed. Don't miss the wonderful fifty-piece collection of Rodin sculptures located on the fifth floor.

*200 EASTERN PARKWAY IN BROOKLYN. Open Wednesday through Friday, 10:00 a.m. to 5:00 p.m.; Saturday and Sunday, 11:00 a.m. to 6:00 p.m. Admission (suggested): $8 for adults, $4 for seniors and students; free for children under 12. Subway: 2, 3 to Eastern Parkway-Brooklyn Museum. 718-638-5000. www.brooklynmuseum.org.*

## 293. Spend a day at the **Museum of Modern Art**.

Less classical than the Met, more traditional than the New Museum, and less specialized than the Whitney, the Museum of Modern Art (MoMA) is a wonderful contradiction of a museum. Since its founding in 1929, MoMA has dedicated itself to being the foremost "modern" museum in the world and has done so in both the literal and artistic senses of the term. The museum exhibits and actively pursues contemporary art and pieces by working artists, and the extensive two-year renovation and architectural redesign has brought MoMA into the twenty-first century; however, the best reason to come here is still to look at the incredible collection of modern masterpieces. This is where you will see Van Gogh's *The Starry Night*, Matisse's *Dance*, and Picasso's *Les Desmoiselles D'Avignon*, which are displayed as part of a wonderful visual survey of artistic movements from the late-nineteenth and twentieth century. Since the renovation, the collection has been reorganized, so now, instead of grouping works by artist, they are presented chronologically by style, unfolding gracefully through two floors of the museum as an exciting tour through Post-Impressionism, Cubism, Surrealism, Dada, Abstract Expressionism, and Pop art. MoMA mounts excellent exhibitions, and in addition to paintings, has galleries for photography and drawings, a film and media department, and a much beloved outdoor sculpture garden. However, unlike many museums, which are either too small or too big to dedicate a day to, MoMA is just the right size and scope to absorb in one marathon visit (which perhaps justifies the notoriously steep admission fee).

*11 WEST 53RD STREET BETWEEN FIFTH AND SIXTH AVENUES IN MANHATTAN. Open Wednesday through Monday, 10:30 a.m. to 5:30 p.m. (until 8:00 p.m. on Friday). Admission: $20 for adults, $16 for seniors, $12 for students, free for children under 16. Free on Friday from 4:00 p.m. to 8:00 p.m. Subway: E, V to Fifth Avenue/53rd Street. 212-708-9400. www.moma.org.*

## 294. Enjoy the **Cooper-Hewitt**, inside and out.

That a museum known for exhibiting progressive, contemporary design is housed in the stately Carnegie mansion seems a little counterintuitive. But nevermind: The collection covers design of all kinds from ancient times through the present day and includes drawings and sketches from examples of decorative art, furniture, jewelry, architectural elements, and industrial and product design, textiles, and wall coverings. The exhibitions focus on modern and contemporary design and development.

At their annual *Solos* exhibition, which showcases contemporary architecture and design, innovative structures—the 2003 edition featured a building made of plastic wrap—are erected in the museum's elegant front garden.

*2 EAST 91ST STREET AT FIFTH AVENUE IN MANHATTAN. Open Monday through Thursday, 10:00 a.m. to 5:00 p.m.; Friday, 10:00 a.m. to 9:00 p.m.; Saturday 10:00 a.m. to 6:00 p.m.; Sunday, noon to 6:00 p.m. Admission: $12 for adults, $7 for students and seniors. Subway: 4, 5, 6 to 86th Street. 212-849-8400. ndm.si.edu.*

## 295. Take a kid to the Forbes Galleries.

This small, idiosyncratic (and free) museum in a series of rooms on the ground floor of the Forbes Building is filled with the personal possessions of Malcolm Forbes and his family. Many of the exhibits are kid-friendly and are accompanied by written commentary and quotes from Malcolm himself. Although the most famous exhibit, the family's gorgeous collection of Fabergé eggs, is gone, there are still plenty of amusing displays of toys and collectibles, like model ships and toy soldiers, correspondence from famous friends, and the family's extensive trove of Monopoly sets—a fitting collection for the famous capitalist. The best part of the museum, however, is what you see before you go through the front door—an elaborate installation of marbles that is hard to take your eyes off of.

*62 FIFTH AVENUE AT 12TH STREET IN MANHATTAN. Subway: 4, 5, 6, L, N, Q, R, W to 14th Street-Union Square. Admission is free.*

## 296. See one of the world's finest personal collections of art at the Frick Collection.

By the time of his death in 1919, Henry Clay Frick had accrued a world-renowned collection of fine art that included Oriental rugs, Asian porcelain, furniture, enamels, silver, drawings, prints, and paintings. In his will, he stipulated that these works become part of a museum to be housed in his opulent mansion on the southern end of Museum Mile, which he also bequeathed to the city. Inside are works by some of the world's most famous artists, such as Goya, Rembrandt, Titian, and Holbein, as well as exquisite pieces of Italian Renaissance sculpture and Ming dynasty vases. The Frick Collection has expanded upon Mr. Frick's initial holdings, and there are more works than can be displayed at one time. But walking around these intimate, quiet galleries and charming courtyards is so enjoyable you'll want to visit every time a new exhibit opens.

*1 EAST 70TH STREET AT FIFTH AVENUE IN MANHATTAN. Open Tuesday through Saturday, 10:00 a.m. to 6:00 p.m.; Sunday, 11:00 a.m. to 5:00 p.m. Admission: $15. Subway: 6 to 68th Street-Hunter College. 212-288-0700. www.frick.org.*

## 297. Walk around (and around) the **Guggenheim**.

The New York branch of this "chain" museum (the other locations are in Bilbao, Spain; Venice, Berlin, and Las Vegas) is most famous for its exterior. Frank Lloyd Wright's conical design literally put the museum on the map and made it one of the most distinguishable features on the Manhattan architectural landscape. Inside, the curving shape allows for a unique way to view art, as works from temporary shows are displayed along a walkway that spirals up the interior. (Particularly fitting for the *Art of the Motorcycle*, a 1998 exhibition of real motorcycles.) The permanent collection—made up of twentieth- and twenty-first-century art—is displayed in galleries that open along the ramp.

*1071 FIFTH AVENUE AT 89TH STREET IN MANHATTAN. Open Friday through Wednesday, 10:00 a.m. to 5:45 p.m. (until 7:45 p.m. on Friday). Open until midnight on the first Friday of every month. Admission: $18 for adults, $15 for seniors and students, free for children under 12. Subway: 4, 5, 6 to 86th Street. 212-423-3500. www.guggenheim.org.*

## 298. See American art at the **Whitney Museum**.

Though not commonly thought of as a "special interest" museum, the Whitney Museum of American Art contains an extensive collection of modern and contemporary American art and is the best place to see the progression of art in this country over the past century. The permanent collection, displayed on a rotating basis, starts with works by early-twentieth-century masters such as Edward Hopper and Alexander Calder, continues through postwar greats like Jasper Johns and Roy Lichtenstein, and ends with late-twentieth-century and contemporary works by artists who include Kiki Smith and Keith Haring. The Whitney Biennial, held every other spring, showcases new works by contemporary artists.

*945 MADISON AVENUE AT 75TH STREET IN MANHATTAN. Open Wednesday, Thursday, Saturday, Sunday 11 a.m. to 6:00 p.m.; Friday 1:00 p.m to 9.00 p.m., 6:00 p.m. to 9:00 p.m. is pay what you wish. Admission: adults $15, children under 12 free. Subway: 6 to 77th Street. 800-WHITNEY. www.whitney.org.*

## 299. Blow your mind at the **New York Hall of Science**.

Chances are that unless you've got a school-age child, you haven't thought of visiting this Queens museum lately. Too bad. The New York Hall of Science is without a doubt one of the most fun places in the city, provided you're not too cool to get excited about science. It can also, of course, be highly informative—when was the last time you thought about microbes and light particles? The museum, which recently underwent another expansion, now boasts more than 400 interactive exhibits, including the world's first hands-on biochemistry lab and a sports center, where you can learn about principles of physics and motion through sports. The museum is definitely geared toward kids, but unlike many children's museums, the exhibits can be just as entertaining (and educational) for adults. So get the kids (or if you don't have any of your own, borrow some) and head out to Queens for a day of mind-bending fun.

*7-01 111TH STREET IN QUEENS. Open Monday through Friday 9:30 a.m. to 2:30 p.m. (Friday until 5:00 p.m.); Saturday and Sunday 10:00 a.m. to 6:00 p.m. N.B.: July and August have different hours. Admission: $11 for adults, $8 for seniors, students, and children. Subway: 7 to 111th Street. 718-699-0005. www.nyhallsci.org.*

## 300. See what's "new" at the **New Museum of Contemporary Art**.

After exploring the classical masterpieces at the **Frick** and the **Met**, the New Museum is the place to check in with today's art scene. From offbeat exhibitions on the photography of John Waters and retrospectives of 1980s East Village art to video and digital displays in the Media Lounge (the only museum space in New York devoted to digital, video, and audio art), the museum definitely has its finger on the pulse. Known for its up-to-date collection and slightly outside-the-mainstream programming, the New Museum is getting, appropriately enough, a new building, scheduled to open in fall 2007. Located on the Lower East Side near the Bowery, the design for the boxy eight-story building looks like the defiant teenage child of the **Whitney**, another New York museum with a bent toward the contemporary. Until the new building opens, however, the museum is located in a temporary space in Chelsea. Pair a visit with an afternoon of **gallery walking** (see page 141), and you'll have a good idea of what art looks like now.

*The new New Museum is scheduled to open in fall 2007 on the Bowery at Prince Street. The temporary space is located at 556 WEST 22ND STREET BETWEEN TENTH AND ELEVENTH AVENUES IN MANHATTAN. Open Tuesday through Saturday, noon to 6:00 p.m. (open until 8:00 p.m. on Thursday.) Admission: $6 for adults, $3 for students and seniors, free for children 18 and under. Thursday from 6:00 p.m. to 8:00 p.m. is pay what you wish. Subway: C, E to 23rd Street. 212-219-1222. www.newmuseum.org.*

## 301. Visit the other "new museum," the **Neue Galerie**.

Located in an exquisite landmark mansion on Fifth Avenue, the Neue Galerie is a relatively recent addition to the New York City museum landscape, but a welcome one. Showing twentieth-century German and Austrian art and design ("neue" is German for new), the museum's small but representative collection is an excellent focused look at the works from this colorful period (including paintings by Klee, Klimt, and Schiele), and the museum is a nice, manageable counterpart to the boundless super-collections at some of the other institutions on Museum Mile. Make sure to save time (and room) for a visit to Café Sabarsky, the museum's excellent Austrian canteen. Chef **Kurt Gutenbrunner** (see page 194) serves excellent renditions of Austrian classics; if liverwurst and goulash are not your thing, then skip right to the *apfelstrudel* and *Linzertortes*, or come for the delicious eggs and Viennese pastries served at breakfast. *1048 FIFTH AVENUE AT 86TH STREET IN MANHATTAN. Open Friday through Monday, 11:00 a.m. to 6:00 p.m. (until 9:00 p.m. on Friday). Admission: $15 for adults, $10 for students and seniors. N.B.: Children under 12 are not admitted and children under 16 must be accompanied by an adult. Subway: 4, 5, 6 to 86th Street. 212-628-6200. www.neuegalerie.org.*

## 302. See Tibetan Art and do tai chi at the **Jacques Marchais Museum** of Tibetan Art.

Staten Island is the unlikely home of the world's largest collection of Tibetan art outside of Tibet. One of only two Himalayan-style monastery buildings in the Western world, this museum houses permanent and changing exhibits of Tibetan artifacts, from gold-leaf paintings to clothing and earthenware. But the exhibits are only one reason to visit. The museum offers a host of different events all year long, such as classes in Tibetan cuisine, painting and crafts workshops, yoga and tai chi classes, and **walking meditations** (see page 303) in the gardens and the Greenbelt of Staten Island. *338 LIGHTHOUSE AVENUE IN STATEN ISLAND. Wednesday to Sunday 1:00 p.m. to 5:00 p.m. Admission: $5 for adults, $3 for seniors and students, children under 6 free. Ferry to St. George; then S74 bus to Lighthouse Avenue. 718-987-3500. www.tibetanmuseum.org.*

## 303. See the python at the **Brooklyn Children's Museum**.

When it was founded in 1899, the Brooklyn Children's Museum was the first museum of its kind, and it remains one of the most fun and educational places in the city to take a child for a day. Everything in the museum invites active participation, so children never get bored or feel like they're being dragged around a gallery. In the Music Mix room, kids can pick up and play all sorts of instruments, from African drums to Fisher-Price xylophones, while the Animal Outpost lets children see, hear, and touch all kinds of animals, with a zoologist on hand to answer questions. The library has books and tapes to keep children thinking, and the museum's educational programming is fun and creative, with regular events like Little Scientist and Artworks which introduce kids to everything from the joys of drawing with crayons to the physics of wet sand. With ramps and stairs to different exhibits, the museum is fun to walk around, too, and a spectacular water flume runs down the center of the building, teaching children the ways of water and letting them float objects down the stream. The star of the show, though, is Fantasia, the 17-foot Burmese python, who has to be seen to be believed.

*145 BROOKLYN AVENUE AT ST. MARK'S AVENUE IN BROOKLYN. Open Tuesday through Friday, 1:00 p.m. to 6:00 p.m.; Saturday and Sunday, 11:00 a.m. to 6:00 p.m. Admission: $4. Subway: 3 to Kingston Avenue; A, C to Nostrand Avenue. 718-735-4400. www.brooklynkids.org.*

## 304. Play with the exhibits at the **Jewish Children's Museum**.

Where can you bake a challah, participate in a pretend game show, and play miniature golf? At the new Jewish Children's Museum in Brooklyn! Located in Crown Heights, a neighborhood with a history of religious and racial tensions, this one-of-a-kind museum combines the educational and commemorative initiatives of a Jewish museum with the approach and technological influences of secular children's museums. Here, children can touch, taste, make, and climb to learn about Jewish history, culture, and customs. The creative, hands-on exhibits (a walk-through Red Sea, a kosher supermarket kids can "shop" in, and a six-hole mini–golf course that teaches them about the Jewish lifecycle) are fun for all religions, ethnicities, and ages.

*792 EASTERN PARKWAY AT KINGSTON AVENUE IN BROOKLYN. Open Sunday through Thursday, 10:00 a.m. to 4:00 p.m. (until 6:00 p.m. on Sunday), and selected Saturday nights. N.B.: The museum is closed on Friday and Saturday in observance of the Sabbath. Admission: $10. Subway: 3 to Kingston Avenue. 718-467-0600. www.jcmonline.org.*

## 305. Get a sense of the past and present of Spanish Harlem at the **Museo del Barrio**.

In the nearly forty years since its opening, El Museo del Barrio has evolved into a leading Latino cultural institution. Located in the Spanish-speaking area of East Harlem (also known as *el barrio*), the museum displays work by young Latin American and Caribbean artists and celebrates the legacies of major influences in Latino art. Its space at the very top of Museum Mile is cool, white, and perfect for displaying the colorful, eclectic collections, which include works in traditional mediums such as painting, drawing, sculpture, and film, as well as more modern forms that include interactive performance pieces and site-specific installations. Past exhibits have featured a chronicle of Latin American portraiture and a full retrospective of the pioneering Mexican photojournalist Casasola. The recent *S-Files* exhibition, a selection of new work by up and coming Latin American artists, included an ingenious piece that told the story of a young Puerto Rican's theft of bubble gum from Wal-Mart—the crime was photographed in stages, the film processed and developed at Wal-Mart's very own photo counter. There is a beautiful pathos to much of the work exhibited here, touching on themes from the grandeur and romanticism of Latin American colonial life to the strength of the Latino community in struggling Harlem projects, and much of it shares a joyousness that invites visitors to celebrate art and the life that inspires it.

*1230 FIFTH AVENUE AT 104TH STREET IN MANHATTAN. Open Wednesday through Sunday, 11:00 a.m. to 5:00 p.m. Admission (suggested): $6. Subway: 6 to 103rd Street; 2, 3 to Central Park North (110th Street). 212-831-7272. www.elmuseo.org.*

## 306. Broaden your horizons at the **Museum for African Art**.

Even in a city that prides itself on its multiculturalism, the Museum for African Art is impressive in its expression of a single culture's art and traditions. The largest museum of its kind in America, the museum's collections include examples of sculpture, portraiture, masks, fabrics, and artifacts from across the African continent. Beautiful, accessible and immediate, much African art has its roots in a spirituality and history that is unfamiliar to Westerners. One recent exhibit explored the ways in which ceramics and domestic arts among the Bamana in Mali reflect the conflicting traditions of their colonial heritage, while another featured examples of the vibrant murals, colorful designs, and symbolic carvings of African architecture. In addition to its temporary galleries in Queens, the museum is using spaces around the city for larger exhibitions until it moves into its new home on Museum Mile on Fifth Avenue in 2008, so check online for seasonal exhibits and locations.

*36-01 43RD AVENUE, 3RD FLOOR, IN QUEENS. Open Monday through Friday, 10:00 a.m. to 6:00 p.m. Admission: $6; free on Monday, Thursday, and Friday from 10:00 a.m. to 11:00 a.m. Subway: 7 to 33rd Street. 718-784-7700. www.africanart.org.*

## 307. Get a taste of New York history at the **Museum of the City of New York**.

The Museum of the City of New York is an interesting blend of exhibitions and archives, chronicling the history of the city and its culture with a collection of more than 1.5 million objects and images. There are exhibitions in many different mediums (such as wartime photographs by photojournalists, contemporary community art projects, costumes from celebrated Broadway shows, and papers that document political scandals), and every collection sheds light on some aspect of New York, its heritage, and its people.

*1220 FIFTH AVENUE AT 103RD STREET IN MANHATTAN. Open Tuesday through Sunday, 10:00 a.m. to 5:00 p.m. Admission (suggested): $9 for adults; $5 for seniors and students. Subway: 6 to 103rd Street. 212-534-1672. www.mcny.org.*

## 308. Brush up your style at the **Museum of the Fashion Institute of Technology**.

The rotating exhibitions at the FIT museum draw on the institute's vast and world-renowned collections of clothing, accessories, and textiles to illuminate every aspect of the fashion world. The exhibits range from whimsical looks at extravagant eighteenth-century haute couture hats to more scholarly examinations of the history of patterned fabrics to sociological evaluations of the miniskirt. The photographic archives contain images of twentieth-century fashion from the obscure to the iconic, and the new, permanent Fashion and Textile History Gallery chronicles the evolution of fashion and our fascination with it over the last 150 years, and includes fabrics worn as long ago as the sixth century. Go for the glimpse of the priceless Balenciaga but stay for the knowledge of how your wardrobe came to be what it is today.
*SEVENTH AVENUE AT 27TH STREET IN MANHATTAN. Open Tuesday through Friday, noon to 8:00 p.m.; Saturday, 10:00 a.m. to 5:00 p.m. Admission is free. Subway: 1 to 28th Street. 212-217-5800. www.fitnyc.edu/museum.*

## 309. Discover folk art at the **American Folk Art Museum**.

You may think you don't know too much about folk art—a broad categorization of works with traditional, cultural, or regional character, by artists who are usually self-taught and have no formal education—but chances are you know *Girl in Red Dress with Cat and Dog*, Ammi Philips's nineteenth-century portrait of a young round-cheeked girl that appears on posters in many living rooms, doctors' offices, and little girls' rooms. That iconic work is just one of the many pleasing surprises at this unpretentious, extremely rewarding museum. Located a few doors down from **MoMA** (see page 121), the museum sits in a slim slice of real estate, modestly occupying its own new building, an amazing 85-foot-tall sliver of a structure, clad in stone-like panels that shimmer metallically, which won the prestigious Arup World Architecture Award for "Best New Building in the World" the year it opened. Inside lies a collection of more than 4,500 unusual paintings and crafts.
*45 WEST 53RD STREET BETWEEN FIFTH AND SIXTH AVENUES IN MANHATTAN. Open Tuesday through Sunday, 10:30 a.m. to 5:30 p.m. (until 7:30 p.m. on Friday). Admission: adults $9, students and seniors $7, free for children under 12; Friday from 5:30 p.m. to 7:30 p.m. is free. Subway: E, V to Fifth Aveneue/53rd Street. 212-265-1040. www.folkartmuseum.org.*

## 310. Learn about the movies at the **Museum of the Moving Image**.

New York has lured so many filmmakers to its streets that movie shoots are just part of the neighborhood, and people don't bat an eye when they wake up to a celebrity's trailer parked on their block. The Museum of the Moving Image celebrates the art of film and animation, and is a great place to learn about its technical side and its changing role in our culture. Exhibits at the museum reveal the mechanisms of this glamorous medium, giving visitors a hands-on, behind-the-scenes look at the processes involved in making everything from cartoons and video games to feature films and TV weather bulletins. Besides its engaging exhibitions, the museum also screens movies on a daily basis, with a program that ranges from Hollywood classics to international documentaries and contemporary art-house films.

*35TH AVENUE AT 36TH STREET IN QUEENS. Open Wednesday and Thursday, 11:00 a.m. to 5:00 p.m.; Friday, 11:00 a.m. to 8:00 p.m.; Saturday and Sunday, 11:00 a.m. to 6:30 p.m. Admission: $10; Friday from 4:00 p.m. to 8:00 p.m. is free. Subway: R, V, G to Steinway Street. 718-784-0077. www.movingimage.us.*

## 311. Watch old TV shows at the **Museum of Television and Radio**.

Watching TV is the thing to do here. The museum has a collection of more than 120,000 radio and television programs and commercial advertisements, which you can watch at consoles in the museum's library. Keep an eye on their programs for special exhibits, seasonal series, and seminars, where you might get to see your favorite TV stars up close.

*25 WEST 52ND STREET BETWEEN FIFTH AND SIXTH AVENUES IN MANHATTAN. Open Tuesday through Sunday noon to 6:00 p.m. Admission: $10 for adults, $8 for students and seniors, $5 for children. Subway: E, V to Fifth Avenue/53rd Street. 212-621-6800. www.mtr.org.*

## 312. See where George Washington really slept at the **New-York Historical Society**.

Calling itself the city's "collective memory," the New-York Historical Society possesses one of the preeminent collections of artifacts, art, and documents of American history, with a focus on New York. The society's library holds more than three million written documents relating to U.S. history, such as newspapers and maps, original Civil War documents, and written correspondence between Alexander Hamilton and Aaron Burr. More than 40,000 items in the society's holdings are on display in the recently opened Henry Luce Center, along with furniture, decorative arts, police and military paraphernalia, and other priceless artifacts. Among all of these historic treasures, it's hard to pick out the particularly notable, but favorites include the 132-piece collection of Tiffany lamps (the world's largest) and George Washington's bed from Valley Forge. *170 CENTRAL PARK WEST AT 81ST STREET IN MANHATTAN. Open Tuesday through Sunday, 10:00 a.m. to 6:00 p.m. Admission: $10 for adults, $5 for seniors, students, and teachers, free for children under 12. Subway: B, C to 81st Street-Museum of Natural History. 212-873-3400. www.nyhistory.org.*

### 313. Live a day in the life of a cop and a firefighter at the New York City Police Museum and the New York City Fire Museum.

For some of us, childhood dreams of heroically fighting fires and valiantly protecting decent citizens from evil villains persist long into adulthood. These museums do a great job of portraying the lives and chronicling the history of New York's emergency forces, and the two can be visited easily in a single day. Exhibits at the New York City Police Museum include a look inside a nineteenth-century police station and a collection of intimidating gear, from uniforms through the ages to the handcuffs and badges used by the earliest New York cops. For further vicarious crime fighting, check out "Suspense in the City," a seasonal series of talks by best-selling mystery writers. The New York City Fire Museum holds a renowned collection of firefighters' equipment and artifacts, which illustrates the history of firefighting in New York from the eighteenth century to the present day, including pre–Civil War hand-pumped fire engines, painted buckets, belts, and the all-important helmets. They also operate an excellent fire safety education program.

**New York City Police Museum.** *100 OLD SLIP BETWEEN WATER AND SOUTH STREETS IN MANHATTAN. Open Tuesday through Saturday, 10:00 a.m. to 5:00 p.m.; Sunday, 11:00 a.m. to 5:00 p.m. Admission (suggested): $5. Subway: 1 to South Ferry; 2, 3 to Wall Street; 4, 5 to Bowling Green; J, M, Z to Broad Street; N, R, W to Whitehall Street-South Ferry. 212-480-3100. www.nycpolicemuseum.org.*

**New York City Fire Museum.** *278 SPRING STREET BETWEEN VARICK AND HUDSON STREETS IN MANHATTAN. Open Tuesday through Saturday, 10:00 a.m. to 5:00 p.m.; Sunday, 10:00 a.m. to 4:00 p.m. Admission (suggested): $5. Subway: C, E to Spring Street. 212-691-1303. www.nycfiremuseum.org.*

### 314. Have a think in the peaceful gardens at the Noguchi Museum.

Toward the end of his life, the acclaimed (and famously private) sculptor Isamu Noguchi decided in the interests of art and education to convert his working studio in Long Island City into a gallery and learning space. The Noguchi Museum remains a uniquely calm and reflective space, with several rooms and a Japanese garden displaying fine examples of his rock and wood sculpture. It's a meditative place to sit and think in the presence of his soothing art, and on the second Sunday of every month,

the museum hosts lectures about Noguchi and his influence on the arts.
*9-01 33ᴿᴰ ROAD AT VERNON BOULEVARD IN QUEENS. Open Wednesday through Friday, 10:00 a.m. to 5:00 p.m.; Saturday and Sunday, 11:00 a.m. to 6:00 p.m. Admission: $10. Subway: N, W to Broadway. 718-204-7088. www.noguchi.org.*

## 315. See brand-new modern art at **PS1**.

PS1, the Queens outpost of the **Museum of Modern Art** (see page 121), is one of the most unusual exhibition spaces in New York. Set in a unique environment in Long Island City that is part converted schoolhouse and part raw installation space, this forward-thinking venue exhibits fresh and creative contemporary art, from light installations that fill entire rooms to pieces of experimental architecture in the museum's outdoor spaces. Galleries of varying shapes and sizes are spread out over the building's five floors, and the eclectic exhibits demand attention in different ways—in one place you're peering down into a dark room full of sculpted figures, and in another you're staring up at a colorful film. Just walking around PS1 can be fun, too: the building is cool and expansive; there are murals in the stairwells; and the views from the windows of the Manhattan skyline and **5Pointz** across the street (see page 137) are surreal and breathtaking.
*22–25 JACKSON AVENUE AT 46ᵀᴴ AVENUE IN QUEENS. Open Thursday through Monday, noon to 6:00 p.m. Admission (suggested): $5. Subway: E, V to 23 Street-Ely Avenue; 7 to 45 Road-Court House Square; G to Long Island City-Court Square. 718-784-2084. www.ps1.org.*

## 316. Celebrate New York's vertical landscape at the **Skyscraper Museum**.

Skyscrapers are New York's signature feature, so it's only fitting that we have a museum dedicated to this particular architectural feat. After operating from several temporary locations, the museum has found a permanent home in the Ritz-Carlton New York, Battery Park Hotel. Ironically, the museum of tall and majestic structures is in a teeny-tiny space on the ground floor, but you won't feel gypped. The one-room museum showcases the history, engineering, design, and social function of tall buildings through several engaging, kid- and novice-friendly exhibits, like a recent show rating the top ten skyscrapers in the city, and several pieces about the World Trade Center towers.
*39 BATTERY PLACE NEAR LITTLE WEST STREET IN MANHATTAN. Open Wednesday through Sunday, noon to 6:00 p.m. Admission: $5 for adults, $2.50 for students and seniors. Subway: 1 to Rector Street or South Ferry; 4, 5 to Bowling Green; N, R, W to Whitehall Street-South Ferry. 212-968-1961. www.skyscraper.org.*

### 317. Learn about New York nautical history at the **South Street Seaport Museum** and the **Red Hook Waterfront Museum**.

Fourscore years ago and more, when people and goods arrived in New York by boat from overseas, the ports of the East River were hives of business and activity. In the late-eighteenth and early-nineteenth centuries, the port at South Street in downtown Manhattan was the country's leading seaport, and the museum located there preserves the memory of the period, with great exhibits of nautical artifacts like seafarers' maps, ships' bells, and the largest fleet of privately maintained historic vessels in the country. Three of the eight ships are permanently moored to the docks and open to the public, and three others offer sailing tours of the waters around the harbor—imagine the year is 1885 and stand on the deck of the *Wavertree* or sail onboard the *Pioneer*. Afterward, you can cross over to Brooklyn and visit the Waterfront Museum, a small and charming gallery of curiosities and artifacts kept aboard a historic vessel moored at Red Hook's Conover Street harbor.

**South Street Seaport Museum.** *207 FRONT STREET AT WATER STREET IN MANHATTAN. Open (summer) Tuesday through Sunday 10:00 a.m. to 6:00 p.m.; (winter) Friday through Monday, 10:00 a.m. to 5:00 p.m. Admission: $8 for adults, $6 for students and seniors, $1 for children ages 5 to 12. Subway: 2, 3, 4, 5, J, M, Z to Fulton Street; A, C to Broadway-Nassau Street. 212-748-8600. www.southstseaport.org.* **Red Hook Waterfront Museum.** *290 CONOVER STREET AT PIER 44 IN BROOKLYN. Open dawn to dusk. Admission: donations accepted. Subway: F to Smith-9th Streets. Bus: B-77 to Conover Street. 718-624-4719. www.waterfrontmuseum.org.*

### 318. Take a tour of the **Lower East Side Tenement Museum**.

When the landlord of 97 Orchard Street died in the late 1980s, the five unused stories of the building above the storefronts he controlled were opened for the first time in fifty years. Inside this time capsule were twenty tenement apartments, left exactly as they were when the landlord closed up the residential part of the building. (He was unable to pay for the fireproofing mandated at the time, so he just boarded them up). Using city records, oral histories, and testimonies from descendents of residents, many of the apartments have been restored to look as they did during particular points of the building's seventy-year tenure as a tenement house, from the 1860s through the 1930s. The result is an unusual "museum," where you can tour different apartments and learn about real former tenants, their occupations, and their lifestyles—sort of like Colonial Williamsburg, New York style. N.B.: The tenement is viewable by guided tour only, and tours do fill up, so it's best to reserve in advance. You can do so online through their Web site or by showing up when the museum opens for same-day tickets.

*108 ORCHARD STREET AT DELANCEY STREET (tenement building is 97 Orchard). Tours run daily, from 11:00 a.m. to 6:00 p.m. Admission: $15 for adults, $11 for students and seniors . Subway: F to Delancey; J, M, Z to Essex Street. For more information, call 212-431-0233 or visit www.tenement.org.*

## 319. Ride a trolley car from the past at the **MTA Transit Museum**.

The Metropolitan Transit Authority operates the biggest public transportation system in the world and has been helping people travel all over the city for more than a century. At the Transit Museum, you can learn about the history of the subways, the mechanics of the trains, and the engineering that has helped shape New York as we know it. In addition to amazing photographic exhibitions—including the recent *On Location*, which used movie stills, photographs, storyboards, film clips, and movie props to explore the pivotal role the MTA has played in New York's cinematic history—there are many engaging interactive exhibits, from the *Memory Project*, where visitors can write, record, or draw something that reflects an experience they had on the subway, to *On the Streets*, a collection of vintage trolley buses that visitors are free to climb aboard.

*BOERUM PLACE AT SCHERMERHORN STREET IN BROOKLYN. Open Tuesday through Friday, 10:00 a.m. to 4:00 p.m.; Saturday and Sunday, noon to 5:00 p.m. Admission: $5. Subway: 2, 3, 4, 5 to Borough Hall; A, C, G to Hoyt Street-Schermerhorn Street; F to Jay Street-Borough Hall; M, R to Court Street-Borough Hall. 718-694-1600. www.mta.nyc.ny.us/mta/museum.*

# Expert Contributor: David Masello

David Masello is the articles editor at *Country Living* magazine and a longtime New York correspondent for *Art & Antiques* magazine. His essays and feature articles about art and architecture have appeared in, among other publications, the *New York Times* and *Boston Globe*, and in several anthologies, including *Best American Essays 2005*. He is the author of two books, *Architecture Without Rules: The Houses of Marcel Breuer* (W.W. Norton) and *Art in Public Places* (City & Company).

## MY FIVE FAVORITE WORKS OF ART IN NEW YORK

### 320. Portrait of Lodovico Capponi *by Bronzino at the Frick Collection* depicts

an attractive young man some might consider haughty and imperious. He is dressed in regal, shimmering Florentine garb of the mid-sixteenth century and even sports a conspicuous codpiece (a fashion of the day). The cameo he grasps in his hand includes the word *"sorte"* (fate, in Italian) and refers to the love he felt for an elusive young woman in the Medici court, whom he eventually married. Try to escape the gaze of his wandering eye.

*For address and information, see entry on the Frick Collection, page 122.*

**321. Bemelmans Bar,** located within the Carlyle Hotel, has the feel of an urban version of the Lascaux Caves, the site in France whose rock walls are covered with prehistoric drawings of beasts. Ludwig Bemelmans, the creator and illustrator of the *Madeline* children's books, lived at the hotel in the mid-1940s and his "gift" to the management was to cover the ochre-colored walls with whimsical paintings of humanlike animals in New York City locales. Many of the drawings hearken to famous personalities of the day, including Jackie Gleason and Conrad Hilton. After your third martini, you might consider starting up a conversation with the animals.

*35 EAST 76TH STREET AT MADISON AVENUE IN MANHATTAN. Subway: 6 to 77th Street. 212-744-1600. www.thecarlyle.com*

**322.** It's a remark uttered frequently by both New Yorkers and visitors that the city streets are filled with some of the handsomest people in the world. One of the most dashing permanent citizens is **Nathan Hale, rendered in bronze, in City Hall Park.** The twenty-year-old revolutionary hero is famous for reputedly saying at his hanging by the British on September 22, 1776, "I only regret that I have but one life to lose for my country." The sculpture was fashioned by Frederick MacMonnies (see entry for statue of **Civic Virtue** on page 140) in 1893. The rope-bound Hale maintains a pose of dignity, his beautiful face and coiffed hair set for all to admire.

*CITY HALL PARK BETWEEN BROADWAY AND PARK ROW, CHAMBERS AND BARCLAY STREETS IN MANHATTAN. Subway: R, W to City Hall.*

**323.** Depending on your state of mind, **Edvard Munch's The Storm, which is part of the Museum of Modern Art's permanent collection,** is either unnerving or just perplexing. Are those six figures in classic Munch pose (arms raised to the sides of their heads) simply fleeing from the moody storm or are they, well, unbalanced? Perhaps it's those unanswerable, impossible-to-resolve qualities about the painting that make it so intriguing. Whatever the interpretation, though, the colors of the stormy sky juxtaposed with the cozy lighted house make this one of New York City's most alluring public paintings.

*For address and information, see entry for MoMA on page 121.*

**324.** It's not uncommon to see people reading the Sunday *New York Times* on one of the benches in the **Astor Court at the Metropolitan Museum of Art.** The tranquil room replicates a Ming Dynasty (1368–1644) residential garden courtyard that is typical of Suzhou, a city in China famous for such spaces. The courtyard is so evocative of the outdoors and of its exotic locale that some New Yorkers use it as an idyllic wee end retreat from the city. And for anyone who doesn't understand the ancient Chinese philosophy of yin and yang, this is the space to learn the lesson: opposites abound, soft and hard surfaces, dark and light areas, natural and man-made details. *For address and more information, see entry for the Met on page 118.*

# Art

## Look for **hidden art**.

In addition to museums, galleries, and open-air public art, New York has some wonderful masterpieces tucked away in less obvious places. Pieces from corporate art collections, commissioned murals in building lobbies, sculptures in plazas, even a decorated piece of the Berlin Wall are all on permanent display in New York—if you know where to look. Accessibility to these semi-public works can be tricky—because many of them belong to corporate collections, they are located in office buildings, banks, and government buildings that do not have specific visiting hours. But rest assured that visiting them—even if you have no other business there—is perfectly legal. That's why they're there. Here are some of our favorites:

### 325. *Piece of the Berlin Wall, outdoor plaza, 520 Madison.*

Down the block from MoMA is a wonderful piece of contemporary art in an unlikely place. On 53rd Street, just west of Madison Avenue, there are several rescued sections of the Berlin Wall decorated with two large, angry-looking faces looming over scrawling graffiti. Just don't be tempted to leave your own mark—though the existing graffiti from Germany is considered part of the piece, further additions are not welcome. *PLAZA OF 520 MADISON AVENUE ON 53RD STREET BETWEEN FIFTH AND MADISON AVENUES IN MANHATTAN. Subway: E, V to Fifth Avenue/53rd Street.*

### 326. *Contemporary art, lobby, 520 Madison.*

Just inside the building are several interesting contemporary artworks from the esteemed art collection of the building's owner, Tishman Speyer. *See address above.*

### 327. *Miró paintings and Giacometti sculpture at 9 West 57th Street.*

You may know the bright, red sculpture of the number "9" outside this building, but also on display in the lobby are several large Joan Miró paintings. The security tends to be stiff and snooty, so expect suspicious looks if you try to get a close-up look, but luckily, the lobby has floor-to-ceiling windows and is well lit, so you can get a good view just walking down 57th Street.

*9 WEST 57TH STREET BETWEEN FIFTH AND SIXTH AVENUES IN MANHATTAN. Subway: N, Q, R, W to 57th Street; N, R, W to Fifth Avenue/59th Street.*

### 328. The sculpture garden, 590 Madison Avenue (formerly the IBM Building).

The atrium at 590 Madison is a true urban oasis, and one of the loveliest, most tranquil spaces in all of Midtown. Located between 56th and 57th Streets, the glass-enclosed public space has both garden and sculptural elements; here, office workers and weary tourists can enjoy a bite to eat amid bamboo trees and a revolving selection of sculpture and large-scale art.

*590 MADISON AVENUE BETWEEN 56TH AND 57TH STREETS IN MANHATTAN. Subway: E, V, to Fifth Avenue/53rd Street.*

### 329. Energy, Result, Workmanship, and Transportation *in the Chrysler Building.*

Though the Empire State Building may eclipse it in height, the Chrysler Building is the city's architectural darling. Inside the exquisite façade lies another Art Deco masterpiece—Edward Turnbull's elaborate 100-by-72-foot ceiling mural. The work celebrates modernity, depicting the workers during the building's construction. Long obscured by poor lighting, the mural was recently restored during the building's renovation.

*405 LEXINGTON AVENUE AT 42ND STREET IN MANHATTAN. Subway: 4, 5, 6, 7, S to Grand Central-42nd Street.*

### 330. Harbors of the World *in the American Express headquarters.*

Commissioned by American Express in the mid-1980s, this ambitious set of murals depicts the world through its major harbor cities. Artist Craig McPherson traveled around the world for a year and then took another four to complete the artwork. The result is a stunning, intricately detailed, eleven-foot-high panorama of the world's waterways.

*3 WORLD FINANCIAL CENTER (BY VESEY STREET) IN MANHATTAN. Subway: E to World Trade Center; A, C to Chambers Street; 2, 3 to Park Place; 1, R, W to Rector Street.*

### 331. *Sculptures at Chase Manhattan Plaza.*

Visitors who make their way through the forest of office buildings that surround this Wall Street complex will be rewarded with several distinguished pieces of public art. The plaza features two large-scale artworks, both referencing the conflict between urban and natural landscapes, and each is stunning in its own way: Jean DuBuffet's forty-two-foot fiberglass sculpture, *Group of Four Trees*, and Isamu Noguchi's *Sunken*

*Plaza*, a circular below-ground water and rock garden, visible from the plaza above, and from the surrounding windows on the lower levels. We suggest going on a Sunday, when the financial district is empty and eerily quiet, so you can really see how well these two faux-natural elements enhance the otherwise bleak concrete landscape. *BETWEEN PINE AND LIBERTY STREETS AND BETWEEN NASSAU AND WILLIAM STREETS IN MANHATTAN. Subway: 2, 3, 4, 5 to Wall Street.*

→ **DID YOU KNOW?** *Noguchi found the seven heavy basalt rocks (each weighing at least a ton) used in* Sunken Plaza *at the bottom of the Uji River in Japan and had them shipped to the United States.*

## 332. Paint something for New York to remember you by at 5Pointz, the Institute for Higher Burnin'.

A landmark visible from the windows of the **7 train into Queens** (see page 67), 5Pointz is a unique space dedicated to the appreciation and encouragement of the art of graffiti. Most of the exteriors of this converted warehouse are covered in the colorful murals and tags of talented graffiti artists from all over the world, and director Jan Meres has plans to convert the interiors into galleries and studios for aspiring and seasoned painters alike. If you'd like to do some painting yourself, you can apply online for a license, or you can just go and walk around the building (including the roof, with spectacular views of Manhattan) to see the work on display. *JACKSON AVENUE AT CRANE STREET AND DAVIS STREET IN QUEENS. Subway: E, V to 23rd Street-Ely Avenue; 7 to 45 Road-Court House Square; G to Long Island City-Court Square. www.5ptz.com.*

## 333. Plunge your hands into fresh soil at the *Earth Room*.

Created by renowned artist Walter De Maria and maintained by the Dia Art Foundation (which is in the process of moving to a new exhibition space by the **Chelsea Highline**—see page 75), the *Earth Room* is a quiet space in the heart of SoHo filled with fresh, dark soil that affords New Yorkers a chance to take a break from the busy asphalt streets below. A glass fence separates you from the 250 cubic yards of earth, so you can stand and inhale the clean, moist air, and visitors are free to plunge their hands into the soil. De Maria's installations often play with relationships that exist between the natural and the man-made: he has exhibited earth rooms twice in Germany, and his *Lightning Field* in New Mexico is acclaimed as one of the late-twentieth century's most significant works of art. Don't be afraid to get your hands dirty—the experience is more refreshing, cathartic, and rewarding than any other hands-on exhibit we can think of.

*141 WOOSTER STREET BETWEEN HOUSTON AND PRINCE STREETS IN MANHATTAN. Open Wednesday through Sunday, noon to 6:00 p.m. Admission is free. Subway: N, R, W to Prince Street. www.earthroom.org.*

### 334. Also on permanent exhibit in **Soho**

is another, equally surreal work by Walter De Maria, the *Broken Kilometer*, a full kilometer's worth of 500 solid brass rods carefully arranged in parallel rows to create a hypnotic illusion of distance and light.

*393 WEST BROADWAY BETWEEN SPRING AND BROOME STREETS IN MANHATTAN. Open Wednesday through Sunday, noon to 6:00 p.m. Admission is free. Subway: C, E to Spring Street.www.brokenkilometer.org.*

### 335. See what's new at the **Armory**.

The International Exhibition of Modern Art of 1913—more commonly known as "the Armory Show," for its location in Manhattan's 69th Regiment Armory—was the first of its kind in this country and is credited with introducing America to what we now refer to as modern art, as it was the first time works by Picasso, Kandinsky, and Duchamp were shown in the U.S. Though no longer held in the Armory, the fair's modern incarnation preserves the same spirit, continuing its legacy by presenting new contemporary works from around the world during its annual five-day run. More than 500 galleries from across the globe jockey for fewer than 150 booths, making for a highly selective show of never-before-seen paintings, sculptures, drawings, photography, mixed-media works, installations, and video art.

*PIERS 90 AND 92 ON THE HUDSON RIVER (BY 50TH AND 52ND STREET) IN MANHATTAN. Late Winter. Admission: $20 per day or $40 for a run-of-the-show pass for adults, $10 for students. Subway: C, E to 50th Street. 212-645-6440. www.thearmoryshow.com.*

### 336. Experience creativity at its most free at the **Flux Factory**.

There are no limits to what goes on at the Flux Factory, an ingenious nonprofit artist's workshop in Long Island City, except for the walls of its homely warehouse space—and even those don't seem to hold things back. At its recent *Cartünnel* exhibit, a maze of colorful tunnels twisted and turned around the gallery, its walls painted with comic book–style environments; at junctions where the passages met, visitors determined the course of their journeys and the stories that accompanied them—a real-life "choose your own adventure." The attitude to art at the Flux Factory is that it should always be interactive, engaging, and thought provoking. *The Novel* exhibit saw three writers locked in glass isolation booths built by young architects for thirty days and thirty nights, their only task to have finished a novel when they emerged at the end of the month—an extreme study in the creative potential of solitude. Exhibits and events at the Flux Factory encompass every medium, from sound and film to writing and the visual arts: one highlight of 2005 was the simultaneous exhibition of *What the Book?*, an eccentric collection of handmade artists' volumes, and the public reading of several classic novels from beginning to end by courageous visitors.

*38-38 43RD STREET IN QUEENS. Hours vary according to exhibit. Admission: donations accepted. Subway: V, R, G to 36th Street. 718-707-3362. www.fluxfactory.org.*

## 337. See what's on (any time of day) at **Broadway Windows**.

This 24-hour viewing space bridges the gap between gallery space and public art, showing continuous revolving exhibitions of contemporary artworks in five professionally lighted street-level windows. The site-specific installations stay up for about two months each and have run the gamut from subtle and ambiguous structures of stone or glass, to brightly colored representational paintings and sculptures, and everything in between. Any artist may submit a proposal, and almost all works are for sale. New York University, which operates the space as a nonprofit gallery, sees it as dual-purpose community service: it provides unrepresented artists with an opportunity to have a gallery show of sorts, and it gives the public free exposure to contemporary and unconventional art they may not see otherwise. Note: NYU also operates the Washington Square Windows, a similar street-side gallery of three windows, on the east side of Washington Square Park.

*BROADWAY AND 10TH STREET, NORTHWEST CORNER, IN MANHATTAN. Subway: 4, 5, 6, L, N, Q, R, W to 14th Street-Union Square; N, R to 8th Street-New York University. 212-998-5751. www.nyu.edu/pages/galleries.*

## 338. Play among the artwork at **Socrates Sculpture Park**.

This quirky open-air exhibition grounds along the East River holds revolving short-term exhibits of large-scale contemporary sculpture, and also hosts other outdoor events including movies and **tai chi classes** (see page 227), as well as children's programs.

*32-01 VERNON BOULEVARD IN QUEENS. Subway: N, W to Broadway. 718-956-1819. www.socratessculpturepark.org.*

## 339. Visit artists in their studios during **NYC Open Studios Weekends**.

New York is full of talented aspiring artists toiling away in private homes and studios. For the month of October, you can meet up-and-coming artists and see their work, one borough at a time, during the Open Studios Weekends. Artists apply to have their studios/workspaces listed on the event map, and each borough is assigned a weekend during the month, during which time the participating artists open their studios, and attendants can pop by during the day to view their work. In addition, there are parties, performances, and a silent auction. The event is sponsored and organized by Emerging Artists International, a nonprofit organization dedicated to promoting contemporary artists and facilitating displays of their work

*October. Admission is free. For more information, maps, dates, and how to apply, visit www.isupportart.org.*

## 340. Get shocked by the statue of *Civic Virtue*.

This 1922 sculpture designed by Frederick MacMonnies was originally erected in Manhattan's City Hall Park. However, its vivid representation of virtue triumphing over temptation (a scantily clad youth with a huge club standing over two trampled sirens languishing at his feet) was deemed by many to be scandalous and insulting to women, which turned the state of *Civic Virtue* into a hotly contested issue around City Hall. "Rough Boy" (or "Tough Boy"), as the sculpture came to be known, was eventually moved to its current location in 1941, when Mayor Fiorello LaGuardia gave it to Queens County on the occasion of the opening of the new Borough Hall, in what can be seen as another example of priceless municipal symbolism.

*QUEENS BOROUGH HALL, 120-155 QUEENS BOULEVARD, BY UNION TURNPIKE, IN QUEENS. Subway: E, F to Kew Gardens-Union Turnpike.*

→ **DID YOU KNOW?** *Despite the controversy surrounding its allegedly lewd depiction,* Civic Virtue *had quite a prestigious provenance. It was sculpted by the Priccirilli Brothers of the Bronx, two of whom also sculpted the lions in front of the* **New York Public Library** *(see page 291) and the Lincoln Memorial in Washington, D.C. The sculpture was, at the time, the largest work designed by an American (MacMonnies) and was said to have come from the largest single block of marble since Michelangelo's* David.

## 341. Catch a glimpse of the **Keith Haring mural**.

Keith Haring was the artist who made New Yorkers learn to love graffiti. His barking dogs and radiant babies were familiar sights in subway stations in the early '80s and they eventually got him noticed by the art world, but even after he became a star artist, he kept drawing on the streets. By the time of his death in 1990, he had created several outdoor murals around the city, mostly in parks and playgrounds. Some of these were not commissioned and have been erased or destroyed, but his 1986 *Crack is Whack!* mural, which is now maintained by the Parks Department, still exists. A personal riff on "Just Say No," the fluorescent orange mural depicts his typical, faceless characters surrounded by skulls and monsters and was Haring's response to the crack epidemic that plagued the city during those years. Located on a handball court at 128th Street and Second Avenue, it is also visible from the FDR Drive, so keep an eye out if you're stuck in traffic.

*128TH STREET BETWEEN SECOND AVENUE AND THE FDR DRIVE IN MANHATTAN. Subway: 4, 5, 6 to 125th Street.*

## 342. Explore the galleries of **west Chelsea**.

In the last decade, the industrial no-man's-land by Chelsea Piers and the West Side Highway has been transformed into a vibrant gallery scene. Today, between two and three hundred galleries lie west of Tenth Avenue, roughly between 20th and 28th Streets, scattered amid taxi depots and warehouses. Attracted initially by lower per-square-foot rents (as compared to SoHo and further uptown) and ample ground-level space (which gallery owners desire), the galleries here also benefit from the large, open spaces that these industrial buildings provide, and visitors benefit from their unbeatable proximity to one another, making it possible to see several shows in a single afternoon—without even having to cross the street.

*To plan a walking tour, or to see what's there, visit www.westchelseaarts.com. They have a list of all the galleries in the area, with addresses, hours, and information on artists they represent. For current shows, you can also check the listings in Time Out New York, New York Magazine, or the New York Times.*

## 343. Peek into **Sotheby's** and **Christie's**.

If you don't have the funds to bid at an **auction** (see page 282), you can still see what's up for sale by visiting the salesrooms of the city's two major auction houses. Both houses display works from major upcoming shows and have pieces from their own holdings on view.

**Christie's.** *20 ROCKEFELLER PLAZA, EAST OF SIXTH AVENUE, IN MANHATTAN. Subway: B, D, F, V to 47th-50th Streets-Rockefeller Center. 212-636-2000. www.christies.com.*

**Sotheby's.** *1334 YORK AVENUE AT 72ND STREET IN MANHATTAN. Subway: 6 to 68th Street-Hunter College. 541-312-5682. www.sothebys.com.*

### 344. Go **sculpture spinning**.

Among our many public treasures, New York City is blessed with not one but two out-door sculptures on rotating axes that turn when pushed. After its mysterious disap-pearance in 2005, Bernard "Tony" Rosenthal's large black cube titled *Alamo, which* had been on Astor Place since the '60s has been returned, hopefully ready for many more spins to come. The other spinning sculpture is Henry Moore's *Three Way Piece* on the **Amsterdam overpass** (see page 76) by Columbia University.
**Alamo.** *ASTOR PLACE BY FOURTH AVENUE AND LAFAYETTE STREETS IN MANHATTAN. Sub-way: 6 to Astor Place.* **Three Way Piece.** *AMSTERDAM OVERPASS BETWEEN 116TH AND 118TH STREETS IN MANHATTAN. Subway: 1 to 116th Street-Columbia University.*

### 345. Dine in the Raleigh Room at **Murals on 54**.

Across the back wall of this small restaurant in the Warwick Hotel, a series of colorful 1937 murals by Dean Cornwall depicts the sixteenth-century British explorer Sir Wal-ter Raleigh and his crew on their way from England to the island of Roanoke. The murals were covered for nearly forty years because, following a dispute with the hotel's owner, William Randolph Hearst, an angered Cornwall added some lewd details. In 2004, as part of the restaurant's renovation project, the murals were restored and are once again the focal point of the Warwick's restaurant.
*63 WEST 54TH STREET BETWEEN FIFTH AND SIXTH AVENUES IN MANHATTAN. Subway: E, V to Fifth Avenue/53rd Street. 212-314-7700. www.murals54.com.*

→ **DID YOU KNOW?** *William Randolph Hearst built the Warwick as a residential hotel in 1927, designating an entire floor for the apartment of his lover, Marion Davies, the actress and Ziegfeld girl. In a stairwell beyond the front desk, there are photo-graphs of some of the hotel's famous guests, including James Dean, Elvis Presley, Eliz-abeth Taylor, the Beatles, Audrey Hepburn, and Cary Grant, a twelve-year resident.*

### 346. **Pick a park** to see some art . . .

On any given day, there are dozens of outdoor sculptures, installations, and other art-works that you can see for free, thanks to the New York Parks Department, the Public Art Fund, the Mayor's Office, and other organizations. Works by artists, famed and unknown, are displayed in city parks across the five boroughs, many of which you can touch, sit on, or play with. You can find a list of the current works and where they are located on the Parks Department's Web site; then go pick a park (or several!) and admire the work from a sunny spot on the grass.
*www.nycgovparks.org/sub_things_to_do/attractions/public_art/public_art.html*

## 347. . . . or enjoy lower Manhattan's "**outdoor museum**" along the Hudson River.

The thirty-plus acres of park area around Battery Park City have one of the city's most interesting public art programs and several dozen permanent artworks have been incorporated into the layout. Pieces by renowned contemporary artists such as Louise Bourgeois, Jim Dine, Sol LeWitt, Andy Goldsworthy, and Tom Otterness are brilliantly integrated into the park and along the esplanade. Temporary artworks also appear throughout the year. One of the highlights is Brian Tolle's *Irish Hunger Memorial*, an elevated landscape in homage to the Irish potato famine of 1845–54, made of stone and native Irish plants with an authentic nineteenth-century Irish cottage that visitors can climb up and roam around.

*Between Battery Park City and the Hudson River, extending from Battery Place to Chambers Street in Manhattan. Subway: 4, 5 to Fulton Street or Bowling Green; N, R to Cortlandt Street; 2, 3 to Park Place; A, C to Chambers Street; E to World Trade Center. www.bpcparks.org. Note: A map with information about the artworks is available at neighborhood museums and businesses.*

## 348. See the rock photographs at the **Morrison Hotel**,

the fine art music photography gallery in SoHo that has bought, exhibited, and sold some of the most famous images in rock music history. Collections of original prints by celebrated music photographers from Henry Diltz to Lynn Goldsmith line the walls, and exhibits change every month or so. The subjects are iconic—recent exhibits have included Elliot Landy's legendary photographs of Bob Dylan and Mick Rock's intimate portrayals of life on the road with David Bowie—and many of the pictures will be familiar to those acquainted with album covers and posters of rock stars. The gallery is popular among musicians, so go on the right day and you might find yourself standing next to some of the famous subjects themselves.

*124 PRINCE STREET BETWEEN WOOSTER AND GREENE STREETS IN MANHATTAN. Subway: B, D, F, V to Broadway-Lafayette Street; 6, C to Spring Street. 212-941-8770. www.morrison-hotelgallery.com.*

## 349. Discover a new artist at the **Washington Square Art Show**.

One spring day during the height of the Depression, a young, cash-strapped, aspiring artist named Jackson Pollock and his friend Willem de Kooning set up some paintings to sell on the street, with the hope of raising enough money to pay the rent for the studio (where he lived) just upstairs. The "show" and its artists got the attention of famous modern art patrons like Whitney and Barr, who worked to turn it into a regular event to showcase the work of living artists. Seventy-five years later, the Washington Square Outdoor Art Exhibition is a biannual juried event and includes categories for sculpture, photography, and crafts. For two consecutive weekends in May and again in September, the streets around Washington Square Park are lined with booths, where artists display their works, many of which are for sale. Whether or not you're interested in buying, this is a great event, so pick a nice afternoon for a stroll around. Who knows, you might become a collector.

*BOOTHS ARE LOCATED ON UNIVERSITY PLACE, FROM 12TH STREET TO WASHINGTON SQUARE PARK, AND THEN ALONG THE EAST SIDE OF THE PARK. Held over two weekends in May and September: Memorial Day and the following weekend; Labor Day and the following weekend. For more information, visit www.washingtonsquareoutdoorartexhibit.org.*

# Music & Dance

### 350. See opera on a small scale (part 1) at the **Amato Opera**.

The Amato is the PBS of the New York opera circuit. Founded in 1948 by an Italian couple passionate about the culture of their homeland, this Lower East Side company produces astonishing performances of classic operas—from Puccini's *Tosca* and other Italian masterpieces to Lehar's *Merry Widow*—and more modern operettas in a tiny venue and on a negligible budget. Still run under the direction of one of the founders, octogenarian Tony Amato, the Amato is true to the less exclusive origins of the art form. Although it lacks the grandeur and magnitude of the **Metropolitan Opera** (see page 149), the shows are tremendous, the theater is intimate, the tickets are affordable, and the passion and commitment to the art is unparalleled.

*319 BOWERY AT BOND STREET IN MANHATTAN. Subway: B, D, F, V to Broadway-Lafayette Street; 6 to Bleecker Street. 212-228-8200. www.amato.org.*

### 351. Go to a concert on **the barge**.

Located on a former working barge moored in the East River, this floating concert hall helped put the Brooklyn waterfront on the map. Opened in 1977, Bargemusic has gained a good reputation for its low-cost chamber music concerts. But people aren't going for the novelty—the 125-seat room is one of the best places to hear solos, duets, trios, and quartets in the city, and Bargemusic attracts top musicians who relish the chance to play in this unique and intimate setting.

*FULTON FERRY LANDING, BY THE BROOKLYN BRIDGE, IN BROOKLYN. Concerts are held year-round, Thursday through Saturday at 7:30 p.m. and Sunday at 4:00 p.m. Admission: $35 to $40 for adults, $30 for seniors, $20 for full-time students. Reservations required, except for free concerts, which are first-come/first-serve. Subway: 2, 3 to Clark Street; A, C to High*

*Street; F to York Street. For more information and concert schedule, call 718-624-2083 or visit www.bargemusic.org.*

---

## 352. Take a trip to **Snug Harbor**.

On the north shore of Staten Island, twenty-six historical buildings set within an eighty-three-acre National Historic Landmark district make up one of New York's more unusual cultural centers. Snug Harbor was originally created as a retirement community for sailors, but its impressive array of Greek Revival, Beaux-Arts, Italianate, and Victorian buildings have been turned into exhibition and performance spaces. Stage productions, art exhibitions, classical concerts, and displays of historic artifacts are presented at the many halls, galleries, and theaters across the park, and the Snug Harbor Cultural Center holds educational events, such as lecture series and classes for kids. On top of everything going on inside the buildings, the park that surrounds Snug Harbor's halls is spacious and beautiful and incorporates wonderful sibling institutions including the Noble Maritime Collection, the Staten Island Children's Museum, and the Staten Island Botanical Gardens.

*1000 RICHMOND TERRACE IN STATEN ISLAND. Hours and admission vary by attraction; contact the center for details about specific exhibits or performances. Staten Island Ferry to the S40 bus. 718-448-2500. www.snug-harbor.org.*

---

## 353. Hear a concert at **Carnegie Hall**.

One of the most famous venues in the world, Carnegie Hall has hosted more than 50,000 events in its 115 years of existence. Since it opened in 1891, the most influential musicians, politicians, thinkers, speakers, and singers of the time have ascended to its stages. This is where Antonin Dvorak's *New World Symphony* premiered, Maria Callas sang her last concert in America, Winston Churchill, Woodrow Wilson; Martin Luther King, and Albert Einstein spoke; and every kind of admired musician—from the New York Philharmonic to the Beatles and Ravi Shankar—has played concerts here. The program is as strong and as glamorous as it has ever been, and there is no better place to hear music in the city.

*57TH STREET AND SEVENTH AVENUE IN MANHATTAN. Subway: 1, A, C, B, D to 59th Street-Columbus Circle; N, Q, R, W to 57th Street. 212-247-7800. www.carnegiehall.org.*

---

## 354. Go to the **CMJ Music Marathon**.

The largest event of its kind in the world, the CMJ Music Marathon takes place at various venues across New York at the end of every summer and brings with it many of the world's top music acts. Aiming to bring artists into closer contact with their audiences, CMJ events include live shows, talks by legendary performers, and film screenings, which take place at concert halls, bars, and theaters. Highlights of the 2005 festival included a special screening of Martin Scorsese's film on Bob Dylan, *No Direction Home*, and a powerful keynote speech from Run DMC's Rev Run on the passing of Jam Master Jay and the state of the music industry today.

*Late summer/early fall. For dates, locations, and performance schedules, visit www.cmj.com/marathon.*

### 355. See opera on a small scale (part 2) at Gotham Chamber Opera.

This six-year-old company is the **Bargemusic** (see page 144) of opera. Gotham's repertoire concentrates on chamber opera, a term that refers to intimate operas written for small casts, small orchestras, and small theaters, which are seldom performed in the city's larger opera houses. But it's not only the programming that's intimate: most of the performances take place in a 350-seat theater, where the distance from the stage to the last row is roughly the distance between the stage and the third row at Lincoln Center.

*466 GRAND STREET AT THE CORNER OF PITT STREET IN MANHATTAN. Subway: F to Delancey Street; J, M, Z to Essex Street. 212-868-4460. www.gothamchamberopera.org.*

### 356. Take your pick of the performing arts at BAM.

Originally founded nearly 150 years ago as a hall for the Philharmonic Society of Brooklyn, the Brooklyn Academy of Music has become one of New York's most illustrious and beloved cultural institutions. Enjoying active support from celebrated patrons and bringing some of the world's most renowned artists to its stages, BAM is a center for excellence in all the performing arts—dance, drama, film, and, of course, music. Its programs maintain a careful balance between the modern and the traditional, alternating between provocative new films and nostalgic retrospectives, modern dance premieres and celebrated classical ballets. One of the annual highlights is the Next Wave festival held each November. The ten-week festival is a showcase of the avant-garde, with performances of all shapes, sizes, and kinds.

*30 LAFAYETTE AVENUE BETWEEN ASHLAND PLACE AND ST. FELIX STREET IN BROOKLYN. Subway: 2, 3, 4, 5, B, Q to Atlantic Avenue; D, M, R to Atlantic Avenue-Pacific Street; N to Pacific Street; BAMbus to and from various locations in Manhattan (see Web site for more information). 718-636-4100. www.bam.org.*

## 357. Go to the Time Warner Center for **Jazz at Lincoln Center**.

As well as offering the city's most celebrated opera, ballet, and classical music, **Lincoln Center** (see page 148) holds one of New York's best and most diverse jazz programs at **Dizzy's Club**, an off-site performance venue in the **Time Warner Center** (see page 63). With renowned house musicians and a roster of incredible performers lighting up its seasons, there is live jazz here every single night of the year. The warm and inviting space has an informal feel that invigorates the performances, from the scheduled weekly acts right through the After Hours Sets, relaxed jams with a wonderful clandestine feel that last well into the night. The Rose Theater and the Allen Room divide between them an eclectic range of visiting acts, from living legends like Yusef Lateef to touring big bands and rising solo stars. An especially fun thing to see is one of the educational shows: as part of the program to teach people to hear, appreciate, and engage in jazz music, artistic director Wynton Marsalis and the Lincoln Center Jazz Orchestra host evenings devoted to legendary artists, genres, or styles of music that let audiences see and hear jazz genius in action. A recent "Who Is Count Basie?" night introduced children, amateur musicians, and jazz enthusiasts to the wonders of the big band and its most celebrated leader. If you arrive early for a show, sit for a moment at the fountains by Columbus Circle and you might catch the house orchestra wheeling their instruments over to the theater.

*BROADWAY AT 60TH STREET IN MANHATTAN. Subway: 1, A, C, B, D to 59th Street-Columbus Circle; 1 to 66th Street-Lincoln Center. 212-258-9800. www.jalc.org.*

## 358. See and support dance at the **Joyce Theater**.

The Joyce Theater is one of the nation's premier modern-dance venues, and it holds the rare distinction of being a gentrification venture that New Yorkers actually approve of. As many longtime city residents remember, its beautiful Art Deco building used to be the Elgin Theater, a popular revival movie house in the '60s and '70s. The Elgin fell on hard times and was forced to close. In 1982, it reopened as the Joyce, a completely renovated 472-seat theater designed to showcase modern dance. In addition to the theater's technical amenities (it is known for its excellent sightlines), the Joyce is also applauded for its charitable programming schemes, and it subsidizes the in-theater costs of two-thirds of the performing dance companies during their runs. The Joyce operates a second space in SoHo, which offers dance companies rehearsal and performance spaces at discounted rates, and it plans to open the 900–1,000-seat International Dance Center in the future Freedom Towers.

*175 EIGHTH AVENUE AT 19TH STREET IN MANHATTAN. Subway: C, E to 23rd Street. 212-691-9740. www.joyce.org.*

## 359. See the **American Dance Theater** perform in its new home.

The nation's best-known dance company, the Alvin Ailey American Dance Theater, has a brand-new, 77,000-square-foot home—the largest facility in the country exclusively devoted to dance. The six-story, state-of-the-art Joan Weill Center for Dance, which opened for the 2006 season, is double the size of the company's previous space at City Center, and it includes a 265-seat "black box" theater, as well as studios, classrooms, a library, a costume shop, and physical therapy facilities.

*405 WEST 55TH STREET AND NINTH AVENUE IN MANHATTAN. Subway: 1, A, C, B, D to 59th Street-Columbus Circle. 212-405-9000. www.alvinailey.org.*

## 360. Check out the indie rock scene at the **Siren Music Festival**.

This free music festival presented by the *Village Voice* showcases the talents of emerging and alternative bands. The all-day concert features multiple bands on two stages by the water at Coney Island. Many of the indie rock bands go on from there to make it into the mainstream; past concerts have featured Death Cab for Cutie, the Yeah Yeah Yeahs, the Shins, and Peaches.

*July. CONEY ISLAND BOARDWALK, MAIN STAGE AND STILLWELL STAGE, IN BROOKLYN. Subway: D, F, N, Q to Coney Island-Stillwell Avenue. For more information, visit www.villagevoice.com/siren.*

# Theater & Performance

## LINCOLN CENTER

Culture reigns supreme in New York, and Lincoln Center is its kingdom. With a school, a library, several exhibition galleries, shops, restaurants, and nearly two-dozen performance spaces, this expansive complex is a village of the performing arts. It is the home of some of the most acclaimed cultural programs in the city (and the world)—including the Metropolitan Opera, the New York Philharmonic, and Juilliard—and hosts annual events, festivals, and, of course, performances of every size, type, and medium under the sun. Its reach, however, extends well beyond the 16.3-acre plaza—some of the facilities are located beyond the main Broadway campus, including the spaces for Jazz at Lincoln Center (see page 147) in the Time Warner Center. Many of the resident organizations give regular concerts and performances off-site, such as the Metropolitan Opera's summer concert series in Central Park (see page 214); and performances can be seen around the country on PBS on *Live from Lincoln Center*, the only televised live performing arts series.

What's best to do at Lincoln Center is subjective and depends on your taste, but the following is a list of our favorite organizations and programs. You can find the full range of offerings (as well as schedules, directions, and additional information) by visiting www.lincolncenter.org. (The following are located on the main campus unless otherwise noted.)

*62ND TO 66TH STREETS BETWEEN COLUMBUS AND AMSTERDAM AVENUES IN MANHATTAN. Subway: 1 to 66th Street-Lincoln Center. Information on all of the following venues and programs can be found by calling 212-875-5000 or visiting www.lincolncenter.org. For Jazz at Lincoln Center, located at the Time Warner Center, see page 147.*

## 361. *Metropolitan Opera*

Now almost 125 years old, the Metropolitan Opera is one of the world's preeminent opera companies, drawing some of the best singers, orchestral musicians, and conductors to its stage. Many masterpieces of opera had their American premieres here, from acclaimed new works like John Harbison's *The Great Gatsby* to Puccini's popular *Il Fanciulla del West,* and several of Wagner's classic works. Under the artistic direction of James Levine since 1976, the Metropolitan Opera stages lavish productions of classic works that are always awe-inspiring to watch, from Mozart's *Marriage of Figaro* to Verdi's *Aida* and Gounod's *Romeo and Juliet.* Astonishing sets and enormous casts contribute to consistently powerful and affecting performances—a recent production of Puccini's *La Bohème* featured a set designed by Franco Zeffirelli. A night at the Met feels grand, decadent, and magical: sip champagne during the interval on its stunning balcony overlooking Lincoln Center Plaza or enjoy a meal at the Grand Tier Restaurant before the show.

*METROPOLITAN OPERA HOUSE AT LINCOLN CENTER LOCATED BETWEEN 62ND AND 65TH STREETS AND COLUMBUS AND AMSTERDAM AVENUES IN MANHATTAN. Subway: 1 to 66th Street-Lincoln Center. For more information, performance schedules, and to purchase tickets, call 212-362-6000 or visit www.metopera.org.*

## 362. *The New York City Ballet*

The New York City Ballet was founded in 1933 by Leonard Kirstein and George Balanchine, with the mission to create a ballet company on par with those in Europe. Today, NYCB is the largest dance organization in America and one of the leading ballet companies in the world, with ninety dancers and a repertory of over 150 works. They perform at Lincoln Center's New York State Theater twenty-three weeks a year, including an annual six-week run of Balanchine's *The Nutcracker.*

*For more information, performance schedules, and to purchase tickets, call 212-870-5570 or visit www.nycballet.com.*

### 363. New York City Opera

The New York City Opera is an interesting combination of the contemporary and the traditional, producing unusual pieces of musical theater and inventive interpretations of classic operas on a grand scale. NYCO productions, which take place in the New York State Theater, tend to have smaller casts than those of the Met Opera and an edgier take on costume and set design. (A recent production of *Tosca* was set in fascist Italy, with dramatic blood-red lighting and a terrifying Scarpia dressed in the black of Mussolini's militia.) The theater itself is wonderful, and intermissions can be spent sipping champagne on the promenade terrace overlooking the fountain and Lincoln Center Plaza.

*NEW YORK STATE THEATER AT LINCOLN CENTER LOCATED BETWEEN 62ND AND 65TH STREETS AND AMSTERDAM AND COLUMBUS AVENUES IN MANHATTAN. Subway 1 to 66th Street-Lincoln Center. 212-870-5570. www.nycopera.com.*

### 364. New York Philharmonic

Avery Fisher Hall is home to the country's oldest symphony orchestra, the New York Philharmonic, which has been performing classical music domestically and abroad since 1842. The orchestra plays 180 concerts a year; in addition to their official September-through-June season at Avery Fisher Hall, they also put on **"Concerts in the Parks,"** an annual series of free outdoor concerts (see page 214). They also hold open rehearsals, which are an interesting and economical way to see a world-class orchestra at work.

*For more information, concert schedules, and to purchase tickets, call 212-875-5656 or visit www.newyorkphilharmonic.org.*

### 365. Film Society of Lincoln Center

Best known for putting on two of the city's major film festivals—the **New York Film Festival** and **New Directors/New Films** (see pages 154-155)—this eminent cinematic organization holds exciting film-related events all year round and has included nearly every major filmmaker of the past thirty-five years in its programs. They hold regular screenings at the state-of-the-art Walter Reade Theater, host conversations, symposia, and discussions, and publish the highly regarded journal, *Film Comment*. Because so many of the events feature advance and exclusive screenings, with high-profile names, many people assume that they're not open to the public. Almost all of them are (with the exception of a handful of annual galas and members-only programs); however, they are extremely popular and often sell out well in advance. The best way to find out what's on is to subscribe to their free e-newsletter, which lets you know about upcoming programs before they are publicized.

*For more information and to sign up for the e-newsletter, call 212-875-5601 or visit www.filmlinc.com.*

### 366. *Lincoln Center Presents*

Lincoln Center Presents is the title of the year-round programming that Lincoln Center for the Performing Arts puts on. Featuring more than 400 performances annually in all twenty-two Lincoln Center venues (as well as outdoor events in plazas and Damrosch Park), it includes concerts, theatrical performances, talks, events for kids, and much more: "Great Performers," a classical music series; "Lincoln Center Festival," their summer performance showcase; "Lincoln Center Out of Doors," a free outdoor summer arts festival; "Live From Lincoln Center"; and "Midsummer Night Swing," a summer-long dance party featuring different performers every night.

*For more information on individual programs and schedules, visit www.lincolncenter.org and click on "Lincoln Center Presents."*

## BROADWAY AND BEYOND

Theaters in New York are classified as "Broadway," "Off-Broadway," and "Off-Off Broadway," but this designation actually has nothing to do with their proximity to the Great White Way. Theaters with more than 500 seats are considered Broadway theaters, 100 to 500 seats are Off-Broadway, and fewer than 100 seats are Off-Off Broadway, regardless of their location. In general, musicals and other popular, large-scale productions appear on Broadway, while serious drama and more offbeat performances start Off-Broadway. (To add to the confusion, successful and critically acclaimed performances will often move to a Broadway theater.) Off-Off Broadway shows tend to be the most experimental and least polished. Many Off-Broadway and Off-Off Broadway theaters are nonprofits, so their productions are usually less commercial than those seen on Broadway. Because going to a show on Broadway is such a classic New York activity in its own right, we've given it its own entry in chapter 1. But here we give you a short list of other favorite theaters and theater companies.

### 367. *The Atlantic Theater*

Founded by David Mamet and William H. Macy, the Atlantic Theater Company puts on a broad range of plays, from classic works by Chekhov, Ionesco, and Pinter, to new plays by modern masters like Martin McDonough, in addition to plenty of Mamet plays. They've also put on plays written and directed by Woody Allen, a theatrical adaptation of John Irving's novel *The Cider House Rules*, and a musical by Duncan Sheik. The theater is located in an old church, which has been converted into a small but well-proportioned theater with good sightlines. (Just make sure to use the bathroom before the play starts—it's located behind the stage.)

*336 WEST 20TH STREET BETWEEN EIGHTH AND NINTH AVENUES IN MANHATTAN. Subway: C, E to 23rd Street. 212-645-1242. www.atlantictheater.org.*

### 368. *Irish Repertory Theater*

For a small country, Ireland has produced a disproportionate number of great play-wrights, and the best place in the city to see their plays performed is the Irish Rep. The theater's mission is to expose American audiences to the wealth of Irish and Irish-American theater, and it puts on an interesting mix of classic and contemporary plays by Samuel Beckett, Brendan Behan, and J. M. Synge, and adaptations of literary works by Yeats and Dylan Thomas. One of its most popular recent productions was *The Irish and How They Got That Way* by Pulitzer Prize–winning author Frank McCourt. The the-ater, located in Chelsea, is typical Off-Broadway, with less-than-spacious seating and a rather awkward layout. But the set designers compensate very well for it, and the acting and direction are typically on par with the impressive plays.

*132 WEST 22ND STREET BETWEEN SIXTH AND SEVENTH AVENUES IN MANHATTAN. Subway: 1 to 23rd Street; F, V to 23rd Street. 212-727-2737. www.irishrepertorytheater.com.*

### 369. *New York Theater Workshop*

The New York Theater Workshop is a unique organization that has been developing and producing plays in the East Village for more than twenty-five years. The shows range from innovative interpretations of well-known plays, such as Henrik Ibsen's *Hedda Gabler* and Tennessee Williams's *A Streetcar Named Desire*, to more experimen-tal modern theater, such as Tony Kushner's *Homebody/Kabul*. One of the theater's claims to fame is that it was where *Rent*, Jonathan Larson's hit rock musical based on *La Bohème*, was first staged. The company nurtures new playwrights, actors, and direc-tors, and invites and appreciates the criticism of its patrons in order to further its mis-sion for theatrical growth and improvement. What ties the productions together is the creative influence of artistic director James Nicola (who has presided over the NYTW since 1988) and his dedication to original and intelligent drama.

*79 EAST 4TH STREET BETWEEN SECOND AVENUE AND BOWERY IN MANHATTAN. Subway: F to Lower East Side-Second Avenue; 6 to Astor Place. 212-780-9037. www.nytw.org.*

### 370. *The Public Theater*

The best known of New York's Off-Broadway venues, the Public Theater is one of the most accomplished theaters in the city, period. Founded in 1954 as the Shakespeare Workshop, the Public is one the premier venues in the city to see Shakespeare, as well as musicals, and contemporary and classical plays. In keeping with its mission as a "pub-lic" theater, it offers free performances (such as **Shakespeare in the Park**, see following entry) and makes an effort to appeal beyond the traditional theater-going audience by representing a diverse array of playwrights, actors, and directors in its productions.

*425 LAFAYETTE STREET BETWEEN ASTOR PLACE AND EAST 4TH STREET IN MANHATTAN. Subway: 6 to Astor Place; N, R to 8th Street-New York University. 212-539-8500. www.publictheater.org.*

## 371. Wait in line to see **Shakespeare in the Park**.

One of New York's most famous theater venues is Central Park's Delacorte Theater, where the **Public Theater** (see previous entry) puts on Shakespeare in the Park. Each summer, hundreds of thousands of people wait in line for countless hours for a chance to see stars like Kevin Kline, Meryl Streep, and Morgan Freeman perform on stage—for free. Tickets for each night's performance become available only on the day of, and the line starts forming around dawn for the box office that opens at 1:00 p.m. For $150, you can be a "summer sponsor," which allows you to reserve a single seat at a performance (proceeds to go toward covering the festival's costs); otherwise, take a morning off and get in line; the wait is worth it.

*THE DELACORTE THEATER, CENTRAL PARK AT THE SOUTHWEST CORNER OF THE GREAT LAWN (AROUND 81ST STREET) IN MANHATTAN. Tickets available at the Delacorte Theater box office or at the Public Theater box office (see address above). Subway: B, C to 81st Street-Museum of Natural History; 4, 5, 6 to 86th Street. For more information on becoming a summer sponsor, contact the Public Theater.*

## 372. **Volunteer to be an usher** for a night.

Ushering for an Off-Broadway show is not only an economical way to see a play, it can also be a fun experience. Broadway theaters mostly use paid, unionized ushers, but almost all Off-Broadway theaters rely on volunteers. The application process is easy, but the competition can be stiff—there are plenty of veteran volunteers out there, mostly unemployed actors and retirees, who are serious about ushering. The procedure varies from theater to theater, but in general, you show up for the performance you're assigned to about an hour before show time wearing all black (or whatever dress code is specified), help seat people, hand out programs, sell concessions—do whatever needs doing—and then you can watch the show from empty seats or from the back of the theater. The insider feel makes it fun, and it can also be a way to see a sold-out hit. However, one drawback is that if the play isn't great, you don't have the privilege of leaving—ushers are usually required to stay afterward to clean up the theater.

*Contact theaters to find out about their specific ushering policies.*

# Film

Note: Many of the cultural centers listed in chapter 8 also have film programs. For outdoor movie series, see "Cinema al Fresco" in chapter 6.

## THE SHOCK OF THE NEW (FILM FESTIVALS)

New York probably hosts more film festivals than any other city in the world—pretty much every cultural society, issue group, and cinematic organization puts one on—and they vary enormously in size, structure, content, and purpose. Although retrospectives and film series on one topic can be great if you happen to be interested in the subject matter, the best festivals are generally those that show new and international films, where you can see American and world premieres of movies that may or may not end up getting a wide distribution.

### 373. *Tribeca Film Festival*

New York's youngest major film festival, the Tribeca was founded in 2002 by neighborhood darling Robert De Niro in an effort to revive optimism following the events of September 11 and to make the New York movie scene more accessible to people in the city. The festival continues to thrive in this spirit, screening an eclectic mix of studio and independent films, foreign and domestic, by first-time filmmakers and well-known directors, from feature films to silent movies to documentaries to freshly restored classics to shorts. For a fortnight each spring, the festival takes over downtown with a series of talks, lectures, and other events accompanying the movies that give new filmmakers a platform to display and discuss their work, and audiences an opportunity to take their favorite directors to task. If you have cinematic ambitions yourself, details of the festival's submission guidelines are listed on its Web site.
*Spring. Screenings are held in various locations around Tribeca. For dates, and details of screenings, talks, locations, and show times, visit www.tribecafilmfestival.org.*

### 374. *New York Film Festival*

In the file of "New York's Best Kept Secrets" is the fact that regular people can go to screenings at the New York Film Festival—and that it's not very hard to do. The most prestigious of the city's film festivals, NYFF is the country's preeminent showcase of new and foreign films, and the line-up is always first-rate. Screenings, most of which are held in Alice Tully Hall, sometimes begin with a bonus short film and almost always end with a question-and-answer session with the actors, director, and/or other crew members. The seventeen-day schedule is announced in August and tickets go on sale later that month—first to members of the **Film Society of Lincoln Center** (see page 150). Two weeks later, tickets go on sale to the public, but you have to act fast, since almost everything sells out within a few days. If you can't get tickets that way, all is not lost: show up early at a screening you want to attend and buy a ticket from someone looking to sell. We can say from personal experience that there is never a shortage of people looking to get rid of spare tickets—even to the most coveted screenings—and this is not the kind of crowd who'd try to scalp them for more than they paid.

*Late September through early October. Most screenings are held at Alice Tully Hall (at Lincoln Center, see page 148 for more), and tickets are available at the Alice Tully Hall box office, by phone at 212-875-5050, or online at www.lincolncenter.org. For more information and upcoming festival dates and schedules, visit www.filmlinc.com/nyff/nyff.htm.*

### 375. New Directors/New Films

The Film Society of Lincoln Center's other major festival is New Directors/New Films, an annual ten-day festival held in conjunction with the **Film and Media Department of the Museum of Modern Art** (see page 157). As its title suggests, this festival showcases the best films by new directors and filmmakers as chosen by a committee from the two hosting organizations. Filmmakers such as Spike Lee, Richard Linklater, Pedro Almodovar, and Steven Spielberg (yes, you read that right) all made their American debuts at ND/NF, and the festival has also introduced many films that have gone on to attain mainstream success, like *Murderball* and the Academy Award–nominated *My Architect*—an impeccable track record that should allay any fears of going in to see an "unknown."

*Spring. Screenings are held in the Walter Reade Theater at Lincoln Center and at the Roy and Niuta Titus Theater at MoMA. For dates, schedules, and more information, visit www.filmlinc.com/ndnf/ndnf.htm.*

### 376. Margaret Mead Film and Video Festival

Held at the **American Museum of Natural History** (see page 118), this annual festival is the premier venue for new documentary film in the U.S. Named in honor of Margaret Mead, the influential anthropologist who was one of the first in her field to recognize the importance of film, the festival showcases the top nonfiction films from around the world in the past year. Many of the films are American or world premieres, and subjects range from global affairs to small, personal stories.

*November. Screenings are $9 each; a twelve-screening "friends of festival" pass is available for $99. Located at the American Museum of Natural History; for dates, schedules, and more information on the museum, visit www.amnh.org.*

### 377. The World According to Shorts

This annual two-day festival shown at BAMcinématek presents the year's best short films made outside of the U.S. The films are usually shown in two programs, each one featuring several ten- to thirty-minute works. The shorts cover the wide spectrum of subject matters and genres as feature films do, so there is comedy and drama, live action and animated. It's a little offbeat, but it's a cool festival to attend because all the screened films have already won international awards, so if you've never seen a short, it's a good introduction to them.

*November. BAMcinématek; for information and directions, see entry for BAM, page 146.*

## 378. See and learn about independent film at **Anthology Film Archives**.

So what exactly is independent film? At Anthology Film Archives, you can learn about the history and development of this outsider art. This museum-library-screening room is devoted to the showing and the preservation of avant-garde and independent film. Anthology also operates a film preservation center and an exhibition gallery for experimental filmmakers who do other arts. This is an excellent resource for anyone interested in film and an interesting place to visit no matter your taste.

*32 SECOND AVENUE AT 2ND STREET IN MANHATTAN. Subway: F, V to Lower East Side-Second Avenue. For more information and screening schedule, call 212-505-5181 or visit www.anthologyfilmarchives.org.*

## 379. Rent a rare movie at **Kim's**.

Kim's is a store New Yorkers love to hate. The salespeople are notoriously judgmental, and customer service often consists of a disapproving look in response to whatever you've asked. But as anyone who has ever tried to find the Italian neorealist section at Blockbuster will tell you, you can't beat Kim's selection of classic, highbrow, and offbeat cinema. This is not the store to come to if you want to rent *Pretty Woman*, but it's a great place to browse and discover some new or forgotten outside-the-mainstream cinema classics. The Avenue A location—infamous for being the surliest—has closed, but you can still get a dose of their signature opinionated retail style at the three other Manhattan stores.

*Multiple locations; see www.mondokims.com for address and information.*

## 380. See a movie on the big screen at **Village East Cinema**.

Now a six-screen first-run cineplex, this East Village theater was built in 1926 and hosted performances of Yiddish-language plays. In addition to lovely architectural details and some Yiddish inscriptions in the lobby, the theater has held on to the grand, full-size auditorium, complete with boxes, orchestra, and mezzanine seating. Five other small screens have been added in the basement, and it's not always easy to guess which one you'll end up in, so if your movie isn't in the big theater, make sure at least to pop your head in. It's a beautiful space in which to watch a movie, with comfortable and roomy seats, and if the movie's dull, you can always look up at the intricately decorated dome ceiling.

*181 SECOND AVENUE BETWEEN 11TH AND 12TH STREETS IN MANHATTAN. Subway: L to First Avenue or Third Avenue. 212-529-6998.*

## 381. Watch movies at **MoMA**.

One of the most impressive holdings of the **Museum of Modern Art** (see page 121) is its film and video collection. Containing more than 22,000 films representing every period and genre, it is considered the strongest international film collection in the U.S. The Film and Media department screens more than 1,000 films annually in the museum's recently renovated, two-screen Roy and Niuta Titus Theater. The programs are much like exhibitions elsewhere in the museum, so films are generally shown in week- or month-long series on particular topics, themes, directors, or eras, and the department often collaborates with institutions in other countries to show their films here. In addition to feature films, animated films, shorts, and even commercials are shown. The theater is well worth a trip, but if you're going to the museum anyway, the deal is terrific: the $20 ticket price includes admission to that day's film.

*Located at MoMA; see page 121 for details.*

## WHEN MAINSTREAM MOVIES GET YOU DOWN, SEE A CLASSIC OR INDEPENDENT FILM.

One thing that New York is blessed with is plenty of places that show movies outside the mainstream, whether it's a good old-fashioned movie (or an obscure art-house film). Here are a few of our favorite venues:

**382. *The Angelika:*** For years, the Angelika was the city's multiplex alternative: it showed independent, arty, and foreign films and revivals on all four of its screens and served cappuccino and panini in the upstairs café. Now that both Italian-style coffee and indie films have made it into the mainstream, the Angelika doesn't seem quite as avant-garde as it once was, but it still shows a good share of foreign films, documentaries, classics, and other movies that a multiplex wouldn't touch with a ten-foot pole. Plus, the Angelika still has one quirk over the newer movie houses: the screens are quite far below street level, so you can feel strong vibrations every time a subway goes by.

*18 WEST HOUSTON STREET AT THE CORNER OF MERCER STREET IN MANHATTAN. Subway: 6 to Bleecker Street; B, D, F, V to Broadway-Lafayette Street. 212-995-2000.*
*www.angelikafilmcenter.org.*

**383. *Cinema Village:*** Cineastes will feel a warm tingle as soon as they turn the corner from the Union Square multiplex and see the authentic, retro, neon marquee on top, with hand-placed letters spelling out the day's offerings. One of the oldest continually operating movie houses in the city, Cinema Village opened in 1963 as a repertory cinema and made its name as a place to see second-run, cult, and classic movies before the advent of VCRs. Since then, it's changed its format intermittently, and in addition to classic and cult films, it also shows first-run art and indie films, documentaries, shorts, and animated features. In the '90s, before kung fu films went mainstream, Cinema Village was the place to see Hong Kong cinema. Today, it's still a place to see the best of the old, and of the new.
*22 EAST 12TH STREET BETWEEN UNIVERSITY PLACE AND FIFTH AVENUE IN MANHATTAN. Subway: 4, 5, 6, L, N, Q, R, W to 14th Street-Union Square. 212-924-3363. www.cinemavillage.com.*

**384. *Two Boots Pioneer Theater & Den of Cin:*** Calling itself a "new but old-fashioned neighborhood theater," the Pioneer shows mostly contemporary independent and foreign films, with some classics mixed in for good measure. The Den of Cin, located underneath the Two Boots video store, shows cult films. Both ventures are run by the same guys who run the Cajun-inspired Two Boots Pizza above it. For kooky, offbeat movies—as well as good pizza—Two Boots is the place to go.
*37 AVENUE A BETWEEN 2ND AND 3RD STREETS IN MANHATTAN. Subway: F, V to Lower East Side-Second Avenue. 212-505-2276. For information, schedules, and addresses of other Two Boots locations, visit www.twoboots.com.*

**385. *Film Forum:*** This three-screen nonprofit movie theater in the West Village shows contemporary first-run art-house and international films, plus repertories and retrospectives of foreign and American classics. Film Forum also has excellent fresh popcorn.
*209 WEST HOUSTON STREET BETWEEN SIXTH AVENUE AND VARICK STREET IN MANHATTAN. Subway: 1 to Houston Street. 212-727-8110. www.filmforum.org.*

**386. *IFC Center:*** The Waverly Cinema's reincarnation as the Independent Film Channel (IFC) Center was a bittersweet moment for city cineastes, but most took comfort in the fact that the beloved eyesore didn't change into something entirely different. Now it's a state-of-the art film center, showing independent movies and equally highbrow snacks (try the popcorn with truffle butter).
*323 SIXTH AVENUE AT WEST 3RD STREET IN MANHATTAN. Subway: A, C, E, B, D, F, V to West 4th Street. 212-924-7771. www.ifccenter.com.*

**387.** *The Quad:* This four-screen family-owned cinema shows mainly first-run art-house and foreign films, as well as occasional revivals and retrospectives. It specializes in films that have shown in festivals but which have not found a U.S. distributor, so many of the movies shown here are ones you *really* won't find anywhere else, even at the city's other art-houses. A recent renovation has shined the twenty-five-year-old theater up a bit, but not much has changed. The décor is still retro-'70s *cinematek*, and the movie screens are still the same size—about the width of a large, flat screen TV.
*34 WEST 13TH STREET BETWEEN FIFTH AND SIXTH AVENUES IN MANHATTAN. Subway: F, V to 14th Street; L to Sixth Avenue. 212-255-8800. www.quadcinema.com.*

**388.** *Landmark Sunshine Cinema:* The New York branch of this art-house movie chain mixes classics of all genres into its independent-slanted film program. Located in a restored vaudeville theater, the films here range from the obscure and foreign to almost mainstream and classics of all eras. The Sunshine also does late-night and **midnight screenings**; for more information, see page 344.
*143 EAST HOUSTON STREET BETWEEN FIRST AND SECOND AVENUES IN MANHATTAN. Subway: F, V to Lower East Side-Second Avenue. 212-330-8182. www.landmarktheaters.com.*

**389.** *Leonard Nimoy Thalia:* Remember the scene in *Annie Hall* when Alvy, Woody Allen's character, takes Annie to see *The Sorrow and the Pity*? Well, they see it at the Thalia. (For more **favorite New York movie scenes**, see page 113.) Like **Cinema Village** (see opposite), the Thalia was a revival movie house, beloved by intellectuals and cinephiles, whose role was undermined by the introduction of home video. After years of deterioration, it was reopened as the Leonard Nimoy Thalia, named for the *Star Trek* star, who was a major benefactor. Part of **Symphony Space** (see page 293), the theater is now used for live performances and readings, as well as for showing a mix of classic, revival, art, animated, short, and documentary films. It is one of the few theaters in the city that still shows double features.
*2537 BROADWAY AT 95TH STREET IN MANHATTAN. Subway: 1, 2, 3 to 96th Street. 212-864-5400. www.symphonyspace.org.*

CHAPTER 5:

# Eating & Drinking

There's nothing better than a fantastic meal, a great bar, or discovering some delicious new kind of food, and this city has a hearty helping of each of these things. New York has the staple ingredients for a thriving gastronomic culture: sizable populations of pretty much every nationality and ethnicity under the sun; talented chefs, both aspiring and established, with boundless imaginations; and a population that both honors history and embraces the next big thing. This mixture has produced a city filled to the brim with eating and drinking pleasures, from the exotic to the gourmet to the place around the corner that makes a great plate of fries. The variety of food- and drink-related activities here is mind-boggling; you can indulge your passion for street food and have an all-out gourmet splurge in the same afternoon—and then go to a bar to play bocce over drinks.

Like all the great things to do, the best eating and drinking activities in New York are those that give you a delightful experience without much effort or aggravation. Eating well here is a cinch—it can easily take more effort to eat a bad meal than an excellent one. But with the bar set so high, we had to look beyond tasty meals to find the best of the best. Unique offerings, particularly welcoming atmospheres, and gorgeous décor are all things that, along with the food and drink, put the following places and experiences in a separate league. The greatest eating and drinking activities are not necessarily exotic or over the top—spotting a Mister Softee truck while you're walking around on a hot day is a pretty great thing in itself—but they go beyond merely filling you up or quenching your thirst. With such an overwhelming amount of terrific eats and drinks, narrowing them down to a succinct list of "bests" was no easy task, but the ones we've chosen for this chapter are the priceless, wholly satisfying experiences that will make you forget every fast-food outlet and chain restaurant there is.

NOTE: We've selected what we think are the best eating and drinking experiences; however, there are additional food-related listings in other chapters. You can find entries for historic eateries in **The Classics** chapter (page 17), a rundown of 24-hour and late-night restaurants in **24 Hour Fun** (page 314), our favorite street treats in **On the Street & Underground** (page 82), and a few quirky specialty joints in **Only in New York** (page 345). For a full list of restaurants and bars, see the index.

## Sample the local cuisine from a **New York chef**.

Several of the city's best (and best-known) chefs have created mini dining empires, with multiple restaurants to their esteemed names. Some stick to the cuisine that they first made their name with, while others confidently branch out to other styles of food and dining experiences in different places. But what unites them across cuisine, genre, and style is their successful expansion across the city's notoriously fickle dining scene, and in doing so, has earned each of the following intrepid men the title of "New York chef." However, their prevalence doesn't necessarily make it any easier to get a taste— no matter how many restaurants the following chefs have, they all seem to be packed.

**390. *Mario Batali:*** "Molto Mario" (as he is affectionately known by millions of Food Network viewers) is the go-to guy for fine Italian food in this city; he's also credited with giving New Yorkers a taste for tripe, offal, pigs' feet, and other exotic meats. But his culinary expertise doesn't stop at the tip of the boot. In addition to his Italian *ristorantes* (Babbo, Lupa, Esca, Otto Enoteca e Pizzeria, and Del Posto), he also owned a French bistro, Bistro du Vent, has a pair of adjoining tapas and wine bars, **Casa Mono** and **Bar Jamon** (see page 191), and is co-owner of the specialty wine store **Italian Wine Merchants** (see page 254). All of his restaurants are wildly popular and perennially cool—and somehow still manage to serve some of the best food in the city.
**Babbo:** *110 WAVERLY PLACE AT WASHINGTON SQUARE IN MANHATTAN. Subway: B, D, F, V, A, C, E to West 4th Street. 212-777-0303.*
**Casa Mono:** *52 IRVING PLACE AT 17TH STREET;* **Bar Jamon,** *125 EAST 17TH STREET, BETWEEN IRVING PLACE AND THIRD AVENUE. Both in Manhattan. Subway: 4, 5, 6, L, N, Q, R, W to 14th Street-Union Square. 212-253-2773.*
**Del Posto:** *85 TENTH AVENUE AT 16TH STREET IN MANHATTAN. Subway: A, C, E to 14th Street; L to Eighth Avenue. 212-774-3680.*
**Esca:** *402 WEST 43RD STREET AT NINTH AVENUE IN MANHATTAN. Subway: A, C, E to 42nd Street-Port Authority Bus Terminal. 212-564-7272.*
**Lupa:** *170 THOMPSON STREET BETWEEN HOUSTON AND BLEECKER STREETS IN MANHATTAN. Subway: 1 to Houston Street. 212-982-5089.*
**Otto Enoteca e Pizzeria:** *1 FIFTH AVENUE AT 8TH STREET IN MANHATTAN. Subway: N, R, W to 8th Street-New York University. 212-995-9559.*
*www.mariobatali.com.*

**391. _Daniel Boulud:_** Daniel Boulud is the reigning king of French cuisine in New York, ruling over his three restaurants here with deft culinary skills and a captivating personality (he also operates outposts in Las Vegas and Palm Beach). Restaurant Daniel, which opened in 1993, revived enthusiasm for _haute cuisine_ with the use of fresh, seasonal ingredients prepared expertly using classic French techniques. Five years later, he opened Café Boulud, named for the country café Boulud's family ran in his hometown outside of Lyon. Café Boulud was also a star, charming patrons with its unusual four-category menu of classic country dishes, seasonal specialties, vegetarian dishes, and a rotating celebration of world cuisines called "Le Voyage." The final piece of the trifecta is DB Bistro Moderne, a more casual, slicked-up bistro whose claim to fame is its **gourmet hamburger** (see page 283).

**Café Boulud:** _20 EAST 76TH STREET BETWEEN FIFTH AND MADISON AVENUES IN MANHATTAN. Subway: 6 to 77th Street. 212-772-2600._

**Daniel:** _60 EAST 65TH STREET BETWEEN PARK AND MADISON AVENUES IN MANHATTAN. Subway: 6 to 68th Street-Hunter College. 212-288-0033._

**DB Bistro Moderne:** _55 WEST 44TH STREET BETWEEN FIFTH AND SIXTH AVENUES IN MANHATTAN. Subway: B, D, F, V to 42nd Street-Bryant Park; 7 to Fifth Avenue-Bryant Park. 212-391-2400._

_www.danielnyc.com_

**392. _David Bouley:_** The city's other DB has a slightly lower profile, but his longtime commitment to downtown Manhattan has made him a most beloved neighborhood figure. Bouley opened his eponymous restaurant in 1987, and the eventual four-star rating put Tribeca on the city's foodie map. Despite its outstanding success, Bouley closed in 1996 to make room for new ventures: Bouley Bakery and the Viennese restaurant Danube. These restaurants were forced to close after September 11, but Bouley, unfazed, immediately opened Green Tarp, a temporary canteen that fed workers at Ground Zero around the clock, and later, used the Bouley Bakery for the same purpose. In 2002, Bouley reopened Danube and opened the next incarnation of Bouley, one block away from the original space. Bouley's latest venture is Bouley Bakery & Market, a three-floor multipurpose culinary destination, with a retail store, cooking classes, and a small dining area upstairs, where you can sometimes catch a glimpse through the open kitchen of the tireless chef at work.

**Bouley:** _120 WEST BROADWAY AT DUANE STREET IN MANHATTAN. Subway: 1, 2, 3, A, C to Chambers Street. 212-964-2525._

**Bouley Bakery & Market:** _130 WEST BROADWAY AT DUANE STREET IN MANHATTAN. Subway: 1, 2, 3, A, C to Chambers Street. 212-219-1011._

**Danube:** _30 HUDSON STREET BETWEEN DUANE AND READE STREETS IN MANHATTAN. Subway: 1, 2, 3, A, C to Chambers Street. 212-791-3371._

_www.bouley.net._

**393. Keith McNally:** To the bafflement of many restaurateurs, Keith McNally seems to have the golden touch: he is the Rumpelstiltskin of the New York restaurant world, who spins ordinary storefronts into critically acclaimed hits time after time after time. It's as if he is in possession of a magic potion that makes his restaurants and bars irresistible to all, rendering patrons powerless to their charming faux-international style, uniformly chic (but not so elite as to be off-putting) clientele, and simple, tasty food. And the potion doesn't wear off—unlike most hot spots, McNally's restaurants continue to attract crowds even a decade after their opening. McNally, who started his career in the service industry as a bellhop in London and a busboy at **Serendipity** (see page 48), made his name on the New York restaurant scene with **Odeon** (see page 46), the bistro that Jay McInerney, a regular patron, immortalized in *Bright Lights, Big City*. No longer affiliated with Odeon, McNally has since opened a string of stylized restaurants, each one more popular than the last. Lucky Strike is his bistro *emeritus*, a stylishly comfortable SoHo canteen that continues to pull in a crowd more than fifteen years after its opening—a grand old age that plenty of New York restaurants never reach. McNally opened the fin-de-siècle–style brasserie Balthazar in 1991, and it has been packed every morning, noon, and night since. Russians and Russophiles protest in vain that the polished Soviet-style décor at Pravda is inauthentic while knocking back caviar and shot after shot of house-infused vodka. At Pastis, a lively bistro in the Meatpacking District, the only complaints concern how long the line is to get in, but they barely register over the constant rumbling chatter—all the better for preventing eavesdropping on the conversations of celebrities, who occupy almost every other table (see page 76). Schiller's Liquor Bar is McNally's take on the British gastro-pub; its timeless charm is irresistible to Lower East Side hipsters and serious foodies alike.

**Balthazar:** *80 SPRING STREET BETWEEN CROSBY STREET AND BROADWAY IN MANHATTAN. Subway: 6 to Spring Street; N, R, W to Prince Street. 212-965-1785. www.balthazarny.com.*

**Lucky Strike:** *59 GRAND STREET BETWEEN WOOSTER STREET AND WEST BROADWAY IN MANHATTAN. Subway: C, E to Spring Street. 212-941-0772. www.luckystrikeny.com.*

**Pastis:** *9 NINTH AVENUE AT LITTLE WEST 12TH STREET IN MANHATTAN. Subway: A, C, E to 14th Street; L to Eighth Avenue. 212-929-4844. www.pastisny.com.*

**Pravda:** *281 LAFAYETTE STREET BETWEEN HOUSTON AND PRINCE STREETS IN MANHATTAN. Subway: 6 to Bleecker Street; B, D, F, V to Broadway-Lafayette Street; N, R, W to Prince Street. 212-226-4944. www.pravdany.com.*

**Schiller's Liquor Bar:** *131 RIVINGTON STREET AT NORFOLK STREET IN MANHATTAN. Subway: F, V to Lower East Side-Second Avenue. 212-260-4555. www.schillersny.com.*

**394. Danny Meyer:** Though he is not actually a chef (he's technically a restaurateur), Danny Meyer has contributed more than enough to the city's restaurant landscape to merit him a place at this table. In the mid-'80s, the area around Union Square was not the thriving neighborhood it is today. The only restaurant was McDonalds, and a little operation called the **Greenmarket** (see page 169) had just started putting up stands in a parking lot around the park. Locals brought their kids to Washington Square Park because the overgrown, drug-infested public space by Union Square— pre-playgrounds, pre–dog runs—could hardly qualify as park. Then an affable twenty-seven-year-old guy from St. Louis opened an upscale restaurant serving food prepared from farm-based ingredients, and the rest is history. Union Square Café is the darling of the city's fine dining scene, a classic that never disappoints, and a place that always makes you feel good about paying it a visit. Meyer used the restaurant's success to bolster the neighborhood by vocally promoting the Greenmarket, using its ingredients at his restaurants, and by slowly peppering the area between Union Square and Madison Square Park with desirable eating establishments: the dark and homey Gramercy Tavern; the grand Eleven Madison Park, with its soaring ceilings, glamorous Art Deco interior, and cosmopolitan atmosphere; Tabla, which serves gourmet Indian food, and its casual, lobby-level Bread Bar, offering Indian street foods; and Blue Smoke, a pitch-perfect pit-barbeque joint, with an adjoining jazz club downstairs called Jazz Standard. In 2005, Meyer ventured out of the neighborhood for the first time to take the helm at the Modern, the fine dining restaurant at the Museum of Modern Art. But Meyer hasn't grown tired of downtown or of revitalizing its amenities: his company, the Union Square Hospitality Group, also operates the Shake Shack, a maddeningly popular, seasonal burger joint that looks like a futuristic roadside dive in Madison Square Park. The company also sponsors the annual **Big Apple Barbeque** (see page 84), whose proceeds benefit the Madison Square Park Conservancy.

**Blue Smoke/Jazz Standard:** *116 EAST 27TH STREET BETWEEN PARK AND LEXINGTON AVENUES IN MANHATTAN. Subway: 6 to 28th Street. 212-447-7733. www.bluesmoke.com.*

**Eleven Madison Park:** *11 MADISON AVENUE AT 24TH STREET IN MANHATTAN. Subway: 6 to 23rd Street; N, R, W to 23rd Street. 212-889-0905. www.elevenmadisonpark.com.*

**Gramercy Tavern:** *42 EAST 20TH STREET BETWEEN BROADWAY AND PARK AVENUE SOUTH IN MANHATTAN. Subway: 6 to 23rd Street. 212-477-0777. www.gramercytavern.com.*

**The Modern:** *9 WEST 53RD STREET BETWEEN FIFTH AND SIXTH AVENUES IN MANHATTAN. Subway: E, V to Fifth Avenue/53rd Street. 212-333-1220.*

**Shake Shack:** *SOUTHEAST CORNER OF MADISON SQUARE PARK(MADISON AVENUE AND 23RD STREET) IN MANHATTAN. Subway: 6 to 23rd Street; N, R, W to 23rd Street. 212-889-6600. www.shakeshacknyc.com. Note: Open April through early December, weather permitting.*

**Tabla Restaurant and Bread Bar:** *11 MADISON AVENUE AT 25TH STREET IN MANHATTAN. Subway: 6 to 23rd Street; N, R, W to 23rd Street. 212-889-0667. www.tablany.com.*

**Union Square Café:** *21 EAST 16TH STREET BETWEEN FIFTH AVENUE AND UNION SQUARE WEST IN MANHATTAN. Subway: 4, 5, 6, L, N, Q, R, W to 14th Street-Union Square. 212-243-4020. For more information, visit Union Square Hospitality Group, www.ushgnyc.com.*

**395. *Jean-Georges Vongerichten:*** He is known simply as Jean-Georges, one of the few chefs with whom people all over the world are on a first-name basis. Yet while he has restaurants on three continents, his home is New York, and the city, in turn, has claimed him as its own, as evidenced by the popularity of his restaurants, and the fact that he has earned more *New York Times* stars than any other chef in the city. A bold chef with a shrewd business sensibility, the Alsatian-born Vongerichten has charmed New Yorkers with restaurant after restaurant, and he seems always to have another trick up his sleeve. After introducing himself to the city with a four-star *New York Times* review at Lafayette restaurant, he left the formal, fine-dining milieu to open JoJo, an intimate, paper tablecloth–adorned bistro in an Upper East Side townhouse. After that, he surprised everyone with Vong, where he mixes his ethereal French cooking with spice from the Far East, followed by another four-star venture, Jean-Georges, along with the Lipstick Café (now closed), a casual spot that catered to the business crowd, and Mercer Kitchen for the SoHo set. He then returned to Asian flavors with 66, an upscale Chinese restaurant, and Spice Market, which serves gourmet renditions of Asian street food in a sexy, dreamlike setting of dark wood and dim lighting. Then, just when we thought we had him pegged, he opened V Steakhouse (also closed), a rococo-decorated steakhouse in the Time Warner Center, and a jewel box of a restaurant called Perry Street, a serene, simply designed dining room inside Richard Meier's glass palaces on the Hudson River. According to Vongerichten, Perry Street is his "casual, neighborhood restaurant." Trying telling that to the reservationist.

**66:** *241 CHURCH STREET BETWEEN WORTH AND LEONARD STREETS IN MANHATTAN. Subway: 1 to Franklin Street. 212-925-0202.*

**Jean-Georges and Nougatine:** *1 CENTRAL PARK WEST BETWEEN 60TH AND 61ST STREETS IN MANHATTAN. Subway: 1, A, C, B, D to 59th Street-Columbus Circle. 212-229-3900.*

**JoJo:** *160 EAST 64TH STREET BETWEEN LEXINGTON AND THIRD AVENUES IN MANHATTAN. Subway: 6 to 68th Street-Hunter College. 212-223-5656.*

**Mercer Kitchen:** *99 PRINCE STREET AT MERCER STREET IN MANHATTAN. Subway: N, R, W to Prince Street. 212-966-5454.*

**Perry Street:** *176 PERRY STREET NEAR THE WEST SIDE HIGHWAY IN MANHATTAN. Subway: 1 to Christopher Street-Sheridan Square. 212-352-1900.*

**Spice Market:** *403 WEST 13TH STREET AT NINTH AVENUE IN MANHATTAN. Subway: A, C, E to 14th Street; L to Eighth Avenue. 212-675-2322.*

**Vong:** *200 EAST 54TH STREET AT THIRD AVENUE IN MANHATTAN. Subway: 6 to 51st Street; E, V to Lexington Avenue/53rd Street. 212-486-9592.*

*www.jean-georges.com.*

# Splurge on an **incredible meal**.

There are many delightful bargains and delicious cheap eats to be had all over the city, but then there are the indulgences—those famous restaurants whose names are known around the world not for trendiness, longevity, or cool design (though they often have those, too) but for the supreme quality of the food. In addition to many of the restaurants we've already listed, here are some other places that live up to their reputation for delivering incredible dining experiences. Yes, all of the following restaurants fall into the very-expensive-to-small-fortune category, but the meals they serve are worth every penny. If you have the means (and a sweet touch with the reservationists), these are the places to go for out-of-this-world gastronomic splurges. Choose your poison:

**396. *Alain Ducasse at the Essex House:*** For ornate French cuisine of the traditional sort, pay a visit to the celebrated chef's grand New York outpost on the ground floor of the Essex House hotel, where you'll be treated like royalty and eat like a king. *155 WEST 58TH STREET BETWEEN SIXTH AND SEVENTH AVENUES IN MANHATTAN. Subway: F to 57th Street; N, Q, R, W to 57th Street. 212-265-7300. www.alain-ducasse.com.*

**397. *Le Bernardin:*** If seafood is your weakness, then the four-star fish-focused *haute cuisine* served here is for you. An offshoot of the equally acclaimed Parisian restaurant of the same name, Le Bernardin holds the distinction of being the only restaurant in New York to have held on to its four-star rating for more than a decade. *155 WEST 51ST STREET BETWEEN FIFTH AND SIXTH AVENUES IN MANHATTAN. Subway: B, D, F, V to 47th-50th Streets-Rockefeller Center. 212-554-1515. www.le-bernardin.com.*

**398. *Chanterelle:*** This Tribeca pioneer does not need to engage in the culinary theatrics of some of the city's other fine restaurants; instead it serves incredible food in a beautiful room with flawless service. *2 HARRISON STREET AT HUDSON STREET IN MANHATTAN. Subway: 1 to Franklin Street. 212-966-6960. www.chanterellenyc.com.*

**399. *Masa:*** Masa is considered the most expensive restaurant in the city at the moment, which is not in itself an illustrious distinction. However, everyone who has eaten here agrees that the money is put to good use (ingredients like truffles and foie gras are thrown around like parsley) and that the experience is never the same twice. (There are no menus; you pay $300 for a prix-fixe selection of what the kitchen is preparing that day.) That said, getting in is a challenge in itself, in more ways than one—securing one of the twenty-six seats is the holy grail of New York dining as we go to press. But if you are lucky enough to make it onto the reservation list, ask to sit at the bar, where you can watch the master, Masa Takayama, at work. N.B.: You can par-

take of Masa's super-gourmet cuisine without submitting to the main restaurant's $350 base fee at Bar Masa, the comparatively economical offshoot next door, which has menus and does not take reservations.
*TIME WARNER CENTER 10 COLUMBUS CIRCLE AT 59TH STREET IN MANHATTAN. Subway: 1, A, C, B, D to 59th Street-Columbus Circle. 212-823-9800. www.masanyc.com.*

**400. *Nobu:*** Nobu can be credited with introducing New York to upscale sushi, and it enjoyed an uncommonly long run as both a hot spot and a foodie mecca. It's been pushed out of the spotlight since Masa and other Japanese mega-restaurants came to town, but even if it's no longer cutting-edge, the sushi is still topnotch. Like Masa, Nobu has a no-reservation offshoot, Nobu Next Door, and it has opened a location in Midtown, Nobu Fifty Seven.
**Nobu and Nobu Next Door:** *105 HUDSON STREET AT FRANKLIN STREET IN MANHATTAN. Nobu: 212-219-0500; Nobu Next Door: 212-334-4445. Subway: 1 to Franklin Street.*
**Nobu Fifty Seven:** *40 WEST 57TH STREET AT FIFTH AVENUE IN MANHATTAN. Subway: F to 57th Street; N, Q, R, W to 57th Street. 212-757-3000. www.myriadrestaurantgroup.com.*

**401. *Per Se:*** Eating at Thomas Keller's exclusive nook on the fourth floor of the **Time Warner Center** (see page 63) is like dying and going to epicurean heaven. Considered the country's best chef, Keller's meals are intricately composed and play out like symphonies of hallelujahs. The otherworldly eating experience is heightened by the incredible bird's-eye view of Central Park and the intimacy (the restaurant has only fifteen tables). Even though the multicourse meals can take as long as a transatlantic flight, diners are still reluctant to leave after their meals, unwilling to return to their earthly existence after experiencing such bliss. Note: Mortals unable to make it into Per Se can sample some of the heavenly delights one floor below at Keller's more plebian Bouchon Bakery.
*10 COLUMBUS CIRCLE AT 59TH STREET, 4TH FLOOR, IN MANHATTAN. Subway: 1, A, C, B, D to 59th Street-Columbus Circle. www.frenchlaundry.com/perse/perse.htm.*

## Engage in a legendary New York City food war.
(Choose your camp and defend its honor to the very last bite.)

### 402. CHEESECAKE: Junior's vs. Veniero's
**Junior's:** *386 FLATBUSH AVENUE AT DEKALB AVENUE IN BROOKLYN. Subway: B, M, Q, R to DeKalb Avenue. 718-852-5257. www.juniorscheesecake.com.*
**Veniero's:** *342 EAST 11TH STREET BETWEEN FIRST AND SECOND AVENUES IN MANHATTAN. Subway: L to First Avenue. 212-674-7070. www.venierospastry.com.*

### 403. *BAGELS: Ess-a-Bagel vs. H&H*

**Ess-a-Bagel:** *359 FIRST AVENUE AT 20TH STREET IN MANHATTAN. Subway: 6 to 23rd Street. 212-260-2252; 831 THIRD AVENUE AT 50TH STREET IN MANHATTAN. Subway: 6 to 51st Street; E, V to Lexington Avenue/53rd Street. 212-980-1010. www.ess-a-bagel.com.*
**H&H:** *2239 BROADWAY AT 80TH STREET IN MANHATTAN. Subway: 1 to 79th Street. 212-595-8000; WEST 46TH STREET AT TWELFTH AVENUE IN MANHATTAN. Subway: A, C, E to 42nd Street-Port Authority Bus Terminal. 212-595-8000. www.hhbagel.com.*

### 404. *STEAK: Smith & Wollensky vs. Peter Luger*

**Smith & Wollensky:** *THIRD AVENUE AT 49TH STREET IN MANHATTAN. Subway: 6 to 51st Street; E, V to Lexington Avenue/53rd Street. 212-753-1530. www.smithandwollensky.com.*
**Peter Luger:** *178 BROADWAY AT DRIGGS AVENUE IN BROOKLYN. Subway: J, M, Z to Marcy Avenue. 718-387-7400. www.peterluger.com.*

### 405. *PICKLES: Guss's vs. The Pickle Guys*

**Guss's Pickles:** *85-87 ORCHARD STREET BETWEEN GRAND STREET AND BROOME STREET IN MANHATTAN. Subway: F to Delancey Street; J, M, Z to Essex Street. 212-334-3616.*
**The Pickle Guys:** *49 ESSEX STREET BETWEEN GRAND STREET AND HESTER STREET IN MANHATTAN. Subway: B, D to Grand Street. 212-656-9739. www.nycpickleguys.com.*

### 406. *CUPCAKES: Magnolia vs. Billy's*

**Magnolia Bakery:** *401 BLEECKER STREET AT 11TH STREET IN MANHATTAN. Subway: A, C, E to 14th Street; L to Eighth Avenue. 212-462-2572.*
**Billy's Bakery:** *184 NINTH AVENUE BETWEEN 21ST AND 22ND STREETS IN MANHATTAN. Subway: C, E to 23rd Street. 212-647-9956. www.billysbakerynyc.com.*

### 407. *HOT DOGS: Gray's Papaya vs. Papaya King*

**Gray's Papaya** *(all locations in Manhattan): 539 EIGHTH AVENUE AT 37TH STREET. Subway: A, C, E to 34th Street-Penn Station. 212-904-1588; 2090 BROADWAY AT 72ND STREET. Subway: 1, 2, 3 to 72nd Street. 212-799-0243; 402 SIXTH AVENUE AT 8TH STREET. Subway: A, C, E, B, D, F, V to West 4th Street. 212-260-3532.*
**Papaya King** *(all locations in Manhattan): SEVENTH AVENUE AT 14TH STREET. Subway: 1, 2, 3 to 14th Street. 212-367-8090; 179 EAST 86TH STREET BETWEEN THIRD AND LEXINGTON AVENUES. Subway: 4, 5, 6 to 86th Street. 212-369-0648; 121 WEST 125TH STREET BETWEEN LENOX AVENUE AND ADAM CLAYTON POWELL BOULEVARD. Subway: 2, 3 to 125th Street. 212-665-5732. www.papayaking.com.*

### 408. *HAMBURGERS: Corner Bistro vs. Blue 9*

**Corner Bistro:** *341 WEST 4TH STREET AT JANE STREET IN MANHATTAN. Subway: 1, 2, 3 to 14th Street; A, C, E to 14th Street; L to Eighth Avenue. 212-242-9502.*
**Blue 9:** *92 THIRD AVENUE AT 12TH STREET IN MANHATTAN. Subway: 4, 5, 6, N, Q, R, W to Union Square; L to Third Avenue. 212-979-0053.*

### 409. *LOBSTER ROLLS: Pearl Oyster Bar vs. Mary's Fish Camp*

**Pearl Oyster Bar:** *18 CORNELIA STREET BETWEEN BLEECKER AND WEST 4TH STREET IN MANHATTAN. Subway: 1 to Christopher Street-Sheridan Square. 212-691-8211. www.pearloysterbar.com.*
**Mary's Fish Camp:** *64 CHARLES STREET AT WEST 4TH STREET IN MANHATTAN. Subway: 1 to Christopher Street-Sheridan Square. 646-486-2185. www.marysfish-camp.com. N.B.: Mary's has a branch in Park Slope called Brooklyn Fish Camp. 162 FIFTH AVENUE BETWEEN DEGRAW AND DOUGLASS STREETS IN BROOKLYN. Subway: M to Union Street; 2,3 to Bergen Street.*

### 410. *DELIS: Carnegie vs. Katz's*

**CARNEGIE:** *854 SEVENTH AVENUE AT 55TH STREET IN MANHATTAN. Subway: N, Q, R, W to 57th Street. 212-757-2245. www.carnegiedeli.com.*
**KATZ'S:** *205 EAST HOUSTON AT LUDLOW STREET IN MANHATTAN. Subway: F, V to Lower East Side-Second Avenue. 212-254-2246. www.katzdeli.com.*

## 411. Go to a **Greenmarket**.

Fresh, seasonal foods from local farmers, at prices that beat the supermarket—need we say more? Greenmarkets are a bountiful blessing in the concrete jungle. The original Union Square market is the largest and the most popular (it's open four days a week, all year round), but there are more than fifty markets across the five boroughs, twenty-three of which operate year-round. Many restaurants buy ingredients there; in fact, if you **get to the Union Square market when it opens in the morning** (see page 334), there's a good chance you'll be surrounded by some of the city's best chefs.

**Union Square Greenmarket:** *WEST SIDE OF UNION SQUARE PARK BETWEEN 14TH AND 17TH STREETS IN MANHATTAN. Open Monday, Wednesday, Friday, and Saturday from 8:00 a.m. to 6:00 p.m. Subway: 4, 5, 6, L, N, Q, R, W to 14th Street-Union Square. For a complete list of other Greenmarket locations, schedules, and the farmers that sell there, visit www.cenyc.org.*

# Eat on the street at an **outdoor food festival**.

Some of our favorites (for information on other great, non-food-centric street fairs and festivals, please see Chapter 3):

**412. *Ninth Avenue International Food Festival.*** As anyone who's ever walked this side of the Port Authority knows, Hell's Kitchen is lined with a more eclectic selection of restaurants than any strip in the city. Get a taste of the melting pot at this massive two-day festival, held each May along Ninth Avenue.
*May. NINTH AVENUE BETWEEN 37TH AND 57TH STREETS IN MANHATTAN. Subway: A, C, E to 42nd Street-Port Authority Bus Terminal. www.hellskitchennyc.com.*

**413. *Bayard's Annual Heirloom Tomato Festival.*** It may not be Bunol, but in early September this historic downtown restaurant hosts New York City's version of La Tomatina, the ecstatic festival and tomato fight that takes place in Spain every summer. The restaurant's executive chef and his wife own a 190-acre organic farm on the North Fork of Long Island, so when the time is ripe, they haul in truckloads of their tomatoes for a big, fat, juicy block party. You can sample many varieties of tomato, on their own or as ingredients in the many salads, soups, and other dishes on display at the stalls.
*September. 1 HANOVER SQUARE BETWEEN PEARL AND STONE STREETS IN MANHATTAN. Subway: 2, 3, 4, 5 to Wall Street; R, W to Whitehall Street-South Ferry. 212-514-9454. www.bayards.com.*

**414. *Taste of Tribeca Street Festival.*** This gourmet food festival showcases the gastronomic treasures of lower Manhattan, complete with live music, entertainment, and neighborhood walking tours. The $45 ticket gets you generously sized tastes of six dishes on offer from more than fifty local restaurants. Sure, it's a bit pricier than a gyro-crepe combo from a regular street fair, but with participants like Chanterelle, Danube, and Bouley, it's a relative bargain—and proceeds benefit local public schools.
*May. DUANE STREET BETWEEN HUDSON AND GREENWICH STREETS IN MANHATTAN. Subway: 1, 2, 3, A, C to Chambers Street. www.tasteoftribeca.org.*

**415. *Dine Around Downtown.*** If $45 sounds a little steep, Dine Around Downtown offers epicures *à la carte* tastes of lower Manhattan cuisine at slightly more affordable prices. Admission is free, and you can sample a slew of menu items for $3 to $5 each.
*May. CHASE MANHATTAN PLAZA, BETWEEN LIBERTY AND PINE STREETS AND NASSAU AND WILLIAM STREETS IN MANHATTAN. Subway: 2, 3, 4, 5 to Wall Street. 212-835-2789. www.downtownny.com.*

**416.** Another food festival of sorts is the annual **Chocolate Show** at the Metropolitan Pavilion. Probably the most enthusiastically anticipated of all the conventions held in the city, the Chocolate Show is like a Willy Wonka–inspired dream come true: four days of seeing, smelling, and, of course, tasting chocolate from all over the world. Though technically a trade show, the chocolate show has plenty of public offerings, including demonstrations, a chocolate fashion show, and free samples galore.
*Early November. THE METROPOLITAN PAVILION, 125 WEST 18TH STREET BETWEEN SIXTH AND SEVENTH AVENUES IN MANHATTAN. Subway: 1 to 18th Street; F, V to 14th Street; L to Sixth Avenue. For more information and ticket prices, call 866-246-2692 or visit www.chocolateshow.com.*

### 417. Get a taste of the Lower East Side's **unique ethnic blend** in a single afternoon.

The Lower East Side of New York is a crossroads of three established ethnic enclaves: Chinatown, Little Italy, and the Jewish neighborhoods that surround them. Though these neighborhoods are no longer the homogenous community centers they once were, the cultural influences remain, and in a few blocks, you can sample authentic treats from each. Start with a bagel or bialy from Kossar's, followed by Cantonese *congee* (rice porridge) at Congee Village, then walk around the block for dessert at Il Laboratorio del Gelato.
*Subway: F to Delancey Street; J, M, Z to Essex Street.*
**Kossar's Bialys:** *367 GRAND STREET BETWEEN ESSEX AND NORFOLK STREETS IN MANHATTAN. 877-4-BIALYS. www.kossarsbialys.com.*
**Congee Village:** *100 ALLEN STREET BETWEEN DELANCEY AND BROOME STREETS IN MANHATTAN. 212-941-1818. www.congeevillage.com.*
**Il Laboratorio del Gelato:** *95 ORCHARD STREET BETWEEN DELANCEY AND BROOME STREETS IN MANHATTAN. 212-343-9922. www.laboratoriodelgelato.com.*

### 418. See how many dumplings you can eat at **Fried Dumpling**.

The scrumptious pork-and-chive-filled dumplings beat the competition and are five for a dollar at this trustworthy dim sum parlor.
*99 ALLEN STREET BETWEEN DELANCEY AND BROOME STREETS IN MANHATTAN. Subway: F to Delancey Street; J, M, Z to Essex Street. 212-941-9975.*

### 419. Have a midnight kebab at **Mamoun's,**

and eat it in one of their cozy wooden booths. No matter the hour, you will never be alone in Mamoun's.

*119 MACDOUGAL STREET BETWEEN BLEECKER AND WEST 3RD STREETS IN MANHATTAN. Subway: A, C, E, B, D, F, V to West 4th Street. 212-674-8685.*

### 420. Devour a cone of Belgian fries from **Pommes Frites,**

smothered in any one of the many delicious sauces: traditional (ketchup, vinegar, or European mayo) or exotic (Vietnamese pineapple, mango chutney, or parmesan peppercorn, to name a few). They also serve a mean *poutine,* the Canadian specialty of fries, gravy, and cheese curds.

*123 SECOND AVENUE BETWEEN 7TH STREET AND ST. MARKS PLACE IN MANHATTAN. Subway: 6 to Astor Place. 212-674-1234. www.pommesfrites.ws.*

### Dinner with **in-house entertainment.**

Now that multiplexes have taken over single-screen movie houses, and tickets cost upward of $10 each, dinner and a movie in New York is no longer as cheap or special as it used to be. Instead, why not try a restaurant that offers a little spectacle along with the meal? The following restaurants cleverly incorporate some signature flourishes into their dinner fare:

**421. *Basta Pasta:*** Order the pasta with parmesan and prosciutto and wait for the whole restaurant to turn to your table and watch a waiter swirl and toss your pasta inside a giant hollow wheel of cheese and scoop it lavishly onto your plate.

*37 WEST 17TH STREET BETWEEN FIFTH AND SIXTH AVENUES IN MANHATTAN. Subway: F, V to 14th Street; L to Sixth Avenue. 212-366-0888.*

**422. *Philippe:*** For twenty-five years, Philippe Chow wowed patrons with his French-Asian cooking and star-studded dining room at his restaurant Mr. Chow's. At his new restaurant, Philippe, another upscale Chinese restaurant on the Upper East Side, he's wowing them with the raw ingredients: there's a live "noodle-pulling" demonstration every night, when a chef turns mounds of dough into noodles and dumpling wrappers before your eyes.

*33 EAST 60TH STREET BETWEEN PARK AND MADISON AVENUES IN MANHATTAN. Subway: N, R, W to Fifth Avenue/59th Street. 212-644-8885. www.philippechow.com.*

**423.** *Churrascaria Plataforma Tribeca:* Order the meat course at this Brazilian restaurant and prepare to eat fifteen different types of meat as they arrive at your table, where steaks, chops, sausages, and ribs are carved and sliced with a flourish before your hungering eyes.
*221 WEST BROADWAY BETWEEN FRANKLIN AND WHITE STREETS IN MANHATTAN. Subway: 1 to Franklin Street. 212-925-6969.*

**424.** *Lucky Cheng's:* We can't really say what the food's like at this drag queen capital of the world; it's the service that's memorable—including comedy, karaoke, and lots and lots of feathers. If you prefer your men *au naturel*, the Savage Men Cover Model Male Revue performs every week on Friday and Saturday nights.
*24 FIRST AVENUE BETWEEN 1ST AND 2ND STREETS IN MANHATTAN. Subway: F, V to Lower East Side-Second Avenue. 212-995-5500. www.planetluckychengs.com.*

---

# Expert Contributor: Andrea Strong

Andrea Strong is the author of *The Strong Buzz* (www.thestrongbuzz.com), a weekly electronic newsletter/blog that offers readers an insider's view into New York City's restaurant world. She also writes a weekly Sunday food column for the *New York Post* and is the co-author, with Katy Sparks, of *Sparks in the Kitchen* (Knopf, 2006).

## MY FIVE FAVORITE RESTAURANTS IN NEW YORK

**425:** *Five Points:* This seasonal Greenmarket-driven American restaurant owned by chef Marc Meyer and his wife, Vicki Freeman, is one of those rare gems that will have you planning your next visit shortly after you walk inside. A cozy, bustling bar area opens to a warmly lit dining room with high ceilings, and an open kitchen turns out signatures like wood-oven roasted pizza topped with thinly sliced Yukon potatoes, Sonoma Teleme cheese, and truffle oil; house-cured double pork chops with cauliflower and braised red mustard greens; and chestnut capellacci with preserved cherries and sage butter. Five Points also serves one of the best brunches in the city. I have three words for you: lemon ricotta pancakes.
*31 GREAT JONES STREET BETWEEN LAFAYETTE STREET AND BOWERY IN MANHATTAN. Subway: 6 to Astor Place. 212-253-5700. www.fivepointsrestaurant.com.*

**426:** *Tia Pol:* A lively bastion of Madrid awaits you at Tia Pol, a sexy sliver of a tapas bar owned by Mani Dawes and Heather Belz, two friends who lived in Madrid after college and vowed one day to open a place that captured the spirit and cuisine of the city's *taperias*. With Tia Pol, and chef-partner Alexandra Raij, they have succeeded. The place is tiny, so it is often standing room only, but the waiters manage to wind their way through the grinning crowds, serving terra cotta *cazuelas* (Spanish cooking dishes) filled with *patatas bravas, jamon croquetteas, chorizo* finished with sherry, and *tortilla d'espana*. The bar helps keep things buzzing with a great selection of Spanish wines and sherries. N.B.: They don't take reservations.

*205 TENTH AVENUE BETWEEN 22ND AND 23RD STREETS IN MANHATTAN. Subway: C, E to 23rd Street. 212-675-8805. www.tiapol.com.*

**427: *Momofuku:*** It would be too simple to say that Momofuku serves the best ramen in the city. It would be true, but it would give you only a small picture of what wonders await at this narrow East Village lunch counter washed in blond wood. Chef-owner David Chang learned the art of noodle making in Tokyo, but he is also a classically trained chef who worked under Craft's Tom Collichio. What this means is that you'll find Greenmarket-fresh ingredients in super-fine signature dishes like spicy kimchi stew, addictive little steamed buns filled with pork belly and slicked with sticky-sweet hoisin sauce, and his signature soul-warming Momofuku ramen—braised Berkshire pork swimming in a rich broth filled with silky ramen. Slurping is encouraged.

*163 FIRST AVENUE BETWEEN 10TH AND 11TH STREETS IN MANHATTAN. Subway: L to First Avenue. 212-475-7899. www.eatmomofuku.com.*

**428. *Beppe:*** New York is not short on Italian restaurants, but I'll take Beppe over any other. First of all, the place is literally Tuscany in the City, a sun-smudged terra cotta façade that opens to a warm room with a fire-breathing hearth, cathedral wood-beamed ceilings, and sturdy tables set with cheerful gingham napkins. As for the food, it's rustic, simple, and straight from the heart. Don't miss the chef's own *norcino*—a housemade "butcher's spaghetti" tossed with a rich ragu made from crumbled pork, garlic, rosemary, tomatoes, and Chianti; or his fat, spicy grilled sausages made in house and served in a cast-iron skillet with stewed artisan beans; or the whole roasted *orata* (sea bass) glossed with olive oil and lemon juice and filled to the gills with fresh herbs. And yes, you must have his Tuscan fries, a mile-high pile tossed with freshly fried rosemary.

*45 EAST 22ND STREET BETWEEN BROADWAY AND PARK AVENUE SOUTH IN MANHATTAN. Subway: 6 to 23rd Street. 212-982-8422. www.beppenyc.com.*

**429. *The Spotted Pig:*** There is always a wait at the Spotted Pig, but I promise you it is always worth it. This convivial gastropub owned by music industry guru Ken Friedman and his brilliant English chef, April Bloomfield, is jammed with hipsters and hotties who wait (and wait, and wait) for the chef's heartbreakingly good food. Bloomfield is known for her *gnudi*—plump buttons of sheep's milk ricotta sauced in brown butter and sage, but you won't want to miss her roasted beet salad with smoked trout and crème fraiche, or her juicy chargrilled burger, topped with Roquefort and tucked inside a brioche bun the size of a catcher's mitt. The crowds are much tamer at lunch, which is the only time you can get your paws on her killer cubano— a toasted baguette stuffed with slow-roasted pork, prosciutto, cheese, and spicy pickled jalapeños. No reservations.

*314 WEST 11TH STREET AT GREENWICH STREET IN MANHATTAN. Subway: A, C, E to 14th Street; L to Eighth Avenue. 212-620-0393. www.thespottedpig.com.*

---

## Pick up a tasty snack or get a meal to go at a **gourmet food market**.

Ranging from vendors of exotic and high-end gourmet ingredients, to places where you can buy restaurant-quality meals to take home, to specialty stores with in-house cafés, New York has no shortage of epicurean markets—Zagat has even dedicated an entire book to them. The following is a list of some of our favorite places to pick up a gourmet snack or prepared meal.

**430. *Agata & Valentina:*** This recently renovated Italian-accented market and café is an established foodie destination, and stands out from others for its truly exotic seasonal delicacies, such as hybrid fruits like "mandarinquats" and "nectacotums." The fresh meat, fish, and cheese counters are among the finest in the city, and if you want to sit down and enjoy your cubed filet mignon and quail's eggs on the spot, there's a companion restaurant and salad bar across the street from the market.

*1505 FIRST AVENUE AT 79TH STREET IN MANHATTAN. Subway: 6 to 77th Street. 212-452-0690.*

**431. *Amy's Bread:*** A stop inside one of Amy's outlets inspires nostalgia for a simpler, tastier time, when carbs were healthy and things with words like "artisanal" and "organic" attached to their names were considered good for you. Hearty loaves of white, wheat, semolina, and specialty breads can be bought to take home, while toothsome sandwiches, quiches, and desserts are best devoured on the spot in the café. Note: The West Village location is right next to the legendary **Murray's Cheese Shop** (see page 295), which makes for an incredible combination.

*Multiple locations; visit www.amysbread.com for addresses and information.*

**432. *Balthazar Bakery:*** This tiny storefront next to the imposing Balthazar restaurant is the best-kept (well, only) secret of the **Keith McNally** empire (see page 163). You can get some of the same menu items served next door (and the famously delicious breads) to take away for less than half the price and unquantifiably less aggravation.

*80 SPRING STREET AT THE CORNER OF CROSBY STREET IN MANHATTAN. Subway: 6 to Spring Street; N, R, W to Prince Street. 212-965-1785. www.balthazarbakery.com.*

**433. The Chelsea Market:** People started trekking to lower Ninth Avenue to go to the Chelsea Market before the Meatpacking District had anything to offer besides, well, meat. Inside the indoor market are nearly two dozen restaurants, specialty markets, and stores, including **Amy's Bread** (see previous page), Ronnybrook Farm Dairy, and the infamous Fat Witch bakery (which gives generous free samples, probably because they know that after one taste, you'll buy as much as they ask you to).
*75 NINTH AVENUE BETWEEN 15TH AND 16TH STREETS IN MANHATTAN. Subway: A, C, E to 14th Street; L to Eighth Avenue. Individual retailers are listed on www.chelseamarket.com; visit Web site for hours and information.*

**434. Eli's & The Vinegar Factory:** The son of legendary Upper West Side grocers, Louis and Lillian Zabar (see entry on **Zabar's**, page 176), Eli Zabar is well established on the Upper East Side as a purveyor of fine foods and drinks. His multiple-location empire includes restaurants, bakeries, a wine store, and two gourmet supermarkets, inspired by the great food halls of Europe.
*Multiple locations on the Upper East Side; for more information on specific outlets, visit www.elizabar.com.*

**435. Le Pain Quotidien:** This Belgian chain bridges the gap between retail and restaurant beautifully, as it is both a good source of fresh bread, pastries, and take-out meals, as well as a charming place to sit down for a meal, snack, or bowl of delicious coffee. There are locations all over the city, so you're never far from a good baguette.
*Multiple locations; visit www.lepainquotidien.com for addresses and information.*

**436. Sahadi's:** You can't eat in, but you can certainly stock up at this popular (and very reasonably priced) Atlantic Avenue market. Dried fruits, nuts, spices, and Middle Eastern foods, spreads, and ingredients are the specialties here, and the prepared foods are excellent. N.B.: Sahadi's is not open on Sundays.
*187 ATLANTIC AVENUE BETWEEN CLINTON AND COURT STREETS IN BROOKLYN. Subway: 2, 3, 4, 5 to Borough Hall; F, G to Bergen Street. 718-624-4550. www.sahadis.com.*

**437. Sullivan Street Bakery:** The breads at this West Village favorite combine Italian recipes and organic baking for some mouthwatering results, like the herb-flecked potato pizza. (There's also a sister location in Hell's Kitchen.)
*Both locations in Manhattan. 73 SULLIVAN STREET BETWEEN SPRING AND BROOME STREETS. Subway: C, E to Spring Street. 212-334-9435; 533 WEST 47TH STREET BETWEEN TENTH AND ELEVENTH AVENUES. Subway: C, E to 50th Street. 212-265-5580. www.sullivanstreetbakery.com.*

**438. *Yura's:*** These Carnegie Hill market-cafés sell a well-edited (and well-done) selection of prepared food and baked goods. The rotating, seasonal menu includes fresh breakfast, lunch, and dinner items, as well as excellent soups (don't miss the carrot ginger), sandwiches, and sweets. The Third Avenue location has a full-service café and attracts a quieter, older crowd eating in, while the atmosphere at the Madison Avenue location is less subdued and caters more to the carryout market driven by its proximity to several prep schools. (The third location, also on Third Avenue, one block up from the restaurant, sells only baked goods.) The weekday after-school rush at the Madison location can get pretty hairy, but during the day it is very civilized and a great place to pick up a picnic lunch on the way to Central Park, which is one avenue over. *All locations in Manhattan. 1645 THIRD AVENUE AT 92ND STREET. 212-860-8060. (Bakery is located at 1659 Third Avenue at 93rd Street and has the same phone.); 1292 MADISON AVENUE AT 92ND STREET. 212-860-8060. Subway (for all locations): 6 to 96th Street; 4, 5, 6 to 86th Street.*

## 439. Play hooky at **Cones** on a sweltering August afternoon.

This Argentinean-owned ice cream shop has developed a cult-like following for its superior scoops—almost chewy, taffy-like ice creams and intensely flavored sorbets—which means that the line can get out of control on summer weekends. What better excuse than that to take an afternoon off during the week?
*272 BLEECKER STREET BETWEEN MORTON AND JONES STREETS IN MANHATTAN. Subway: 1 to Christopher Street-Sheridan Square; A, C, E, B, D, F, V to West 4th Street. 212-414-1795.*

## 440. Try an ice cream flavor you didn't think existed from the **Chinatown Ice Cream Factory**.

Lychee, red bean, black sesame, and taro are among the exotic offerings at this Chinatown institution, alongside more traditional American staples, such as cookies-and-cream to mint chocolate chip.
*65 BAYARD STREET BETWEEN MOTT AND ELIZABETH STREETS IN MANHATTAN. Subway: 6, N, Q, R, W, J, M, Z to Canal Street. 212-608-4170. www.chinatownicecreamfactory.com.*

## 441. Join the **food club** . . .

Two things that New Yorkers really love are good food and getting to do things before anyone else. Culinary Insiders is a club that combines these two passions by offering rare, one-of-a-kind, private events with New York restaurants, like dinners with chefs, kitchen tours, tastings at not-yet-opened restaurants, and foodie field trips outside of the city. The club works with some of the city's most respected chefs to organize events—including Daniel Boulud and Jean-Georges Vongerichten (see entries above). Membership gets you early bookings for all events, plus reduced admission fees; events are also open to the public, subject to availability, so you can attend one before you join.

*Annual membership: $125 and up. For more information and a schedule of upcoming events, call 212-330-9080 or visit www.culinaryinsiders.com.*

## 442. . . . or join the **hamburger club**.

O'Neill's Irish Bar has a burger-of-the-month club, which entitles members to one special burger at the restaurant each month, served with fries and a matched beer. The burger and beer changes each month, but provided you don't mind toppings like cheese, bacon, or guacamole, you won't be disappointed. You can sign up for a year, a half-year, or a single month—however much your waistline will permit.

*729 THIRD AVENUE AT 45TH STREET IN MANHATTAN. Subway: 4, 5, 6, 7, S to Grand Central-42nd Street. 212-661-3530. www.irishpubny.com.*

## 443. Slurp up a **Ralph's Italian ice**.

On a hot, sticky day, enjoying an Italian ice ranks pretty high on the list of all-time best things to do in New York. Alas, the once seasonally ubiquitous pushcarts seem to have gone the way of the subway token and are hard to come across these days. However, great Italian ices can still be procured from Ralph's, which has been selling this delicious treat since 1928. At the original Staten Island location and the other locations in Queens, you can find dozens of flavors of traditional Italian ice, sherbet, and ice cream. They also have a few low-carb/low-sugar varieties, something no self-respecting pushcart would be caught selling.

*Multiple locations in Staten Island and Queens. For information, visit www.ralphsices.com.*

## 444. Get taken to lunch in the **Condé Nast cafeteria**.

Frank Gehry's sleek, futuristic cafeteria is the most exclusive lunch spot in town—no matter who you are, or how much you'll spend, the only way to get in is if someone who works there invites you. But if you can't swing a meeting with Anna Wintour, it's worth trying to bribe one of the numerous editorial assistants for a trip inside. After you've made it past the security desk in the lobby, take the elevators up to the fourth floor and follow the crowd. If you actually want to eat, you'll have to buy a card from one of the machines by the entrance—the only form of payment the cafeteria accepts—otherwise, you'll have to content yourself with the visual feast. Past the dark servery and cash registers is the glass-and-tan seating area filled with undulating lines of leather booths and blue titanium. The space is small and oddly shaped, but the rise and fall of Gehry's elevated seating areas separated by glass panels make the room look bigger than it is (even when it's packed), and the canteen he created has an eye-catching visual appeal that echoes that of the slick magazine conglomerate. The food offerings are appropriately lavish: an abundant salad bar packed with premium produce and sumptuous prepared dishes; a daily hot meal that reads like the menu of a three-star restaurant; freshly baked breads, bagels, muffins, and pizzas; plus soups, sandwiches, sushi, fruit, and even a self-serve frozen yogurt machine. Still, that doesn't stop a disproportionate amount of the magazines' staff from congregating around the piles of undressed lettuce and egg whites, so you'll have no problem getting to the more exciting items. Lest you think that you'll blend right in, the aisles up to the bulbous seating areas—compared, inevitably, to catwalks—are sloped and slippery and can send all but the most seasoned fashion editor for a spill in front of the entire staff.

*4 TIMES SQUARE AT 42ND STREET, 4TH FLOOR, IN MANHATTAN. Subway: 1, 2, 3, 7, N, Q, R, W, S to Times Square-42nd Street.*

---

## 445. Escape and rejuvenate at **Hangawi**.

Behind a pair of heavy wooden doors on 32ND Street lies the single most transporting dining experience in the city. Leave your earthly existence along with your shoes at the entrance and let yourself be whisked away by the soothing music, smooth sake and plum wine, and incredible vegetarian Korean cuisine. It is the closest thing to true bliss that is easily accessible by subway.

*12 EAST 32ND STREET BETWEEN FIFTH AND MADISON AVENUES IN MANHATTAN. Subway: B, D, F, V, N, Q, R, W to 34th Street/Herald Square. 212-213-0077. www.hangawirestaurant.com.*

---

## Have dinner in a restaurant's back garden.

Eating outdoors in the middle of this thriving metropolis always feels like an unusually decadent pleasure. From the first unseasonably warm day in April, any restaurant with decent curb space will throw open the windows, schlep out tables, and string some lights for giddy patrons eager to bask in the long-awaited spring air. However, not all outdoor eateries are created equal. Sidewalk cafés can be good for people- watching, but they've got nothing on the transporting, deliciously smug feeling that comes from eating your meal tucked away in a back garden. Here are a couple of great ones.

**446. *Pure Food and Wine:*** On a sultry summer day, there's nothing more refreshing than a glass of organic sangria in Pure's backyard, followed by some of the gourmet raw dishes. (Skeptics and carnivores take note—it may

not have the heft of a steak, but what these people can do with a tomato will blow your mind.)
*57 IRVING PLACE BETWEEN 17TH AND 18TH STREETS IN MANHATTAN. Subway: 4, 5, 6, L, N, Q, R, W to 14th Street-Union Square. 212-477-1010. www.purefoodandwine.com.*

**447. Yaffa Café:** One of the few places left in the East Village where you can have a legitimately good meal for under $10. The backyard is loud, lively, and feels kind of like a keg party sometimes—as it should.
*97 SAINT MARKS PLACE BETWEEN FIRST AVENUE AND AVENUE A IN MANHATTAN. Subway: L to First Avenue; 6 to Astor Place. 212-677-9001.*

**448. 5 Ninth:** This sophisticated restaurant nestled in a townhouse stands out among the many loud, brightly lit attractions of the Meatpacking District. In addition to the far-out meat preparations from acclaimed chef Zak Pelaccio, one of the city's rising-star chefs, the enclosed backyard seating area behind the restaurant is another of its great charms. If you can't get a seat outside, the three-story nineteenth-century brownstone that houses the restaurant is pretty nice, too.
*5 NINTH AVENUE BETWEEN GANSEVOORT AND LITTLE WEST 12TH STREETS IN MANHATTAN. Subway: A, C, E to 14th Street; L to Eighth Avenue. 212-929-9460. www.5Ninth.com.*

**449. Paradou:** Also in the Meatpacking District, this charming French bistro is the antithesis of **Pastis** (see page 163): it's calm, cozy, and meant for relaxation. Dining on cassoulet and crepes in their lovely back garden, you can easily lose track of what country you are in. They put walls around part of the garden in the winter, so half of it is open year-round.
*8 LITTLE WEST 12TH STREET BETWEEN NINTH AVENUE AND WASHINGTON STREET IN MANHATTAN. Subway: A, C, E to 14th Street; L to Eighth Avenue. 212-463-8345. www.paradounyc.com.*

**450. Sherwood Café/Robin des Bois:** Hands down, the most romantic garden you can eat in anywhere in the city. Try the Sherwood Special (a combination of the cheese and charcuterie platters), with plenty of wine....
*195 SMITH STREET BETWEEN BALTIC AND WARREN STREETS IN BROOKLYN. Subway: F, G to Bergen Street. 718-596-1609. www.sherwoodcafe.com.*

**451. Home:** They have gas lamps on the outdoor deck, so this is a good choice if you just can't wait another night for spring to begin—or if you want to stretch summer out as long as possible. The garden is open year-round, and diners who brave the cold for an al fresco meal in the winter are inducted into the Polar Bear Diner Club, and receive special buttons that congratulate them as "fearless eaters under the heaters"

*20 CORNELIA STREET BETWEEN BLEECKER AND WEST 4TH STREETS IN MANHATTAN. Subway: 1 to Christopher Street-Sheridan Square. 212-243-9579.*

**452.** *Barolo:* Only if the owners opened the gates from the cool Italian-style garden onto Thompson Street would you know you're not in Tuscany.

*398 WEST BROADWAY BETWEEN SPRING AND BROOME STREETS IN MANHATTAN. Subway: C, E to Spring Street; N, R, W to Prince Street. 212-226-1102.*

**453.** *Bohemian Hall & Beer Garden:* This truly bohemian hangout in Queens (it was started as a community center for Czech and Slovak immigrants in the early twentieth century) is the home of the city's only outdoor beer garden. The décor isn't flashy (picnic tables are pretty much it) and the food's not very fancy (Eastern European staples from the kitchen inside or burgers and dogs from the grill outside), but it's big, lively, and well worth a trip.

*29-19 24TH AVENUE IN QUEENS. Subway: N to Astoria Boulevard. 718-274-4925. www.bohemianhall.com.*

## 454. Have a blintz from **Teresa's**.

For some, a blintz has the same power to spark as much passionate competition and unwavering preference as any bagel, steak, pickle, or pizza, and the ones turned out at Teresa's are about as good as they come. Best eaten as soon as they are served, they are warm, crispy, and the soft cheese filling is perfectly balanced between sweet and savory.

*103 FIRST AVENUE BETWEEN 6TH AND 7TH STREETS IN MANHATTAN. Subway: L to First Avenue. 212-228-0604. 80 MONTAGUE STREET AT HICKS STREET IN BROOKLYN. Subway: N, R to Court Street-Borough Hall; 2, 3 to Clark Street. 718-797-3996.*

## 455. Visit the **Brooklyn Brewery**.

Thanks to a large influx of German immigrants, Brooklyn was once one of the nation's beer-producing capitals; one hundred years ago, it was home to nearly fifty breweries. By the second half of the twentieth century, however, all of these family-owned breweries had closed, forced out of business by the bigger breweries in the Midwest. After years of basement brewing, hand labeling, and distributing out of their van, the local brewers who made Brooklyn Lager revived the borough's brewing tradition when the Brooklyn Brewery opened in 1996. You can tour the brewery for free every Saturday (tours run between twenty and thirty minutes and are held hourly from 1:00 p.m. to 4:00 p.m.). The brewery also hosts happy hours (Friday, 6:00 p.m. to 11:00 p.m.; a selection of eight beers is available for $3 each), concerts, parties, and other events. *1 BREWERS ROW, 79 NORTH 11TH STREET IN BROOKLYN. Subway: L to Bedford Avenue. 718-486-7422. www.brooklynbrewery.com.*

### 456. Buy a bottle of wine at **Punch & Judy**.

Pick a complementary red, stretch out on a sofa in the secluded back room, and spend an entire night dipping fresh fruit into their amazingly decadent chocolate fondue. *26 CLINTON STREET BETWEEN HOUSTON AND STANTON STREETS IN MANHATTAN. Subway: F to Delancey Street; J, M, Z to Essex Street. 212-982-1116.*

### 457. Have a champagne date at the **Bubble Lounge**.

Champagne can turn any evening into an occasion. So with the price of a cocktail pushing $15 at hot spots around town, why not let it? This Tribeca lounge offers more than 300 kinds of champagnes and sparkling wines, in a classier, cozier, and more welcoming setting than the trendy bars. Perfect for a romantic rendezvous, a celebration, or a regular after-work drink. *228 WEST BROADWAY BETWEEN FRANKLIN AND WHITE STREETS IN MANHATTAN. Subway: 1 to Franklin Street. 212-431-3433. www.bubblelounge.com.*

### 458. Swing with your steady on the lovers' seats at **Bowery Bar** and **Down the Hatch**,

probably the only bars left in the city where you can indulge playground romance. Swing in the breeze in the patio garden at Bowery Bar, or stake out the swing for a whole night at Down the Hatch—it's the only peaceful corner of the bar. **Bowery Bar, aka B-Bar & Grill:** *40 EAST 4TH STREET BETWEEN BOWERY AND LAFAYETTE STREET IN MANHATTAN. Subway: 6 to Astor Place; B, D, F, V to Broadway-Lafayette Street. 212-475-2220.* **Down the Hatch:** *179 WEST 4TH STREET BETWEEN SIXTH AND SEVENTH AVENUES IN MANHATTAN. Subway: A, C, E, B, D, F, V to West 4th Street. 212-627-9747.*

### 459. Have a rendezvous at the **Cellar Bar** at the Bryant Park Hotel.

Cavernous tiled walls, arched and candlelit hallways, and powerful cocktails mean seduction is inevitable.

*40 WEST 40TH STREET BETWEEN FIFTH AND SIXTH AVENUES IN MANHATTAN. Subway: B, D, F, V to 42nd Street-Bryant Park. 212-869-0100. www.bryantparkhotel.com.*

### 460. Indulge in a greasy soul food breakfast with classic jukebox accompaniment at the **M&G Diner**.

M&G Diner is a local favorite and something of a celebrity haunt, with Harlem faces like Mary J. Blige and Bill Clinton among the regular customers. Look smart and go on a Sunday morning for an amazing breakfast, the best jukebox in Harlem, and a crowd of beautifully dressed locals who show up hungry after church.

*383 WEST 125TH STREET AT ST. NICHOLAS AVENUE IN MANHATTAN. Subway: A, C to 125th Street. 212-864-7326.*

## Travel the world, table by table.

Many cities boast one or two signature "imported" cuisines, but nowhere else will you have the variety—and for the most part, the authenticity—of so many different types of food, in so many different settings, from so many different places.

With such an abundance of nonindigenous delights, it's hard to contain international food under one heading; we easily could have devoted an entire chapter to the topic. There are excellent restaurants specializing in cuisines both familiar and exotic; there are fancy fine dining establishments, specialty shops, take-out joints, and holes-in-the-wall; there are neighborhoods famous for their authentic foreign food and less familiar enclaves that boast equally delectable delights. In this section, we've chosen our favorite dining spots for a dozen popular foreign cuisines. However, don't limit your travels to the restaurants whose cuisines you already know—there's so much more out there! After all, you don't have to be a particularly sophisticated New Yorker to be familiar with food from Thailand, Brazil, or Vietnam; what about Uruguay, Guyana, Yemen, Sri Lanka, or Eritrea? You'll find restaurants from these countries, along with others from lands you may never even have heard of. Finding out about them (and finding them), however, can be just as hard as locating their native countries on a map. *The Food Lover's Guide to the Best Ethnic Eating in the City,* by *Village Voice* food columnist Robert Sietsema, gives information on the ethnic cuisines of almost eighty countries and cultures that can be enjoyed in restaurants around the five boroughs. If you're up for an adventure, we recommend using this book to take a trip to somewhere you've never been.

# CHINESE

As many foodlovers know, "Chinese food" in America is made up of many different regional cuisines and specialties. While there are countless good Chinese restaurants of all kinds all over the city, it can be hard to tell which are authentic (meaning they serve dishes actually eaten in the region). Here are some favorites:

**461.** Have Hong Kong–style dim sum, a seemingly limitless range of dumplings, spring rolls, and milk teas, with all the flourishes at the **Golden Unicorn**.
*18 EAST BROADWAY AT CATHERINE STREET IN MANHATTAN. Subway: 4, 5, 6 to Brooklyn Bridge-City Hall; J, M, Z to Chambers Street. 212-941-0911.*

**462.** Go celebrity-spotting while you enjoy the best ribs in Chinatown at **Hop Kee**. The famous lemon fried flounder has kept the likes of Bill Cosby, Conan O'Brien, and Bill Clinton coming back time and again.
*21 MOTT STREET AT MOSCO STREET IN MANHATTAN. Subway: 1 to Franklin Street; A, C, E to Canal Street. 212-964-8365.*

**463.** Devour a basket of explosive soup dumplings at **Joe's Shanghai**, the restaurant that claims to have invented them. You don't even have to ask for them specifically; they'll know.
*9 PELL STREET BETWEEN BOWERY AND MOTT STREET IN MANHATTAN. Subway: B, D to Grand Street; 6, J, M, Z, N, Q, R, W to Canal Street. 212-233-8888.*

**464.** Order the duck at the **Peking Duck House**. Even vegetarians have been known to enjoy watching the waiters carve the duck here. (Don't be alarmed by the sleek new look: the décor may say twenty-first-century SoHo, but the food is still Chinatown, all the way.)
*28 MOTT STREET AT PELL STREET IN MANHATTAN. Subway: 6, J, M, Z, N, Q, R, W to Canal Street. 212-227-1810.*

**465.** Order the Shanghai banquet at **Shanghai Pavilion**. It looks like a regular Chinese restaurant, but critics and aficionados of Chinese cuisine vouch that the dishes at this Upper East Side joint are authentic, and some consider Shanghai Pavilion the best Chinese food outside of Chinatown. You must call a day in advance to request certain specialties, like beggar's chicken, a stuffed chicken baked in clay; but you also won't want to miss the soup dumplings—the restaurant's owner used to work at the venerable dumpling purveyor, Joe's Shanghai (see above).
*1378 THIRD AVENUE BETWEEN 78TH AND 79TH STREETS IN MANHATTAN. Subway: 6 to 77th Street. 212-585-3388.*

# ITALIAN

With the extreme variety in look, taste, and price, Italian cuisine in this city defies categorization. Like Chinese cuisine, each region of Italy has its own style and specialties; something that's prepared authentically at a Neopolitan restaurant may not taste the same at a Tuscan trattoria or an enoteca (although they all may be equally good). In addition, the restaurants range broadly in character, from those that specialize in certain foods (pizza, pasta, or panini), to authentic and firmly regional restaurants (like Manducatis or the restaurants on Arthur Avenue in the Bronx), to Italian-inspired fine dining (such as L'Impero and Mario Batali's Babbo, mentioned above). We've considered each of these under the umbrella of Italian food and selected some of the best. (See also our list of the best pizza places on page 203.)

***Arthur Avenue.*** The neighborhood of Belmont, high in the Bronx between Fordham Road and Crotona Park, has been a dense and popular Italian enclave for close to a century. Running through its center is Arthur Avenue, a street of Italian storefronts and restaurants that has been drawing local residents and traveling epicureans for as long as anyone can remember. Aside from its gastronomic attractions, Belmont is a charming little corner of the Bronx, where church bells ring out every quarter of an hour, Old World traditions meet contemporary American attitudes, and kids play in playgrounds while men and women sit in street cafés talking over cappuccinos. Go by day, and the neighborhood around Arthur Avenue and East 187th Street is a great place to stroll and pick up some of the best quality Italian foods, from fresh pastas to meats, vegetables, breads, cheeses, and herbs. Go by night, and choose from a host of busy restaurants, where you can enjoy these fresh ingredients cooked with genuine Italian-American flair, whether it's a slice to go at **Full Moon** (see page 204) or a sumptuous feast at Pasquale's Rigoletto. Note: All listings below are in the Bronx.

**466. Biancardi's:** An authentic Italian butcher offering everything from rabbit and veal to salami and smoked meats.
*2350 ARTHUR AVENUE BETWEEN CRESCENT AVENUE AND FRANK SIMEONE SQUARE. 718-733-4058.*

**467. Borgatti's:** A maker of genuine fresh egg pasta and ravioli that has won over locals and food critics alike.
*632 EAST 187TH STREET BETWEEN HUGHES AVENUE AND BELMONT AVENUE. 718-367-3799.*

**468. Egidio's Patisserie:** A bakery whose windows are so full of extravagant cakes and Italian sweets they're impossible to resist.
*622 EAST 187TH STREET AT HUGHES AVENUE. 718-295-6077.*

**469. Umberto's:** One of Arthur Avenue's largest restaurants and the only one devoted entirely to fresh Italian seafood dishes.
*2356 ARTHUR AVENUE BETWEEN CRESCENT AVENUE AND FRANK SIMEONE SQUARE. 718-220-2526.*

**470. Pasquale's Rigoletto:** The biggest and liveliest of the restaurants on Arthur Avenue, and the perfect place for a rollicking dinner party.
*2311 ARTHUR AVENUE BETWEEN CRESCENT AVENUE AND FRANK SIMEONE SQUARE. 718-365-6644.*

*The popular part of Arthur Avenue runs from East 184TH Street to East 188TH Street, and many more great markets and cafés can be found on 187TH Street, across Arthur Avenue to Cambrelleng Avenue. Bus: Bx55 from anywhere along Third Avenue to St. Barnabas's Hospital, Third Avenue and East 183rd Street (one block from the base of Arthur Avenue). Subway: 4, D to Fordham Road, then Bx12 bus east; 2, 5 to Pelham Parkway, then Bx12 bus west. N.B.: www.arthuravenuebronx.com has directions, recipes, and facts about Arthur Avenue and Belmont. Information on some of the stores and merchants listed above can also be found there.*

**471.** For true Italian home cooking the way Nonna used to make, head to **Manducatis** (rumor has it they close one month each summer to can tomatoes in Italy). Reward yourself for making the trip to Long Island City with exceptional pastas and entrees, rare Italian wines from the owner's collection, and a celebrity sighting or two.
*13-27 JACKSON AVENUE AT 47TH AVENUE IN QUEENS. Subway: 7 to Hunters Point Avenue; G to 21st Street. 718-729-4602.*

**472.** For classic Italian cuisine in a more formal setting, head to the darkened dining room of **Il Mulino.** Too far north and west to be part of Little Italy, Il Mulino is located on a busy corner of the Village and is one of the oldest and finest Italian restaurants in the city. While the menu is short and straightforward, the food is carefully and authentically prepared and draws inspiration largely from the recipes and flavors of central Italy's mountainous provinces. Simple pastas with traditional lamb or veal ragus are especially good—differing notably from other restaurants in the quality of the meats used—and the classic, herbed seafood dishes are wonderful.
*86 WEST 3RD STREET BETWEEN SULLIVAN AND THOMPSON STREETS IN MANHATTAN. Subway: A, C, E, B, D, F, V to West 4th Street. 212-673-3783. www.ilmulinonewyork.com.*

**473.** For elevated Italian, go to **L'Impero.** Foie gras may not sound Italian, but it's one of the house specialties at this upscale Tudor City restaurant. Other choices range from the rare and rarified roasted goat to the simply sublime spaghetti with tomatoes and basil. The $48 prix-fixe lunch ($58 at dinner) lets you eat like a prince for a relatively

modest sum, allowing you to choose any four courses from the entire menu.
*45 TUDOR CITY PLACE BY 43RD STREET AND FIRST AVENUE IN MANHATTAN. Subway: 4, 5, 6, 7, S to Grand Central-42nd Street. 212-559-5045. www.limpero.com.*

**474.** For true Italian coffee, go to ***Tarallucci e Vino***. Though the name means "biscuits and wines," coffee connoisseurs consider the espresso to be on par with the cafés in Italy.
*163 FIRST AVENUE BETWEEN 10TH AND 11TH STREETS IN MANHATTAN. Subway: L to First Avenue. 212-388-1190. 15 EAST 18TH STREET BETWEEN FIFTH AVENUE AND BROADWAY IN MANHATTAN. Subway: 4, 5, 6, L, N, Q, R, W to 14th Street-Union Square. 212-228-5400.*

## FRENCH

Yet again, there's plenty to choose from, along a particularly broad spectrum on the elegance scale. On the high end are those restaurants featuring classic French gourmet cooking mentioned in the "splurges" section (see page 166). But work your way down a bit, and there are bistros, brasseries, patisseries, creperies, and chocolatiers that excel in particular specialties and regional delights.

**475.** Get a crepe from the little window at ***Shade To Go*** and eat it in **Washington Mews** (see page 100)—Paris without the jet lag.
*241 SULLIVAN STREET BETWEEN BLEECKER AND WEST 3RD STREETS IN MANHATTAN. Subway: A, C, E, B, D, F, V to West 4th Street. 212-982-6275.*

**476.** Forget Paris, and have a less traditional but just as scrumptious crepe at the ***Creperie***. You may not be able to sit, but crepes like the spinach and feta are worth standing for—and they make a perfect snack while you're waiting for a table at 'inoteca, the popular Italian restaurant next door.
*135 LUDLOW STREET BETWEEN RIVINGTON AND STANTON STREETS IN MANHATTAN. Subway: F to Delancey Street; J, M, Z to Essex Street. 212-979-5543.*

**477.** Order the *galette des rois* at ***Gavroche***. There are many wonderful French bistros in this city, but we wanted to single this one out because it is one of the very few that serve the *galette des rois*, the almond cake with a charm baked inside that the French serve during the Feast of the Epiphany. The person whose slice contains the charm (called "la feve" because they used to use a dry bean; today, charms are usually figurines) is crowned the king or queen of the day, and gets to wear a paper crown. During the first week of January, this bistro serves the cake (which is quite tasty), complete with charms. You can have it by the slice or, to increase your odds, bring a group and buy the entire cake.
*212 WEST 14TH STREET BETWEEN SEVENTH AND EIGHTH AVENUES IN MANHATTAN. Sub-*

way: 1, 2, 3 to 14<sup>th</sup> Street; A, C, E to 14<sup>th</sup> Street; L to Eighth Avenue. 212-646-8553.

**478.** Get a taste of Provence at **Nice Matin**. The Upper West Side is no longer the gastronomic wasteland that it once was, and Nice Matin stands out among the area's many good restaurants as a sunny spot of solid regional cooking. Traditional dishes like *soupe à pistou* (a vegetable and bean soup) and *pissaladière* (a thin, pizzalike onion tart for which Nice is famous) allow you to experience the Mediterranean flavor that separates the cuisine of southern France from that of the rest of the country. *201 WEST 79TH STREET AT AMSTERDAM AVENUE IN MANHATTAN. Subway: 1 to 79<sup>th</sup> Street. 212-873-6423. www.nicematinnyc.com.*

**479.** Have a pastry at **Café Fauchon**. The Manhattan outpost of the famed French *boulanger et traiteur* (to call it a "food hall" seems disrespectful) has an adjoining café where excellent French pastries and treats are served, including perfect croissants and mouthwatering *macarons*, flavored cream-laced puffs, flown in from Paris. *442 PARK AVENUE AT 56TH STREET IN MANHATTAN. Subway: 4, 5, 6 to 59<sup>th</sup> Street; N, R, W to Lexington Avenue/59<sup>th</sup> Street. 212-308-5919. www.fauchon.com.*

**480.** Have a meal—and then a pastry—at **Payard Patisserie & Bistro**. Eating a meal at Payard is like the joyous reunion of two old friends. Order traditional French dishes—savory tarts, terrines, and bouillabaisse—in the full-service bistro, and then on your way out, pick up scrumptious Napoleons, milles feuilles, opéras, éclairs, petit fours, chocolates, or other sweet confections in the patisserie. (The bistro also has a dessert menu, but we suggest holding out for the pastries, if you can.) The meals are all top-notch, and while we're not sure, we don't think it's actually possible to leave without eating dessert. The patisserie also serves excellent brioches, croissants, and pain au chocolat in the morning. *1032 LEXINGTON AVENUE BETWEEN 72ND AND 73RD STREETS IN MANHATTAN. Subway: 6 to 77<sup>th</sup> Street. 212-717-5252. www.payard.com.*

**481.** Savor a single piece of chocolate from **Maison du Chocolat**. The chocolates made by this Paris-based chocolatier may taste disarmingly bitter to a palette accustomed to Hershey's or Godiva, but anyone who loves the robust flavors of European chocolate will appreciate the satisfying richness of each piece crafted here. *Both locations in Manhattan. 1018 MADISON AVENUE BETWEEN 78TH AND 79TH STREETS. Subway: 6 to 77<sup>th</sup> Street. 212-744-7117. 30 ROCKEFELLER CENTER AT 49TH STREET. Subway: B, D, F, V to 47<sup>th</sup>-50<sup>th</sup> Streets-Rockefeller Center. 212-265-9404. www.lamaisonduchocolat.com.*

# ENGLISH

**482.** Have a proper English tea at *Tea & Sympathy*, a cozy little tearoom where pots of Yorkshire Gold and tiers of finger sandwiches and scones never look out of place. For heartier appetites, or those craving classic British cooking, they also prepare a nice Yorkshire pudding, bangers and mash, treacle pudding, and, of course, beans on toast.
*108 GREENWICH AVENUE BETWEEN SEVENTH AND EIGHTH AVENUES IN MANHATTAN. Subway: A, C, E, to 14th Street; L to Eighth Avenue. 212-807-8329. www.teaandsympathynewyork.com.*

**483.** Get some fish and chips at *A Salt and Battery*, considered the most authentic taste of home for many wandering Britons (the imported chip-cutter from London helps, as does the Capital Radio and Virgin U.K. soundtrack, broadcast via the Internet). *Both locations in Manhattan. 112 GREENWICH AVENUE BETWEEN SEVENTH AND EIGHTH AVENUES. Subway: A, C, E, to 14th Street; L to Eighth Avenue. 212-691-2713. 80 SECOND AVENUE BETWEEN 4TH AND 5TH STREETS. Subway: F, V to Lower East Side-Second Avenue. 212-254-6610. www.asaltandbattery.com.*

**484.** Throw caution to the wind, and indulge in one of the cheekiest imported treats: a deep-fried Mars bar from the *ChipShop*. (Those watching their carbs can try the "dietetic" version made with an Atkins bar.) British expats starved for their tabloids can get their fix by visiting the restroom at the Park Slope location, which is wallpapered with clippings from England's finest dailies.
*Both locations in Brooklyn. 383 FIFTH AVENUE AT 6TH STREET. 718-832-7701. Subway: F to 4th Avenue; M, R to 9th Street. 129 ATLANTIC AVENUE BETWEEN CLINTON AND HENRY STREETS. 718-855-7775. Subway: 2, 3, 4, 5 to Borough Hall; N, R to Court Street-Borough Hall; F to Bergen Street. ww.chipshopnyc.com.*

# INDIAN

The Queens neighborhood of Jackson Heights, which extends beyond Sunnyside up Roosevelt and 37th Avenues between 72nd Street and Junction Boulevard, is known as Little India. While there is a heavy Indian presence in East Midtown and the East Village in Manhattan, Little India is the densest Indian enclave in the five boroughs. Powdered spice stores, beautiful sari makers, and video shops carrying everything Bollywood line the streets, and the restaurants make this area the place to go for a true and varied taste of Indian food, whether you're looking for a quiet snack in a local curry house, a feast of tandoori meats in one of the larger restaurants, or a sample of authentic Indian desserts to take home.

**485.** Where else but in Jackson Heights can you find top-notch Indian food in a place that calls itself a diner? Grab a window seat at the enormous **Jackson Diner** and enjoy great South Indian cooking in one of the busiest and most strikingly decorated restaurants in New York.

*37-47 74TH STREET BETWEEN 37TH AND ROOSEVELT AVENUES IN QUEENS. Subway: 7 to 74th Street-Broadway; E, F, G, R, V to Jackson Heights-Roosevelt Avenue. 718-672-1232.*

**486.** For a quieter experience, visit the **Delhi Palace**. Go hungry—there is such a vast selection of starters and sweets that you'll have no choice but to order a bunch and taste as many as you can.

*33-73 74TH STREET IN QUEENS. Subway: 7 to 74th Street-Broadway; E, F, G, R, V to Jackson Heights-Roosevelt Avenue. 718-507-0666.*

**487.** Embrace the madness of Midtown at **Curry in a Hurry**—something of a fast-food place for Indian cuisine, but the food (in particular the chutney) is very good.

*119 LEXINGTON AVENUE AT 28TH STREET IN MANHATTAN. Subway: 6 to 28th Street. 212-683-0900.*

**488.** Feast like a king (or a queen) at **Dawat**. Far from the bustling restaurant rows of 6th Street, Murray Hill, and Jackson Heights lies this excellent, upscale Indian fine dining establishment. Dawat means "invitation to a feast," and you should accept without question. The food is top notch, the décor refined, and the service on par with the city's most elegant restaurants. Order one of the tasting menus—called "the king" or "the queen"—and then relax as you are served dish after tantalizing dish of the chef's specialties.

*210 EAST 58TH STREET BETWEEN SECOND AND THIRD AVENUES IN MANHATTAN. Subway: 4, 5, 6 to 59th Street; N, R, W to Lexington Avenue/59th Street. 212-355-7555.*

**489.** Let yourself be courted by the "callers" at **Milon** and **Panna II**, two Indian restaurants on First Avenue. Though they allegedly share a common kitchen, the doormen of this neighboring pair of incredibly bright, colorful restaurants do their utmost to make the distinction between dining rooms seem profound. Each has a full and cheap menu of Indian and Bengali dishes, and each is so full of dangling chili lights and tinsel that the world outside seems dull by comparison. Tip: whichever restaurant you choose, make sure you tell the waitstaff that it's someone's birthday—the "surprise" celebrations are elaborate and happen three or four times a night.

*Milon (on the left at the top of the stairs) and Panna II (on the right): 93 FIRST AVENUE BETWEEN 6TH AND 7TH STREETS IN MANHATTAN. Subway: L to First Avenue; 6 to Astor Place; F, V to Lower East Side-Second Avenue. Milon: 212-228-4896; Panna II: 212-598-4610.*

**490.** Stock up on spices and more at *Kalustyan's*. Though it carries products of all different kinds—snacks, tea, cosmetics, prepared food, chutney, and sweets galore—from all over the world, one sniff inside Kalustyan's will send you straight to the spices. Choose from nearly 900 varieties, from dill, cumin, and nearly a dozen kinds of curry powder to more exotic offerings not found anywhere else.
*123 LEXINGTON AVENUE BETWEEN 27TH AND 28TH STREETS IN MANHATTAN. Subway: 6 to 28th Street. 212-685-3451. www.kalustyans.com.*

# SPANISH

**491.** For tapas, head to *Casa Mono*. This airy, corner taverna and the small bar next to it, *Bar Jamon*, are owned by **Mario Batali** (see page 161), the city's venerable Italian chef who's masterfully rendered this traditional Spanish concept for the city's dining scene. A meal at Casa Mono is both an excellent choice for tapas, and a low-risk, cost-effective way to sample Batali's characteristically adventurous, meat-laden cuisine. The menu is not translated into English, so vegetarians (or less adventurous carnivores) who don't speak Spanish should ask for a translation before ordering; if not, dive in for a feast of unfamiliar flavors and ingredients. Casa Mono serves small plates of formidable foodstuff, so if you've ever been curious about offal or cockscombs, this is the place to experiment. There is a long list of wines and sherries which can help calm your nerves if you're anxious about headcheese.
*Both in Manhattan. CASA MONO: 52 IRVING PLACE AT 17TH STREET. BAR JAMON, 125 EAST 17TH STREET BETWEEN IRVING PLACE AND THIRD AVENUE. Subway: 4, 5, 6, L, N, Q, R, W to 14th Street-Union Square. 212-253-2773. www.mariobatali.com.*

**492.** Dig into the paella at *El Pote Espanol*. This excellent Spanish restaurant has been serving an authentic blend of Spanish and South American cuisine for nearly a quarter of a century. The atmosphere is more formal than some of New York's lively sangria and tapas bars, and the menu is heavy on rich, savory meat and seafood dishes. The flavorful vegetable dishes (from fresh asparagus to buttery artichokes and stuffed mushrooms) are outstanding, but it's the colorful and rich paella that keeps people coming back.
*718 SECOND AVENUE BETWEEN 38TH AND 39TH STREETS IN MANHATTAN. Subway: 6 to 33rd Street. 212-889-6680. www.elpote.com.*

**493.** Take a date to *El Cid*. Although El Cid is predominantly a tapas bar, it's a great and comfortable place to enjoy an intimate supper. Focus on the chicken or the shellfish dishes, all deliciously garlicky and flavorful, add an order of sweet sangria, and make sure you leave enough room to try the *torrejas*, a traditional Spanish dessert

akin to bread pudding in spiced wine and served with ice cream.
*322 WEST 15TH STREET BETWEEN EIGHTH AND NINTH AVENUES IN MANHATTAN. Subway: A, C, E to 14th Street; L to Eighth Avenue. 212-929-9332.*

## RUSSIAN

Brighton Beach, the stretch of beach and boardwalk that links Coney Island to Sheepshead Bay, is home to one of the largest and most intense ethnic communities in New York. Known locally as "Little Odessa," Brighton is populated almost entirely by Russians and Ukrainians, and it is simply *the* place to go for borscht, caviar, honey cake, and all things reminiscent of the USSR. (The nightlife's not bad either.) Street signs, papers, and menus are in Russian, delis and street vendors sell fresh sour-cherry and cranberry juices, and everyone brings his or her own bottle of vodka to the table.

**494.** Eat smoked-fish salad and grilled meat on the boardwalk at **Tatiana**, the grandest and most extravagant of the restaurant-nightclubs in Brighton. They'll bring you blankets if it's windy and umbrellas if it's raining, so you can sit outside and watch the Russians on the beach all year round.
*3152 BRIGHTON 6TH STREET AT THE BOARDWALK IN BROOKLYN. Subway: B, Q to Brighton Beach. 718-646-7630.*

**495.** Try a plate of traditional veal dumplings (*pelmeni*) and a bottle of pear soda at **Stolovaya**, the most authentic Russian diner in Brooklyn. Be warned: they do not speak English, but will understand a request for an English menu.
*813 AVENUE U BETWEEN 8TH AND 9TH STREETS IN BROOKLYN. Subway: F, Q to Avenue U. 718-787-0120.*

**496.** Indulge in caviar at **Petrossian**. Although it is only twenty years old, this sibling of the Paris restaurant founded in the 1920s has already become a Midtown institution. The décor is dark and sophisticated and strongly reminiscent of an indulgent Old Europe, and the service makes you feel positively aristocratic. The menu is extremely rich and dominated by beluga, ossetra, and sevruga caviar, salmon roe, and various smoked fish. The best thing to do is to order the chef's tasting menu and sample a little of everything with a cocktail or glass of cold champagne.
*182 WEST 58TH STREET AT SEVENTH AVENUE IN MANHATTAN. Subway: 1, A, C, B, D to 59th Street-Columbus Circle. 212-675-2681. www.petrossian.com.*

**497.** Have the house-infused vodkas at the **Russian Vodka Room**. This scruffy theater district haunt doesn't have the look of authenticity one might expect of an "ethnic" place,

but rest assured that if vodka's your thing, you've come to the right place. There are many exotic flavors of house-infused vodka—such as apple and pomegranate, and garlic, pepper, and dill—which you can have in a mixed drink or in a generously sized shot.
*265 WEST 52ND STREET BETWEEN EIGHTH AVENUE AND BROADWAY IN MANHATTAN. Subway: C, E, to 50th Street; 1 to 50th Street. 212-307-5835.*

# POLISH

The Brooklyn neighborhood of Greenpoint is the most densely Polish part of New York and the place to go if you've got a hankering for kielbasa and cabbage salad. Walk around the area between Manhattan Avenue, Greenpoint Avenue, and Nassau Avenue, and you'll discover a whole community of Polish butchers, bakeries, cafés, and restaurants serving genuine Polish cuisine with unceremonious authenticity. If you're looking for Polish treats to take home, try Jaslowiczanka Bakery (163 Nassau Avenue, 718-389-0263) for fresh rolls and pancakes, and Poznanski's (668 Manhattan Avenue, 718-383-3908) for delicious smoked and treated meats. If you're looking for a place to sit down and eat Warsaw-style, it's best to stroll Manhattan Avenue and try one of the following places.
*Subway: G to Greenpoint Avenue or Nassau Avenue; L to Bedford Avenue.*

**498. *Stylowa:*** *694 MANHATTAN AVENUE AT NORMAN AVENUE IN BROOKLYN. 718-383-8993.*

**499. *Christina's:*** *853 MANHATTAN AVENUE AT GREENPOINT AVENUE IN BROOKLYN. 718-383-4382.*

# GREEK

**500.** If you're looking for fish so fresh it's practically swimming, head to the ***Greek Captain Fish Market*** in Long Island City.
*32-10 36TH AVENUE IN QUEENS. Subway: 7 to 45 Road-Courthouse Square; G to Long Island City-Court Square. 718-786-6015.*

**501.** For an excellent Greek meal that's less fish focused, visit ***Periyali.*** The atmosphere at this Flatiron restaurant is more subdued than what you might expect of a Greek restaurant, as befitting the excellent, refined renditions of traditional dishes and Greek home cooking.
*35 WEST 20TH STREET BETWEEN FIFTH AND SIXTH AVENUES IN MANHATTAN. Subway: N, R, W to 23rd Street; F, V to 23rd Street. 212-463-7890. www.periyali.com.*

# GERMAN AND AUSTRIAN

**502.** Eat upscale Austrian at one of **Kurt Gutenbrunner's** restaurants. A native of Austria, Chef Gutenbrunner has carved a tasty niche in the New York City food scene for this formerly underrepresented cuisine with four high-profile Austrian restaurants. His first, *Wallsé*, named for the small village near the Danube where he grew up, endeared New York foodies to dishes like spätzle, wiener schnitzel, and *kavalierspitz*, a boiled beef dish. At *Thor*, a restaurant in the Hotel on Rivington (the restaurant name is a play on the hotel's acronym and the Norse god of thunder), the food is more Austrian-influenced than outright authentic, and it specializes in small plates, so newcomers can sample several regional specialties before committing to a full, traditional meal. Gutenbrunner's newest restaurant, *Blaue Gans*, is a casual *wirsthouse*, the Austrian equivalent of a brasserie, with lots of sausage, sauerkraut, and schnitzel, along with German and Austrian wines. He also runs *Café Sabarsky*, the elegant Viennese *kaffeehaus* in the **Neue Galerie** (see page 124), one of the loveliest museum eateries in the city, where you can enjoy savory and sweet Viennese treats for breakfast, lunch, or a midday snack.

**BLAUE GANS:** *139 DUANE STREET BETWEEN WEST BROADWAY AND CHURCH STREET IN MANHATTAN. Subway: 1, 2, 3, A, C to Chambers Street. 212-571-8880.*

**CAFÉ SABARSKY:** *1048 FIFTH AVENUE AT 86TH STREET IN MANHATTAN. Subway: 4, 5, 6 to 86th Street. 212-288-0665.*

**THOR:** *107 RIVINGTON STREET BETWEEN ESSEX AND LUDLOW STREETS IN MANHATTAN. Subway: F to Delancey Street; J, M, Z to Essex Street. 212-796-8040. www.hotelonrivington.com.*

**WALLSÉ:** *344 WEST 11TH STREET AT WASHINGTON STREET IN MANHATTAN. Subway: A, C, E to 14th Street; L to Eighth Avenue. 212-352-2300. www.wallse.com.*

**503.** Eat at the *Silver Swan*. Lacking the fanfare that announces the provenance of many international restaurants, this low-key Flatiron bar and restaurant is as popular with locals as an after-work spot as it is with tried-and-true German food fans seeking national specialties like schnitzel, sausage, and potato pancakes. Instead of polka music and waiters dressed in lederhosen, the Silver Swan validates itself by the authenticity of its food and drink, which features an extensive imported beer selection. We suggest you eat at the bar, and chat with the friendly bartenders and munch on the delicious hand-rolled sourdough pretzels—just try not to fill up! (For more on our favorite **bar snacks**, see page 199.)

*41 EAST 20TH STREET IN MANHATTAN. Subway: 6 to 23rd Street. 212-254-3611.*

# SCANDINAVIAN

**504.** Enjoy a purist's Scandinavian dining experience at *Aquavit.* To eat at Aquavit is to immerse yourself in Scandinavian culture, from the rich and varied regional menus to the cool, transporting interiors. Aquavit spreads across three separate rooms, each distinguished by the particular type of Scandinavian cuisine it serves. In the bar, small savory snacks like salted herring accompany good European wine and beer, and drinkers lounge on sleek modernist furniture by Arne Jacobsen. The café has an informal, local feel, with a light menu that includes seafood salads and other perfect lunch dishes from cauliflower soup to cold fish sandwiches. The restaurant's main dining room is light and elegant, an austere and refreshing setting for an extravagant menu that mixes Scandinavian tradition with West European flavors, from foie gras with cherry chutney to indulgent seafood samplers, heavily salted ox tongue, and one of the best lobster rolls in the city (served with trout roe, apples, and a bacon and egg dressing). We recommend you try the Sunday smorgasbord buffet, Aquavit's perfect sampler of meats, fish, cheeses, and breads. A new café location recently opened in **Scandinavia House** (see page 301), serving meatballs, *vasterbotten* quiche, and other regional snacks to hungry culture vultures.
**AQUAVIT:** *65 EAST 55TH STREET BETWEEN PARK AND MADISON AVENUES IN MANHATTAN. Subway: 6 to 51st Street; E, V to Lexington Avenue/53rd Street. 212-307-7311. www.aquavit.org.*
**SCANDINAVIA HOUSE:** *58 PARK AVENUE AT 38TH STREET IN MANHATTAN. 212-847-9727. Subway: 4, 5, 6, 7, S to Grand Central-42nd Street.*

**505.** Get out of the weekday lunch rut with an authentic Scandinavian meal at *Smorgas Chef.* You can trade in steam tables and salad bars for an authentic smorgasbord, along with other Nordic delicacies like North Sea shrimp, meatballs with jam, and, of course, herring.
*All locations in Manhattan. 53 STONE STREET BETWEEN BROAD STREET AND HANOVER SQUARE. 212-422-3500; 924 SECOND AVENUE AT 49TH STREET. 212-486-1411; 283 WEST 12TH STREET AT WEST 4TH STREET. 212-243-7073. For more details on locations and directions visit www.smorgaschef.com.*

# JAPANESE

**506.** Take a trip to *Village Yokocho.* This slice of Japan on Stuyvesant Street is like a quiet Tokyo neighborhood that has been transported to the second floor of a building in the East Village, incorporating a restaurant, bar, and grocery store. **Yajirobei**, the restaurant on the second floor, is lively and comfortable, and the food is authentic and delicious. Though the atmosphere is distinctly Japanese, the menu is pan-Asian and ranges from traditional fish, rice, and noodle dishes to skewered meats and vegetables, which you can eat seated at a wooden bar around the grill. Afterward, walk through the restaurant to the wooden door at the end, which discreetly leads into one of the East Village's best-kept secrets: **Angel's Share**, a dark, sophisticated cocktail bar with a Japanese accent and huge windows overlooking the street (bear in mind that you may have to wait in line: Angel's Share admits on a one-in/one-out basis). Right next door to Yajirobei, above the **St. Mark's Bookshop** (see, page 341), is the **Sunrise Mart**, New York's finest Japanese supermarket. Stocking everything from Japanese candy to fresh fish, fruit, vegetables, and prepared foods for lunch, it is the best place for authentic Japanese ingredients—and it's the most colorful grocery store in the city by a mile.

**Village Yokocho and Angel Share:** *8 STUYVESANT STREET BETWEEN THIRD AVENUE AND EAST 9TH STREET IN MANHATTAN. Villate Yokocho: 212-598-3041. Angel Share: 212-777-5415.*

**Sunrise Mart:** *4 STUYVESANT STREET BETWEEN THIRD AVENUE AND EAST 9TH STREET IN MANHATTAN. 212-598-3040. Subway: 6 to Astor Place.*

**507.** Have afternoon tea with an Eastern influence at *Cha An*, a peaceful refuge of restorative tea and freshly prepared food. At Cha An, tea is prepared and served in traditional Japanese style and with meticulous care and precision. Choose a tea from the extensive menu, which explains the background and flavor of each variety. Match it with one of the set teas, which include anything from a Japanese take on scones and clotted cream to fresh salmon, tea-infused rice cakes, vegetable dishes, and culture-clash desserts like a sesame seed–encrusted crème brulée. The staff is among the most courteous and thoughtful in the city; presentation is beautiful, and there is no calmer atmosphere in town. (Don't miss **Cha An's restrooms**—see page 351.)

*230 EAST 9TH STREET BETWEEN SECOND AND THIRD AVENUES IN MANHATTAN. Subway: 6 to Astor Place. 212-228-8030. www.cha-an.com.*

**508.** Eat where cultures meet at *Bond Street*. Situated above its trendy sister bar on a pretty cobbled street, Bond Street is beautifully laid out across two floors, with minimalist décor and low lighting that create a cool but surprisingly comfortable and lively atmosphere. The menu is a daring mix of traditional Japanese fish, sushi, and sashimi dishes, and rich, Western savory flavors: try the foie gras with seared tuna, the truffled arctic char, or the shrimp and bacon seaweed rolls.

*6 BOND STREET BETWEEN BROADWAY AND LAFAYETTE STREET IN MANHATTAN. Subway: 6 to Bleecker Street; B, D, F, V to Broadway-Lafayette Street; N, R, W to Prince Street. 212-777-2500.*

**509.** Brave the lines at *Tomoe Sushi*. Depression-era lines are usually enough to knock any restaurant out of consideration for this book, but as any local sushi fan will tell you, this reservation-adverse restaurant has the freshest ingredients in the city. If you want the highest quality sushi in the city, well, get in line.
*172 THOMPSON STREET BETWEEN BLEECKER AND HOUSTON STREETS. Subway: A, C, E, B, D, F, V to West 4th Street. 212-777-9346.*

**510.** Spend the night eating your fill at *Donguri*. This beautiful and stylish yet traditional Japanese restaurant is small enough to maintain a warm, cozy atmosphere, but offers food that is at once true to Japanese tradition and among the most sophisticated in the city. The décor is coolly soothing, with exposed brick walls and dark wood furniture, and the place feels like an oasis of calm amid the busy blocks of the Upper East Side. Every dish, from finely balanced sashimi to deliciously savory grilled meats and sweet boiled vegetables, is meticulously prepared and beautifully presented. Rather than ordering a full meal at once, the chef's recommendation is that you sit and order one or two dishes at a time. Ask for assorted sashimi, and cross your fingers that the day's special is oysters.
*309 EAST 83RD STREET BETWEEN FIRST AND SECOND AVENUES IN MANHATTAN. Subway: 4, 5, 6 to 86th Street. 212-737-5656.*

### 511. Meet a friend for a long, boozy lunch in the middle of the week at **Old Town Bar**.

The "timeless" (read: ungentrified) décor and crew of regulars at the bar are conducive to midweek drinking, and the high-backed wooden booths offer excellent cover in case your boss walks by.
*45 EAST 18TH STREET BETWEEN BROADWAY AND PARK AVENUE SOUTH IN MANHATTAN. Subway: 4, 5, 6, L, N, Q, R, W to 14th Street-Union Square. 212-529-6732.*

### 512. Pretend you're in the movie business at **Relish**.

A former restaurant that was closed for decades, it opened its doors only for directors and cameramen who used its classic interiors as sets for countless New York movies. Relish has reopened and is one of the nicest places in Brooklyn for late-night snacks or all-day breakfasts. Far enough from the Bedford strip to be quieter than most of Williamsburg's hip eateries but still good enough to warrant lines on a weekend, it's as big and spacious as something you'd find on a highway a thousand miles west of the city, and has a menu to fit. Classic diner dishes from eggs and omelets to burgers and tuna melts are infused with spicy Spanish and Cajun flavors, so even the comfort food packs a punch, and the milkshakes are particularly tasty. Come late, approaching the neon lights and the rounded chrome roof in the dark, and hunker down in a cozy booth—you'll feel like you're in a movie yourself. (Note: though Relish is a diner, it's not open round the clock. For our favorite **24-hour diners and eating establishments,** see page 335.)

*225 WYTHE STREET AT NORTH 3RD STREET IN BROOKLYN. Subway: L to Bedford Avenue. 718-963-4546.*

### 513. Have a different hot chocolate shot every day of February at **City Bakery**.

It sounds like a gimmick, but as anyone who's ever tried to take on a full cup can tell you, one shot is really all you need. City Bakery's hot chocolate is sinfully rich and deliriously tasty; a shot topped with one of their homemade marshmallows is pretty much the best thing going in the winter months. During hot chocolate month in February, they offer a different flavored variety every day.

*3 WEST 18TH STREET BETWEEN FIFTH AND SIXTH AVENUES IN MANHATTAN. Subway: 1 to 18th Street. 212-366-1414. www.thecitybakery.com.*

### 514. Turn any piece of candy into a special treat at **Wrappers Delight**.

Whether it's an exquisite chocolate from Jacques Torres or Maribelle, or a good old Swedish fish, you can buy it here and have it boxed, wrapped, ribboned, and bowed. If you just want to treat yourself, there are generous free samples of sticky, sweet, and scrumptious treats. (For more on **food freebies**, see page 285.)

*152 FIFTH AVENUE BETWEEN DEGRAW AND DOUGLASS STREETS IN BROOKLYN. Subway: 2, 3, 4, 5, B, Q to Atlantic Avenue; D, M, R to Atlantic Avenue-Pacific Street; N to Pacific Street. 718-399-6400. www.wrappersdelight.org.*

### 515. Have a cheese plate at **Artisanal**, New York's undisputed favorite fromagerie. This Midtown bistro is dedicated to cheese, from hundreds of varieties available in the cheese cave to the dishes on the menu, which include addictive *gougères* (French cheese puffs), macaroni and cheese, and excellent fondues. For a real treat, go to the cheese counter, and have them fix you a personalized plate. But take our advice and plan carefully, or risk waking up the next morning with a fromage hangover.

*2 PARK AVENUE AT 32ND STREET IN MANHATTAN. Subway: 6 to 33rd Street. 212-725-8585.*

### 516. Check out a new restaurant during **Restaurant Week**.

Though we've got four-star restaurants, plenty of celebrity chefs, and some famously inventive cooking, the prices (or the month-long waits for reservations) discourage many of us from trying them out. But twice a year, New Yorkers get a chance to taste what the critics are writing about. During the two Restaurant Weeks, usually held in January and July, restaurants all over the city—from the fanciest and the trendiest to neighborhood joints and old-time classics—offer prix-fixe three-course meals at lunch and/or dinner for bargain prices (around $20 for lunch, $35 for dinner). How good a deal it is depends on the restaurant and your taste, and reservations at the more upscale places can still be tough to get. But a three-course meal for under $40 anywhere in the city is a pretty good deal.

*For more information, dates, prices, and a list of participating restaurants, visit www.NYCVisit.com.*

---

## 517. Vive l'apéritif!

Apéritif à la Francaise is a relatively low-profile annual festival that promotes French food and culture. That means free nibbles and goodies at participating New York bars and restaurants, as well as parties, tastings, and other special events.

*Held for one week in June. For information, participating venues, and a schedule of events, visit www.frenchcocktailhour.com.*

---

## 518. Dinner and a song at Asia Roma . . .

There are plenty of good karaoke spots around town, but this restaurant and underground karaoke bar on the cusp of Chinatown and Little Italy has a unique bicultural flair. Look out for the resident house singer, a veritable Chinese Sinatra in white gloves, who is only too happy to step up to the mic when the crowd falls quiet.

*40 MULBERRY STREET BETWEEN BAYARD AND WORTH STREETS IN MANHATTAN. Subway: 1 to Franklin Street; A, C, E to Canal Street. 212-385-1133.*

## 519. . . . or if you're looking for a seedier sing-song, head to Winnie's,

a smaller bar near the courthouse, where Winnie, the glamorous proprietress, presides over a colorful cast of karaoke characters who rock the mic in Mandarin and Michael Jackson.

*104 BAYARD STREET BETWEEN MULBERRY AND BAXTER STREETS IN MANHATTAN. Subway: A, C, E to Canal Street. 212-732-2384.*

---

## Feast on bar snacks . . .

Bar owners struggle like aspiring Broadway stars to make it on the NYC nightlife scene, so it should come as no surprise that they even get creative about the snacks they serve. Forgo peanuts and potato chips and sample some of following bar-top delights:

**520. *Hot dogs at Rudy's Bar & Grill.*** Unbelievably, this old-school, red-leather, jukebox-sporting dive bar dispenses free hot dogs—as many as you want, whenever you want them. Order seven, just because you can, then eat them off a paper plate in the pig-themed backyard with a pitcher of Rudy's special red beer. Around $3 a pint, that's a bargain in itself.

*627 NINTH AVENUE BETWEEN 44TH AND 45TH STREETS IN MANHATTAN. Subway: 1, 2, 3, 7, N, Q, R, S to Times Square-42nd Street; A, C, E to 42nd Street-Port Authority Bus Terminal. 212-974-9169. Note: If the grill is empty at Rudy's, head down a block to Circus (615 Ninth Avenue), which is also owned by the Rudy's folks and offers the same free dogs.*

**521. *Goldfish crackers and wasabi peas at Tom & Jerry.*** If you don't see them on the bar, ask the bartender and you'll get a huge bowl of good old-fashioned Goldfish crackers and wasabi peas to help your beer go down.

*288 ELIZABETH STREET BETWEEN HOUSTON AND BLEECKER STREETS IN MANHATTAN. Subway: 6 to Bleecker Street; B, D, F, V to Broadway-Lafayette Street. 212-274-8787.*

**522. *Pizza at Buttermilk.*** On Wednesday nights (and on the occasional quiet Sunday), the staff at this friendly Park Slope bar order pizza from a local take-out place for all to enjoy. To go with your slice, ask for Connect 4, Battleship, or any of the classic board games kept behind the bar, and then grab a booth for a low-key, low-cost evening out.

*577 FIFTH AVENUE AT 16TH STREET IN BROOKLYN. Subway: F to 15th Street-Prospect Park. 718-788-6297.*

## . . . or get dinner **delivered to the bar** where you're drinking.

Sometimes you need something more substantial than snacks while you're drinking. Like everywhere else, many New York restaurants have bar menus, and many bars have kitchens. But if you prefer something simple and greasy, you're in luck, too. Plenty of laid-back dives keep a stack of delivery menus behind the bar; all you have to do is ask. They're happy to have you order in from a neighborhood joint if it keeps you drinking there. What you get depends on the area, but when you're two sheets to the wind, it's hard to go wrong with pizza or Chinese. However, there are some bars that benefit from their proximity to some particularly good take-out grub. Two good pairings:

**523.** Drinking beer in the garden at the ***Gate,*** and ordering fish and chips wrapped in newspaper from the **ChipShop** (see page 189).

*321 FIFTH AVENUE AT 3RD STREET IN BROOKLYN. Subway: F to 4th Avenue; M, R to 9th Street. Phone: 718-768-4329.*

**524.** Drinking and listening to bands at the legendary **Arlene's Grocery,** and ordering hot sandwiches from **Katz's** (see page 169).
*95 STANTON STREET BETWEEN LUDLOW AND ORCHARD STREETS IN MANHATTAN. Subway : F, V to Lower East Side-Second Avenue. 212-995-1652. www.arlenesgrocery.net.*

## 525. Find **Freeman's**.

Freeman's is an unusual restaurant in every way, a hidden treasure among the hipster hangouts on the Lower East Side. Finding it is part of the fun: turn off Rivington Street just west of the Bowery onto Freeman Alley. The giant wooden doors at the alley's end open into one of the coolest and most inviting restaurants in the city. The real treat, however, is the spectacular display of taxidermy that decorates the walls. Depending on what you order, you may find a relative of your supper staring down at you while you eat.
*END OF FREEMAN ALLEY, OFF RIVINGTON STREET, BETWEEN BOWERY AND CHRYSTIE STREET IN MANHATTAN. Subway: F to Delancey Street; J, M, Z to Essex Street. 212-420-0012. www.freemansrestaurant.com.*

## 526. Thursday night spaghetti and meatballs at **Frank**.

Show up early for free antipasti, and stay late for the lightest atmosphere this side of the Mediterranean. Spaghetti's not the only thing on the menu, but we recommend you take advantage of their celebrated Thursday night special and try the fresh, flavorful meatballs.
*88 SECOND AVENUE BETWEEN 4TH AND 5TH STREETS IN MANHATTAN. Subway: F, V to Lower East Side-Second Avenue. 212-420-0202. www.frankrestaurant.com.*

## 527. Treat yourself to boeuf bourgignon at the counter of **Chez Brigitte**.

Eating out alone is commonplace in this city, and you can find solo diners enjoying their meals at restaurants all over town. But the truly intimate Chez Brigitte (they can seat fewer than a dozen diners at a time) elevates the experience of eating alone to fine dining. Here, single diners are in the majority, and are not treated like second-class citizens. Instead of tossing them appetizers at the bar, Chez Brigitte treats their mostly solo clientele to French "comfort food" at very reasonable prices; the $8 boeuf bourgignon is among the best deals in town.
*77 GREENWICH AVENUE AT SEVENTH AVENUE SOUTH IN MANHATTAN. Subway: 1, 2, 3 to 14th Street; A, C, E, B, D, F, V to West 4th Street. 212-929-6736.*

### 528. Play bocce while you drink at **Floyd NY**.

In true melting-pot style, this unpretentious Brooklyn bar serves bourbon and beercheese and also sports an indoor bocce court. Try your hand on the forty-foot clay court while you munch on the Kentucky beercheese, a highly addictive blend of cheese, beer, and spices.

*131 ATLANTIC AVENUE BETWEEN HENRY AND CLINTON STREETS IN BROOKLYN. Subway: 2, 3, 4, 5 to Borough Hall; N, R to Court Street-Borough Hall. 718-858-5810. www.floydny.com.*

### 529. Eat lamb by the fireplace at **Patois**.

One of Brooklyn's best French restaurants, this Carroll Gardens bistro gets unusually young and tender lamb through a special arrangement with a farmer upstate. Dishes like the rustic rack of lamb and the minted lamb shank are complemented and intensified by the smell of softly burning wood from the fireplace.

*255 SMITH STREET BY DEGRAW STREET IN BROOKLYN. Subway: F to Carroll Street. 718-855-1535. www.patoisrestaurant.com.*

### 530. Let sake bring out your literary inclinations, and compose poems on the wall at **Decibel**.

Though this underground sake den has an illicit feel, go ahead and write on the walls. They're cool.

*240 EAST 9TH STREET BETWEEN SECOND AND THIRD AVENUES IN MANHATTAN. Subway: 6 to Astor Place; L to Third Avenue; N, R to 8th Street-New York University. 212-979-2733.*

### 531. Have lunch in the **Delegates Dining Room** at the UN.

Forget Nobu—if you really want to impress someone, take him or her to lunch at the Delegates Dining Room at the **UN** (see page 19). Though it's open to the public (with reservations), this refined commissary feels elite, exclusive, cosmopolitan, and miles away from Midtown midday madness (perhaps that's because the UN is technically an international territory). For $25, you get an abundant lunch buffet, as well as the chance to rub shoulders with some real international superstars—plus a superb view, courtesy of the wall-to-ceiling windows that overlook the East River.

*Lunch is served weekdays from 11:30 a.m. to 2:30 p.m. Reservations should be made a day in advance by calling 212-963-7625. No jeans or sneakers allowed; jacket required for men. All diners must bring a photo ID. Use the visitor's entrance on FIRST AVENUE AT 46TH STREET IN MANHATTAN. Subway: 4, 5, 6, 7, S to Grand Central-42nd Street. For more information, visit www.aramark-un.com or www.un.org.*

## 532. Feed nature and yourself at the **New Leaf Café** . . .

Set in a stone structure between the **Cloisters** (see page 120) and the main entrance of Fort Tryon Park, the New Leaf Café is a uniquely pleasant dining experience that benefits more than just your stomach. Proceeds from the café support the upkeep of the park.

*ONE MARGARET CORBIN DRIVE, FORT TRYON PARK IN MANHATTAN. Subway: A to 190th Street. 212-568-5323. www.nyrp.org/newleaf.*

## 533. . . .or feed your sweet tooth for a good cause at the **Sweet Things Bake Shop**.

This shop is run by the Lower East Side Girls Club, and all the goodies here are made by girls enrolled in an entrepreneurial baking program, Sweet Things. So the cookie you buy supports educational and skill-building programs for local children. And who knows—the girl who baked it might go on to be New York's next master chef.

*136 AVENUE C BETWEEN 8TH AND 9TH STREETS IN MANHATTAN. Subway: L to First Avenue. 212-982-1714. www.girlsclub.org/programs/SweetThings05.html.*

## Slices of New York.

Though we didn't come up with it ourselves, pizza was long ago adopted by New Yorkers and raised as one of our own. The ingenious invention of Italian immigrants more than a century ago, pizza is the perfect meeting of old Italian cuisine and the New York lifestyle. While it can be found all over the world, and different places have different styles, we know that our version is the best. There are pizzerias and take-out pizza parlors all over the five boroughs, and with so many varieties of pie out there, we thought we'd throw in our two cents and give you a shortlist of what we consider the ten best pizzas in town (also see **Lombardi's**, on page 48):

**534. *Arturo's:*** Almost as old as **Lombardi's**, and almost as good, eating at Arturo's feels like being in a friend's kitchen.
*106 WEST HOUSTON STREET AT THOMPSON STREET IN MANHATTAN. Subway: 6 to Bleecker Street; B, D, F, V to Broadway-Lafayette Street. 212-677-3820.*

**535. *Grimaldi's:*** You can't get pizza like this in Manhattan—really—the coal ovens they use are illegal in the borough. Go for the meat toppings.
*19 OLD FULTON STREET UNDER THE BROOKLYN BRIDGE IN BROOKLYN. Subway: A, C to High Street. 718-858-4300. www.grimaldis.com/Brooklyn.htm.*

**536. John's of Bleecker Street:** Legendarily delicious pies, but remember: they don't sell by the slice.
*278 BLEECKER STREET BETWEEN SIXTH AND SEVENTH AVENUES IN MANHATTAN. Subway: 1 to Christopher Street-Sheridan Square; A, C, E, B, D, F, V to West 4th Street. 212-243-1680. www.johnsofbleeckerstreet.com.*

**537. Full Moon:** What looks like an unremarkable pie-by-the-slice parlor serves some of the tastiest pizzas in the city.
*600 EAST 187TH STREET AT ARTHUR AVENUE IN THE BRONX. See page 186 for full directions. 718-584-3451.*

**538. L'asso:** This unassuming pizzeria on the fringes of Little Italy has delicious pies with surprising toppings: try the smoked tartufo.
*192 MOTT STREET AT KENMARE STREET IN MANHATTAN. Subway: 6 to Spring Street; F to Delancey Street; J, M, Z to Essex Street. 212-219-2353. www.lassonyc.com.*

**539. Franny's:** The garden at this popular spot is as comfortable as your own backyard—if your backyard served some of the best pizza in the city.
*FLATBUSH AVENUE BETWEEN ST. MARK'S AVENUE AND PROSPECT PLACE IN BROOKLYN. Subway: 2, 3 to Bergen Street; B, Q to Seventh Avenue. 718-230-0221. www.frannysbrooklyn.com.*

**540. Pie by the Pound:** It might not look like much, but the pizza here is surprisingly good and extremely filling. Good for a hefty snack.
*Both locations in Manhattan. 1542 SECOND AVENUE BETWEEN 80TH AND 81ST STREETS. Subway: 4, 5, 6 to 86th Street. 212-517-5017; 124 FOURTH AVENUE BETWEEN 12TH AND 13TH STREETS. Subway: 4, 5, 6, L, N, Q, R, W to 14th Street-Union Square. 212-475-4977. www.piebythepound.com.*

**541. Patsy's:** Another of the oldest pizzerias in the city, Patsy's represents the upper crust with amazing ingredients, perfectly cooked pies, and great salads.
*Multiple locations. Call 212-688-5916 or visit patsyspizzeriany.com for specific addresses and information.*

**542. Joe's:** Pizza that manages to be both incredibly crispy and amazingly heavy with cheese and toppings.
*7 CARMINE STREET AT SIXTH AVENUE IN MANHATTAN. Subway: A, C, E, B, D, F, V to West 4th Street. 212-255-3946.*

**543.** *Viva Herbal Pizzeria:* Pizza purists should not scoff at Viva's unconventional vegetarian pizzas. The monstrous slices are just as messy as those at any of the other joints on our list, and they certainly don't taste virtuous. Try a slice with green tea-infused tofu, mountains of vegetables, and pesto on a spelt crust. (Viva's is kosher, too.)
*179 SECOND AVENUE BETWEEN 11TH AND 12TH STREETS IN MANHATTAN. Subway: L to First or Third Avenues. 212-420-8801.*

CHAPTER 6:

# The Great Outdoors

Despite being the greatest metropolis in the world, New York isn't all sidewalks and skyscrapers. We've got an ocean, rivers, lakes, wildlife refuges, and nearly 30,000 acres of parks and gardens across the five boroughs—not bad for a place known as a concrete jungle. In addition, we've got plenty of people with different athletic pursuits and passions; the same diversity and vivaciousness that's responsible for the city's wide variety of arts and culture also colors the out-of-doors, so along with all of the traditional activities (baseball, basketball, running, cycling, and gardening), we've got cricket leagues, bocce tournaments, and a trapeze school.

In this chapter, we cover the best of outdoor fun, including parks and gardens; nature, wildlife, and zoos; water-related activities; and outdoor sports. One of the interesting things about outdoor activities in New York is how, in different ways, they combine the available natural resources—rivers, beaches, the ocean, and green spaces—with the unique qualities the city has to offer. Outdoor activities in New York are not pathetic, shrunken versions of their natural selves; rather, they are adapted for and enhanced by the particular conditions of city living. We have special Urban Rangers to protect our parks, a state-of-the-art riverfront sports complex on top of a waste treatment plant, and excellent beaches and golf courses only a subway ride away. In fact, one of the most amazing things about the outdoor pursuits around the city is how easily accessible they are. You don't need a car or a long weekend to visit a wildlife center, or go horseback riding, surfing, or canoeing—every activity you can imagine is right here.

Another wonderful part of New York's outdoor culture is how we turn some urban, typically indoor activities outside when the weather gets nice. Outdoor movies, yoga and tai chi classes, concerts, readings, and fairs and festivals abound during the warmer months (for street fairs and festivals, see chapter 3). Enjoying the arts al fresco can also be a great way to see exciting, world-renowned performances without breaking the bank, since many of these events are free.

There is a wealth of opportunities for enjoying the outdoors across the five boroughs, all year long, from cross-country skiing in the streets after a blizzard to swimming in the ocean or one of the city's public pools during the dog days of summer. The activities we've listed below are the best of hundreds we discovered all over town. So next time you hear someone talking about the lack of open spaces and natural beauty here, just take them outside.

## Parks & Gardens

No matter where you are in New York, you're never far from greenery or floral beauty. There are more than 1,700 parks across the city, including playgrounds and ball fields as well as forests and woodlands, and many exquisite gardens, from the botanic gardens found in three of the five boroughs (Brooklyn, the Bronx, and Staten Island) to the lovely community gardens maintained by various volunteer and neighborhood groups.

These bucolic oases are perfect for unstructured retreats, but they also offer organized activities that anyone can take advantage of. The Parks Department, which oversees all of the city parks, runs sports lessons and education programs for kids and adults, gives walks and tours, and puts on hundreds of events, most of which are free. Their Web site (www.nyc.gov/parks) has a list of facilities and programs for all of the parks in the five boroughs, plus maps, opening hours, calendars of events, and much more.

### 544. Stop and **smell the flowers** all around the city.

If you think that the freshest flowers in New York come from the **Greenmarket** (see page 169), you're in for a shock. Our parks have a surprising amount of floral variety. The Parks Department has created a Citywide Blooming Guide, so you can find out what's in bloom and where to find it. This online guide lists the names of local flora and where they are located (with pictures, for novices), arranged by month. Pick a park, and then see how many you can identify; or, when you come across an unfamiliar blossom in an unlikely place, look it up on the site.

*www.nycgovparks.org/sub_things_to_do/highlights/blooming_calendar/citywide_ blooming_calendar.html*

### 545. Get inside **Gramercy Park**.

This old-fashioned and entirely undemocratic gated park is an exceptional detail on the New York City landscape, and its exclusivity is part of its charm—and history. In 1831, Samuel Ruggles purchased a piece of swampland to develop into real estate. At the time, few New Yorkers wanted to live so far uptown, but Ruggles attracted an elite demographic with the creation of a pristine private park reserved for residents of his development, believing that the well-heeled would be enticed by the promise of a beautiful, well-manicured outdoor space in Manhattan (this was two decades before Central Park) that was off-limits to the less fortunate. Today it is still New York's only private park, belonging, as per Ruggles's arrangement, to the inhabitants of the homes and apartments surrounding it as a sort of shared front yard. Each building is allotted a certain number of park keys, which residents (renters and owners) are free to use; additional keys for individual residents may be purchased for $350 each. Key holders are understandably protective of their pristine outdoor space, so there are plenty of rules on permissible activities, conduct, and entrants. But though it doesn't welcome the type of freewheeling fun you'll find in most parks, it does offer a rare sense of calm and is a true urban escape—to anyone who can get in. The park is open to the public on Christmas Day, Yom Kippur, and on certain other days of the year for neighborhood events. Otherwise, you'll have to make friends with someone with a home around the park. Just don't try to sneak in behind a key holder—they tend to get litigious.

*20TH TO 21ST STREETS BETWEEN LEXINGTON AVENUE AND IRVING PLACE IN MANHATTAN. Subway: 6 to 23rd Street.*

---

### 546. Walk the length of the **Battery Park City parks**, and explore all the secret coves and hidden harbors along the way.

The parks, pathways, and gardens of Battery Park City cover a long and scenic stretch of the lower West Side, running beside the Hudson River from Wagner Park at the southernmost tip of Manhattan to Rockefeller Park and the piers around Chambers Street. While Battery Park City is a burgeoning neighborhood of new apartments, quiet offices, and cultural offerings, the parks along the Hudson remain relatively peaceful and extremely pleasant to roam around. As well as the popular tree-lined esplanades, there are a number of lesser-known and almost hidden gardens that are great fun to discover along the way. Look out for the old cast-iron benches hidden in the trees above the pathway at South Cove, the chess tables in Rector Park, and the secret "scholar's garden" off the busy harbor at North Cove. There are also some interesting **public artworks**—for more on those, see page 142.

*BATTERY PARK CITY PARKS FROM WAGNER PARK TO ROCKEFELLER PARK IN MANHATTAN. Subway: 1, 2, 3, A, C to Chambers Street (to walk south along the water); 1 to Rector Street (to walk north along the water). www.bpcparks.org.*

---

### 547. Listen to **jazz outdoors** in two of the city's nicest parks.

In honor of Charlie Parker, one of the jazz world's greatest and most lasting influences, a full weekend in late summer each year is devoted to the music he wrote, played, and inspired. Because Parker divided his working life between Harlem and the East Village, the **Charlie Parker Jazz Festival** begins on Saturday in Marcus Garvey Park and concludes on Sunday in Tompkins Square Park. Although the event draws some of the best and most respected new talent in the world to its stage—recent players have included Vanessa Rubin, Jimmy Heath, and Geri Allen—the weekend is all about being outside in the fresh air, and the musicians seem to enjoy the summer sunshine as much as the audiences. The festival takes place at the same time as the **Howl! Festival** (see page 85), so there are plenty of other things going on in the neighborhood that weekend as well.

*The Charlie Parker Jazz Festival is held annually on the last weekend in August. Marcus Garvey Park is just south of 125th Street in Harlem. Subway: 2, 3, 4, 5, 6 to 125th Street. Tomkins Square Park is between Avenues A and B, running from East 7th to East 10th Streets. Subway: F, V to Lower East Side-Second Avenue; L to First or Third Avenues. www.cityparksfoundation.org.*

---

### 548. Sunbathe on the promenade in **Hudson River Park**.

You can stay on the "shore" (i.e., the promenade and the grassy lawns behind it), or pick a pier and stretch out surrounded by water.

*WEST SIDE OF MANHATTAN BETWEEN 59TH STREET AND BATTERY PARK. Subway: A, C, E to 14th Street, 34th Street, 42nd Street-Port Authority Bus Terminal, or 59th Street; 1 to Christopher Street-Sheridan Square, Houston Street, Franklin Street, or Chambers Street.*

---

### 549. Skip stones on the water between the Brooklyn and Manhattan Bridges at **Brooklyn Bridge Park**.

This small, little-known public space on the Brooklyn shore was rejuvenated in 2003 and is now one of the most beautiful parks in the city—and one of the only places that brings you within touching distance of the water of the East River. With dramatic views of the bridges, the East River, and the Manhattan skyline in front, and with the striking remains of a nineteenth-century tobacco warehouse and the storehouses of DUMBO behind, the park is a refreshing place to spend an afternoon. Unstructured leisure activities like aimless strolls and skipping stones are great ways to appreciate the gorgeous scenery and secluded feel, but should you desire something more organized, the park hosts a bevy of outdoor events, including **outdoor movies** (see page 212), **yoga classes** (see page 225), performances, and firework displays.

*EAST RIVER BETWEEN THE BROOKLYN AND MANHATTAN BRIDGES IN BROOKLYN. Subway: 2, 3 to Clark Street; A, C to High Street; F to York Street. For more information on the park and development project, call 718-802-0603 or visit www.bbpc.net.*

## Borrow a neighborhood park for a **moment of calm**.

They may be big, green, and beautiful, but on a pretty weekend day, the big parks like **Central** and **Prospect** (see pages 216 and 219) and some of the others listed in this chapter are anything but peaceful. But there are many smaller parks that make excellent escapes from the city hubbub, no matter the day or time. The best are hidden in residential areas, frequented only by locals or those in the know. Here are several particularly beautiful, lesser-known parks and gardens tucked away from busy streets and avenues.

**550. *Cobble Hill Park:*** Pick up a coffee and a pain au chocolat at Delicatessen on the corner and then enjoy your breakfast in the park. *VERANDAH PLACE BETWEEN CONGRESS AND CLINTON STREETS IN BROOKLYN. Subway: F, G to Bergen Street.*

**551. *Tudor City Gardens:*** A peaceful retreat from 42nd Street, and the perfect lunch spot for Midtown's desk-bound workers. *SECOND AVENUE AT 42ND STREET IN MANHATTAN. Subway: 4, 5, 6, 7, S to Grand Central-42nd Street.*

**552. *Gardens of Saint John the Divine:*** The grounds are as striking and serene as the Cathedral itself, with herbs, a fountain, a rose garden, and peacocks in the summertime. *1047 AMSTERDAM AVENUE NEAR 110TH STREET IN MANHATTAN. Subway: 1 to 110th Street; B, C to Cathedral Parkway (110th Street). 212-316-7490. www.stjohndivine.org.*

**553. *Liz Christy Gardens:*** The first community garden in New York, named for the local gardener whose efforts brought the park to life more than thirty years ago. *EAST HOUSTON STREET AND BOWERY IN MANHATTAN. Subway: F, V to Lower East Side-Second Avenue. www.lizchristygarden.org.*

**554. *City Hall Park:*** Legend has it that Jack London lived rough for a while in this pretty downtown park, earning his way by telling stories around the fountain at night. *BETWEEN BROADWAY, PARK ROW, AND CHAMBERS STREET IN MANHATTAN. Subway: 4, 5, 6 to Brooklyn Bridge-City Hall; J, M, Z to Chambers Street.*

## 555. Climb the steps in **Morningside Park**.

Carved into the dramatic rock face that defines one side of the park, the steps that lead up to Amsterdam Avenue are a rugged reminder of the city's natural foundations. While you're catching your breath at the top, relax on a bench and gaze out over Harlem. The view is well worth the trek.
*MORNINGSIDE AVENUE AT 110TH STREET IN MANHATTAN. Subway: 1 to Cathedral Parkway (110th Street); B, C to Cathedral Parkway (110th Street).*

## 556. Check out the foliage at **Wave Hill** in Riverdale.

This twenty-eight-acre garden and cultural center includes ten acres of second-growth forest and plenty of native plants and trees. Homesick New Englanders and foliage junkies can celebrate nature's fireworks here each September during the annual Plant Pigment Weekend, with walks, garden demonstrations, and other activities. Afterward, you can check out a nature-focused art exhibit at the Glyndor Gallery, explore the grounds (which include Wave Hill House, a former residence of Mark Twain and the Roosevelts), or enjoy a picnic.

*WEST 249TH STREET AND INDEPENDENCE AVENUE IN THE BRONX. Subway: 1 to 231st Street; A to 207th Street, then Bx 7 or Bx 10 bus. Open year-round, Tuesday through Sunday, though hours vary seasonally. Admission: adults $4, students and seniors $2. Free on Tuesdays and Saturdays from 9:00 a.m. to 12:00 p.m., and throughout December, January, and February. For information on visiting, programs, and hours, call 718-549-3200. www.wavehill.org.*

## 557. Watch a cricket match in **Van Cortlandt Park**.

Believe it or not, cricket's popularity in the U.S. once rivaled that of baseball, and legend has it that Mayor Van Cortlandt designated a portion of his Bronx estate for the purpose of playing cricket. Today, the park that bears his name has thirteen cricket pitches, where you can watch area leagues and teams play this elaborate gentleman's sport. In addition to cricket, the nearly 1,150-acre park has a track stadium, the city's **oldest golf course** (see page 232), a freshwater lake (the Bronx's largest), as well as fields for soccer, football, bocce, and, of course, baseball.

*WEST 240TH STREET AND BROADWAY IN THE BRONX. Subway: 1 to Van Cortlandt Park-242nd Street; 4 to Woodlawn.*

→ **DID YOU KNOW?** *Stephanus Van Cortlandt was New York's first native-born mayor, who ran the city from 1677 to 1678 and 1686 to 1688.*

## 558. Take a breather by the **Ghandi statue** in Union Square Park.

The surrounding garden acts as a buffer from the traffic on 14th Street, and the beautiful statue depicting the beloved pacifist will smooth over any rage of the day.

*UNION SQUARE PARK WEST BETWEEN 14TH AND 15TH STREETS. Subway: 4, 5, 6, L, N, Q, R, W to 14th Street-Union Square.*

## 559. Soak up the rays beneath the "**LONG ISLAND**" and "**PEPSI-COLA**" signs.

You know the ones—you see them all the time across the East River from Manhattan. They're relics from the area's former incarnation as an industrial center, which has been transformed into a waterfront park. If you go early enough on a warm day, you can snag a wooden chaise lounge underneath these beloved New York landmarks. The park is also a great place to **watch the fireworks** on July 4 (see page 26).

**GANTRY PLAZA STATE PARK.** *474 48TH AVENUE IN QUEENS. Subway: E, V to 23rd Street-Ely Avenue; 7 to 45 Road-Court House Square; G to Long Island City-Court Square.*

## 560. Surf the net at **Bryant Park** . . .

How appropriate that this Midtown oasis is hooked up for wireless Internet access. On a warm summer day (when the boss is out of the office for the afternoon), take your laptop and work at one of the little tables or sprawl out on the lawn for as long as your battery lasts. (Sorry, no wireless outlets yet.)

*40TH TO 42ND STREETS BETWEEN FIFTH AND SIXTH AVENUES IN MANHATTAN. Subway: 7 to Fifth Avenue-Bryant Park; B, D, F, V to 42nd Street-Bryant Park. www.bryantpark.org.*

### 561. . . . or downtown.

The Downtown Alliance, a community advocacy group, has rigged eight downtown "hot spots" for Wi-Fi, including the South Street Seaport and the **Winter Garden** in the World Financial Center (see page 350).

*For more information and exact locations, check the map at www.downtownny.com.*

## Cinema al fresco

The Big Apple's answer to the classic small-town drive-in is the summer movie series shown in different parks around New York. They are one of the most universally beloved of the city's outdoor activities, and why not? They're fun, free, and an easy, pleasant way to spend a couple of hours in the outdoors, especially after a long day cooped up inside. A few good ones:

**562. *Bryant Park:*** Probably the best known (and most consistently crowded) of the outdoor movie series. During the ten-week series (late June through August), classic films are screened on the lawn each Monday. The film starts at dusk (usually 8:00 or 9:00 p.m.), but the lawn opens to blanketers at 5:00 p.m., and it's best to get there early and bring a picnic. The park's proximity to Midtown means that it gets pretty packed on not-toostifling summer nights, but it's a great way to see classics like *The Philadel-phia Story, Rear Window,* or *Jaws* on the big screen. (Though screenings tend to be crowded, a perk of this festival is **ample and clean restrooms**—for more information, see page 351.)

*For address, see opposite. Subway: 7 to Fifth Avenue-Bryant Park; B, D, F, V to 42nd Street-Bryant Park. For schedules and information, call 212-768-4242 or visit www.bryantpark.org.*

**563. *RiverFlicks at Hudson River Park:*** RiverFlicks runs two outdoor film series each summer, from the beginning of July through August. On Wednesday nights, they show general movies on an annual theme, and on Friday nights there's a special kids' series. The films are shown on Piers 46 (near 10th Street) and 54 (near 14th Street), and there is seating and free pop-corn! (Showtime is at dusk. There are public restrooms in the park.)

*For address and directions, see page 209. For schedules and information, call 212-627-2020 or visit www.hudsonriverpark.org.*

**564. *Movies with a View at Brooklyn Bridge Park:*** A themed six-week series takes place at this lovely waterfront park. A DJ starts spinning tunes at 6:00 p.m.; movies start at dusk. Free popcorn, too! (Restrooms located near the park's entrance, off Water Street.)

*For address and directions, see page 209. For schedules and information, call 718-802-0603 or visit www.bbpc.net.*

**565.** You can also attend the ***grand finale of the Manhattan Short Film Festival***, which is held each September in Union Square. Films are shown on multiple screens throughout the park, and after the screening, viewers can vote for their favorite, and the winner is announced.

*September. FROM 14TH AND 17TH STREETS BETWEEN BROADWAY AND PARK AVENUE IN MANHATTAN. Subway: 4, 5, 6, L, N, Q, R, W to 14th Street-Union Square. For schedules and information, call 212-529-8640 or visit www.msfilmfest.com.*

## Outdoor Music

Like the movies, outdoor concerts are an excellent way to enjoy the out-of-doors in an otherwise urban environment. On evenings and weekends during warmer months, it's hard to find a park that *doesn't* have some music going on, with informal performances by musicians of all kinds playing for your aural enjoyment. Many parks, of course, have extensive, organized concert series, such as:

**566. *Summerstage:*** A legend, an institution, the festival that started it all. Since 1986, Summerstage has been putting on excellent free events in Central Park all summer long. The schedule also includes dance performances, spoken word events, and a few films, but most of the offerings are musical performances that run the gamut from rock and pop, to classical and instrumental, to experimental, and tributes. Admission is first-come, first-served, so be prepared to line up for more popular acts.

*Concerts are held in Central Park on Rumsey Playfield. For more information, visit www.summerstage.org or call 212-360-2756.*

**567. *Philharmonic in the Park:*** Every year, the **New York Philharmonic** (for full entry, see page 150) performs outdoor concerts in parks around the five boroughs. They're both an opportunity to hear the Philharmonic for free and a pleasant way to enjoy a summer evening outside, with soundtrack provided. Tip: the real classical music aficionados tend to sit in the front, and the atmosphere generally gets increasingly more relaxed the further back you go.

*For more information, call 212-875-5656 or visit www.newyorkphilharmonic.org.*

**568. *Met in the Park:*** Like the Philharmonic, **the Met** (see page 149) performs two operas from its current season at a park in each of the boroughs.

*For more information, call 212-362-6000 or visit www.metopera.org.*

**569.** During the ***River to River*** festival, there are free concerts and musical performances of all kinds almost daily all summer long, at eight lower Manhattan parks.

*For more information, call 212-627-2020 or visit www.rivertorivernyc.com.*

**570. *Bryant Park*** hosts several different concert and music series each summer, including "Broadway in Bryant Park," "Piano in the Park," and, for early birds, the *Good Morning America* concert series (start time is 7:00 a.m.).

*For more information, call 212-768-4242 or visit www.bryantpark.org.*

**571. *Lincoln Center Out of Doors***, a series of free concerts and performances at Lincoln Center Plaza in August and September, is an annual part of **Lincoln Center Presents** (for full entry, see page 151). One of the highlights is Midsummer Night Swing, a month long outdoor dance party featuring different bands each night.

*For more information, call 212-875-5000 or visit www.lincolncenter.org.*

## 572. Commune with nature at the New York Botanical Gardens.

The largest and best known of the city's three botanical gardens, this 250-acre park has rivers and ponds, hills, rocks, and fifty acres of preserved forest—not to mention forty-eight separate gardens. Take a day and lose yourself in these dramatic and beautiful natural surroundings.

*200TH STREET AND KAZIMIROFF BOULEVARD IN THE BRONX. Subway: 4 to Bedford Park Boulevard-Lehman College; B, D to Bedford Park Boulevard, then Bx 26 bus east to Garden entrance gate. NYBG is also accessible by Metro-North; take the Harlem line to Botanical Garden station. 718-817-8700. www.nybg.org.*

## Brooklyn Botanic Garden

It's hard to believe that this exquisite, vividly colored piece of land was the site of an ash dump in the nineteenth century. Though not as large as the gardens in the Bronx, there's more than enough floral beauty here to make you forget your urban troubles. Here are our favorite spots.

*1000 WASHINGTON AVENUE IN BROOKLYN. Subway: B, Q to Prospect Park; 2, 3 to Eastern Parkway-Brooklyn Museum. 718-623-7200. www.bbg.org.*

### 573. Follow the Celebrity Path. Brooklyn's answer to Hollywood's Walk of Fame, featuring plaques for famous Brooklynites. Harvey Keitel is from Brooklyn? Who knew? (New names are added on "Welcome Back to Brooklyn" Day each June.)

### 574. Test your sense of smell in the Fragrance Garden.
Originally designed as a place of beauty for the blind, this garden is full of the most wonderfully scented plants around, from chocolate flowers to spearmint leaves and herbs.

### 575. Take a walk down the Cherry Esplanade around bloom time.
The site of more than 200 blossoming cherry trees is the perfect way to celebrate spring's arrival. The annual *sakura matsuri* (cherry blossom festival) is one of the garden's most beloved events, a weekend-long Japan-themed celebration that includes samurai sword demonstrations!

### 576. Go to Bluebell Wood in May.
A lesser-known rival of to the Cherry Esplanade, Bluebell Wood is a beautiful, secluded spot just south of the cherries that is transformed into the most magical, enchanted glade every spring, when more than 45,000 blue-

bells cover the forest floor in color. A path wanders between magnificent old oak, birch, and beech trees, and for a stretch of the way, you find yourself surrounded by nothing but bright blues and violets.

**577.** Lose yourself in thought in the Chinese Scholar's Garden, or just lose yourself in Connie Gretz's Secret Garden at the **Staten Island Botanical Garden**.
Yet another hidden treasure in the low-profile fifth borough is the Staten Island Botanic Garden, which is on the grounds of the **Snug Harbor Cultural Center** (see page 145) and boasts several unique attractions. One is the Chinese Scholar's Garden, which is the only one its kind in the United States. The garden is a sanctuary of sculptures, waterways, and perennial greens inspired by the traditionally tranquil private gardens of ancient China. Another is Connie Gretz's Secret Garden, which is modeled on the garden in the children's book by Frances Hodgson Burnett. The garden is surrounded by a hedge maze (the only one of its kind in New York), so the "secret" is finding it.
*1000 RICHMOND TERRACE IN STATEN ISLAND. Subway: 1 to South Ferry; ferry to Staten Island; then S40 bus to Snug Harbor and the Botanic Gardens. 718-273-8200. www.sibg.org.*

## Central Park

When people think "outdoors" in New York, chances are the first image that pops into their heads is Central Park. Olmsted and Vaux's 150-year-old park is an urban masterpiece, 843 acres of varied bucolic terrain (including lakes, woodlands, hills, and lawns) that literally runs right through the middle of the city. In addition to the sheer beauty of this verdant oasis, Central Park is also New York City's backyard, and for plenty of Manhattanites, close proximity to "the park" is a non-negotiable condition of residence. This is where people from all over the city come to play, relax, learn, hang out, work out, and meet up. Here are some of our favorite things about it.
*Subway: 1, 4, 5, 6, A, B, C, D, N, R, W to various points; see www.mta.info for subway map. For more information on the park, call 212-310-6600 or visit www.centralparknyc.org.*

**578.** *Watch the giant turtles swim in Turtle Pond.* You can see frogs, fish, and waterbirds there, too.
*MIDDLE OF THE PARK, BETWEEN 79TH AND 80TH STREETS (at the base of Belvedere Castle). Subway: B, C to 81st Street-Museum of Natural History.*

**579. *Go rowboating on the lake.*** You'll have to brave the tourists, but it's worth it. It's tons of fun, a great way to cool off, and at $10 an hour, it's a pretty good deal!
*EAST SIDE BETWEEN 74TH AND 75TH STREETS. Rowboats can be rented from March through October, weather permitting. Subway: 6 to 77th Street.*

**580. *Ride a horse.*** You can reserve a horse at Claremont Stables, and go riding on the park's bridle paths.
*175 WEST 89TH STREET. Subway: B, C to 86th Street. Contact Claremont Stables for more information at 212-724-5100.*

**581. *Ride the carousel for old times' sake . . .*** The carousel that operates today is actually the fourth to occupy this spot. (The previous ones all burned down.) The first one, built in 1870, was animal powered. The subsequent three, however, have been steam powered.
*MIDDLE OF THE PARK, NEAR 64TH STREET. Subway: 6 to 68th Street-Hunter College; B, C to 72nd Street.*

**582. . . . *or have a full-fledged amusement park outing at Victorian Gardens.*** Think you have to leave the city to ride the teacups? Not anymore. From May through September, Wollman Rink is transformed into a good old-fashioned carnival, with all the cotton candy, face painting, and rides of traditional traveling summer carnivals.
*WOLLMAN RINK, EAST SIDE OF THE PARK BETWEEN 62ND AND 63RD STREETS. Subway: N, R, W to Fifth Avenue/59th Street. For more information on hours and admission, visit www.victoriangardensnyc.com.*

**583. *Watch the "disco skaters" strut their stuff by the Bandshell.*** There are no official hours or performance times; just enter the park on the east side, around 64th Street, and follow the music!
*Subway: N, R, W to Fifth Avenue/59th Street.*

**584. *Work on your own skating (and stopping) for free at the Skate Patrol Stopping Clinic.*** The Central Park Skate Patrol offers free lessons in inline skate braking on weekends from April through October. They also operate a skate school, offering classes taught by certified Skate Patrol instructors, where you can learn more advanced skills, like turns, crossovers, and skating backwards, for a reasonable $25 per class.
*Stopping Clinic is open weekends from April through October, 12:30 p.m. to 5:30 p.m.*

*WEST 72ND STREET, JUST INSIDE CENTRAL PARK. No reservations. Skate School operates weekends from April through October. Classes are available for beginners through advanced and cost $25 each. Classes meet at BLADES, 120 WEST 72ND STREET, BETWEEN COLUMBUS AVENUE AND BROADWAY. Subway: 1, 2, 3 to 72nd Street. For more information, or to register for Skate School, call 212-439-1234 or visit www.skatepatrol.org.*

**585. Have drinks at the Boathouse.** It's a mob scene at brunch, and dinner is pricey—and the urban lakeside dining idea is pretty gimmicky. But it's a gimmick with a great view, and well worth the price of a cocktail or two.
*CENTRAL PARK DRIVE NORTH AT EAST 72ND STREET. Subway: 6 to 68th Street-Hunter College. 212-517-2233. www.thecentralparkboathouse.com.*

**586. Watch lawn sports.** There are two kept greens in the park reserved for lawn sports like bocce and croquet. If you go on a nice spring or summer day, you can see experienced players, dressed in traditional whites and engaged in intense competition. (If you want to play, however, you need a permit.)
*Fields are located near West 69th Street. For more information on permits, call 212-408-0226 or visit www.centralparknyc.org.*

**587. Go fishing in the Harlem Meer.** Just beyond the Conservatory Gardens at the northeast corner of the park is the Harlem Meer. You can fish there free of charge—poles and corn kernel bait are available for use at the Dana Center. Fishing is catch-and-release, so everything must be thrown back—not that you'd really be tempted to eat what you catch anyway.
*CHARLES A. DANA CENTER. 110TH STREET AND LENOX AVENUE. Subway: 2, 3 to Central Park North (110th Street). Equipment available Tuesday through Sunday from April through October.*

**588. Skating at Lasker Rink.** Another gem in the lightly traveled northern end of the park. Not surprisingly, it is much less crowded here than at Wollman Rink—and much cheaper. In the summer, the rink converts to a public pool.
*MID-PARK BETWEEN 106TH AND 108TH STREETS. Subway: 2, 3 to Central Park North (110th Street). Skating from November through March. For more information, call 917-492-3857 or visit www.wollmanskatingrink.com/main_lasker.htm.*

**589. Discover the Conservatory Gardens.** Tucked away in the northeast corner of the park, shielded from the commotion of the throngs below, this breathtaking six-acre garden is an oasis of calm in the city's most beloved open space. The name comes from a huge glass conservatory that stood there from 1898 until 1934, when it was demolished and replaced by the garden. This is the only formal garden in the park, and it is comprised of three distinctly landscaped sections: Italian, French, and English. Few park visitors make the trek so far north, so aside from weddings and the occasional painter or two, you'll be able to drink in the exquisite floral beauty in peace. You can enter either by walking up from within the park, or through the gates on Fifth Avenue at 105th Street. The wrought iron gates once stood at the entrance to the Vanderbilt Mansion on Fifth Avenue and 58th Street (the spot where **Bergdorf Goodman** sits today; see page 240); they were moved to the park in 1927. Just inside lies the Italian garden, with its well-manicured lawns and hedges, crab apple trees, and a wrought-iron pergola with a fountain in front of it. (Check out the medallions on the walkway under the pergola—they are inscribed with the names of each of the thirteen original colonies.) The French garden to the north has the most stunning floral displays—20,000 tulips bloom each spring, from new bulbs planted the previous fall. There's also the beautiful sculpture of the three dancing maidens that encircles the fountain at the center. The English garden to the south has the best year-round floral display, and a lovely reflecting pool with water lilies and another fountain. This fountain is known as the Burnett Fountain, for the bronze sculpture of two children from Frances Hodgson Burnett's book, *The Secret Garden*—an appropriate touch for the park's own secret garden.

*FIFTH AVENUE AND 105TH STREET. Subway: 2, 3 to Central Park North (110th Street).*

## Prospect Park

Prospect Park is to Brooklyn what Central Park is to Manhattan: a rambling park space overflowing with natural beauty and outdoor amenities. Also designed by Olmsted and Vaux, it shares many similarities with its sister park in Manhattan, but Prospect has its own distinct character and features. Divided by hills, woods, and waterways, the terrain varies from the picturesque lake with its Victorian boathouse to the wilderness of the ravine, the busy field of baseball diamonds, and the small zoo contained in its center. Here we list a few of the very best things to do in Prospect Park.

*Subway: 2, 3 to Grand Army Plaza; B, S/Franklin Avenue Shuttle to Prospect Park; F to Seventh Avenue; Q to Parkside Avenue. www.prospectpark.org*

**590. *Hire a pedal boat on the lake.*** Compared to its crowded counterpart in Manhattan, the lake at Prospect Park is like the open sea, a palatial sixty acres of uncharted water for the few happy explorers who make the most of the pedal boats every summer. Follow turtles, watch the herons perched on the islands, and move from open sunlit waters to the shade of bulrushes in a few easy strokes.
*Pedal boat rentals at Wollman Rink. Use the Ocean Avenue/Parkside entrance and follow signs to Wollman Rink. Subway: B, S/Franklin Avenue Shuttle to Prospect Park; Q to Parkside Avenue.*

**591. *Try to catch the prize fish in the annual Macy's fishing contest.*** An annual event since 1947, the Macy's fishing contest sees Brooklyn's youngest fishermen compete to catch a huge, tagged bass named for R. H. Macy. The waters of Prospect Park are full of fish, from bass to porgies, and prizes are awarded for the first and biggest catches of the day, as well as for Macy, the tagged bass (everything caught in Prospect Park must be thrown back). There are exhibits and classes held at the Audubon Center throughout the day to teach kids about the fish they're after.
*July. Audubon Center is just inside the Lincoln Road/Ocean Avenue entrance to the park. Subway: B, Q, S/Franklin Avenue Shuttle to Prospect Park.*

**592. *Ride the carousel.*** These painted horses have provided nearly a century of fun for kids, from their original home at Coney Island in 1912 to their beautiful present reincarnation in the "Children's Corner" of Prospect Park.
*Just inside the Willink entrance at Ocean Avenue, Flatbush Avenue, and Empire Boulevard. Subway: B, Q, S/Franklin Avenue Shuttle to Prospect Park.*

**593. *Get lost in the wooded ravine.*** Brooklyn's only forest runs across the middle of Prospect Park, bringing a glimpse of the rocks, streams, and shady treetops of the Adirondacks to the city.
*Middle of the park between Long Meadow and Nethermead; accessible from the Grand Army Plaza entrance or from the Ninth Street entrance on Prospect Park West. Subway: 2, 3 to Grand Army Plaza; F to Seventh Avenue.*

**594. *Hide undisturbed in the Vale of Cashmere,*** a cool, shaded garden and pond sunk down behind the Long Meadow. It is entirely possible to spend a whole day in the Vale of Cashmere without seeing another living soul.
*Enter at Grand Army Plaza and head toward the Audubon Center; look for signs to the vale. Subway: 2, 3 to Grand Army Plaza.*

**595. See the sun shine through the stained-glass ceiling of the Concert Grove pagoda**, whose Oriental pavilion is one of the prettiest buildings in Brooklyn. The grove is full of whimsical bronze sculptures of famous composers—Beethoven is depicted with a deep frown—which inspires local musicians to play here on warm days.
*Near the Ocean Avenue/Parkside entrance. Subway: B, S/Franklin Avenue Shuttle to Prospect Park; Q to Parkside Avenue.*

**596. Skate to the best old-school roller-disco music at the "other" Wollman Rink.** Between the Concert Grove and the lake, Prospect Park's popular ice rink has clean ice, floodlights, and the best soundtrack this side of the **Roxy** (see page 333).
*Just inside the Ocean Avenue/Parkside entrance. Follow signs to Wollman Rink. Subway: B, S/Franklin Avenue Shuttle to Prospect Park; Q to Parkside Avenue.*

**597. Watch pups splash about on Dog Beach.** No jokes about the doggie paddle—this little pond by the ball fields in the Long Meadow is for canines only. Even if you don't have a dog, it's a quirky urban attraction that's good for at least one "Awwww."
*Long Meadow, by 9th Street. Off-leash hours and rules apply. Subway: F to Seventh Avenue.*

**598. Make a rooftop garden (or if your building won't let you, make friends with someone who's got one).**
A rooftop garden is a great way to get out of the city without technically leaving your apartment, whether it is full of massive seasonal plantings, or just a few potted plants and a glider chair. Stock up on urban gardening gear at the **Chelsea Garden Center**, or if you really want to go all out, try the posh **Marston & Langinger** shop, where you'll find everything you need to create a proper English country garden right here in the city.
*Chelsea Garden Center: 499 TENTH AVENUE AT 38TH STREET IN MANHATTAN. Subway: A, C, E to 42nd Street-Port Authority Bus Terminal. 212-727-7100. www.chelseagardencenter.com.*
*Marston & Langinger: 117 MERCER STREET BETWEEN PRINCE AND SPRING STREETS IN MANHATTAN. Subway: 6 to Spring Street; N, R, W to Prince Street. 212-965-0434. www.marston-and-langinger.com.*

**599. Take a canoe ride up the Gowanus Canal.**
The Gowanus Dredgers Canoeing Club has canoes, paddles, and life jackets available

for public use, and offers tours up and down the canal during the season (May through October). Waterfront tours are by appointment and are 90 minutes long; other tours and special events are 15 to 20 minutes long and are posted on the Web site's calendar. The equipment and tours are free, though contributions are encouraged. (The organization works to maintain the Gowanus Canal and encourages public use and awareness of local waterways). Try to go in the evening—the sunset on the canal is surprisingly romantic.

*Most canoeing events depart from 2ND STREET NEAR BOND STREET. Subway: F, G to Carroll Street; R to Union Street. For more information, call 718-243-0849 or visit www.waterfrontmuseum.org/dredgers/home.html.*

## 600. Go fishing off a real fishing boat in Sheepshead Bay.

Catch a boat from one of the piers along Emmons Avenue, and head into the Atlantic for an early-morning or a late-night trip. If you're especially brave, you can try selling your catch to the restaurants along the Bay.

*EMMONS AVENUE ALONG SHEEPSHEAD BAY IN BROOKLYN. Prices range from $24 to $40 per trip. Subway: B, Q to Sheepshead Bay.*

## 601. Kayak on the **Hudson River** (and don't fall in!).

The Downtown Boathouse offers several public small-crafts programs, the most popular of which is free kayaking on the Hudson. They provide kayaks, paddles, life jackets, and supervision—the only thing you need to know is how to swim. In addition to the public kayak rentals, they also hold three-hour guided trips up the Hudson, and free kayaking lessons on Wednesday evenings.

*HUDSON RIVER AT PIER 40 IN MANHATTAN (Houston Street: Subway: 1 to Houston Street); PIER 96 (56th Street: Subway: 1, A, C, B, D to 59th Street); 72ND STREET (Subway: 1, 2, 3 to 72nd Street). For more information, call 646-613-0375. www.downtownboathouse.org/links.html.*

## 602. Take the subway to the **beach**.

Take your pick: Brighton Beach, Coney Island, Manhattan Beach, and Rockaway are all accessible by subway, and free, so a day at the beach will cost you only the price of a MetroCard. Each beach has its own character, but they're all fun and well maintained, so choose between the crowded funfair atmosphere of Coney Island, the Russian expanses of Brighton Beach, the quieter Spanish flavor of Manhattan Beach, or the surfer's paradise of Rockaway.

*Subways maps at www.mta.info.*

## 603. Take the **Yankee Clipper** to a game.

More peaceful than driving, more comfortable than the train, and much quicker than you would expect. Departs from various points along the East River in Manhattan. *$18 dollars round-trip for adults, $14 for children under 12. For more information, call 800-53-FERRY. www.nywaterway.com.*

## 604. Go sailing off **City Island**, the premier resort town of the Bronx.

Many people live in New York for years and never visit City Island, but it's worth the small voyage—especially if you like fish. With all sorts of boats for hire, fishing trips on the nearby waters, and fresh seafood available at cafés along the shore, City Island is a surprisingly lively seaside resort, and a pretty sight from the deck of a sailboat in the sound. Follow up your maritime expedition with fish and chips from **Johnny's Famous Reef** (page 325) and a browse through **Mooncurser Records** (page 276). *Subway: 6 to Pelham Bay Park; BX29 bus to City Island. For information on visiting City Island, sailing, restaurants, and other entertainment, visit www.cityisland.com.*

## 605. See if you can train a telescope on one of the bald-headed eagles that live at the **Inwood Hill Nature Center**.

Inwood Hill Park, the beautiful stretch of land at the northernmost tip of Manhattan, is a great place to visit when you want to get off the beaten path. Walking through its winding forests and along its rocky cliffs, and looking out across the Hudson brings you as close to nature as you can get without leaving the island. The Nature Center within the park is a great place to observe and learn about the few wild animals that make Manhattan their home. *INWOOD HILL PARK, 218TH STREET AND INDIAN ROAD IN MANHATTAN. Open Wednesday through Sunday. Subway: A to Inwood-207th Street. 212-304-2365.*

## 606. Get up close and personal with shorebirds at the **Jamaica Bay Wildlife Refuge**.

More than 300 species of birds spend their summers at this 9,000-acre refuge. From mid- to late-August, the pond is teeming with young birds that aren't yet afraid of people, so you have the rare opportunity to get within petting distance of beautiful wild birds. *GATEWAY NATIONAL RECREATION AREA, FLOYD BENNETT FIELD IN BROOKLYN. Subway: A to Broad Channel. For more information, see entry for Floyd Bennett Field, page 236. 718-318-4340. www.nps.gov/gate.*

## 607. Watch an octopus prepare its dinner at the New York Aquarium.

To keep the animals as nimble and alert as they would be in the wild, the aquarium staff uses various "enrichment games," like putting food in closed containers or hiding it in a toy. You can watch an octopus use a couple of its arms to open a jar filled with tasty fish at feeding times.

*SURF AVENUE AND WEST 8TH STREET IN BROOKLYN. Subway: D to Stillwell Avenue; F, Q to West 8th Street-New York Aquarium. For feeding times, call or check online. 718-265-FISH. www.nyaquarium.com.*

## 608. See lions, tigers, bears, and much more at the Bronx Zoo.

The Bronx Zoo is the largest metropolitan zoo in the world, and one of the most important conservation sites. Opened in 1899, the zoo has pioneered many educational and zoological programs, such as taking animals out of cages and putting them into simulations of their natural environments. The zoo's first conservation project was the American bison, whose numbers, by the turn of the century, had dwindled from millions to 1,000. The zoo founded the American Bison Society, which successfully accomplished the breeding and reintroduction of bison into natural habitats all over the country. Now, under the auspices of the Wildlife Conservation Society (WCS), the Bronx Zoo has been integral in preserving species all over the world, and is still on the forefront of zoological technology and design. You can see the fruits of their labor in the highly detailed, replicated natural habitats that fill the 265-acre park, from the Himalayan Highlands, where red pandas, snow leopards, and other rare, endangered animals roam through a forest with authentic natural adornments made by Tibetan monks, to the beautiful Butterfly Garden and greenhouse, where thousands of butterflies roam. The zoo's most recent innovation is the Congo Gorilla Forest, an amazing 6.5-acre replica of an African rain forest that is home to more than 300 native animals (including gorillas, monkeys, and snakes); it is also the first zoo exhibit to involve visitors in the conservation effort by giving them the option to have the zoo donate their admission fee toward rainforest conservation. And that's only the beginning. The number of amazing things to do and see could fill an entire chapter, from daily feedings and enrichment demonstrations where you can watch zookeepers play with the animals, to the Skyfari tram ride that gives an overview of the entire zoo.

*FORDHAM ROAD AT THE BRONX RIVER PARKWAY IN THE BRONX. Subway: 2 to Pelham Parkway; 2, 5 to West Farms Square-East Tremont Avenue. For hours, admission prices, and other details, call 718-367-1010 or visit www.bronxzoo.com.*

## 609. Go horseback riding **on the beach**.

You can trot up and down a private three-mile stretch of the Brooklyn coast on a horse hired from the Jamaica Bay Riding Academy.

*7000 SHORE PARKWAY IN BROOKLYN. Group trail rides and private rides available. Subway: B, Q to Sheepshead Bay; taxi to the academy. For specific directions, call 718-531-8949. www.horsebackride.com/jb/home.html.*

## Give your yoga a **breath of fresh air**.

In the nicer weather, certain yoga instructors break out of the studio and bring their classes outside to parks around the city. For devoted practitioners, these classes offer a change of pace without changing activity; for newcomers, they are a way to try yoga in a setting that may be less intimidating than a studio. Following is a list of parks that host yoga classes in the warm weather; most are seasonal, but some are offered year-round and shift to indoor spaces elsewhere in the park during the winter months. The days and times of all of these are subject to change, so contact the park or check their Web sites for the most current information.

**610. *Brooklyn Bridge Park:*** Offers sunset yoga classes on the boardwalk several times during the summer at 7:00 p.m. Classes are free, but you must bring your own mat, and you should arrive half an hour early to sign up.
*See full entry on page 209.*

**611. *Bryant Park:*** Hosts a free open class conducted by the Yoga Project NYC on Thursday evenings, 6:00 p.m. to 7:00 p.m., May through August. Classes are held on the southwest corner of the lawn. Mats available to borrow.
*See full entry on page 212.*

**612. *Central Park:*** Holds several different classes year-round at the North Meadow Recreation Center (mid-park near 97th Street); in the summer, some classes venture outside. Fee is $7 per class; mats available to borrow with photo ID.
*See full entry on page 216.*

**613. *Greenbelt Nature Center:*** Holds an eight-week session July through August, with weekly morning classes. (Cost is per session.)
*700 ROCKLAND AVENUE AT BRIELLE AVENUE IN STATEN ISLAND. For information, schedules, and directions, call 718-351-3450 or visit www.sigreenbelt.org, or the Parks Department Web site: www.nyc.gov/parks.*

**614. *Inwood Hill Park:*** Hosts "Fun in the Setting Sun," a series of free weekly Vinyasa classes organized by Inwood Peace Yoga Center during the summer. Classes are Monday evenings from 7:00 p.m. to 8:30 p.m.; sign-in starts at 6:30 p.m. (Mats available for purchase only.)
*NEAR 218TH STREET AND INDIAN ROAD IN MANHATTAN. Subway: 1, A to 207th Street. For information and schedules, call 212-304-YOGA or visit www.inwoodpeaceyoga.com.*

**615. *Riverside Park:*** Holds a free weekly evening Hatha yoga class for all levels, June through September. (Bring your own mat.)
*BETWEEN 72ND AND 158TH STREETS AND THE HUDSON RIVER IN MANHATTAN. For information on schedule and location, visit www.riversideparkfund.org.*

**616. *Socrates Sculpture Park:*** Holds free Kripalu (a form of Hatha yoga) classes on the park grounds on Saturday mornings from 11:00 a.m. to 12:00 p.m., May through August. (Bring your own mat.)
*32-01 VERNON BOULEVARD IN QUEENS. Subway: N, W to Broadway. 718-956-1819. www.socratessculpturepark.org. For more on the park, see page 139.*

**617. *Rooftop yoga*** is another out-of-studio option. **Laughing Lotus** holds a weekly sunset class on top of Greenwich House during the summer. Mats available to rent for $2.
*27 BARROW STREET AT SEVENTH AVENUE SOUTH IN MANHATTAN. Subway: 1 to Christopher Street-Sheridan Square. For more information and schedules, call Laughing Lotus at 212-414-2903 or visit www.laughinglotus.com.*

## Outdoor **Tai Chi**.

If you've ever walked through a park in the early morning and noticed a group of people in a trancelike state performing slow, mesmerizing movements in tandem, you've probably witnessed an outdoor tai chi class. Like yoga, there are plenty of studios at which to study tai chi in the city, but going outside can give your practice a pleasant new perspective. Some classes are seasonal, while others are year-round and held outdoors during the warmer months.

**618. *Brooklyn Botanic Garden:*** Holds weekly classes for different levels on Fridays, from September through November. Beginner classes are held indoors at the Visitor's Center; intermediate and advanced classes are held on the grounds at the Cherry Esplanade, weather permitting.
*See full entry on page 215.*

**619. *Bryant Park:*** Holds free open classes on Thursday mornings, 7:30 a.m. to 8:30 a.m., May through August, at the Fountain Terrace.
*See full entry on page 212.*

**620. *Central Park:*** Classes held on Saturdays, 10:00 a.m. to 11:30 a.m., at the North Meadow Recreation Center (mid-park at 97th street). The class runs year-round and is held outdoors, weather permitting. The cost is $7 per class.
*See full entry on page 216.*

**621. *Socrates Sculpture Park:*** Holds free weekly classes on Sunday mornings, May through August.
*See full entry on page 139.*

**622. *Wave Hill:*** Holds classes on Saturday mornings at 10:00 a.m. (beginners) and 11:00 a.m. (intermediate). Classes are held year-round, either on the grounds or in Wave Hill House. The fee is $10 for the public and $7 for members.
*See full entry on page 211.*

## 623. Join the **New York Road Runners Club**.

This nearly fifty-year-old running club is probably most commonly associated with the **New York City Marathon** (see page 29), and membership gives you access to training groups and increases your chances for entry into the marathon. But the club's focus is to facilitate running in the New York area, and it offers plenty for less serious (or complete novice) runners. There are clinics and lectures on running-related topics, and classes in other physical activities like biking, yoga, and strength training to complement your running (open to non-members as well). The club can also help you find a running partner or answer your training questions online (members only). The many offerings, flexibility of participation, and supportive community make this a great organization for athletes of any level, with a variety of interests.
*Annual membership starts at $35. For information on programs and how to join, call 212-860-4455 or visit www.nyrrc.org.*

## 624. Learn to run with **Nike**.

You may question the company's ethics, but you can't question its commitment to sports. Nike runs free running clinics in **Central Park** (see page 216) all year round, complete with coaches, training plans, and post-run snacks and hydration. In 2006, the clinic met four evenings a week at 6:30 p.m., and Saturday mornings at 9:00 a.m. The meeting point is either at the Niketown Store (57th and Madison) or Columbus

Circle, where everyone starts with a group stretch. Then runners break off into groups, from which you can choose your pace (10-minute mile, 9-minute mile, etc.) and distance (between three and seven miles). The clinics are open to runners of all levels, but this is a particularly good opportunity for novices who want to "learn" how to run. You'll have access to professional trainers, and receive discounts and coupons for things like shoe fittings and free Nike gear.

*For more information, visit www.nikerunning.com.*

## 625. Take a run with the **Hash House Harriers**.

No applications, no fitness qualifications, no abstentious track stars at this quirky, international fun-and-run-loving social club. Just show up at the appointed time and place, and follow the path (or pack) until you reach the "on-in" (their version of the finish line, usually a bar). The route changes each time and is marked in chalk on the street by the "Hare" (the Hasher who makes up the course). The routes are intentionally broken up, forcing the faster runners to stop and figure out where the trail continues and allowing the slower runners time to catch up, so everyone finishes the run around the same time. Then there's pizza and beer for all. Hash runs occur several times a week, at different locations around the city.

*For more information, call 212-HASHNYC or visit www.hashnyc.com.*

## 626. Explore New York **by bike**.

The New York Cycle Club (NYCC) and the Five Borough Bicycle Club (5BBC) offer several rides every weekend day and on certain weekdays to various destinations throughout the five boroughs. Rides range from slow to serious, and some have a strong sightseeing bent. They can be a really great way to see parts of the city that you've never been to (and perhaps never even heard of).

*Membership to each of the clubs is about $20 per year. For more information, visit www.nycc.org or www.5bbc.org.*

## 627. The annual **New York Century Ride**

is another great way to see New York by bike, as well as a cycling challenge for riders of all levels. There are five different routes of varying distances—15, 35, 55, 75, and 100 miles—which take you through as many as four of the five boroughs. We prefer the New York Century over the Five Boro Bike Tour, another annual ride popular with cyclists of various levels, because the Century attracts only a fraction of the Five Boro participants (5,000 vs. 30,000), and the starts are staggered by the different distance groups, so there isn't the same backup at the start.

*September. Ride start and finish are in Central Park (see page 216). For more information and to register, visit www.transalt.org.*

## 628. Ride **Manhattan island** from tip to tip.

A continuous bike path running the length of Manhattan was long the Manifest Destiny of city cyclists, but the dream has been realized through a series of interconnecting parks, which allow for an uninterrupted waterfront path. Start at Pier A at Hudson River Park, by Battery Park City, and continue up through Riverside Park, the "Cherry Walk" (a cherry tree–lined section of the path between 100th and 125th Streets), Fort Washington Park, and arrive at the George Washington Bridge. Stop for a break at the top by the Little Red Lighthouse, the hero of the beloved children's classic, *The Little Red Lighthouse and the Great Gray Bridge.* (You can't miss it—it's directly under the bridge—for more information, see page 73.) Then you can turn around and head back, or, if you're feeling adventurous, you can cross the bridge and continue riding on 9W, a picturesque bike route popular with area cyclists.

## 629. Go on a **Critical Mass Ride.**

On the last Friday of every month, cyclists (and some rollerbladers) congregate in more than 300 areas around the world to participate in a Critical Mass ride, a lively celebration of bicycles and other nonpolluting modes of transportation. In New York, the ride meets at the north end of Union Square Park at 7:00 p.m. Though they're technically a form of activism, the rides aren't organized protests; they're spirited, leisurely paced group rides. Critical Mass is a movement, not an organization, so there's no one "organizing" or "administering" the rides, and you don't have to be committed to the cause to participate; just showing up because you like to ride is support enough. The rides last about two hours, although you can jump in or out anytime, and there's no registration. Though the spirit is usually good-natured, peaceful, and respectful of traffic and cars, the activist streak does rear its head from time to time— most notably in 2004, when the August ride held during the Republican National Convention created conflict with the police and led to many arrests and several lawsuits. Most of the time, though, it's all fun due to the freeform and welcoming character of the rides. The local environmental organization Time's Up! often organizes coinciding activities like after-parties and theme nights for certain holidays and events; check their Web site for information about events for upcoming rides.

*Last Friday of every month at 7:00 p.m. Departs from UNION SQUARE AND 17TH STREET IN MANHATTAN. Subway: 4, 5, 6, L, N, Q, R, W to 14th Street-Union Square. Note: Although this is the "official" starting point, groups also leave from other parks and areas in Manhattan. Check the Time's Up! Web site for more details: www.times-up.org.*

### 630. Explore the city on a social skate with the **Empire Skate Club**.

Empire Skate is an in-line skating club that holds regular events for skaters of all different levels. It organizes group skates on Tuesday and Thursday nights (Thursday for open levels, Tuesday for more experienced skaters) around Central Park; day and half-day skates to other boroughs and further afield on weekends; and two- and three-day skating getaways. The events are free, but for $25 you can become a member and receive a free private skating lesson, discounts at local skate shops, and more.

*For more information, call 212-774-1774 or visit www.empireskate.org.*

### 631. Put on your blades for **Wednesday Night Skate**.

New York's largest regular group skate is Wednesday Night Skate, a free two-hour evening skate that takes different routes through the city each week. Routes are planned in advance, tested for obstructions and obstacles, and led by volunteers. Each skate covers about ten to twelve miles of city streets, so participants should be comfortable with skating in traffic and with cars, but otherwise, these events are open to anyone—all you have to do is show up.

*Skaters meet at 7:45 p.m. (for 8:00 p.m. departure) at UNION SQUARE AND 14TH STREET IN MANHATTAN. Wednesday evenings, from April through October. (Canceled in rain or bad weather.) Subway: 4, 5, 6, L, N, Q, R, W to 14th Street-Union Square. For more information visit www.weskateny.org.*

### 632. Skate with a view at **Riverbank State Park**.

The only state park in Manhattan is a twenty-eight-acre park and recreation area built on top of a wastewater treatment facility. (Yes, you read that right.) But there's nothing second-rate about this park—Riverbank has some of the city's nicest athletic facilities, including a unique elevated ice- and roller-skating rink. The rink boasts panoramic views of the Hudson River for skaters to admire as they whiz around, and it also has a canopy (good for keeping ice skaters safe from sleet in the winter and roller skaters out of the baking sun in the summer). The rink is small, so it does get crowded during prime hours, but even so, it's much calmer than the scene at some of the city's better-known rinks—and is less than half the price.

*679 RIVERSIDE DRIVE NEAR 140TH STREET IN MANHATTAN. Subway: 1 to 145th Street. 212-694-3600. nysparks.state.ny.us/parks/info.asp?parkID=75.*

## 633. Go **cross-country skiing** up and down the empty avenues right after a big snowstorm.

Following a major snowfall, there's a tiny window of opportunity when all regular activity is suspended, and the city is at peace. With cars immobilized, pedestrians scarce, and fresh white powder covering every surface, the best way to enjoy this complete urban calm is to put on some skis and take to the streets. It may not look like Vermont, but this rarity has its own kind of wonderment. If you'd prefer a slightly more bucolic setting, you should go to the Great Lawn or Sheep Meadow in **Central Park** (see page 216).

*Anywhere you want!*

## 634. Swim in one of the city's **outdoor pools**.

There are more than fifty pools scattered across the five boroughs, and all of them are free. Many also offer swimming lessons and team training. Try the one in Astoria Park, the nicest and largest in the city system, which hosted the Olympic trials for the U.S. swimming and diving teams in 1936 and 1964. All pools are open from the end of June through Labor Day, usually from 11:00 a.m. to 7:00 p.m.

*ASTORIA PARK, BETWEEN DITMARS AVENUE AND HOYT AVENUE SOUTH, AND 19TH STREET AND THE EAST RIVER IN QUEENS. Subway: N, W to Astoria-Ditmars Boulevard. For other pool locations and information, visit: www.nycgovparks.org/sub_things_to_do/facilities/ af_pools.html.*

## 635. Surf **Rockaway Beach**.

There's not a palm tree in sight, but this strip between 88th and 90th Streets in Far Rockaway is a bona fide surfing beach. It is New York's only surf-specific spot, the one place where you can take to the waves without having to dodge swimmers. Though the scenery may not be as picturesque as Sunset Beach, surfers say the waves hold their own, and it's an easy subway ride from Manhattan and Brooklyn.

*SURF BEACH IS BETWEEN THE JETTIES, BETWEEN 88TH AND 90TH STREETS AT ROCKAWAY BEACH IN QUEENS. Subway: A to Beach 90th Street.*

## 636. Unleash your inner acrobat at **Trapeze School**.

If you want to get "out" of the city but don't have time for a trip upstate, try soaring above it. The Trapeze School of New York offers classes in "aerial arts" for all levels at its waterfront location in Hudson River Park. In the flying trapeze class, students jump from a twenty-three-foot-high platform and fly through the air hanging by their arms or knees, eventually working up to maneuvers like "catches" (the flyer grabs on to a "catcher" and lets go of his trapeze). The benefits (besides fun) include gains in physical fitness, endurance, and self-esteem, as well as stress relief. Can you think of a better way to let loose? You'll feel liberated and invigorated—and far away from the commotion and concrete below.

*ON THE HUDSON RIVER, SOUTH OF CANAL STREET, BETWEEN PIERS 26 AND 34 IN MAN-HATTAN. For information, class schedules, and prices, call 212-678-0728 or visit www.trapezeschool.com.*

## 637. **Tee off** in the boroughs.

There are a dozen golf courses in four of the five boroughs (all except Manhattan), many of which are accessible by subway or bus. A hop, skip, and a jump from the 86th Street R stop in Brooklyn is the **Dyker Beach Golf Course**, now a favorite destination among area golfers, thanks to a recent refurbishing. There are plenty of trees, and even a large lake—you wouldn't know you're in the middle of Brooklyn except for the street noise and exquisite views of the Verrazano-Narrows Bridge. A little further out in Brooklyn is the **Marine Park Golf Course**. You can still get there by public transportation, but it's a little more complicated—and for that reason, a bit less crowded. The course's proximity to the ocean makes for some gusty breezes from time to time, and on a cool, windy day, you could swear you were at St. Andrew's. In the Bronx, **Van Cortlandt Park** (see page 211) boasts two golf courses: the 110-year-old eighteen-hole **Van Cortlandt Golf Course** and the smaller nine-hole **Mosholu Golf Course**. Both of these are also convenient to subway stops. Queens and Staten Island have three and four courses, respectively.

*DYKER BEACH: 86TH STREET AND 7TH AVENUE IN BROOKLYN. Subway: R to 86th Street. 718-836-9722.*

*MARINE PARK: 2880 FLATBUSH AVENUE IN BROOKLYN. Subway: 2, 5 to Brooklyn College-Flatbush Avenue, then Q-35 Green bus. 718-338-7149.*

*VAN CORTLANDT & MOSHOLU GOLF COURSES are both located in Van Cortlandt Park in the Bronx. Van Cortlandt Golf Course is at VAN CORTLANDT SOUTH AND BAILEY AVENUES. Subway: 1 to Van Cortlandt Park-242nd Street. 718-543-4595. Mosholu is at JEROME AND BAINBRIDGE AVENUES. Subway: 4 to Mosholu Parkway or Woodlawn. 718-655-9164. For a list of all of the city's courses, with information on hours, fees, and directions, visit nycgovparks.org/sub_things_to_do/facilities/af_golf.html.*

## 638. **Work yourself out** in the park.

*Self* magazine's annual health and beauty field day, the Self Workout in the Park, has achieved the highest physical fitness coup there is: it makes working out fun. Really, extremely, surprisingly fun. Now held each spring on Central Park's Rumsey Playfield, the day is packed with activities such as free group exercise classes, massages, personal training sessions, and outdoor rock-climbing simulations, plus a field's worth of sponsors handing out goodies and samples. But what really makes this a great event is that despite the obvious sponsorship, there is a somewhat spontaneous and infectious atmosphere generated by hundreds of people who are clearly having a lot of fun. Well, that and the fact that with all the freebies, you won't have to buy soap or granola bars for at least a year. (Note: While men can attend, it's clearly geared toward women.)

*The Self Workout in the Park is held each spring. RUMSEY PLAYING FIELD, CENTRAL PARK, IN MANHATTAN. Tickets are available at the event or online at www.condenastdirect.com/self-workout_in_the_park.*

## 639. Swing on the rings at **Riverside Park**.

At this grown-up playground by 105th Street, you can swing on the rings, or do chin-ups or gymnastics on the bars in full view of the patrons of the Hudson Café. Just be warned—it's not as easy as it looks.

*TRAVELING RING TOWER, RIVERSIDE PARK AT 105TH STREET IN MANHATTAN. Subway: 1 to 103rd Street. For tips on how to swing for beginners, visit www.swingaring.com.*

## 640. Go to the track for horse races at the **Aqueduct**.

If you prefer watching your horses rather than riding them, spend a day in the sunshine at the thoroughbred races in Queens. Aqueduct is the only racetrack within New York City, and it hosts several great races such as the annual Wood Memorial in April, which is part of the warm-up trail for horses competing for the illustrious Triple Crown. Grandstand admission is only $1—and you could come back a big winner!

*110-00 ROCKAWAY BOULEVARD IN QUEENS. Subway: A train to Aqueduct-North Conduit Avenue. 718-641-4700. www.nyra.com/aqueduct.*

## 641. Join a **ZogSports team**.

Combining sports, socializing, and charity, ZogSports organizes activities and sports leagues for regular New Yorkers with a philanthropic bent. You can get a group of friends together to form your own team, or sign up individually and be assigned to one. Each team designates a charity, and the top performing teams in each league receive a donation for their chosen charity. The entry fee, which varies depending on which sport you're interested in, covers equipment, refs, and a contribution. ZogSports runs teams all year long for soccer, softball, kickball, and touch football, among others (they also have indoor leagues), and the divisions vary from very competitive to "extremely casual." Less pressure than a company softball team and more fun than meeting at a bar (though they do that, too), the teams are a great way to have fun, get outside, make friends, and benefit others.

*For information and schedules, visit www.zogsports.com.*

## Take a walk in one of the city's biggest and most beautiful graveyards.

If you've never done it, you may find it hard to believe, but taking a walk in a grave-yard is a very pleasant thing to do. They're the most reliably peaceful of outdoor spaces—you're pretty much guaranteed that a cell phone won't go off while you're taking your breather. New York cemeteries offer the additional draw of their wide open green spaces—as well as, of course, a roster of impressive inhabitants. Two favorites:

**642. *Woodlawn Cemetery:*** Woodlawn is well known as one of the most impressive burial grounds in the world, both for the number of notable names it contains and for the grand monuments that adorn the graves. As the first cemetery "local" to the city, Woodlawn was the chosen resting place of many artists, musicians, and other enter-tainers looking to be among friends. Miles Davis, Lionel Hampton, and Duke Ellington are just three from the long list of jazz legends buried here. Woodlawn was designed on a landscape-lawn plan that encouraged families to create monuments, center-pieces, and sculpture for their loved ones. Take a walk through the winding paths, check out the amazing mausoleums, and explore the memorials (but don't forget to get a photograph permit before you snap).

*WEBSTER AVENUE AND EAST 233RD STREET IN THE BRONX. Subway: 4 to Woodlawn; 2 or 5 to 233rd. 718-920-0500. www.thewoodlawncemetery.org.*

**643. *Green-Wood Cemetery:*** This beautiful cemetery sits atop the highest point in Brooklyn; from the top of Battle Hill, you can see downtown Manhattan, the Statue of Liberty, and much of the five boroughs stretching out around you. Late greats who've come to their eternal rest beneath Green-Wood's beautiful lawns include Leonard Bernstein, Jean-Michel Basquiat, Bill "the Butcher" Poole (Daniel Day-Lewis's character in *Gangs of New York*), and one of America's greatest heroes, Charles Feltman (the first guy ever to put a hot dog in a bun).

*500 25TH STREET IN BROOKLYN. Subway: R to 25th Street. 718-768-7300. www.green-wood.com.*

## 644. Take a day trip to Roosevelt Island.

It is possible (even likely) to have lived in New York for years without ever having con-sidered visiting Roosevelt Island. But this quirky strip of land between Manhattan and

Queens has an interesting (and bizarre) history and remnants of some incredible, obscure landmarks, including: an abandoned smallpox hospital; Blackwell House, the vacant home of the island's former owners, the Blackwell family; ruins of an infamous lunatic asylum; and a decommissioned lighthouse (whose original purpose was not to direct ships but to light up the aforementioned lunatic asylum and prevent escapes). Get the drift? You can walk from tip to tip in a couple of hours, and there's a great guide to the island's landmarks online at www.riwalk.com. If you get tired of walking, the bus that runs on the island still operates on a 25-cent fare. To get there, you can take the **tram** (see page 68), drive, or take the F train.

*Subway: F to Roosevelt Island.*

### 645. See a sheep-shearing demonstration at the **Queens Farm Museum**.

If days in the city have you longing for some good old-fashioned fun, you can hop on the subway and pay a visit to a farm. The Queens Farm Museum is a real working farm, located on forty-seven acres of undisturbed farmland in eastern Queens. And this is no modern theme-farm for city slickers—it is the longest continually farmed site in the entire state, dating back to 1697. In addition to tours of the historic farmhouse, planting fields, and greenhouse, you can participate in traditional agrarian events and activities: hayrides (April–October), sheep shearing, an Easter Egg hunt, a country fair (September), an Indian powwow (July), a corn maze (late summer–early fall), a haunted house, plus apple and berry festivals, pumpkin picking, and other harvest events.

*73-50 LITTLE NECK PARKWAY IN QUEENS. Subway: E, F to Kew Gardens/Union Turnpike. 718-347-3276. www.queensfarm.org.*

### 646. Go on a walk with the **Shorewalkers**.

Think you have to go up (or out of) state for a good hike? Think again. The Shorewalkers is a nonprofit group dedicated to promoting and preserving the city's shore areas—which are much larger than you might think! The group leads walks nearly every weekend to different exotic-sounding destinations, including the Rockaway Peninsula, Inwood Hills, and the **Gowanus Canal** (see page 221). Walks are open to the public with a suggested $3 contribution, or you can join Shorewalkers for around $25 for a year of unlimited walks. The Great Saunter, an annual walk around the perimeter of Manhattan, is the biggest and most popular event. If you still want to get out of the city, no problem: thanks to the Shorewalkers, you can walk from Manhattan to Bear Mountain in the Hudson Valley on the Batt to Bear trail, a fifty-mile scenic hike along the Hudson River.

*For information, schedules, and membership policies, visit www.shorewalkers.org.*

### 647. Celebrate New York's contribution to aviation history at **Floyd Bennett Field**.

While it would surprise plenty of New Yorkers to know that there is a 26,000-acre national park within the city limits (also see **Jamaica Bay Wildlife Refuge** on page 223), even lesser known is that within the park, there stands one of the most important landmarks in American aviation history. Named for the man (a New York native) who piloted the first flight over the North Pole, Floyd Bennett Field was the first municipal airport in New York, with runways dating back to the late 1920s. Although it never succeeded as a commercial airport, because of its long runways and isolated location, Floyd Bennett Field was favored by what were then called "experimental pilots" during the golden age of aviation. Many historic and record-breaking flights took off or landed here in the 1930s, such as round-the-world flights by Wiley Post and Howard Hughes, and the "accidental" transatlantic trip that earned "Wrong Way" Corrigan his nickname. In 1941, the airport was turned over to the U.S. Navy, which used it through both World War II and the Cold War, and it was actively used by the Coast Guard until 1998. If you call in advance, you can arrange for a park ranger to give you a tour of the hangar (Tuesday, Thursday, and Saturday), which houses historic aircraft and other aviation memorabilia. Tip: you can drive, but visiting Floyd Bennett Field is a lovely stop on a bike ride around the parkland.

*Floyd Bennett Field is located in GATEWAY NATIONAL PARK, JAMAICA BAY UNIT. For directions, maps, and information on visiting, contact the National Park Service at 718-338-3988 or visit www.nps.gov/gate.*

→ **DID YOU KNOW?** *Gateway National Recreation Area is also home to a clothing-optional beach that is the only one of its kind in a National Park Service facility. Gunnison Beach is located in the Gateway's Sandy Hook unit, which is actually in northern New Jersey (and therefore can't technically qualify as an entry for our book). However, it is one of the few (if not only) nude beaches in the area, so if you live in New York City and want to sunbathe au naturel, this is your best option. (For more information, visit www.gunnisonbeach.org.)*

## Expert Contributor: Francisco Liuzzi

**Francisco Liuzzi is a certified personal trainer, cycling coach, and sports nutrition specialist. He is part-owner of Nutri-FitNYC (www.nutri-fitnyc.com), a New York City personal training company that approaches physical fitness as a combination of proper exercise and proper diet education.**

# MY FIVE FAVORITE OUTDOOR SPORTS IN NEW YORK

**648.** *Pick-up basketball in the park:* The best thing about New York City outdoor basketball is that you have the chance to play against someone who can actually do a 360-degree dunk in almost any park. That and the trash talk. Nothing says New York City ball in the park more than being crossed over and dunked on while being made fun of. It sounds harsh but it's the way they play. To watch a game: the courts at West 4th Street are the best. If you plan to play, bring an A game and a thick skin. One missed lay-up and you inherit a nickname you don't want. Passersby line the fence and they get to hear it all. To play: Tompkins Square Park. The competition can get pretty mean, but more courts mean it's easier to get into a game.

**WEST 4TH STREET COURTS:** *WEST 4TH STREET AND SIXTH AVENUE IN MANHATTAN. Subway: A, C, E, B, D, F, V to West 4th Street.*

**TOMPKINS SQUARE PARK COURTS:** *BETWEEN 7TH AND 10TH STREETS ON AVENUE A IN MANHATTAN. Subway: L to First Avenue.*

**649.** *Biking through the city:* A view from your bicycle while sliding through pedestrians and traffic will give you an appreciation for the rhythm of the city that you can't really pick up on foot. Though not for everyone, riding uptown in the middle of Sixth Avenue, patting taxis on the side if they get too close and screaming "Heads up!" at pedestrians as they walk across the street staring at cell phones and iPods is strangely relaxing. Less risky is riding "the loop" in Central Park: 6.2 miles of gently rolling hills affords an up-close look at the charms of Central Park, as well as great views of the Midtown skyline. Celebrity sightings are common and even the "regular" people in the park are fun to look at. (For more on people-watching in the park, see page 216).

*CENTRAL PARK LOOP, BETWEEN 59TH AND 110TH STREETS, FIFTH AVENUE AND CENTRAL PARK WEST IN MANHATTAN. Subway: check map, depending on location.*

**650.** *Jogging over the Brooklyn Bridge:* Starting at the base of the Manhattan side of the Brooklyn Bridge, run to the Brooklyn side and back. Some of the city's best views come from the middle of the **Brooklyn Bridge** (see page 66): all of Brooklyn, all of the skyscrapers of Midtown and downtown Manhattan, and the South Street Seaport, as well as the Statue of Liberty. The run isn't very long, with slight inclines as you come up both sides. The feeling of crossing the East River while running in the open air of the bridge's top level, as the city unfurls in front of you, is enough to make you forget you're exercising.

*Subway: (for Manhattan) 2, 3 to Fulton Street; 4, 5, 6 to Brooklyn Bridge-City Hall; A, C to Broadway-Nassau Street; J, M, Z to Chambers; (for Brooklyn) A, C to High Street.*

**651. *Wallball in the city:*** "Wallball," or handball as it more commonly known, is one of the more popular activities at nearly all city parks and playgrounds. Few outdoor activities, including basketball, have as competitive a following as handball. Your hand is your racket, so pretty much anyone can play. It's just as fun to watch though, because the small court space gives great advantages to skilled players with a variety of trick serves. Older players frequently compete with younger ones, and trash talk is generational. Wallball is a good way to get a feel for a neighborhood. Any city court or park will have a wall, so there are games all over, but again, the **basketball courts of West 4th Street and Sixth Avenue** (see page 237) are among the most intense. *For a list of parks, visit www.nyc.gov/parks.*

**652. *Frisbee on the Great Lawn:*** Throwing a Frisbee in the middle of the Great Lawn on a sunny day in the city is hard to beat, regardless of one's athletic ability or taste. The Great Lawn is fun for numerous reasons: endless amounts of grass to run on; people of all shapes, sizes, and degrees of strangeness to watch; and an ability to make the hectic problems of the city vanish, for a little while. Even when it's crowded, there is plenty of space, and you don't even have to bring your own Frisbee—someone will always let you jump in. Actually, knowing how to throw a Frisbee isn't even required—just watch your head.
*CENTRAL PARK BETWEEN 79TH AND 85TH STREETS IN MANHATTAN. Subway: 4, 5, 6 to 86th Street; 6 to 77th Street; B, C to 81st Street-Museum of Natural History or 86th Street.*

CHAPTER 7:

# Bargains & Splurges

With a countless number of stores in more sizes, shapes, and styles than you can imagine, New York City is truly a shopping mecca, drawing people from around the world eager to escape the monotony of their local malls and familiar chains and partake in the splendid array of exemplary, unique, and thrilling shopping opportunities. But the wonderful thing about shopping in New York is not just the amount and variety of what can be bought; it's also how enchanting the experience can be, whether it is ascending the floors of one of the glamorous department stores, discovering delightful anachronisms like Aphrodisia or The Hat Shop, or scoring a $600 suit for $199 at a sample sale.

In this chapter, we've chosen our favorite New York shopping experiences, from unique treasures that can be found in particular stores, to the best neighborhoods for wandering and window-shopping, to some out-of-the-ordinary retail setups, like a mobile clothing shop that drives around the city and the wonderfully eclectic designers' markets. Of course, one of the most distinctive (and intriguing) elements about buying things in New York is the highs and lows. You can buy a beautiful bouquet of flowers for $10 and then spend $100 on a hamburger—and both will exceed your expectations. For this reason, we've also highlighted the city's best bargains and splurges, pitted against each other, to show the manic, crazy, and wonderful niches and extremes that can be found here.

## Department Stores

Paris may take credit for inventing the department store, but New York made them her own. Through the twentieth century, New York's department stores touted modernity and luxury, each with its own seductive charm. Although department stores are no longer the epitome of modern shopping, and several of the city's greatest names in retail (Gimbel's, A&S, B. Altman) are gone, the ones that are left retain some of their glamorous sheen or have acquired a new patina. Decades after their heyday, they are the grandes dames of New York shopping and occupy a place in city lore, from the specter of the Vanderbilt Mansion that haunts the site of today's Bergdorf's to the Macy's of *Miracle on 34th Street*. Unlike the rest of the country, where they are often swallowed up into the bellies of malls, department stores in New York still have a distinct presence and potent allure, different from the other shops and boutiques in the city. Here are our favorite things to do inside them.

## 653. Use the stairs at **Henri Bendel**.

Though it's named for a man, Bendel is distinctly feminine: petite, ladylike, and perfectly done-up. The ornate architecture and diminutive width make it feel more like a private townhouse than a mother ship, making Bendel the most fun of the department stores to explore. There are elevators, but if you ascend via the marble staircases, you're in for a real treat. Each floor unfolds in a series of nooks, full of sartorial treasures, and you can easily lose your way wandering from room to dazzling room—which is exactly what we recommend doing. This is not the best place to shop when you need to find something specific quickly, but it is a pleasure to wander around, and the sense of discovery if you do spy something is infinitely more satisfying than if you were to find the same item laid out in plain view at one of the other department stores.
*710 FIFTH AVENUE BETWEEN 55TH AND 56TH STREETS IN MANHATTAN. Subway: E, V to Fifth Avenue/53rd Street; N, R, W to Fifth Avenue/59th Street. 212-247-1100.*

## 654. Look but don't touch at **Bergdorf Goodman**.

For pure uptown sophistication, nothing beats a trip to Bergdorf's. The Zola-esque exaltation of luxury retail is apparent from the moment you walk in, when you see the jewelry and fine accessories presented in display cases like works of art. The behind-the-glass atmosphere can take the fun out of shopping (this really doesn't seem like a place where the salespeople like you to try things on), but if you think of it as a museum of luxury rather than a retail outlet, the works on view can be quite thrilling. Our favorite spot is the recently renovated seventh-floor home department, a maze-like collection of extravagant and stylishly anachronistic décor items, where you can see elaborate taxidermy animals and sample fancy French chocolates.
*754 FIFTH AVENUE BETWEEN 57TH AND 58TH STREETS IN MANHATTAN. Men's store: 745 Fifth Avenue at 58th Street. Subway: E, V to Fifth Avenue/53rd Street; N, R, W to Fifth Avenue/59th Street. 212-753-7300. www.bergdorfgoodman.com.*

→ **DID YOU KNOW?** *The Bergdorf building was formerly the site of the mansion of Cornelius Vanderbilt. Before the department store opened in 1928, the mansion's front gates were moved uptown, to Central Park's Conservatory Gardens (see page 218).*

## 655. Shop and refuel at **Bloomingdale's**.

Though it stands apart from the elite Fifth Avenue retail palaces both in neighborhood and in prestige, Bloomingdale's is well worth a detour. With a large information kiosk situated prominently in the lobby and an entrance to the store located in the subway station, it has a decidedly more plebeian feel than places like Henri Bendel and Bergdorf Goodman—although that's not to say that there aren't plenty of items well within splurge territory. Bloomingdale's carries medium- and high-end clothing for men, women, and children, as well as furniture, bedding and housewares, shoes, accessories, and cosmetics, and the atmosphere is welcoming and unpretentious, making it a great place to actually shop. It's also got the best places to eat of any department store in the city. Of the numerous eateries in the store, our favorites are 40 Carrots and Burke in the Box. More of a lunch counter than a restaurant, 40 Carrots is like a health-conscious cafeteria circa 1980, with tasty soups and salads served with melba toast, simple sandwiches served on grainy bread, and what many consider the best frozen yogurt in the city. A recent renovation spiffed up the slightly dated look but thankfully preserved the menu and recipes. The frozen yogurt is really yogurt, and the tangy plain and coffee flavors are a million miles away from Tasti D-lite. If you're in the mood for something cutting edge, try Burke in the Box, chef David Burke's new prepared-food café on the ground floor, where you can try items like mini-sandwiches served in tennis ball canisters and cheesecake lollipops.

*1000 THIRD AVENUE BETWEEN 59TH AND 60TH STREETS IN MANHATTAN. 212-705-2000. Subway: 4, 5, 6 to 59th Street; N, R, W to Lexington Avenue/59th Street.*

Note: Bloomingdale's now has a SoHo location, which carries a nice selection of trendy and high-end fashions, but no 40 Carrots or Burke in the Box.

*504 BROADWAY BETWEEN SPRING AND BROOME STREETS IN MANHATTAN. Subway: 6 to Spring Street; N, R, W to Prince Street. 212-729-5900. www.bloomingdales.com.*

## 656. Buy something cool at **Barneys**.

Some longtime downtown New Yorkers have never forgiven Barneys for its treasonous act of 1996: forsaking the original 17th Street store to preserve the uptown Madison Avenue location. With its air of exclusivity (some would say snootiness), Barneys fits in well among the other upscale Madison Avenue boutiques. Its emphasis on cutting-edge designers gives the feel (or the illusion) that you are getting a glimpse of the latest styles before they go mainstream. And though the vibe is now thoroughly uptown, Barneys has cashed in on its original edgy, downtown image with the edgy, downtown-looking styles of Co-op, the store's "casual" department. Co-op has spawned several freestanding boutiques, including, ironically, a large store within spitting distance of the original Seventh Avenue location.

**BARNEYS:** *660 MADISON AVENUE AT 61ST STREET IN MANHATTAN. Subway: N, R, W to Fifth Avenue/59th Street. 212-826-8900.*
**CO-OP CHELSEA:** *236 WEST 18TH STREET BETWEEN SEVENTH AND EIGHTH AVENUE. Subway: 1 to 18th Street. 212-593-7800. For addresses of other Co-op locations, visit www.barneys.com.*

→ **DID YOU KNOW?** *The 17th Street space that used to be the Barneys department store is now a museum of Himalayan art.*

## 657. Shop for cosmetics and rest your feet at **Takashimaya**.

The term "department store" conjures the image of a flurry of cosmetic pushers greeting customers with sales pitches and perfume baths before they escape to other floors. One of the ways that luxury department stores can signal their elite status is by getting rid of this bazaar-like atmosphere in the entryway, and moving the beauty products to a less obtrusive space (at Barneys and Bergdorf's, for instance, the makeup counters are on the basement levels). At Takashimaya, the New York outpost of the posh Japanese department store, they've dispensed with the entire counter concept and moved the beauty items to a calm, comfortable shopping area on the store's top level. The entire floor is bathed in a dim, flattering light, with products from high-end international brands like Babor and Santa Maria Novella displayed on one side of the floor, and a sitting area with couches at the other end. There are even several treatment rooms, where you can enjoy facials, massages, manicures, and pedicures featuring their products with no appointment necessary (although you do have to pay, of course). The sales people are fluent in human body language, and always seem to know the perfect instant to approach you—never a moment too soon, and nary a product push in sight. They carry only a small number of very exclusive brands, several of which are exclusive to Takashimaya, and all of which are of such high quality, they make Crème de la Mer look like Noxzema. On your way downstairs, stop on the other floors and browse the modest but eclectic selection of clothing, jewelry, and housewares. On the first floor, make sure to stop by the small flower department in the front to admire the floral designs by famed French florist Christian Tortu.
*693 FIFTH AVENUE BETWEEN 54TH AND 55TH STREETS IN MANHATTAN. Subway: E, V to Fifth Avenue/53rd Street. 212-350-0100.*

## Buy discounted designer clothing at a **sample sale**.

Sample sales are the fashion-conscious New Yorker's best-kept secret. These hidden caches of discounted designer clothing stock plenty of fashionable New York closets, and keep many a young fashion or magazine assistant in office-appropriate apparel.

Technically, most of the clothing sold at the sample sales listed here isn't actually designer samples, as they once were when the term "sample sale" was coined. The clothes you find at a sample sale are usually overstock from inventory; after designers ship that season's merchandise to stores, they sell what's left over to what are essentially clearing houses, at a big discount, which offer it to the public through sample sales. This means that, one, the stuff tends to be from the current season; and, two, there's usually a range of sizes.

Sample sales take place all the time. Many are held in the Garment District, at designer showrooms, but others are held in stores or other spaces around the city. *Time Out New York*, *New York Magazine*, and *DailyCandy* (www.dailycandy.com) list current sample sales and are good places to check to see who's offering what, where, and when. The following are some favorite places for sales:

**658. Clothingline:** This large warehouse in the Garment District gets new merchandise regularly, all year round, from a wide range of well-known designers such as Theory, Tocca, Ben Sherman, White & Warren, among many, many others. The selection and variety of the sizes are particularly good, and there is a huge communal dressing room for women. You can sign up on their Web site (www.clothingline.com) to receive a weekly e-mail that will notify you about upcoming sales.
*261 WEST 36TH STREET, SECOND FLOOR, BETWEEN SEVENTH AND EIGHTH AVENUES IN MANHATTAN. Open according to schedule, but usually Monday through Friday, from 10:00 a.m. to 6:00 p.m.; weekend sales are held occasionally. Subway: 1, 2, 3, A, C, E to 34th Street-Penn Station.*

**659. Find Outlet:** Find is a "chain" outlet—it has branches in Chelsea and NoLita, as well as New Jersey and Los Angeles. If Clothingline resembles a department store, with a sometimes overwhelming amount of brands and sizes, Find is the boutique of the New York discount fashion world. Both Manhattan outposts operate out of small storefronts, but the "sale" mentality prevails, on weekends especially, with people crowding the racks and trying on items in the aisles when the dressing rooms are full. The offerings lean toward up-and-coming labels rather than established high-fashion brands, so it's a great place to discover new designers before they make it big. If you go during the week, or happen to hit an off time, you're bound to come out with, well, a good find.
**Chelsea:** *361 WEST 17TH STREET BETWEEN EIGHTH AND NINTH AVENUES IN MANHATTAN. Subway: A, C, E to 14th Street; L to Eighth Avenue. Open Thursday through Sunday, noon to 7:00 p.m. 212-243-3177.*
**NoLita:** *229 MOTT STREET BETWEEN PRINCE AND SPRING STREETS IN MANHATTAN. Hours are the same as the Chelsea location. Subway: 6 to Spring Street; N, R, W to Prince Street. 212-226-5167. www.findoutlet.com.*

**660. *Barneys Warehouse Sale:*** If you've ever been walking around Chelsea at 7:00 a.m. on a Thursday morning and wondered what throngs of poshly dressed women could possibly be waiting for at that hour, chances are you've encountered the line for the opening day of the Barneys Warehouse Sale, the department store's legendary week-long housecleaning. Twice a year, in February and August, Barneys opens its warehouse to the public and sells off the remaining stock from that season at incredibly discounted prices to make room for the next season. The difference between this and a sample sale is that the clothes come from the store rather than the designers, but in practice there's no difference in merchandise or price, except that the February sale will feature mostly fall and winter clothes, and the August sale will offer mostly spring and summer clothes. Basically, you can expect to see all of the designers carried at Barneys and Co-op, and some of the exact clothing that was on the racks just the week before, for between 50 and 80 percent off, with markdowns occurring throughout the week. (Shoes and men's clothing available too.) Caution: this sale is not for the faint of heart—you need to be a hearty shopper to take it on. You will be pushed and shoved, you will pick through bins of clothing, you will try on clothes in the aisle, and you had better keep an eye on whatever treasures you find because everything is fair game until you hand over your credit card. By the end of the week, they are practically giving the clothes away, but most of the good stuff is long gone by the second morning. We suggest going on opening day, around 10:00 a.m. or 11:00 a.m.—the initial opening rush at 8:00 a.m. thins out as people leave for work, so you'll have a good hour or so before the lunchtime crowd descends.

*August and February. 255 WEST 17TH STREET BETWEEN SEVENTH AND EIGHTH AVENUES IN MANHATTAN. Subway: 1 to 18th Street. For exact dates and hours, visit www.barneys.com.*

## 661. Buy designer clothing for a discount at **Century 21**.

Century 21 is a department store—but it's a department store where the merchandise is half the price it would be at other department stores. From Prada and Pucci to Champs and Fruit of the Loom, you can find every type of clothing, shoe, accessory, or houseware, high- and low-end, in a relatively well-organized setting. Sure, the racks are crammed with clothes, customer service consists of the promise of a $25 credit if you're not given a receipt, and there is not a dependable selection of size and merchandise, but considering what you're getting (top-quality and high-fashion goods for a fraction of what they're normally sold for), it's amazingly easy to browse the racks. (And browse is what you'll want to do, since inventory varies greatly.) And though it pretty much always feels like the day before Christmas, recent renovations like an expanded shoe section and women's dressing rooms (well, cubbies) on the third floor have significantly enhanced the shopping experience. It's a particularly good place to stock up on underwear and socks, and for sizable discounts on coats

and men's suits. (There's also a location in Bay Ridge, Brooklyn.)
*22 CORTLANDT STREET BETWEEN CHURCH STREET AND BROADWAY IN MANHATTAN. Subway: 2, 3, 4, 5, J, M, Z to Fulton Street; A, C to Broadway-Nassau Street; R, W to Cortlandt Street. 212-227-9092. Brooklyn location: 472 EAST 86TH STREET BETWEEN FOURTH AND FIFTH AVENUES. Subway: R to 86th Street. 718-748-3266. www.c21stores.com.*

## 662. Fantasize about your dream house at **ABC Carpet & Home**.

ABC is the king of the city's shelter stores, and a wonderful example of the American dream come true. ABC was born in 1897, out of a pushcart on the Lower East Side, where Max Weinrib, an Austrian immigrant, sold used carpet and odd fabrics. In the generations since, it has grown into the world's biggest rug and carpet store, and today, it is run by Max's grandson and great-granddaughter. Occupying two landmark buildings on opposite sides of lower Broadway, ABC flanks the avenue, as if signaling your arrival downtown, where it rules by taste and confidence (its influence can be seen in the aesthetic and merchandise in many downtown stores and boutiques). On the west side of Broadway, the 881 building houses carpets and rugs, more than 35,000 from around the world, including antiques and Oriental rugs several centuries old, and new, modern rugs from ABC's own collection. At the home store across the street, the riches are laid out over six stories of lavishly designed departments, selling furniture, antiques, vintage and new fabrics, bedding and linens, breathtaking lamps and sconces, toys, books, drapes, scarves, jewelry, spiritual aids ... the amount of beautiful merchandise is literally staggering. ABC Home is by far the most opulent store in New York, eschewing minimalist chic in favor of wearing its riches on its sleeves, and while the carpet store may be of interest only to those looking to buy, the home store is actually best visited if you're not looking for anything in particular. Explore, and let yourself be seduced by the treasures that unfold floor after floor. Listen and you may hear a single piece calling your name, beckoning you for a closer look, and—should you have the resources—offering you the privilege of taking it home. (Should you lack the resources, ABC also has an outlet in the Bronx. For more information, visit the Web site below.)
*881 AND 888 BROADWAY AT 19TH STREET IN MANHATTAN. Subway: 4, 5, 6, L, N, Q, R, W to 14th Street-Union Square. 212-473-3000. www.abchome.com.*

## 663. Take a trip down memory lane (without breaking the bank) at **Reminiscence**.

Bursting at the seams with kitsch, Reminiscence proves that there is always a steady market for Pez dispensers and Hawaiian shirts. Opened in 1971, it began selling novelty items and vintage camp T-shirts long before other retailers started mass-manufacturing them. Their stuff, however, is authentically tacky. Up front, there is a selection of toys and games right out of *Pee Wee's Playhouse*, including Tom Tierney paper dolls, plastic Lolita sunglasses, Magic 8-Balls, retro cartoon character lunchboxes, and the largest assortment of car air fresheners we've ever seen. In the back, they sell vintage clothes—and this is a great place to shop for them because, one, unlike most vintage stores, the prices are quite cheap; two, the area with the clothes is roomy and never too crowded; and, three, there isn't an overwhelming amount of stuff, so you can browse through the entire selection easily, without worrying that the Hawaiian shirt you just found will be snatched out from under you.

*50 WEST 23RD STREET BETWEEN FIFTH AND SIXTH AVENUES IN MANHATTAN. Subway: F, V to 23rd Street. 212-243-2292.*

## 664. Find the perfect pair of jeans at **What Comes Around Goes Around**.

Although it's been open only since 1993, WCAGA has revolutionized the way people see and buy vintage clothes in New York. Housing the largest collection of vintage denim in the United States, the SoHo retail location looks more like an uptown boutique than a secondhand store, with shelves upon shelves of pristinely folded jeans, cases of accessories from boots to belt buckles, and racks of well-kept leather and woolen coats and jackets. The store's philosophy is that buying vintage clothes should be more exciting, more reliable, and more selective than picking through the racks at thrift shops, and the success of WCAGA lies in the fact that the selection is so broad and in such good condition that you have the fun of picking out a hard-to-find classic cut without the frustration of sifting through moth-eaten riffraff. They've even extended this philosophy to their showroom, which holds one of the most impressive and comprehensive collections of vintage clothing in the world, from western wear to sportswear and military outfits, as well as a library of vintage textiles, periodicals, and historical fashion memorabilia.

**WCAGA (RETAIL):** *351 WEST BROADWAY BETWEEN BROOME AND GRAND STREETS IN MANHATTAN. Subway: 6 to Spring Street; N, R, W to Prince Street. 212-343-9303.*
**WCAGA (SHOWROOM):** *13-17 LAIGHT STREET, NO. 28, BETWEEN VARICK AND CANAL STREETS, FIFTH FLOOR, IN MANHATTAN. Subway: 1, 2, 3, A, C, E to Canal Street. 212-274-8340. www.nyvintage.com.*

## 665. Buy some New York City shoes at **Sacco**.

Why, out of all of the shoe stores in the city, have we chosen this one as the place where you should buy your shoes? Because in New York, you need shoes that look good and you need shoes you can walk in, and Sacco is where you can buy one pair to serve both purposes. Sacco carries beautiful shoes that are designed to be worn (as in walked, run, and subwayed in), but that look like—though not derivative of—shoes from Gucci, Prada, and other high-end designers. Sacco has its own line, designed and manufactured in Italy, and adheres to special design guidelines to make each pump, sandal, and boot comfortable to walk in; the stores also carry styles from a few other brands, specially chosen for their high standards of style and comfort. And it gets better—for the quality, the shoes are shockingly inexpensive, around $100 to $250 for heels and loafers, and $150 to $300 for boots. Sacco adheres to another great European tradition and holds excellent sales in January and July.

*Multiple locations throughout Manhattan. Call 212-243-2070 or visit www.saccoshoes.com for store locations.*

## 666. Try the coffee at the **Bodum store**.

Nobody makes a French press like Bodum, the Danish kitchenware designer whose tasteful teapots, milk-frothers, espresso cups, garlic presses, cheese cutters, whisks, and glasses brighten the kitchens of many sophisticated New Yorkers. As if browsing for cappuccino machines and sleek chrome fondue sets wasn't enough of an urbane pleasure, the Bodum store also offers weary shoppers samples of coffee made in the one-of-a-kind machines—boiled, brewed, and served in the café-ware of your choice. There is also an in-store café for light savory meals and snacks.

*413 WEST 14TH STREET BETWEEN NINTH AND TENTH AVENUES IN MANHATTAN. Subway: A, C, E to 14th Street; L to Eighth Avenue. 212-367-9125. www.bodum.com.*

## 667. Get your dollar back at the **Music Inn**.

The proprietors of this wonderful, museumlike shop have accrued so much musical paraphernalia that to sift through it would take days—and considerable athleticism. All manner of musical instruments, from wooden flutes and xylophones to ukuleles and castanets, fill the hallways, clutter the floor, and hang from the ceiling. Shelves of vintage vinyl records line the walls, and sheet music, reeds, metronomes, and other accoutrements take up any leftover space. The owners are frighteningly knowledgeable on virtually every aspect of music, and will dig around upon request for just about anything you might desire. In order to enter the Music Inn, visitors must pay one dollar, which will be returned if they make a purchase at the store. Our advice is to make the most of this eccentric treasure, make a selection, and get your buck back at the checkout.

*169 WEST 4TH STREET BETWEEN SIXTH AND SEVENTH AVENUES. Subway: 1 to Christopher Street-Sheridan Square; A, C, E, B, D, F, V to West 4th Street. 212-243-5715.*

### 668. Seek out the **Manolo Blahnik store**.

The Manolo Blahnik store is hidden in the middle of a quiet block in Midtown, directly behind the **Museum of Modern Art** (see page 121). The store's sign is a tiny plaque, no bigger than those used on street-level doctor's offices, and though shoes are displayed in the window, there is no name-brand fanfare, no autographed pictures from *Sex and the City*, no distinguished marquee, nothing that calls out to shoppers on Fifth Avenue. It's not that they don't want you inside—everyone from the security guard/doorman who lets you in to the well-coiffed salespeople is surprisingly warm and amiable. It's that self-promotion is—apologies to the other stores—clearly beneath them. For this reason, Manolo Blahnik is a truly special store, and one of the few boutiques in the city that radiates luxury without being snooty or offensively exclusive. Even if there's no way in a million years that you'd actually buy a pair of these iconic sartorial treasures, the store is well worth a detour off Fifth Avenue's main drag. Come to experience, admire, and try for yourself, if you dare…

*31 WEST 54TH STREET BETWEEN FIFTH AND SIXTH AVENUES IN MANHATTAN. Subway: E, V to Fifth Avenue/53rd Street. 212-582-3007.*

### 669. Delight a friend with a gift from **Hable Construction** …

This West Village boutique carries Hable's beautiful and unique home accessories, which, while not dirt cheap, are a lot closer to reasonable than you might expect from a brand that is regularly featured in top fashion and shelter magazines. Textiles, bedding, gardening tools, and other décor elements are made from distinctive patterned fabrics of the owner's design, or in wool-felt by a Hungarian women's collective. The look is cheery but not cheesy, modern but not minimalist, and the store is full of charming knickknacks that would make delightful hostess gifts, housewarming tokens, or birthday presents.

*117 PERRY STREET BETWEEN GREENWICH AND HUDSON STREETS IN MANHATTAN. Subway: A, C, E to 14th Street; L to Eighth Avenue. 212-989-2375. www.hableconstruction.com.*

### 670. … or from **Auto**.

If you want to impress someone with your good taste, you can't go wrong at Auto. Hanging out on the fringes of the Meatpacking District, Auto is like the cool loner you always wanted to befriend in high school: it's proud to be outside the mainstream, and intriguing and stylish in its own way. Inside the store, you'll find slick, high-design lifestyle accessories like silkscreen cooking aprons, customizable nesting dolls, funky winter caps and mittens, and a well-edited selection of art and design books. The store is definitely geared toward the hip urban family, so you'll see plenty of cool baby gear, like tomato-shaped beanbag chairs, a hyper-stylized bouncy chair, and stuffed animals made of brightly colored cashmere. Auto recently expanded into the store next door, which sells jewelry and women's clothing. The prices are about what you'd expect from a place that carries cashmere teddy bears (expensive, though not outrageous), and even if this kind of mod luxury isn't your style, just being in the store will make you feel a little cooler.

*803 AND 805 WASHINGTON STREET BETWEEN GANSEVOORT AND HORATIO STREETS IN MANHATTAN. Subway: A, C, E to 14th Street; L to Eighth Avenue. 212-229-2292. www.thisisauto.com.*

## 671. Buy a gift for a kid or something unique for yourself at **Blue Tree**.

When Blue Tree opened up in the space vacated by the beloved toy store Penny Whistle on the Upper East Side, many adults and children who had lamented the loss of the neighborhood's one fun place to shop nearly jumped for joy. Blue Tree isn't exactly a toy store, although it does carry plenty of toys. It's more like a chic curiosity shop, overflowing with unique and exotic treasures scattered about in a delightfully topsy-turvy bi-level space. Children and former children will find something to tickle their fancy, like funky skateboards, a solar-powered rotating globe, ladies' purses made to look like yearbooks and doctor's manuals, and complete sets of Shakespeare's plays in adorable leather-bound mini-books. Store owner Phoebe Cates (a neighborhood mom who is married to the actor Kevin Kline) and her staff dart about the store like little sprites, going up and down the stairs, pulling hidden treasures out of nooks and crannies and chatting with customers. But lest the carefree atmosphere make you forget where you are, one look at the price tags will bring you right back— the cheapest item we found was the $9 pair of cashmere infant socks.

*1283 MADISON AVENUE BETWEEN 91ST AND 92ND STREETS IN MANHATTAN. Subway: 4, 5, 6 to 86th Street. 212-369-BLUE. www.bluetreeny.com.*

## 672. Earn a bottle of Cristal at **Sable's**.

The Upper East Side has long been home to many Eastern Europeans, and among the plethora of German and Hungarian delicatessens, Sable's Smoked Fish has for years been the most respected supplier of caviar, salmon, and all manner of Baltic treats. It's best to go on an empty stomach: the exceptionally generous staff will hand you samples of everything from thin slices of smoked mackerel to delicious lashings of lobster salad, served on a crispy square of toast. It's not cheap, but with a vast range of caviar, fish, cheese, bread, and traditional potato pancakes, it's difficult to leave with your wallet intact. That's not to say that there isn't a deal to be had: spend $1,500 in one visit, and you get a bottle of Dom Perignon champagne. Not bad, but we recommend you go the distance—spend $2,000 and earn a gleaming bottle of Cristal as your reward.

*1489 SECOND AVENUE BETWEEN 78TH AND 79TH STREETS IN MANHATTAN. Subway: 6 to 77th Street. 212-249-6177. www.sablesnyc.com.*

### 673. Equip yourself like a paparazzo at **B&H Photo**.

A Midtown institution for thirty years, B&H Photo is a photographer's gourmet supermarket, an emporium of camera and film supplies like no other in the world. B&H carries virtually everything a photographer could conceivably need, from a huge range of cameras, flashes, camcorders, and microphones to the broadest selection of film, editing equipment, and Polaroid accessories in the city. The store stocks every new item from every major brand, as well as vintage pieces and secondhand equipment, so there's something to fit every photographer's budget and taste, and amateurs, professionals, and collectors are all catered to. The process of actually purchasing something at B&H is unique as well—orders are placed at different counters and items are then picked up at the checkout, where they arrive by a system of overhead conveyor belts and pulleys.

*420 NINTH AVENUE BETWEEN 33RD AND 34TH STREETS IN MANHATTAN. Subway: 1, 2, 3, A, C, E to 34th Street-Penn Station. 212-444-6615. www.bhphotovideo.com.*

### 674. Furnish your apartment (or any small space) at **Tiny Living**.

Though New York has Crate and Barrel, Pottery Barn, and even a Home Depot, plenty of residents can't help feeling a little put out that most of the items sold at these popular chains wouldn't fit in their tiny living spaces. Tiny Living specializes in apartment-style home décor, and offers ingenious solutions to small-space constraints. Compact gadgets like collapsible wine racks and two-decker cheese graters will help apartment dwellers find functional space they didn't even know they had. And even if you live in a mansion, you can still enjoy some of Tiny's itty-bitty versions of regular doodads, like the mini–martini shaker and a Ping-Pong set that looks like it was designed for Tom Thumb.

*125 EAST 7TH STREET BETWEEN FIRST AVENUE AND AVENUE A IN MANHATTAN. Subway: L to First Avenue; 6 to Astor Place. 212-228-2748. www.tiny-living.com.*

### 675. Pluck and strum at **Mandolin Brothers**.

One of Staten Island's lesser-known attractions is Mandolin Brothers, Ltd., one of the greatest guitar stores in the world. With close to a thousand instruments in its vast showroom, Mandolin Brothers really carries every fretted instrument you can imagine, from classic acoustic and electric guitars to banjos, ukuleles, twelve-strings, pedal steels, bass guitars, and, of course, mandolins. There are new and used instruments at reasonable prices and rare collectibles from antique Gibsons to beloved Telecasters and one-of-a-kind Martins, and there is even an entire lefty section devoted to south-paw players. The golden rule of Mandolin Brothers' showroom is that you can pick up and play any instrument you want, without fear of frowns or comments from the staff. *629 FOREST AVENUE BETWEEN PELTON AND OAKLAND AVENUES IN STATEN ISLAND. Staten Island Ferry to Staten Island, then 48 Forest Avenue bus to Pelton Avenue. 718-981-8585. www.mandoweb.com.*

---

## 676. Stop in and be pampered at **Mayle**.

Jane Mayle's elegant and chic designs make her boutique on Elizabeth Street one of NoLita's gems. At first glance, her clothes look as if they could be vintage pieces—and in fact her boutique's previous incarnation, Phare, sold vintage clothes as well as new ones—but closer inspection reveals a sophisticated line of simply cut, colorful, and retro-inspired attire. Her dresses are pretty and feminine, and her coats and sweaters are thick and warm without being overly heavy—but the highlights of her collection are invariably her tops, which are often detailed with beads, sequins, and beautiful patterns without ever being cutesy or over-the-top. The store itself is small and cozy, and the staff is so unobtrusively helpful that trying on clothes makes you feel like a princess with ladies-in-waiting.
*242 ELIZABETH STREET BETWEEN HOUSTON AND PRINCE STREETS IN MANHATTAN. Subway: 6 to Spring Street; N, R, W to Prince Street. 212-625-0406.*

---

## 677. Have an intimate encounter with precious jewels at **Harry Winston**.

A block down from **Tiffany** (see page 25) is the flagship store of another legendary jeweler. Harry Winston does not have the same fame or iconic clout as the home of the little blue box, but its jewels are no less impressive. The store is calm and quiet as a boutique, and while that intimacy might make it more intimidating to browse in, it also lends a pleasant, furtive feeling, like being inside a life-size treasure chest right on Fifth Avenue. Winston, who was the last owner of the Hope Diamond (he donated it to the Smithsonian), was known for his intricate, artistic designs, and you can see examples of his masterpieces displayed in the store. (You could also try to strike up a musical number, like **Ed Norton in *Everyone Says I Love You***; for more great movie scenes, see page 113.)
*718 FIFTH AVENUE AT 56TH STREET IN MANHATTAN. Subway: E, V to Fifth Avenue/53rd Street; N, R, W to Fifth Avenue/59th Street. 212-245-2006. www.harrywinston.com.*

### 678. See jewels in a less rarified setting (no pun intended) in the **Diamond District**.

West 47th Street between Fifth and Sixth Avenues is home to more than 2,000 independent jewelers, many of them operating out of "exchanges," which are ground-level halls filled with up to 100 booths where different jewelers operate. The setting isn't luxe, but what it lacks in ambience it makes up for in expertise—since 47th Street is where diamonds come when they arrive in the United States, the jewelers here are some of the most experienced in the world. In addition to diamonds, you can also find wedding bands, watches, and regular gold, silver, and platinum jewelry. (This is also an excellent place for jewelry repairs.) The offerings here are not known for being particularly on the cutting edge (again, pun not intended) of style, but if you want to comparison shop, this is the best way to do it, and even if you're not in the market for a gem, it's fascinating to watch how this enclave of independent merchants does business. To help you navigate, the district operates an excellent Web site (see below) with information about the Diamond District and what is sold there, a directory of jewelers in the area, and buyer's guides for jewelry and diamonds.

*WEST 47TH STREET BETWEEN FIFTH AND SIXTH AVENUES IN MANHATTAN. Subway: B, D, F, V to 47th–50th Streets–Rockefeller Center. For more information, visit www.47th-street.com.*

### 679. Get yourself some Rem Koolhaas designs at **United Nude**.

When is a shoe not a shoe? When it's designed as an interpretation of architecture or an iconic object. To really get the gist, visit United Nude, the New York outpost of this shoe-producing European design company. Co-founded by shoemaker Galahad J.D. Clark and architect Rem D. Koolhaas (nephew of the Pritzker Prize–winning architect of the same name), United Nude produces elegant, architecturally inspired footwear that look as likely to turn up in *Dwell* as in *Vogue*. Their signature "concept" (the United Nude term for style) is the Mobius, a wedge sandal made from a single strip that forms a Mobius band and inspired by Mies van der Rohe's famous Barcelona chair. They also make a high-heeled pump called Naked, which doesn't have any covering over the shoe's construction and reinforcements. Although the design is high-concept, the shoes are surprisingly down-to-earth: all of the styles are comfortable enough to walk around in, and are reasonably priced. United Nude is currently in the process of expanding its line to include bags, clothing, eyewear, and, not surprisingly, furniture.

*260 ELIZABETH STREET BETWEEN PRINCE AND HOUSTON STREETS IN MANHATTAN. Subway: 6 to Spring Street. 212-274-9010. www.unitednude.com.*

## 680. Spoil your dog at **Trixie and Peanut**.

Trixie and Peanut is the Barneys of the city's pet boutiques, with designer dog clothes, personalized rhinestone collars, "Chewy Vuitton" fuzzy purses, and bottles of "Dog Perignon" (there is also stuff for cats). But what really makes this store stand out is the attention lavished on each and every furry diva. Even if you've got an overweight bulldog with questionable breath, they'll make you feel like he or she is the cutest pet in world.

*23 EAST 20TH STREET BETWEEN BROADWAY AND PARK AVENUE SOUTH IN MANHATTAN. Subway: 6 to 23rd Street. 212-358-0881. www.trixieandpeanut.com.*

## 681. Buy a bottle or two from **Acker, Merrill, and Condit**.

Many of us would like to know more about wine than we do, and most of us would like to drink more wine than we do. Both goals are possible at Acker, Merrill, and Condit, the oldest wine shop in America and a paradise for anyone with a taste for the grape. Founded in New York in 1820, Acker is still a family-run business and makes its customers' happiness top priority. Shopping for wine at this Upper West Side store is wonderfully unlike looking around a regular liquor store: for one thing, the selection is unrivalled, drawing on wines from most every vintage and continent; and for another, the people who work here are passionate and knowledgeable about wine, and can provide customers with anything from a history of a particular region to good advice on what goes best with butternut squash. AM&C holds a number of live and Internet auctions throughout the year, giving connoisseurs a chance to bolster their collections, and curious newcomers a chance to pick up a good bargain. The company philosophy—that experts and amateurs should enjoy wine together—extends to their Wine Workshop, which holds tastings and other events designed to spread knowledge and enjoyment of wine to as many people as possible.

*160 WEST 72ND STREET BETWEEN BROADWAY AND COLUMBUS AVENUE IN MANHATTAN. Subway: 1, 2, 3 to 72nd Street; B, C to 72nd Street. 212-787-1700. www.ackerwines.com.*

## 682. Avoid divulging how much you know about wine (and how much you can spend) at **Discovery Wines**.

It's a gimmick, but it might be the best gimmick in town: this East Village wine store has several computer stations where you can search the inventory by price, type, or region, and avoid the interaction with a store clerk that many people dread. The computers have a food-matching feature, where you enter the type of food and what kind of wine you want to serve (red, white, or sparkling), and it will list all the viable options. Finally, there's a scanner that you use to scan the barcode of a bottle to find out where it's from and what it pairs well with.

*10 AVENUE A AT HOUSTON STREET IN MANHATTAN. Subway: F, V to Lower East Side-Second Avenue. 212-674-7833. www.discoverywines.com.*

### 683. If you have to talk to a salesperson at a wine store, the Chelsea Wine Vault is the place to do it.

This store is as unpretentious as they come, and with more than 3,000 bottles, there really is something in every price and taste range. The people who work here are unabashedly enthusiastic about wine—a far cry from the aloof oenophiles in many wine stores. Grab a salesperson and describe what you're looking for, and he or she will likely launch into a discussion about a small wine or newly discovered producer. Tastings are similarly lively, with the staff eager to share the featured bottles, and it's hard not be infected by their oeno-exuberance.

*75 NINTH AVENUE BETWEEN 14TH AND 15TH STREETS IN MANHATTAN. Subway: A, C, E to 14th Street; L to Eighth Avenue. 212-462-4244. www.chelseawinevault.com.*

### 684. Bring the family to the wine store at Bottlerocket.

Believing that "buying wine should be as pleasurable as drinking it," Bottlerocket Wine & Spirits is a user- and family-friendly wine store, with a playspace for kids, treats for dogs and candy for under-agers, a large reading room in back, and some very friendly wine sellers. To keep things easy, the store stocks only 365 bottles at a time, arranging featured wines in several themed kiosks in the middle of the store. Wines for meat, vegetables, chocolate, celebrations, gift-giving, and other occasions are grouped in different stations, with easy-to-read tasting summaries, storage tips (don't keep open bottles of wine on the fridge door!), and edifying facts. There are also sheets of seasonal recipes for customers to take, or if you don't feel like cooking, there's a take-out kiosk, complete with menus from local delivery joints.

*5 WEST 19TH STREET BETWEEN FIFTH AND SIXTH AVENUES IN MANHATTAN. Subway: 4, 5, 6, L, N, Q, R, W to 14th Street-Union Square. 212-929-2323. www.bottlerocketwine.com.*

### 685. Add to your wine cellar at Italian Wine Merchants.

At the top end of the wine store spectrum is this sophisticated shop, specializing in very fine Italian wines and serving many connoisseurs and collectors. Co-owned by chef **Mario Batali** (see page 161), IWM is an authority on food, wine, and cellar management. To maintain quality control, only one bottle of each type of wine is on display; the rest is kept in a temperature-controlled cellar. Although the store sells single bottles of "everyday wine," IWM's real strength is in helping people begin or develop their own collections, and as a place to find special gifts (they even have a wine registry for couples). They have an extensive selection of well-chosen gift baskets and wine clubs for the novice through connoisseur. And though IWM is upscale, the attitude is one of appreciation rather than exclusion. They offer seminars and will arrange private tastings in their Studio del Gusto and Vintage Tasting room.

*108 EAST 16TH STREET BETWEEN IRVING PLACE AND UNION SQUARE EAST IN MANHATTAN. Subway: 4, 5, 6, L, N, Q, R, W to 14th Street-Union Square. 212-473-2323. www.italianwinemerchant.com.*

## 686. Try before you buy at **Vintage New York**.

Anything that uses a legal technicality to get customers what they want when they want it qualifies as a best thing to do, in our opinion. While plenty of wine stores offer scheduled tastings of specific wines from time to time, Vintage New York is the only place in the city where you can taste any wine in the store any time you want. That's because the shops are owned by Rivendell Winery in the Hudson Valley, which, as a "farm winery," is permitted to operate its two stores as off-site "tasting rooms," where patrons can taste and buy. What that means for you is that, unlike regular wine stores, they're free to uncork any bottle from the large selection of New York State wines whenever they choose, so customers can taste whatever they want. All of the wines are from New York State, so if you've never had local wine, this is place to try it.

*Both locations in Manhattan. SoHo: 482 BROOME STREET AT THE CORNER OF WOOSTER STREET. Subway: 1, 2, 3, 6 to Canal Street; J, M, Z, N, Q, R, W to Canal Street. 212-226-9463. Upper West Side: 2492 BROADWAY AT THE CORNER OF 93RD STREET. Subway: 1, 2, 3 to 96th Street. 212-721-9999. www.vintagenewyork.com.*

## 687. Shop for history at **Argosy**.

For eighty years, Argosy has exhibited and sold valuable autographs, rare books, and antique maps to serious collectors and intrigued passersby in their book-filled storefront. Occupying seven floors of a building near Bloomingdale's, Argosy is a museum, library, gallery, and history lesson rolled into one: you can see centuries-old maps, priceless first editions, rare inscribed copies of works by authors from Hemingway to Boccaccio, and letters from authors, critics, playwrights, composers, and other cultural notables that reveal much more than just a valuable signature. But such illustrious provenances don't come cheap: while some of the more common books and prints are comparatively affordable, you can expect prices for the rarer items to start in the thousands.

*116 EAST 59TH STREET BETWEEN PARK AND LEXINGTON AVENUES IN MANHATTAN. Subway: 4, 5, 6 to 59th Street; , N, Q, R, W to Lexington Avenue/59th Street. 212-753-4455. www.argosybooks.com.*

### 688. Fantasize about decorating your apartment with vintage posters from **La Belle Epoque**.

Art and advertising have long gone hand in hand, and the classic works on display at this esteemed Upper West Side gallery are testament to the golden age of poster art. La Belle Epoque claims to hold the largest collection of rare and vintage advertising posters in the world, with more than three thousand pieces on sale that date from the mid-nineteenth century to the end of the twentieth century. Each poster is an original, and the collection encompasses everything from the earliest English fashion magazine covers to Parisian exhibition posters, Warhol montages, post-Impressionist drawings by Henri Toulouse-Lautrec, and Art Deco masterpieces by Alphonse Mucha. Prices range from $500 to over $20,000, so shopping at La Belle Epoque is serious business—but the colorful gallery is fascinating to visit with or without your checkbook.

*280 COLUMBUS AVENUE AT 73RD STREET IN MANHATTAN. Subway: 1, B, C to 72nd Street. 212-362-1770. www.la-belle-epoque.com.*

### 689. Flip through racks of fine lingerie at **La Petite Coquette**.

Never has buying underwear been more comfortable for girls and easier for their boyfriends than at La Petite Coquette ("the little flirt"), a stylish boutique devoted to fancy lingerie and solid, friendly service. Racks that might otherwise hold paintings, posters, or samples of fabrics display underwear in all shapes, sizes, cuts, and colors, so prospective shoppers can flip through and coordinate exactly which print they want their particular cut of thong to come in. And if G-strings aren't the order of the day, La Petite Coquette carries plenty of other sexy, stylish, and even some comfortable pieces from a wide range of sophisticated brands, from ribbon-decorated creations by Mary Green and slips from La Perla, to comfy pajamas and simple boyshorts from Andre Sarda, and everything in between. (If you like La Petite Coquette and prefer to avoid the larger underwear emporia altogether, you should also check out Le Corset, a small and very sexy boutique in SoHo that carries an exceptionally fine range of classic, delicate lingerie.)

**LA PETITE COQUETTE:** *51 UNIVERSITY PLACE BETWEEN 9TH AND 10TH STREETS IN MANHATTAN. Subway: 4, 5, 6, L, N, Q, R, W to 14th Street-Union Square. 212-473-2478. www.thelittleflirt.com.*

**LE CORSET:** *80 THOMPSON STREET BETWEEN SPRING AND BROOME STREETS IN MANHATTAN. Subway: C, E to Spring Street. 212-334-4936.*

## 690. Save yourself some money at **National Wholesale Liquidators**.

It's difficult to explain the appeal of a place like National Wholesale Liquidators, but the concept is simple. A consumer-friendly, family-owned company, it buys every-thing—and we mean *everything*—at wholesale prices, and sells it to you for far less than anybody else. With more than 120,000 items in stock at any one time, most of it closeout merchandise from well-known brands, there is always a little bit of every-thing in the store. Shopping here is like going through a department store on fast-forward: there are videotapes, sneakers, sewing machines, toaster ovens, tote bags, inflatable swimming pools, pet toys, umbrellas, perfumes, stationery, stereos, T-shirts, video games, jewelry, lamps, storage containers, toothbrushes, barbecues, towels, and more, all lined up in aisle after aisle after aisle. On second thought, maybe it's not so difficult to explain how great this place is. With locations in Staten Island and Long Island City as well as Manhattan, this is the place to go when you need … anything.
*632 BROADWAY BETWEEN HOUSTON AND BLEECKER STREETS IN MANHATTAN. Subway: 6 to Bleecker Street; B, D, F, V to Broadway-Lafayette Street. 212-979-2400. See Web site for details on stock and other New York locations: www.nationalwholesaleliquidators.com.*

## 691. Stock up on everything Asian at **Pearl River Mart**.

Although **Century 21** (see page 244) coined the motto "New York's Best Kept Secret," Pearl River Mart was for years an underground shopping destination, an emporium of cheap and unusual goods, furniture, and clothes well off the beaten path. For those unacquainted with this strange and wonderful land, Pearl River Mart is a Chinese department store, which started nearly thirty years ago as a small retail outlet for immigrants in Chinatown to get products from home. Pearl's reputation as a place to find exotic and well-priced clothes and gifts eventually traveled uptown, and it became a legendary offbeat shopping stop, until finally, several years ago, it moved from the dingy location on Canal Street to a brand-new, airy, bi-level space complete with a café and the most **sparkling public restrooms** in the area (see page 351). For about as much as you would spend at Bed, Bath and Beyond (or less), you can furnish your home with beautiful porcelain dish sets, colorful lamps, rustic straw hampers, and silk bedding. And speaking of silk, the clothing and apparel section features tra-ditional Chinese jackets, dresses, skirts, pajamas, slippers, and robes. And then there are bags and shoes, food, tea and snacks, toys and dolls, beauty and health products, and, of course, the accessories and gifts. Suffice it to say that pretty much anything you could ever want or need can be found here, including information on feng shui so you can arrange all your new purchases favorably in your home.
*477 BROADWAY BETWEEN BROOME STREET AND GRAND STREET IN MANHATTAN. Subway: 6, J, M, Z, N, Q, R, W to Canal Street. 212-431-4770. www.pearlriver.com.*

## 692. Hang out at the **Williamsburg mini-mall**.

Along the main shopping drag of **Bedford Avenue** (see page 280) is this street-level collection of stores, the Williamsburg version of the suburban strip mall. Located in a converted industrial building (the former Realform Girdle Factory), the utilitarian looking mini-mall contains a coffee shop (an independent one, of course), a wine store, a cheese store, a bookstore, three women's clothing boutiques (one hippie, one trendy, and one wacky), an Internet center, a yoga studio, and a computer store. Most of the stores have entrances on the street, but you can also go from one to the other via the enclosed public area, the mall's defining element. Here you'll find a couple of benches, a very high-concept trash can, and a Neoprint photo machine, where for $3 you can get a sheet of miniature sticker-photos of you and your friends against animated backgrounds.
*BEDFORD AVENUE BETWEEN N. 4TH STREET AND N. 5TH STREET IN BROOKLYN. Subway: L to Bedford Avenue.*

## 693. Pretend you're a chef at **Broadway Panhandler**.

Whether your idea of cooking is making a soufflé from scratch or warming up a can of soup, Broadway Panhandler will make you feel like a pro—or that you could be, if you had the right equipment. With top-of-the-line pots and pans, obscure cooking gadgets, sleek kitchen accessories, and the best knife selection in town, this SoHo store will bring out every culinary inclination you have. If that's not enough inspiration, the lively in-store demonstrations by chefs and cookbook authors might convince you to throw away your take-out menus for good.
*477 BROOME STREET AT THE CORNER OF WOOSTER STREET IN MANHATTAN. Subway: 6, J, M, Z, N, Q, R, W to Canal Street. 866-266-5927. www.broadwaypanhandler.com.*

## 694. Find a companion at **Mogu**.

A recent import from Japan, Mogu is a home design store with a difference. Each of its pillows, cushions, chairs, beanbags, and other furnishings are made with a soft, malleable, Styrofoam center that molds easily to fit any shape, and everything is covered either in a soft, stretchy, Lycra-based material or in an even softer imitation fur. This makes the objects comfortable furnishings for the home and incredibly tactile and fun to play with. You can get heart-shaped cushions, crosses, donuts, or spectacularly huge basketballs, in an array of blindingly bright colors. Favorites include the enormous hanging tube cushions, which are suspended from the ceiling and seem to be there just for you to squeeze as you walk around; and the soft, life-size, person-shaped pillow, to keep you company on lonely winter nights.
*258 ELIZABETH STREET BETWEEN HOUSTON AND PRINCE STREETS IN MANHATTAN.*

*Subway: 6 to Bleecker Street; B, D, F, V to Broadway-Lafayette Street. 212-625-2444.*
*www.mogu.com.*

## 695. Break the mold with something from **Patricia Field**.

Way back in 1966, a young Patricia Field opened an eponymous boutique in Green-wich Village to sell her line of fresh and hip clothes to savvy New Yorkers. Thirty years later, Patricia Field—still younger at heart than most of her fashion contemporaries—moved into a salon in SoHo called Hotel Venus, a haven of sexy, provocative, and chic clothes for the downtown crowd. With a successful history of forays into high fashion, tongue-in-cheek political T-shirts, and an Emmy Award–winning career as a costume designer (she dressed the stars of *Sex and the City*), Field has achieved legendary sta-tus as a true pioneer and visionary of the New York fashion scene. Her designs for women are bright, sassy, and colorful, from tiny miniskirts and iconic T-shirts to tightly cut jeans and striped legwarmers. In addition to a growing range of cool, understated designs for men, Hotel Venus stocks a host of accessories ranging from stylish hats, sunglasses, and personalized tote bags to novelty items and other mysterious "white trash treats."

*302 BOWERY AT HOUSTON STREET IN MANHATTAN. Subway: 6 to Bleecker Street; B, D, F, V to Broadway-Lafayette Street. 212-925-2741. www.patriciafield.com.*

## 696. Bring back a souvenir from **Roberta Freymann**.

If a trip to Kasmir, Marrakech, or Hanoi isn't in your future, a visit to Roberta Freymann can have you looking like you just got back from an exotic holiday. Tucked away on the first and second floors of a townhouse on the Upper East Side, this boutique is packed to the brim with colorful clothing and accessories from far-flung reaches of the world. Madison Avenue will feel very far away when you look at the price tags, so you can stock up on gorgeous kimonos and wraps, unusual printed skirts and dresses, jewelry, beach gear and more—without having to worry about how you'll fit everything in your suitcase.

*153 EAST 70TH STREET BETWEEN LEXINGTON AND THIRD AVENUES IN MANHATTAN. Sub-way: 6 to 68th Street. 212-585-3767*

## 697. Add some weight to your library at **Bauman Rare Books**.

The Bauman galleries divide their monumental and world-renowned collection of rare and antique books between New York and Philadelphia. Anybody who's serious about getting hold of a particular edition of anything, from Chaucer to Fitzgerald, will be able to find it here—for a hefty price, of course, generally starting in the thousands.

Recently seen in the New York gallery: a first edition of Tolkien's *The Hobbit* for $65,000; an inscribed edition of Bertrand Russell's *Principia Mathematica* for $45,000; and a specially illustrated edition of Arthur Rimbaud's *Season in Hell* for $20,000. Besides rare books, the Bauman gallery has original musical scores, handwritten manuscripts from poets, novelists, and playwrights, and autographs.

*535 MADISON AVENUE BETWEEN 54TH AND 55TH STREETS IN MANHATTAN. Subway: 6 to 51st Street; E, V to Lexington Avenue/53rd Street. 212-751-0011. www.baumanrarebooks.com.*

### 698. Get a shopping bag from **Brooklyn Industries**.

This Brooklyn-born clothing store is like the NYC version of **American Apparel** (see page 317), selling basic streetwear like T-shirts, corduroy pants, sweaters, and down vests, all in bright colors. But an additional incentive to buy something here is the shopping bags. These huge, reusable totes have an outside pocket and are big and sturdy enough to carry a week's worth of laundry or a stack of library books. They are hands down the best shopping bags in the city, and are well worth the cost of what you'll buy to get one. (If they don't give you one with your purchase, just ask.)

*Multiple locations; for information, call 800-318-6061 or visit www.brooklynindustries.com.*

### 699. See stripes at the **Paul Smith boutique**.

One of England's finest fashion exports, Paul Smith has consignments in department stores all over the world, but only a handful of freestanding boutiques. Shopping at Paul Smith can be as fun as the clothes themselves, which stand out as among the most colorful and charismatic in a world of otherwise dark and serious menswear. His store on lower Fifth Avenue—hidden on a quiet corner just south of the big flagship chain stores—is a lively yet comfortable place to browse through wooden shelves of shirts, T-shirts, jeans, suits, and more. The powerful combination of his style and humor shows most in his accessories: everything from hats and ties to wallets and cufflinks is decorated with bright colors, iconic imagery, and the ubiquitous multicolored stripes. The impeccably dressed staff is always friendly and can be constructively critical if you ask. Make a point to visit during the winter and summer sales, and look out for the beautiful store dog.

*108 FIFTH AVENUE AT 16TH STREET IN MANHATTAN. Subway: 4, 5, 6, L, N, Q, R, W to 14th Street-Union Square; F, V to 14th Street; L to Sixth Avenue. 212-627-9770. www.paulsmith.co.uk.*

### 700. Try on shoes at the **Camper store**.

Camper, the stylish Majorcan shoe company, is known for its whimsical sensibility, like its line of "Twins" shoes, where the two shoes in a pair don't quite match. Fittingly, the store in SoHo has a few playful touches as well. The shoes are displayed on a stage against a red painted wall on one side of the store; on the other side is a series of rubbery-looking, slightly inflated disks, which are the seats you can use while trying on shoes. It feels like you're sitting on a whoopee cushion, but don't worry—the air isn't going to come out. It might take a second or two to get your balance, but once you do, you'll be treated to the sweetest seat in the neighborhood.

*125 PRINCE STREET AT THE CORNER OF GREENE STREET IN MANHATTAN. Subway: N, R, W to Prince Street. 212-375-9786. www.camper.com.*

## 701. Sift through forgotten classics at **Bookleaves**.

Virtually hidden among the winding streets of the far West Village, Bookleaves is a wonderful old-fashioned bookshop full of first editions, rare old nonfiction books, and tattered copies of classic novels. The store is cluttered, cozy, and warm, and the selection is so varied that you could leave with a cheap, well-loved paperback thriller or a beautiful vintage hardcover art book. The store has worn leather chairs and an owner with an inexhaustible knowledge of world literature, and there are few more pleasurable things to do in the colder months than retreat into this little treasure and warm up with a book.

*304 WEST 4TH STREET AT BANK STREET IN MANHATTAN. Subway: 1, 2, 3 to 14th Street; A, C, E to 14th Street; L to Eighth Avenue. 212-924-5638.*

## 702. Complete your comic book collection (or start one) at **Midtown Comics**.

Among the largest and best-stocked comic book stores in the world, Midtown Comics sells every single trade comic book in print, and a whole lot more besides. Spread out over two huge locations are mainstream brands like Marvel and Dark Horse to manga books, independent publishers, and comic-related trade paperbacks. In addition to their up-to-date selection of new titles, the stores share a collection of more than half a million back issues, as well as toys, statuettes, and figurines of all your favorite characters.

*Both locations in Manhattan. **Times Square:** 200 WEST 40TH STREET AT SEVENTH AVENUE. Subway: 1, 2, 3, 7, N, Q, R, W, S to 42nd Street-Times Square; A, C, E to 42nd Street-Port Authority Bus Terminal.*

***Grand Central:** 459 LEXINGTON AVENUE AT 45TH STREET. Subway: 4, 5, 6, 7, S to Grand Central-42nd Street. 800-411-3341. www.midtowncomics.com.*

### 703. Spoil your bicycle at **Conrad's**.

Conrad's is anomalous in several ways: it's a bike store that has thrived in the posh no-man's-land of Tudor City for thirty-five years; it's a mom-and-pop shop, but has a cutting-edge inventory; and despite the notoriously high turnover in retail, it has employed the same mechanics for two and a half decades. But it is exactly these reasons that city cyclists in the know make the trek to Tudor City Place when their precious Treks and Cannondales need some TLC.

*25 TUDOR CITY PLACE NEAR 41ST STREET IN MANHATTAN. Subway: 4, 5, 6, 7, S to Grand Central-42nd Street. 212-697-6966.*

### 704. Sip lemonade in the garden at **Darling**.

Darling is without question one of the loveliest boutiques in the city, a special place where you leave yourself in the salesperson's hands, and you'll be cared for like an eagerly anticipated guest. Located in a landmark townhouse at the top of the West Village, the boutique occupies the ground and basement levels, with a beautiful garden out back, where in warmer weather you can drink fresh lemonade while you chat with the staff. Owner Ann French Emonts, a costume designer and costume teacher whose former students include fashion designer Zac Posen, handpicks every piece in the store, including new, vintage, and her own one-of-a-kind designs. The look is feminine but not cutesy, with an emphasis on pieces with original or hand-sewn details. The women who work here are like no other salespeople in the world—they are enchanting and sweet, like gracious hostesses who make you feel completely at home in their delightful abode. On Thursday nights, the store stays open late, and you can join them for champagne while you shop.

*1 HORATIO STREET AT EIGHTH AVENUE IN MANHATTAN. Subway: A, C, E to 14th Street; L to Eighth Avenue. 646-336-6966. www.darlingny.com.*

### 705. Impress your friends with a bag from **Peter Hermann**.

What's so special about this cramped Thompson Street bag store? Take a closer look at the merchandise inside. Those with a taste for European fashion will surely recognize the names on the labels—and be shocked. This boutique, which carries bags and leather goods from European designers, many of which are hard or impossible to find anywhere else in the U.S., is a well-kept secret among New York Europhiles. Hermann himself is often in the store, but any probing into how he gets the merchandise over here will likely be met with a brush-off or vague explanation, so don't bother. Ten years ago, this was one of the few places where you could find bags from French brands like Longchamp and Herve Chapellier. Hermann still carries a good selection of both those brands, but today, the hot finds are the bags from Mandarina Duck, an Italian brand whose purses are extremely hard to get in this country.

*118 THOMPSON STREET BETWEEN PRINCE AND SPRING STREETS IN MANHATTAN. Subway: C, E to Spring Street. 212-966-9050.*

## 706. Prepare for a trip—pretend or real—at Flight 001.

This funky West Village store specializes in cool travel gear, from sleek luggage and travel accessories to useful travel gadgets. Even if you are not going away, you may be tempted by the unusual bags from chic designers like Orla Keily and Un Après-Midi de Chien; leather wallets and accessories from Tusk; and skin care products from Korres and Dr. Hauschka. All told, the selection is a little random, but it's a lot of fun to browse through, and it's a great place to go to feel like part of the jet set. Afterward, practice being abroad by stopping by **Tea & Sympathy** (see page 189).

*96 GREENWICH AVENUE AT JANE STREET IN MANHATTAN. Subway: A, C, E to 14th Street; L to Eighth Avenue. 212-989-0001. www.flight001.com.*

## 707. Join in Finnegan's Wake at the Gotham Book Mart.

Eighty-five years ago, a woman named Frances Steloff opened the Gotham Book Mart, a monument to literature and an oasis of calm in Midtown that remains one of the most impressive and pleasant bookstores in New York. Guided by a commitment to literature, Steloff for years challenged censors, and championed the experimental, becoming a well-known and leading supplier of controversial works by novelists such as Henry Miller, D. H. Lawrence, and James Joyce. Joyce himself used to order books from Gotham, and the store is home to both the James Joyce Society and the Finnegan's Wake Society of New York. Spread over two floors, Gotham sells a mix of new and used books, specialist journals, and rare and out-of-print editions, and also holds exhibitions of notable books and artworks in its upstairs gallery. The poetry, fiction, and biography sections are particularly strong, and the helpful staff is full of arcane literary knowledge. Whether you go to join the Joyce enthusiasts, or simply to leaf through the finest collection of Edward Gorey books in the city, Gotham is an important place to visit.

*16 EAST 46TH STREET BETWEEN FIFTH AND MADISON AVENUES IN MANHATTAN. Subway: B, D, F, V to 47th-50th Streets-Rockefeller Center. 212-719-4448. www.gothambookmart.com.*

## 708. Hook yourself up at J&R.

Though much of the technology it started out selling is now obsolete, J&R has remained a fixture of New York retail for thirty-five years. In 1971, J&R opened a store on Park Row selling LPs, eight-tracks, and quadraphonic hi-fi equipment. In 2006, the J&R stores occupy an entire block of Park Row, and between them carry absolutely every kind of electronic product imaginable. A rare example of a family-run super-store, J&R is an authorized dealer of virtually everything it carries and yet still main-tains the kind of small-business relationships that keep its prices among the lowest in the city. You can get anything from laptops and cameras to iPods, VCRs, stereo equipment, camcorders, DVD players, musical instruments and recording equipment, computer software, CDs, video games . . . and all those unnamed leads, plugs, and accessories that you need to hook things up. The knowledge of the staff extends beyond the products in the store to great advice on what you have at home and what you might need in the future. On top of all this, J&R holds a special place in the hearts of New Yorkers: it's been a loyal, successful, and dependable retailer integral to the downtown community since it opened, and has been a major player in the sup-port and rejuvenation of lower Manhattan in the wake of 9/11. Keep an eye out for the live music events J&R brings to City Hall Park.

*PARK ROW BETWEEN BEEKMAN AND ANN STREETS IN MANHATTAN. Subway: 2, 3 to Park Place or Fulton Street; 4, 5, 6 to Brooklyn Bridge-City Hall; A, C to Broadway-Nassau Street; J, M, Z to Fulton Street; N, R, W to City Hall. 212-238-9000. www.jr.com.*

## 709. Sharpen up at **Duncan Quinn**.

After only a couple of years in SoHo, trend-setting menswear designer Duncan Quinn's stylish Spring Street boutique has become one of downtown's hottest shop-ping destinations. Aptly described by *GQ* magazine as "rock 'n' roll meets Savile Row," Quinn's sense of style is the picture-perfect product of an appreciation for the refine-ment of traditional English tailoring and a youthful flair for the edgier side of modern fashion. While not straying far from the familiar lines and close-fitting cuts of the clas-sic gentleman's suit, his colorful linings, bold ties, fitted shirts, and lively cufflinks and accessories inject a sharp, modish flavor. Besides suits and formal wear, Duncan Quinn sells a wide range of less serious but equally smart clothing, from brightly colored cashmere sweaters to T-shirts, socks, underwear, and even a small selection of ladies clothes. Best of all, Duncan Quinn offers a bespoke tailoring service, which will fit you with a sharp new look in the handcut cloth of your choice.

*8 SPRING STREET AT ELIZABETH STREET IN MANHATTAN. Subway: 6 to Spring Street; B, D, F, V to Broadway-Lafayette Street; N, R, W to Prince Street. 212-226-7030. www.duncanquinn.com.*

## 710. Have a fragrance made for your sweetheart at **Creed** . . .

The Creed family has been making beautiful, sophisticated fragrances for its elite clientele in Paris since 1760, counting Oscar Wilde, Audrey Hepburn, and Napoleon

Bonaparte as former customers. At their small boutique on Bond Street, and now in a new location on Madison Avenue, New Yorkers can follow in these elegant footsteps and request that the sixth generation of the Creed family—Olivier Creed—make a unique perfume for a lucky someone. The staff will take into account any details of character and taste you wish to share, and will then put centuries of secrets to use in crafting a scent just for the recipient. If the $20,000 price tag seems too high, bottles of Creed's delicious ready-made creations are available for sale at the much friendlier price of $150.

*Both locations in Manhattan. 9 BOND STREET AT LAFAYETTE STREET. Subway: 6 to Bleecker Street; B, D, F, V to Broadway-Lafayette Street. 212-228-1940. 897 MADISON AVENUE BETWEEN 71ST AND 72ND STREETS. Subway: 6 to 68th Street-Hunter College. 212-794-4480.*

## 711. . . . or create your own scent at **Jo Malone**.

British perfumer Jo Malone does not have one signature scent. Instead, she is known for her delicate technique of fragrance combining, designing her scents to be layered over one another to create an individual "fragrance wardrobe." At her Flatiron store, you can develop your own perfume in the fragrance kiosk, with buttons that release different scents (and if you need help, you can arrange for a personal fragrance consultation). Other luxurious in-store services include home fragrance and skin care combining consultations, plus hand and arm massages.

*949 BROADWAY AT 22ND STREET IN MANHATTAN. Subway: N, R, W to 23rd Street. 212-673-2220. www.jomalone.com.*

*N.B.: There is also a Jo Malone boutique at Madison Avenue, but it does not have a fragrance booth: 946 MADISON AVENUE BETWEEN 74TH AND 75TH STREETS IN MANHATTAN. Subway: 6 to 77th Street. 212-472-0074.*

## 712. Find a replacement for a missing button at **M&J Trimming**.

This Garment District staple has a literally mind-boggling selection of trimming paraphernalia. Ribbons, beading, buttons, buckles, and sequins in every shape, size, color, and material are displayed along ceiling-high racks. For the crafty and DIY set, M&J is the haute couture of trimming, a step above the other trim stores in the area, offering only the best materials (crystal rhinestones, silk Jacquard, velvet ribbons) imported from Europe, Asia, and all over the world. For the rest of us, it is a sight to behold, and a store where you are guaranteed to find something you need—or suddenly must have.

*1008 SIXTH AVENUE BETWEEN 37TH AND 38TH STREETS IN MANHATTAN. Subway: B, D, F, V, N, Q, R, W to 34th Street-Herald Square. 800-9-MJTRIM. www.mjtrim.com.*

### 713. Treat your dog to happy hour at **Zoomies' biscuit bar**.

You and your pet will feel right at home at Zoomies, thanks to the warm atmosphere and welcome of the owners, Susan and Angelique. Susan, a former executive at Christian Dior, and Angelique, who owned a restaurant in Paris, combined their expertise and love of dogs (they are the proud owners of an adorable pup named Chouchou) to create this charming West Village boutique. Susan designs a line of dog beds and accessories, and Angelique runs the biscuit bar, which is full of homemade dog treats. They will make a fuss over your dog and keep him or her busy as you browse the merchandise, displayed on beautiful French antiques (another passion of theirs). Afterward, have a biscuit at the bar (Angelique says they're OK for humans, too), and if the weather's nice, take your pup out to the back garden to run around.
*434 HUDSON STREET BETWEEN LEROY AND MORTON STREETS IN MANHATTAN. Subway: 1 to Houston Street. 212-462-4480. www.zoomiesnyc.com.*

### 714. Improve your home with something from the **Vitra Design Store**.

This small showroom offers iconic modern furniture and accessories to design professionals and discerning Manhattanites. Along one side of the store runs a platform of elegant, utilitarian chairs from designers that include Charles and Ray Eames, Jean Prouve, Frank Gehry, and George Nelson, and the shop floor is decorated with Karim Rashid tables, Noguchi stools, and Philippe Starck lamps. There is a small selection of high-brow design books, which are housed in a chic shelving system that at first glance looks like an exhibit too carefully arranged to touch, but which can be browsed through in comfortable chairs nearby. Most of the pieces are not only attractive, useful pieces of home furniture, but also celebrated artifacts of design history. The prices aren't low, but they aren't extravagant either, so this is a good place to start if you're looking to smarten up your living quarters.
*29 NINTH AVENUE BETWEEN 13TH AND 14TH STREETS IN MANHATTAN. Subway: A, C, E to 14th Street; L to Eighth Avenue. 212-463-5750. www.vitra.com.*

### 715. Step back in time at the **Lascoff Apothecary**.

Between the Duane Reades on every corner and treasures like **Bigelow** (see page 266), New York City is a hypochondriac's dream—and Lascoff completes the picture. Housed in a beautiful old room of dark wood shelves and glass casements are Parisian soaps, English bubble baths, Dead Sea salts, Italian flu medicines, and arcane bottles of Swedish mouthwash. Every pharmaceutical taste is catered to, whether you scrub with pumice and oils or shave with a bowl of lather and a badger-hair brush, and the major new brands can be found alongside classic boutique fragrances and little-known interna-

tional specialties. The Lascoff Apothecary hasn't changed much since moving to its current location in the early 1930s (the store has been in business on Lexington Avenue since 1899, first on 84th Street, and its 82nd Street incarnation is run by the third Lascoff generation), and shopping here is like rummaging through a grandfather's house for treasure. You have to hunt for things by opening the cupboards and drawers around the room (there are even some hidden behind an old leather couch). Be sure to check out the drugstore's history in the beautiful sepia photographs that stand in the windows.
*1209 LEXINGTON AVENUE AT 82ND STREET IN MANHATTAN. Subway: 4, 5, 6 to 86th Street. 212-288-9500.*

---

### 716. Get yourself that *shtreimel* you always wanted at **Shtreimel Center**.

Nowhere else on earth do the forces of style and Orthodox Judaism come together more perfectly than at this Brooklyn men's hat emporium. Shtreimel Center is a place like no other, an extravaganza of Hasidic headwear that caters to more kinds of religious aesthetics than one would have thought existed. Taking their names from letters of the Hebrew alphabet, Hasidic hats often tend toward the fedora shape and are limited to blacks and browns, but there is a surprising variety of styles, covering everything from wide-brimmed and felt to tall, round, and furry. Whether you're buying your soft velvet *pey*, trilby-esque *gimel*, or bowler-style *ayen* out of professional necessity, spiritual enthusiasm, or simple sartorial taste, Shtreimel Center is a sight to behold, and the only place to go for a sweet *alef beyz*.
*5707 NEW UTRECHT AVENUE, BETWEEN 57TH AND 58TH STREETS IN BROOKLYN. SUBWAY: D, M, N to New Utrecht Avenue. 718-436-4037.*

---

### Discover a new designer at a **designer market**.

New York has an embarrassment of artists and clothing designers whose work has yet to hit the mainstream. You can take advantage of this at two excellent designer markets, regularly occurring flea market–style covered markets brimming with vendors selling clothes, jewelry, handbags, and other pieces of their own design:

**717. TheMarketNYC** is held in the Saint Patrick's youth center on Mulberry Street, every Saturday and Sunday, from 11:00 a.m. to 7:00 p.m. The vendors are "emerging designers," who sell mostly jewelry and clothes, and the looks do not stray too much from those of the boutiques a block over.
*268 MULBERRY STREET BETWEEN HOUSTON AND PRINCE STREETS IN MANHATTAN. Subway: 6 to Bleecker Street; B, D, F, V to Broadway-Lafayette Street; N, R, W to Prince Street. 212-580-8995. www.themarketnyc.com.*

**718. Artists and Fleas** has a wider range of goods for sale, in a smaller space. Located in an old warehouse on **N. 6th Street** (see page 280), the vendors here run the gamut from clothing and jewelry designers like the ones at MarketNYC, to artists, secondhand and antiques dealers, and even some people selling homemade goodies to munch on while you shop. In addition to the goods, this market is a lot of fun to browse because there is a DJ who plays Madonna, doo-wop, and other hip retro favorites.

*129 N. 6TH STREET BETWEEN BEDFORD AVENUE AND BERRY STREET IN BROOKLYN. Subway: L to Bedford Avenue. 917-541-5760. www.artistsandfleas.com.*

## 719. Go bold or minimalist at the MoMA Design Store.

MoMA's museum shop is such a good place to shop that it expanded out of the museum into a freestanding store. In addition to the two locations by the museum (one inside the museum and one across the street), there is one in SoHo, which more than holds it own against the other design heavyweights in the neighborhood, and it is the best of the three to shop in because it's the least crowded. Inside the stores, you'll find traditional gift shop fare (books, calendars, and museum-related tchotchkes) as well as furniture, jewelry, and housewares from cool classic and contemporary designers. There are Eames chairs in bold colors, high-concept kitchen gadgets, contrasting wallets and card cases from the colorful British line Designers Guild, and creative games and toys for kids. MoMA recently started to carry Muji, the mid-priced, severely minimalist Japanese line of home accessories and office supplies popular in Europe. Now you can finally buy the cardboard speakers and plain aluminum business card cases that your friends in Paris and Tokyo have.

**MUSEUM LOCATION:** *11 AND 44 WEST 53RD STREET BETWEEN FIFTH AND SIXTH AVENUES IN MANHATTAN. Subway: E, V to Fifth Avenue/53rd Street. 212-767-1050.*

**SOHO LOCATION:** *81 SPRING STREET AT THE CORNER OF CROSBY STREET IN MANHATTAN. Subway: 6 to Spring Street; N, R, W to Prince Street. 646-613-1367. www.momastore.org.*

## 720. Try some of Britain's most beloved delicacies at Myers of Keswick.

British expats can enjoy a scotch egg and some fresh chipolata sausage, and then stock up on tins of Heinz beans, bottles of H.P. sauce, Walker's crisps, and other treats from home. Those unfamiliar with English gastronomic jewels should start with McVities chocolate digestive biscuits. Myers supplies sausages, meats, and other ingredients to several of the city's **best English restaurants** (see page 189).

*634 HUDSON STREET BETWEEN HORATIO AND JANE STREETS IN MANHATTAN. Subway: A, C, E to 14th Street; L to Eighth Avenue. 212-691-4194. www.myersofkeswick.com.*

## 721. Set up your own bakery at **New York Cake and Baking Supply**.

This professional-grade supply store has everything you could possibly need to make a dessert. There's no sugarcoating on the store itself, but what it lacks in ambience, it more than makes up for with a selection that will satisfy cooks and pastry chefs, and boggle the minds of everyone else. Even those whose ovens are filled with shoes and wine bottles will want to try their hands at baking when they see things like a cool-but-scary-looking crème brûlée set, complete with mini blowtorch, and the rows of beautiful edible decorations, which can come in handy even if, in the end, you decide to go with store-bought.

*56 WEST 22ND STREET BETWEEN FIFTH AND SIXTH AVENUES IN MANHATTAN. Subway: F, V to 23rd Street; N, R, W to 23rd Street. 212-675-2253. www.nycake.com.*

## 722. Deck out your studio with art supplies from **New York Central**.

This supplier of the New York art world celebrated its centennial in 2005, but among city artists, it is as popular as ever. New York Central is a wonderful, labyrinthine, old-fashioned art store that has absolutely the best range of art supplies around, from the largest selection of fine arts papers in the country (there are more than 3,000 papers, cards, and vellums) to etching and wood-carving tools, silk screen supplies, and hand-made sketchbooks. They carry more than one hundred canvasses and thousands of brushes, many of which are antiques that date back to the 1920s and 1930s. Every member of the staff in the store is an artist, and under the rule of legendary, charming, and outspoken owner Steven Steinberg, the service is second to none, with personal attention and firsthand knowledge doled out in equal measure. Everyone from private enthusiasts to New York notables like Lichtenstein and Warhol has made New York Central their favorite place for art supplies; it would be surprising if this unique store isn't celebrating its bi-centennial.

*62 THIRD AVENUE AT 11TH STREET IN MANHATTAN. Subway: 4, 5, 6, L, N, Q, R, W to 14th Street-Union Square; L to Third Avenue. 212-473-7705. www.nycentralart.com.*

## 723. Buy sneakers at **Paragon**.

There's no shortage of places to buy sneakers in this city—in fact, there are more than a dozen within ten blocks of this store—but if you want your sneakers to do more than just look good, Paragon is the place to go. This independent sporting goods store has been around since 1908, so they're experts on New Yorkers' diverse range of athletic needs—from everyday pavement pounding to the most unusual niche sport—and their footwear department has the best selection of sneakers and other sports shoes in the city. From aquasocks to wrestling shoes, they carry shoes for every possible athletic pursuit, in a wide range of styles, brands, and prices. The staff in the shoe department, located on the lower level, is knowledgeable about both shoes and sports, and will help you choose from dozens of options to find the one that's right for you. Paragon is also an excellent place to find camping and ski gear, and the staff takes the outdoors very seriously, so they won't make you feel silly for buying a high-tech North Face in the middle of Manhattan.

*867 BROADWAY AT 18TH STREET IN MANHATTAN. Subway: 4, 5, 6, L, N, Q, R, W to 14thStreet-Union Square. 212-255-8889. www.paragonsports.com.*

→ **DID YOU KNOW?** *Paragon's distinctive black exterior played a supporting role in the sitcom* Mad About You *as Buchman's Sporting Goods, the store owned by Paul's family.*

## 724. Buy your favorite movie art at **Posteritati**.

With a collection that encompasses many thousands of pieces, Posteritati is a store devoted to the timeless art and iconic imagery of movie posters. The depth of the selection is what sets Posteritati apart—you can find all the quaint and colorful international versions of your favorite movie art here, as well as a rich stock of classic Hollywood and independent movie posters. The gallery hosts changing exhibitions of artwork from different periods and genres of film, from the Eastern European avant-garde to Bollywood, Japanese new wave, and the Hammer horror classics. The store also sells books on film art and other movie memorabilia, which together with the exhibitions, make this a fun place to visit even if you are not in the market to buy.

*239 CENTRE STREET BETWEEN BROOME AND GRAND STREETS IN MANHATTAN. Subway: 1, 2, 3, 6, A, C, E, N, Q, R, W to Canal Street. 212-226 2207. www.posteritati.com.*

## 725. Browse artists' books at **Printed Matter**.

Printed Matter is a nonprofit organization whose purpose is to promote and disseminate works by artists in book format. What that means is that this Chelsea store contains thousands of unusual artworks for you to admire, touch, and explore (and purchase, too, if you are so inclined). Printed Matter specializes in artists' publications, what they call "artwork on the page," produced in large, inexpensive editions meant for dissemination (rather than the more precious "book objects" that artists sometimes produce). However, "large editions" is a relative term, and you're probably not going to find too many things that would be in the art section of a regular bookstore. Most books are priced around $20, though there are many that cost even less.

*195 TENTH AVENUE BETWEEN 21ST AND 22ND STREETS IN MANHATTAN. Subway: C, E to 23rd Street. 212-925-0325. www.printedmatter.org.*

## 726. Get a last-minute Halloween costume at **Ricky's**.

The stores we've chosen for this section are almost all New York originals, and for the most part, we've stayed away from outright, interstate chains, which Ricky's by definition is. (There are currently twenty-one locations, including two in Miami Beach, which would not be surprising to anyone who's familiar with Ricky's flamboyant aesthetic.) However, as anyone who was around in the '80s can tell you, Ricky's is a New York shopping institution and the kind of place that can expand its number of outlets but still remain one of a kind. Ricky's is a drugstore—you can buy shampoo, toiletries, and cosmetics—but it's a drugstore with a wild streak. When it comes to what they sell, they've got a very different agenda than CVS: there's a disproportionate amount of hairbrushes and styling tools, the most extensive hair-dye department we've ever seen (and we're not talking just Clairol), and a wide selection of wigs and costumes. And while you can't get a prescription filled, you can get a makeup consultation or a wig fitting from a transvestite professional behind the counter. In addition to being the best place to come if, say, you want to cover your gray hair with pink, Ricky's is a great place to shop for a Halloween costume. Ricky's goes all-out on Halloween, with nearly as good a costume selection as the regular costume stores, and an even better selection of glitter makeup, hair dye, fake lashes, and risqué hosiery. On the big night, you can still find ghosts and goblins and French maids at Ricky's putting the finishing touches on their costumes, long after the other costume shops have closed.

*Various locations in Manhattan. For addresses, visit www.rickys-nyc.com.*

## 727. Pick out a valuable relic at **Skyline Books**.

No matter how many times you've visited, there are always corners of this small and cluttered used bookshop that remain to be discovered. Although there are respectable fiction, poetry, and biography sections, it's the more obscure treasures that stand out: the store has a surprising collection of signed copies and first editions by Beat writers, from Ginsberg to Burroughs, locked in glass cases; and the travel section is a gold mine of charming Victorian travelogues, antiquated guides to New York City, and essays by celebrated traveling raconteurs, from Mark Twain to Bill Bryson. Browse this store and **Books of Wonder** (see page 277), on the same block, for a delightful literary interlude.

*13 WEST 18TH STREET BETWEEN FIFTH AND SIXTH AVENUES IN MANHATTAN. Subway: F, V to 14th Street; L to Sixth Avenue. 212-759-5463.*

### 728. Step into the limelight at **Colony Records**.

For nearly sixty years, Colony Records has been supplying Broadway wannabes with all the materials they need to recreate their favorite scenes from smash hit musicals in their own homes. Colony has a vast collection of CDs, sheet music, and special karaoke versions of every Broadway show under the sun—if you've ever seen a show and wanted to take the soundtrack home, this is the place to find it. They even carry the "hardware" for the job, too: microphones and karaoke machines for the living room.

*1619 BROADWAY AT 49TH STREET IN MANHATTAN. Subway: 1 to 50th Street; N, R, W to 49th Street. 212-265-2050. www.colonymusic.com.*

### 729. Concoct a witch's brew at **Aphrodisia**.

If it seems improbable that a spice and herb store, of all things, survived the Bleecker Street gentrification, consider that it might have had something to do with the store's merchandise. With jars and vials of alternative remedies lining the wall, each hand-labeled in beautiful, grade-school-teacher–style script, Aphrodisia looks like a musty hippie hangout, and quite frankly, it seems exactly the kind of place that gets taken over by stores like L'Occitane and L'Oliver & Co., which have moved in across the street. Whether it's a coincidence or a great advertisement for whatever concoction they make to ward off evil spirits, we can't say, but it's a priceless relic, and definitely an interesting place to browse whether you're looking for a magic potion or a new tea.

*264 BLEECKER STREET BETWEEN CORNELIA AND MORTON STREETS IN MANHATTAN. Subway: 1 to Christopher Street-Sheridan Square; A, C, E, B, D, F, V to West 4th Street. 212-989-6440.*

### 730. Pick a card–any card–at **Tannen's Magic Superstore**.

Even sorcerers need a place to shop, and for New York's magic circle that place is Tannen's Magic Superstore. Every magic wand, loaded dice, trick sword, multicolored handkerchief, and fifty-one-card deck that an aspiring magician might ever need is here, along with a huge range of bizarre masks and outfits, surprising toys, and any other conjuror's tools you can imagine. The store is unique in the city—and there aren't too many that compare to it anywhere in the world—and it has supplied tricks and treats to everyone from TV show prop departments and professional illusionists to kids looking to master their very first disappearing-coin act. Ask a member of the staff for a demonstration—you'll be blown away.

*45 WEST 34TH STREET, SUITE 608, BETWEEN FIFTH AND SIXTH AVENUES IN MANHATTAN. Subway: B, D, F, V, N, Q, R, W to 34th Street-Herald Square. 212-929-4500. www.tannens.com.*

→ **DID YOU KNOW?** *Tannen's, which opened in 1929, was featured in Michael Chabon's 2001 novel,* The Amazing Adventures of Kavalier and Clay.

## 731. Buy organic at **Whisker's Holistic Pet Care** (and have it delivered).

Whisker's Holistic Pet Care is about as different from the city's pet boutiques as you would expect from a place with the word "holistic" in the name. Instead of designer dog clothes and gourmet treats, this store carries tons of nontoxic and chemical-free food, toys, and supplies for dogs, cats, and birds, all crammed into an East Village storefront. Everything on offer meets high holistic standards, from the organic pet food to the homeopathic remedies, odor neutralizers, and a mysterious potion that even some nonpet owners might be interested in called Mouse-B-Gone. The staff is friendly and knowledgeable, and there is free delivery to anywhere in Manhattan, Brooklyn, Queens, and certain locations in the Bronx.

*235 EAST 9TH STREET AT SECOND AVENUE IN MANHATTAN. Subway: 6 to Astor Place. 212-979-1455. www.1800whiskers.com.*

## 732. Curl up with a book at **Ursus**.

Now that Ursus Rare Books has absorbed its old Chelsea branch into the location upstairs at the Carlyle Hotel, it is indisputably the best place in the city to look for art books of all shapes and sizes. After nearly thirty-five years in the business, the selection is comprehensive, high-end, and up-to-date, with everything from books of critical essays to the latest, glossiest coffee table books and exhibition catalogs from museums around the world. There is a separate room for rare and out-of-print books—one of the most impressive collections of its kind in the city. Inside, it's peaceful and quiet, with soft cushions on the windowsills inviting you to sit back and leaf through the books while gazing out over Madison Avenue. When the shop closes for the night, you can continue the literary theme by heading downstairs to **Bemelmans Bar** to see the Madeline murals (see page 134).

*981 MADISON AVENUE BETWEEN 76TH AND 77TH STREETS IN MANHATTAN. Subway: 6 to 77th Street. 212-772-8787. www.ursusbooks.com.*

## 733. Shop a **pop-up**.

Though few New Yorkers like to admit it, you can't quite get *everything* here. There are still some stores, from popular international labels to some of the country's largest retailers that, for better or for worse, have yet to stake out turf for a New York store. However, a few clever companies have gotten around that little technicality. The biggest retail phenomenon to hit New York City streets in the last few years have been the "pop-up" shops, mobile or temporary stores from brands without a permanent New York City address that open during the holidays or other strategic times. Target won over city shoppers with its floating pop-up on a barge in the Hudson River in 2002, and a year later, the budget airline Song introduced itself to the city with a SoHo pop-up. Since then, we've seen pop-ups from chic foreign brands like Japan's Uniqulo and Iceland's 66° North, and a Fashion Week outlet for As Four, hip local designers. While some shoppers may resent the pop-ups' inherent "limited time only" policy as a marketing gimmick, we think the ephemeral nature makes them fun. *Any time, any place—keep your eyes open!*

## 734. Shop the **Caravan**.

Speaking of mobile retail, the Caravan is another retail gimmick that we can't help loving. This "boutique on wheels" stocks trendy clothing and accessories for men and women in a kitted-out silver van, and drives around to different locations in the city. You can find out where they'll be parked on their Web site or by calling them, but given its itinerant nature, it's not really worth the trouble of seeking it out. Instead, if you happen to see an oversize silver van with its doors wide open parked on a street near you, don't hesitate to jump in.

*For more information, call 917-613-8409 or visit www.shopcaravan.com. N.B.: If tailgating isn't your style, they also have a fixed store at 2 GREAT JONES STREET IN MANHATTAN. Subway: 6 to Bleecker Street. 212-260-8189.*

## 735. Buy a hat—and keep the box—at the **Hat Shop**.

Stocking only hats made by New York milliners—most from the city, some from upstate—the Hat Shop is a bastion of style, taste, and class in the home of the Yankee cap. A Wall Street broker turned millinery maven, owner Linda Pagan believes resolutely in the power of a hat to breathe new life into anybody's look, and the range of styles on display extend from the quiet dignity of a well-made felt fedora to the flamboyant extravagance of a decorated cocktail hat. Although the days are gone when hats were requisites of city society, it is never too late to invigorate your outfits with some snappy headwear, and the Hat Shop is the place to go for anything from a straw summer boater to an elaborate Art Deco–inspired piece. Before you go, brush up on your milliner's lexicon, so instead of fumbling around for an explanation of the feathery thing with ribbons and a hair net at the back, you can ask directly for a canotier with aigrettes, ruching, and a snood.

*120 THOMPSON STREET BETWEEN PRINCE AND SPRING STREETS IN MANHATTAN. Subway: 6 to Spring Street; C, E to Spring Street. 212-219-1445.*

# Vinyl Sources

Record collectors and people who amass music as others collect books or antiques will travel all over the world to fill the holes in their libraries, but lucky New Yorkers have no shortage of places carrying classic LPs, EPs, and 45s, if they know where to look. There are scores of independent, new and used record stores across the city to keep vinyl enthusiasts of all kinds happy, but to find the best ones you'll have to roam the length and breadth of the five boroughs and scour the streets of some unlikely neighborhoods. The five we've chosen to highlight are special not only for keeping astonishing collections of vinyl, from classic oldies to life-changing rarities, but also for being unique places that are worth the journey in itself.

## 736. Consult the oracles of used CDs and records at **Academy**.

Dividing its vast collections between two locations, Academy Records & CDs is an institution among New York's music and movie hunters. The Chelsea location takes a utilitarian approach, and stocks hundreds of used CDs and DVDs of all genres alongside the traditional collector's choices of classical vinyl LPs, while the East Village store is devoted entirely to jazz, pop, rock, soul, and reggae records. While everything at Academy is likely to be in great working condition, neither location stocks too many rarities or mint items, so prices are reasonable, and the selections at both are fluid and comprehensive. *Both locations in Manhattan.* **Academy Records & CDs:** *12 WEST 18TH STREET BETWEEN FIFTH AND SIXTH AVENUES. Subway: 1 to 18th Street; F, V to 14th Street; L to Sixth Avenue. 212-242-3000.* **Academy LPs:** *77 EAST 10TH STREET BETWEEN THIRD AND FOURTH AVENUES. Subway: 4, 5, 6, L, N, Q, R, W to 14th Street-Union Square. 212-780-9166. www.academy-records.com.*

## 737. Rediscover the old-school at **Beatstreet Records**.

Two flights down in the middle of the Fulton Mall is the largest record store in Brooklyn, housing one of the biggest and most comprehensive collections of hip-hop, soul, R&B, and reggae records in New York. Stocking everything from old-school classics to brand-new hits, from legendary soul albums to rare mixes of new singles, Beatstreet is a DJ's paradise, and a great store for anyone looking to find on vinyl what most places only have on CD. The people here know their stuff, and the records range from standard new releases to specially pressed twelve-inch compilations of hard-to-find tunes. There are computers that allow you to search the stocklist for anything you might want, from a particular Al Green album to Biz Markie's entire back catalog, and there are even decks set up for the braver among you to spin your records for the crowd in the store before you buy.

*494 FULTON STREET BETWEEN HOYT STREET AND ORATORY PLACE IN BROOKLYN. Subway: 2, 3 to Hoyt Street-Fulton Mall; A, C, F to Jay Street-Borough Hall. 718-624-6400. www.beatstreet.com.*

### 738. Rummage through the crates at **Mooncurser Records**.

When people think of **City Island** (see page 233), most think of sailing or fish and chips, but if you like music, Mooncurser is another good reason to make the trek across the water. Mooncurser is a legend among secondhand record stores. Run by charismatic octogenarian Robert Roberge, the store has been selling everything from priceless rarities to bargain reissues for more than thirty years. Mooncurser has 100,000-plus records, specializing in Latin and soul and including 45s and 78s, and while very few are less than twenty years old, everything is kept in good condition and is more than likely to be worth the asking price. But know your limits: hip-hop act Naughty By Nature is said to have spent $40,000 here on 12,000 records in just one afternoon.

*229 CITY ISLAND AVENUE BETWEEN CENTRE AND SCHOFIELD STREETS ON CITY ISLAND IN THE BRONX. Subway: 6 to Pelham Bay Park, then the Bx29 bus to City Island. 718-885-0302.*

### 739. Think of a record, and then find it at **House of Oldies**.

Of the handful of wonderful vinyl record stores that run along Carmine Street, the legendary House of Oldies deserves special mention. With a vault of more than a million records in the store itself and in the basement below, you can walk in and request almost any rock, pop, soul, blues, jazz, country, funk, reggae, or dance record from the 1950s through the 1980s and expect to find it. Many of the records are in mint or excellent condition, so prices are suitably high, but the selection is hard to beat, in New York or anywhere.

*35 CARMINE STREET BETWEEN BLEECKER AND BEDFORD STREETS IN MANHATTAN. Subway: 1 to Houston Street; A, C, E, B, D, F, V to West 4th Street. 212-243-0500.*

### 740. Mingle with reggae greats at **Coxsone's Music City**.

In the early 1980s, legendary Studio One reggae producer Coxsone Dodd opened a record store in (appropriately enough) Jamaica, Queens, devoted entirely to reggae, ska, dub, and dancehall records. Although Coxsone is sadly no longer with us, his store remains the best place in New York to look for reggae records, from classic early recordings to brand new Jamaican hits, and albums from big name artists like Bob Marley and Gregory Isaacs to harder-to-find rarities and dub remixes. Many of Coxsone's friends, including reggae icons like Alton Ellis and Derrick Harriott, are frequent visitors to the store. N.B: If Queens is too far for you to go, check out **Jammyland** in the East Village for Manhattan's best stock of reggae records.

**Coxsone's Music City:** *3135 FULTON STREET BETWEEN NORWOOD AND HALE STREETS IN QUEENS. Subway: A, C to Euclid Avenue; J, Z to Norwood Avenue. 718-277-4166.*

**Jammyland:** *60 EAST 3RD STREET BETWEEN FIRST AND SECOND AVENUES IN MANHATTAN. Subway: F, V to Lower East Side-Second Avenue. 212-614-0185. www.jammyland.com.*

---

## Expert Contributor: Laura Dave

Laura Dave is a writer and New York native. She is the author of the novel, *London is the Best City in America,* and regularly writes for *Glamour, Self,* and *ESPN the Magazine.*

### MY FIVE FAVORITE BOOKSTORES IN NEW YORK

**741. *Books of Wonder:*** This children's bookstore is just the kind of store that I dreamed of as a little kid. I love perusing the aisles, and will forever hope to bring home one of BOW's hard-to-come-by first editions, like *When We Were Very Young* (for only $4,500!).
*18 WEST 18TH STREET BETWEEN FIFTH AND SIXTH AVENUES IN MANHATTAN. Subway: 1 to 18th Street. 212-989-3270. www.booksofwonder.net.*

**742. *Three Lives and Company:*** A West Village touchstone, Three Lives is a favorite stomping ground of mine because the literature-savvy folks behind the counter use words like "chaser" in pairing two books for you. It is a good place for literary stargazing, because many local authors and editors like to frequent the store, and are occasionally invited to do a stint as a guest bookseller. You might see Michael Cunningham checking out the new arrivals, or Jonathan Safran Foer playing salesman for a day.
*154 WEST 10TH STREET AT WAVERLY PLACE IN MANHATTAN. Subway: 1 to Christopher Street-Sheridan Square; A, C, E, B, D, F, V to West 4th Street. 212-741-2069. www.threelives.com.*

**743. *Housing Works Used Book Café:*** You'd be hard-pressed to find a bookstore anywhere doing this much good. One hundred percent of Housing Works's profits go to homeless New Yorkers living with HIV and AIDS. Moreover, the store is spacious and lovely and hosts terrific live events like in-store concerts and performances.
*126 CROSBY STREET BETWEEN HOUSTON AND PRINCE STREETS IN MANHATTAN. Subway: 6 to Bleecker Street; B, D, F, V to Broadway-Lafayette Street; N, R, W to Prince Street. 212-334-*

3324. www.housingworks.org.

**744. *Barnes & Noble (Chelsea Branch):*** There is just something about the Chelsea branch of B&N. It might be the enormous-even-for-a-chain literature section; or the travel section you can get lost in; or the upstairs café, where I have whittled away many mornings. But I think it's mostly that, by the time I leave, I'm always anxious to put pen to paper.
*675 SIXTH AVENUE AT 21ST STREET IN MANHATTAN. Subway: F, V to 23rd Street. 212-727-1227. www.barnesandnoble.com.*

**745. *The Corner Bookstore:*** This intimate Upper East Side establishment is a throwback to old-school bookshops: full of charm and love, where each book feels handpicked and gratefully cared for. I have *never* left here empty-handed. And the in-store readings are among the best and most personal in the city. This may be my favorite bookstore—not just in Manhattan, but anywhere.
*1313 MADISON AVENUE AT THE CORNER OF 93RD STREET IN MANHATTAN. Subway: 6 to 96th Street. 212-831-3554.*
*See page 291 for a list of stores with live reading programs.*

## Shopping Excursions

Though all of the stores listed in this chapter offer wonderful individual shopping experiences, perhaps the most special thing about shopping in New York is the pleasant, pedestrian-oriented adventure of strolling the streets, discovering new stores, revisiting favorites, and experiencing the unique atmosphere that each neighborhood has to offer. And despite the ongoing homogenization of retail to the detriment of long-standing independents, and the presence of a few mall-like behemoths, there are still several areas that have retained—and, in some cases, have enhanced—their own special, thoroughly urban shopping character. Here are our five favorites:

**746. *Fifth Avenue (part 1):*** Though it's become increasingly mall-ish over the last few years, Fifth Avenue has not lost its majesty, and feels anything but run-of-the-mill. From 42nd Street to where the park starts at 59th Street, grand flagship stores grace practically every address, each more impressive than the last. Even stores not known as "luxury brands" (the Gap, H&M, Abercrombie & Fitch) pull out all the stops with their multilevel retail palaces, as if to pay their respects to this legendary shopping strip. Walking up from 42nd Street, you'll hit three legendary department stores (Saks, **Henri Bendel**, **Bergdorf Goodman**), elegant jewelers (Cartier, H. Stern, **Harry Winston**, and **Tiffany**), famous European designers (Versace, Armani, Louis Vuitton), the exotic and opulent **Takashimaya**, and many more. Should all of this capitalist grandeur inspire a wave of piety (or guilt), you'll also pass the majestic **Saint Patrick's Cathedral** (see page 21).

*FIFTH AVENUE BETWEEN 42ND AND 59TH STREETS IN MANHATTAN. Subway: 7 to Fifth Avenue-Bryant Park; B, D, F, V to 42nd Street-Bryant Park; E, V to Fifth Avenue/53rd Street; N, R, W to Fifth Avenue/59th Street.*

**747. Madison Avenue: Barneys** (see page 241) marks the transition of Madison Avenue, from its plebeian, middle-of-the road-Midtown strip, to the exclusive-feeling upscale boutiques of the Upper East Side. Between 60th Street and the 80s, where smaller, neighborhood stores (read: for older, wealthier, family types) occupy the avenue, Madison has a quiet and stylish grandeur reminiscent of the established shopping districts of Paris or London, with a number of uptown outposts of downtown boutiques, a few major fashion houses, and a handful of single-outpost stores. Along with Armani (760 Madison), Prada (841 Madison), Dolce & Gabbana (825 Madison), Moschino (803 Madison), and Miu Miu (831 Madison) stores, you'll pass the Emanuel Ungaro boutique (792 Madison) and the two huge Ralph Lauren/Polo mansions (867 and 888 Madison), with their luxurious rooms complete with sofas and fireplaces that are like living rooms. There are more specialized boutiques, too, like La Perla (803 Madison) for underwear, Jimmy Choo (716 Madison) for glamorous Upper-East-Side heels, and the wonderful **Maison du Chocolat** (1018 Madison) for hot chocolate and truffles. Other highlights include Sherry-Lehmann (679 Madison), an old-time New York wine store that is a good place to pick up a special bottle; Zitomer (969 Madison), the enormous pharmacy that is like a small department store, with toys, clothes, and all sorts of other baubles; Floris of London (703 Madison), which has been selling the superior fragrances of this distinguished old English perfumer for twenty years; the bars and bookstore of the **Carlyle Hotel** (at 76th Street); and Clearly First (980 Madison), which sells chic, unusual Scandinavian goods. We recommend you start at 60th Street and work your way uptown, so that when you're ready to wind down, the frenzy of Midtown is far behind you, and you can enjoy tea or a drink at the Mark (just off Madison on 77th) or Carlyle hotels, or find a seat at one of the quiet cafés and restaurants that dot the avenue.

*MADISON AVENUE BETWEEN 61ST AND 80TH STREETS IN MANHATTAN. Subway: 4, 5, 6 to 59th Street.*

**748. Bleecker Street:** The stretch of Bleecker Street that runs from Hudson Street in the West Village through the eastern edge of SoHo has an eclectic character and a cozy, neighborhood feel that create the perfect setting for shopping or browsing. Start at the corner of Bleecker and Hudson Streets, where a small farmer's market occupies the picturesque intersection on Saturdays, and begin walking east, keeping your eyes open. You'll pass trendy boutiques, cute cafés, gourmet food stores, old music stores, and some great places to find antiques and one-of-a-kind knickknacks all along the way. You can get anything from antique furniture and picture frames to vintage globes and Art Deco lampshades in shops such as Les Pierre (369 Bleecker), Clary & Co. (372 Bleecker), and the wonderful Old Japan (382 Bleecker), whose century-old kimonos make amazing gifts (for people small enough to wear them). There are a couple of excellent record stores en route—Rebel Rebel (319 Bleecker), which is better for rock and punk LPs, and Bleecker Street Records (239 Bleecker), which keeps a huge selection of both new and old records—plus one of the city's better guitar shops, Matt Umanov Guitars (273 Bleecker). Take a breather from the serious fashion of Marc Jacobs (385 Bleecker), Ralph Lauren (women's store: 380 Bleecker; men's store: 381 Bleecker), and Intermix (365 Bleecker) by stopping in the Lulu Guinness store (394 Bleecker) for a breath of whimsy or Blush (333 Bleecker). Also fun are the offbeat little shops like Verve (353 Bleecker), filled with clothes, accessories, and other odds and ends that are always nice to browse through. If you need snacks along the way, you can brave the lines for the famous cupcakes at **Magnolia** (401 Bleecker), or try the mythic pizzas at **John's** (278 Bleecker), the great Italian meats at **Faicco's** (260 Bleecker), and the cheese at **Murray's** (254 Bleecker); or you can try to revive yourself with some herbs at **Aphrodisia** (264 Bleecker). Wherever you go, our advice is to go early on a Saturday or Sunday, when you can see the street and the farmer's market in the prettiest light, and then walk up Bleecker Street before the crowds descend. *BLEECKER STREET BETWEEN HUDSON AND CARMINE STREETS IN MANHATTAN. Subway (to start at Hudson Street): A, C, E to 14th Street or L to Eighth Avenue; (to start at Carmine Street) 1 to Houston Street.*

**749. Bedford Avenue:** Shopping in Williamsburg is fun because it has a rough, rather unfinished feel, sort of like the Brick Lane and Spitalfields Market areas of London. And while it seems a bit off the beaten path, it is also very user-friendly, even if you don't know Williamsburg at all. The Bedford Avenue subway stop lets you out on Bedford and N. 7th Street: between there and Metropolitan Avenue (which runs perpendicular to Bedford, right below N. 3rd Street), there are several dozen boutiques, restaurants, and the **mini-mall**. The stores cover all shopping bases, from stylish home lifestyle gear at Spacial Etc (199 Bedford) to the flowing Tibetan clothing at Pema (225 Bedford); from independent bookstores (Spoonbill and Sugartown, in the mini-mall) to the antique and secondhand furniture at Ugly Luggage (214 Bedford). Being Brooklyn, there's also hip baby store, Sam & Seb (208 Bedford), where you can buy toddler-sized Velvet Underground and Che Guevara shirts. Take a detour on your way back to the subway on N. 6th Street, east of Bedford, and you'll find another little enclave of shops: The Future Perfect, a cool furniture store that sells a lot of independent designers (115 N. 6th Street); Sleep, a cheeky lingerie-and-linen boutique—what

a good idea to combine the two! (110 N. 6th Street); a popular secondhand children's shop called Flying Squirrel, where you can get high-fashion kiddie gear at bargain prices (96 N. 6th Street); and **Artists & Fleas** (129 N. 6th Street). Also in the area and worth checking out are Beacon's Closet (88 N. 11th Street, a block east of Bedford), an excellent secondhand store with a wide selection of used, vintage, and contemporary clothing and accessories, and **Brooklyn Industries** (162 Bedford).
*BEDFORD AVENUE, BETWEEN N. 7TH AND METROPOLITAN AVENUE, AND N. 6TH STREET, BETWEEN BEDFORD AND WYTHE AVENUES, IN BROOKLYN. Subway: L to Bedford Avenue.*

**750. *Fifth Avenue (part 2):*** Surprise! Manhattan's Fifth Avenue does not have a monopoly on good shopping—Fifth Avenue in Brooklyn also has a great strip. Shopping here is a little like shopping in Williamsburg, with lots of independent boutiques and not a chain store in sight, but whereas Williamsburg has a bit of a gritty feel like North London, Park Slope is more like Notting Hill: well-off, but not ostentatious, with a charming residential feel. Between Flatbush Avenue and Ninth Street (about twenty blocks) lies a quaint, tree-lined stretch of stores. You can easily cover them in one stroll by darting back and forth across the avenue, which is relatively narrow, and has very light traffic. Most of the stores are quite small, even for boutiques, but what they lack in size they more than make up for in charm. Frilly women's clothing shops like Flirt (93 Fifth), Goldy & Mac (219 Fifth), and Eidolon (233 Fifth) are like stepping into a modern boudoir, with friendly feminine chatter that will make girls feel right at home (but might be a little intimidating for a guy). Cog and Pearl (190 Fifth) is a wonderful home store that sells handmade gifts and accessories, while Scaredy Kat (229 Fifth) has great cards—both printed and custom-made—and gifts for children and adults. Speaking of kids, there are also several children's stores, including Romp (145 Fifth), which sells modernist-looking toys, including sleek rocking horses and preservative-free wooden drums, and Lulu's (48 Fifth), a kiddie barber shop that smartly features a big toy selection. 3R Living (276 Fifth) is an interesting home store that carries "future friendly products"—housewares, cookware, toys, pet accessories and cleaning products that are eco-friendly, made with sustainable manufacturing techniques, fairly traded, and packaged in an environmentally conscious way. If you haven't run out of steam, head two blocks east to Seventh Avenue, which also has a lot of stores but is a bit busier and not quite as pleasant to amble around.
*FIFTH AVENUE BETWEEN FLATBUSH AVENUE AND 9TH STREET IN BROOKLYN. Subway: 2, 3, 4, 5, B, Q to Atlantic Avenue; D, M, R to Atlantic Avenue-Pacific Street; F to Fourth Avenue; N to Pacific Street.*

# On the Cheap and All Out

We've got the highest highs, and the lowest lows, and one of the best things to do is to check out what you can get at either end:

**751.** *One pound of bulk chocolate or the candy of your choice at Economy Candy (between $2.99 and $5.99) vs. a box of Taittinger champagne truffles from Jacques Torres ($50 for thirty pieces).* Tip: Economy Candy isn't just for bulk candies. They also have an excellent selection of European chocolate bars and treats available by the bar or piece.

**Economy Candy:** *108 RIVINGTON STREET AT ESSEX STREET IN MANHATTAN. Subway: F to Delancey Street; J, M, Z to Essex Street. 800-352-4544. www.economycandy.com.*

**Jacques Torres:** *350 HUDSON STREET AT HOUSTON STREET IN MANHATTAN; Subway: 1 to Houston Street; 212-214-2462; and 66 WATER STREET BETWEEN THE BROOKLYN AND MANHATTAN BRIDGES IN BROOKLYN; Subway: A, C to High Street; F to York Street. 718-875-9772. www.mrchocolate.com.*

**752.** *Bidding on a vintage oak armoire (around $200) or a Gucci jacket (around $60) at the Housing Works auctions vs. bidding on an Impressionist painting at an auction at Christie's or Sotheby's (starting at $20,000 to more than $95,000,000).*

**Housing Works:** *Various locations. Check Web site for schedule and locations: www.housingworksauctions.com.*

**Christie's:** *20 ROCKEFELLER PLAZA, 49TH STREET BETWEEN FIFTH AND SIXTH AVENUES, IN MANHATTAN. Subway: B, D, F, V to 47th-50th Streets-Rockefeller Center. 212-636-2000. www.christies.com.*

**Sotheby's:** *1334 YORK AVENUE AT 72ND STREET IN MANHATTAN. Subway: 6 to 68th Street-Hunter College. 212-606-7000. www.sothebys.com.*

**753.** *One dozen roses from any corner deli (around $10) vs. an arrangement by Michael George ($100 and up).* George's customers include fashion designers, magazine editors, and the doyenne of décor, Martha Stewart.

**Michael George:** *5 TUDOR CITY PLACE, 40TH STREET BETWEEN FIRST AND SECOND AVENUES, IN MANHATTAN. Subway: 4, 5, 6, 7 to Grand Central-42nd Street. 212-883-0304. www.michaelgeorgecustomfloral.com.*

**754.** *Lunchtime manicure at Bloomie Nails ($10, including a short back rub) vs. the Guinot Paris manicure at the Buff Spa in Bergdorf Goodman ($55).*

**Bloomie Nails:** *Multiple locations.*

**Buff Spa:** *See page 240 for Bergdorf Goodman.*

**755.** *Massage at a street fair ($10 for 10 minutes) vs. the "Purva Kama Four-Hand Synchronized Massage" ($570 for 1 hour and 50 minutes) at the Spa at the Mandarin Oriental.*

**Street fair massages:** *See page 83.*

**The Spa at the Mandarin Oriental:** *80 COLUMBUS CIRCLE AT 60TH STREET IN MANHATTAN. (Also see entry on page 63.) Subway: 1, A, C, B, D to 59th Street-Columbus Circle. 212-805-8880. www.mandarinoriental.com.*

**756.** *"Recession special" from Gray's Papaya (two franks and a drink for $2.75) vs. the black truffle burger (in season) from DB Bistro Moderne ($60 for a burger with a single portion of truffles; $120 for a double).*

**Gray's Papaya:** *Multiple locations. 539 EIGHTH AVENUE AT 37TH STREET: Subway: 1, 2, 3, A, C, E to 34th Street-Penn Station; 212-904-1588. 2090 BROADWAY AT 72ND STREET: Subway: 1, 2, 3 to 72nd Street; 212-799-0243. 402 SIXTH AVENUE AT 8TH STREET: Subway: A, C, E, B, D, F, V to West 4th Street; 212-260-3532.*

**DB Bistro Moderne:** *55 WEST 44TH STREET BETWEEN FIFTH AND SIXTH AVENUES IN MAN-HATTAN. Subway: B, D, F, V to 42nd Street-Bryant Park. 212-391-2400. www.danielnyc.com. Also see entry on Daniel Boulud on page 162.*

**757.** *The AirTrain between Manhattan and JFK ($5 plus subway fare, one way) vs. US Helicopter ($159, one way).* AirTrain travel time: about sixty minutes to or from Manhattan via the subway (including the five-minute transfer between subway and AirTrain platforms). Helicopter travel time: less than ten minutes (no transfers). *AirTrain departs regularly from the Howard Beach and Sutphin Boulevard-Archer Avenue stations. Subway: A to Howard Beach or J, Z, E to Sutphin Boulevard-Archer Avenue. For more information on AirTrain, visit www.panynj.gov/airtrain. N.B.: US Helicopter departs every hour on the hour from 7:00 a.m. to 7:00 p.m. from the downtown and Midtown heliports. Reservations are required. For more information and to make reservations, call 877-262-7676 or visit www.flyush.com.*

# Cheap Thrills: Top five things to do when you are feeling strapped for cash.

### 758. Go to a museum on a **free** or **pay-what-you-wish day**.

Almost all of the museums in New York designate a couple of hours each week as free or "pay what you wish" time, which is a great way to visit a certain collection or exhibition without feeling like you have to spend the entire day there. Some museums, such as the **Brooklyn Museum** (see page 120), offer free programs and performances during these times. Also, the **Met** (see page 118) is always pay-what-you-wish, so if you don't have time to make a marathon visit that would justify the suggested $15 admission fee, you can pop in for an hour and pay what you feel is appropriate.

*See chapter 4 for a list of favorite museums, and contact the museums for information on hours and special programs.*

### 759. Take an **introductory yoga class**.

Some yoga studios offer free classes to new students, which, unlike free trials at gyms, don't come with the expectation that you'll shell out a lot of money to sign up in the future. Jivamukti, a popular downtown yoga center, has a regularly scheduled free class for new students held the last Sunday of every month. Studio newcomers of all levels are invited to come and try out for free the serious, traditional practice and peace-inducing environment that has had people making pilgrimages to the center for more than twenty years.

*Jivamukti: 841 BROADWAY, AT 13TH STREET IN MANHATTAN. Jivamukti's free introductory class is held the last Sunday of every month, at 4:00 p.m. Available to first-time visitors to Jivamukti only, but all levels welcome. The class is first-come, first-served, and it is recommended that you arrive at least half an hour in advance. Subway: 4, 5, 6, L, N, Q, R, W to 14th Street-Union Square. 212-353-0214. www.jivamuktiyoga.com. For information on Jivamukti's New Year's Eve celebration, see entry page 322. For other free introductory classes, contact individual centers for listings.*

### 760. Get free haircuts for life at **Bumble & Bumble**.

This one has achieved something of an urban myth status, but we swear it's true— and if you're willing to forsake some control and pampering, it's not that hard to do. Bumble & Bumble, one of the most famous hair companies in the industry, runs an ongoing training school that is constantly in need of models. To become a model, you first have to fill out the online application, which consists mostly of biographical information and a few questions about your hair. Provided you don't have any bizarre hair issues, you should receive an e-mail telling you to attend a model call, where your hair will be assessed for one of about a half-dozen cuts that is being taught at that time. Then you book an appointment for the cut, which occurs in groups of sixteen, with an instructor present. The cuts are free (no tipping either), models get free samples of Bumble & Bumble products, and they will offer you a cut with a professional if you're unhappy with what you receive. Just don't lose sight of what you're actually doing. The stylists are there for themselves, not for you, so don't expect any pampering, and the appointment is run as a class, so personal attention is at a minimum. And most of all, don't be late—they overbook appointments for these classes on purpose, so if you're not among the first sixteen people in the door, you don't get a cut, even though you had an appointment. Once you're in the program, you can call in whenever you want a cut for another of the same style, or come back to the model call to see if you can be assigned a new one.

*For more information, call 866-7-BUMBLE or visit www.bumbleandbumble.com.*

---

### 761. Hang out in the "cold room" at **Fairway**.

If it's 100 degrees in the shade, you don't have air conditioning, and you can practically feel your skin frying, head to Fairway. The 10,000-square-foot "cold room" is a continually refrigerated section, where meat, fish, dairy products, and fresh pasta are kept. It is a sight to behold any time of the year, and a godsend for those without air conditioning in the middle of August. Not only is it free, unlike many other reliable air-conditioned venues, but it is really, really cold (around forty degrees) all the time, no matter what's happening outside.

*2328 12TH AVENUE BY 129TH STREET IN MANHATTAN. Subway: 1 to 125th Street. 212-234-3883. www.fairwaymarket.com.*

---

### 762. Gorge on **food freebies**.

Our favorite place for free noshing is **Dean & Deluca** (see page 41), where generous samples of breads, pizzas, prepared food, cakes, and pastries are displayed for the taking, and it's usually too busy for anyone to notice if you're scarfing down a few of each. Both the Gourmet Garage and Garden of Eden also put out trays of free samples sporadically, and both almost always have cheese and bread bits to nibble on. There are now several more new Williams-Sonoma stores in the city, almost all of which have in-store kitchens, where staff members whip up tasty concoctions like chestnut stuffing and chocolate chip blondies throughout the day that you can wash down with a small cup of coffee, mulled cider, hot chocolate, or lemonade. One little-known sample-giving outlet is the Streit Matzo factory on the Lower East Side, which hands out pieces of matzo (fresh from the oven) to bystanders. Finally, to complement your gratis meal, pretty much every wine store has regular "tastings," where you pick up some wine freebies and crackers. Best Cellars on the Upper East Side is a good one to try; they have wine tastings (sometimes with cheese) every night from Monday through Friday, 5:00 p.m. to 8:00 p.m.; and on Saturdays from 2:00 p.m. to 4:00 p.m. They offer free wine and food pairings with dishes made by restaurant chefs from around the city. Speaking of the Upper East Side, some of the best gourmet freebies come from **Sable's** (see page 249), where you will be treated to generous samples of caviar.

**Dean & Deluca:** *560 BROADWAY AT PRINCE STREET IN MANHATTAN. Subway: N, R, W to Prince Street. 212-226-6800. www.deananddeluca.com.*

**Streit Matzo Factory:** *148-154 RIVINGTON STREET AT SUFFOLK STREET IN MANHATTAN. Subway: F to Delancey Street; J, M, Z to Essex Street. 212-475-7000. www.streitmatzos.com.*

**Best Cellars:** *1291 LEXINGTON AVENUE BETWEEN 86TH AND 87TH STREETS IN MANHATTAN. Subway: 4, 5, 6 to 86th Street. 212-426-4200. www.bestcellars.com.*

**Gourmet Garage:** *Multiple locations. www.gourmetgarage.com.*

**Williams-Sonoma:** *Multiple locations. www.williamsonoma.com.*

**Garden of Eden:** *Multiple locations. Check the yellow pages for locations.*

## 763. Wash up at **Kiehl's**.

A not-very-well-kept secret about this 150-year-old apothecary is that they will give you pre-packaged samples of anything—and we mean anything—in the store, and as many different products as you want. Cast a look in the skin care direction, and you'll be showered with samples of face wash, moisturizer, and eye cream; step over to the hair care section, and the staff will pick out a shampoo and conditioner for your hair type to try. Fortunately for freeloaders, there is a branch on the Upper West Side now, so you can split your time between there and the Village store to avoid looking too conspicuous. (Kiehl's also has counters in department stores, but those do not offer samples.)

**East Village:** *109 THIRD AVENUE AT 13TH STREET IN MANHATTAN. Subway: 4, 5, 6, L, N, Q, R, W to 14th Street-Union Square. 212-677-3171.*

**Upper West Side:** *150 COLUMBUS AVENUE AT 69TH STREET IN MANHATTAN. Subway: 1 to 66th Street-Lincoln Center or 1, 2, 3 to 72nd Street. 212-799-3438.*

# Deluxe Treatment: Top five things you can do/buy when money is no object

## 764. Order the zillion dollar lobster frittata at **Norma's**.

This gourmet omelet is available for $100 with one ounce of caviar, or with ten ounces for $1,000. The menu dares you to expense it.

*LE PARKER MERIDIEN HOTEL, 118 WEST 57TH STREET, BETWEEN SIXTH AND SEVENTH AVENUES IN MANHATTAN. Subway: N, Q, R, W to 57th Street; F to 57th Street. 212-708-7460. www.parkermeridien.com.*

## 765. Have a private dinner at the **Cellar Room at 21**.

Up to twenty-two of your friends and family can have a private meal in the famous Cellar Room at the 21 Club, the famous wine cellar that the Feds never found during Prohibition, with its 2½-ton door that is unlocked by slipping an eighteen-inch wire through the wall. To have dinner in New York's most famous secret vault costs $450 per person for a seven-course meal. (They also serve lunch in the Cellar Room Monday through Friday at the considerably more reasonable price of $110 per person.)

*21 WEST 52ND STREET BETWEEN FIFTH AND SIXTH AVENUES IN MANHATTAN. Subway: E, V to Fifth Avenue/53rd Street. 212-582-7200. www.21club.com.*

→ **DID YOU KNOW?** *The Cellar Room at the 21 Club is technically not part of "21"— it's the cellar of the building next door at no. 19. The cellar was "borrowed" from the neighbors during Prohibition to hide their alcohol, so when 21 employees were asked if there was any liquor on the premises, they could truthfully answer "No."*

## 766. Have your jeans custom-made at **Earnest Sewn**.

In a city glutted with high-end denim, the zenith is this Meatpacking District store, where you can have jeans custom-made while you wait. For upwards of $300, customers can choose from one of the exclusive denims, and then select pocket designs and buttons, and the jeans are cut and sewn on-site for your personal fit.

*821 WASHINGTON STREET AT GANSEVOORT STREET IN MANHATTAN. Subway: A, C, E to 14th Street; L to Eighth Avenue. 212-242-3414. www.earnestsewn.com.*

## 767. Have the **World Cocktail** or the **Jewel in the Glass**.

The signature cocktail at the bar in the Trump World Tower is a $50 mix of Veuve Cliquot, Remy XO and white grape and lemon juices—all topped with a twenty-three-carat garnish. For another $30, you can get the **Pen-Top's** $80 Cristal-based Jewel in a Glass, along with one of the best rooftop views in the city (see page 57).

**WORLD BAR:** *Trump World Tower, 845 UNITED NATIONS PLAZA, FIRST AVENUE AT 48TH STREET IN MANHATTAN. Subway: 6 to 51st Street; E, V to Lexington Avenue/53rd Street. 212-935-9361. www.hospitalityholdings.com.*

**PEN-TOP:** *PENINSULA HOTEL, 700 FIFTH AVENUE AT 55TH STREET IN MANHATTAN. Subway: E, V to Fifth Avenue/53rd Street; F to 57th Street. 212-956-2888. www.newyork.peninsula.com.*

## 768. Open a house account with **Posy Floral Design**.

For between $200 and $2,000 per week, this haute Upper East Side floral boutique will deliver fresh flowers to your home and have them arranged by their top-notch floral designers. After an initial personalized consultation with the designers in your home, the designers can also help you choose vessels and vases in which to display the flowers. (They can also do arrangements for hotel rooms.)

*145 EAST 72ND STREET NEAR LEXINGTON AVENUE IN MANHATTAN. Subway: 6 to 68th Street-Hunter College. 212-744-7788. www.posyflowers.com.*

CHAPTER 8:

# Enrichment & Renewal

Learning, experiencing, and experimenting are an integral part of the culture in New York. This city encourages open minds and active bodies by opening itself to any class, discipline, sport, or pastime that seeks a place, and attracting dynamic, talented people from all over the world to share their creativity and expertise. The experience of trying something new is easy to come by here—so easy, in fact, that you may very well stumble onto something (a bookstore reading, free introductory yoga class, public lecture or performance) without even looking. This in itself is one of the best things about New York.

This chapter is devoted to the best of the city's many wonderful resources for improving one's well-being with education, relaxation, and recreation. From degree programs at prestigious universities to classes in art, dance, language, or martial arts; from lectures, talks, and readings by renowned leaders and scholars to informal discussions and gatherings, the opportunities for learning are limitless and constantly changing. At the same time, there are plenty of ways to refresh, relax, and rejuvenate, whether at spas, meditation sessions, or through exercise. No matter where your interests lie, there's a wealth of resources in this city to help you get what you need to nurture yourself—mind and body.

Note: We've included several forms of exercise and athletics in this chapter, but for more outdoor sports and activities, see chapter 6, "The Great Outdoors."

## Literature & Spoken Word

### 769. Listen to stories at **the Moth**.

There are eight million stories in the Naked City, as the saying goes, but only the best ones make it to the Moth. Cooler than a comedy club, more studied than improv, the Moth is an urban storytelling group that showcases this slightly obscure but very particular (and incredibly entertaining) art form. Each season, the organization hosts twelve storytelling events, which feature a different roster of performers, selected by the Moth curator, who deliver unscripted, ten-minute stories on a chosen theme (past themes include "Call of the Wild," "Sex and Money," and "Near Death Experiences"). Former storytellers have included big-name celebrities, local writers, journalists, and comedians, as well as regular New Yorkers who happen to have a gift for the gab. The Moth also puts on biweekly "Story Slams," in which average Joes compete in an audience-determined storytelling showdown. Both kinds of events are enjoyable and edifying—and their unpredictability makes you realize how thrilling it is to watch a spontaneous, live performance.

*Events are held at different venues around the city. For more information and a list of upcoming events, visit www.themoth.org.*

## 770. A poetry slam at **the Nuyorican**

is another event that explores the possibilities of the spoken word. Even if you haven't read a poem since high-school English, give poetry slams a try—they're anything but dull. The Nuyorican Poets Café started out as a living room poetry salon, and it has evolved into a vibrant, multi-medium art and performance space. And though the poetry slams are still what the venue is best known for, it also holds jazz and hip-hop concerts, theatrical performances, film and video events such as movie screenings, and screenplay readings. With multiple events taking place every night of the week, there's always something on, so either check out the monthly calendar (available online), or just head downtown and see what's happening.

*236 EAST 3RD STREET BETWEEN AVENUES B AND C IN MANHATTAN. Poetry slams held Friday night at 10:00 p.m. Subway: F, V to Lower East Side-Second Avenue. 212-505-8183. www.nuyorican.org.*

## 771. Commune with writers at the **Poetry Project at Saint Mark's**.

A longstanding institution of the New York literary scene, the Poetry Project counts Allen Ginsberg, Alice Walker, Patti Smith, and Michael Ondaatje among the many people who have shared their work here. One of the large number of community programs housed in Saint Mark's Church in-the-Bowery, the Poetry Project runs a vibrant roster of literary programs, including three weekly reading and events series; workshops in poetry and writing; and events such as the annual New Year's Day Marathon Reading, which draws in more than a hundred writers and other creative types for a day of performances, discussions, and, of course, readings. There is something for everyone here, no matter how, what, or how often you read.

**SAINT MARK'S CHURCH IN-THE-BOWERY:** *131 EAST 10TH STREET AT SECOND AVENUE IN MANHATTAN. Subway: 6 to Astor Place. 212-674-0910. www.poetryproject.com.*

## 772. Catch up on your personal correspondence at **Freebird Books**.

This beloved Brooklyn bookstore holds letter-writing evenings on the first Wednesday of every month from 7:00 p.m. to 9:00 p.m. There's no presentation or instruction, just a casual get-together hosted to keep this dying art alive. In addition to letters, it's also a perfect opportunity to plow through some thank-you notes, or take care of your holiday cards. Freebird supplies pens, paper, and envelopes, and also has stamps and a lovely selection of notecards and postcards for sale. Afterward, reward yourself for your diligence with a selection from the store's large inventory of new and used books, or a treat from the café.

*123 COLUMBIA STREET BETWEEN KANE AND DEGRAW STREETS IN BROOKLYN. Subway: F to Bergen Street. 718-643-8484. www.freebirdbooks.com.*

## 773. Spend a day in one of the beautiful reading rooms at the **New York Public Library**.

The Humanities and Social Sciences Library, one of four research libraries in the NYPL system, is the one people know best, located in the majestic Beaux-Arts building with the lion sculptures, next to Bryant Park. If you take the small trouble of obtaining an access card (in person at the library), you can visit the library's special collections, surround yourself with shelves of wonderful old books, sink into a comfortable chair, and read to your heart's content. Especially recommended is the Pforzheimer Room, an amazing collection of English romanticism in a cozy room with plush, red velvet chairs.

*FIFTH AVENUE AND 42ND STREET AT BRYANT PARK IN MANHATTAN. Subway: B, D, F, V to 42nd Street-Bryant Park; 7 to Fifth Avenue-Bryant Park. 212-930-0830. www.nypl.org.*

→ **DID YOU KNOW?** *The original names of the lions that stand outside the New York Public Library on Fifth Avenue were Leo Astor and Leo Lenox, after the library's founders, John Jacob Astor and James Lenox. During the Great Depression, Mayor Fiorello LaGuardia renamed them Patience and Fortitude.*

## Go to a literary reading.

It often seems like everyone in New York has either published a novel, or is working on one. That may be a slight exaggeration, but between the Pulitzer Prize winners and the struggling writers, there are literary readings to attend pretty much any night of the week. The particular setting, caliber of writer, and quality of the audience make some better than others. Our favorite spots:

**774.** *Housing Works Used Book Café* hosts readings and other literary events year-round. These are interesting because, unlike readings at other bookstores, theirs tend not to be limited to individual authors promoting a new book. Instead, they host discussions between writers, invite several writers to read on a certain theme, or have speakers on topics related to books and literature. (They also have a monthly concert series called "Live From Home.") They attract some fairly big names, but the environment is always cozy and laid-back. Most events are free, but there is a suggested donation to benefit Housing Works, the nonprofit organization that provides services to homeless New Yorkers living with HIV and AIDS. (One hundred percent of the bookstore's profits fund the same cause.)
*126 CROSBY STREET BETWEEN HOUSTON AND PRINCE STREETS IN MANHATTAN. Subway: 6 to Spring Street; B, D, F, V to Broadway-Lafayette Street; N, R, W to Prince Street. 212-334-3324. www.housingworks.org/usedbookcafe.*

**775.** *192 Books,* an independent bookstore in Chelsea, hosts readings, signings, and art exhibitions throughout the year. Although the owners call 192 a general-interest bookstore, the store has a distinctly arty vibe (Paula Cooper, one of the store's owners, also operates a nearby gallery) and therefore attracts many artistic types to the readings.
*192 TENTH AVENUE AT 21ST STREET IN MANHATTAN. Subway: C, E to 23rd Street. 212-255-4022. www.192books.com.*

→ **DID YOU KNOW?** *In 2004, novelist Paul Auster read* Oracle Nights *in its entirety over the course of two four-hour sessions at 192 Books.*

**776.** *The Corner Bookstore* (see page 278) on the Upper East Side hosts readings and book parties throughout the year, sometimes as many as two or three a week during the fall and spring. The authors that read are often customers, so the events have a cozy, neighborhood feel. Complimentary wine and cheese is another perk. The best way to find out what's scheduled is by picking up a calendar of events at the store.
*1313 MADISON AVENUE AT THE CORNER OF 93RD STREET IN MANHATTAN. Subway: 6 to 96th Street. 212-831-3554.*

**777.** At Amanda Stern's series at *Happy Ending*, all readers are required to take a "public risk" (in addition to reading from their own work in front of a crowd). Held biweekly in the lower level of this quirky Lower East Side bar, Stern adds a bit of a mischief to the typical author reading. Authors tend to be on the younger side, many of them first-time novelists, and if they take themselves too seriously, the lively, informal atmosphere, plus the prospect of cracking open a coconut or making sea monkeys perform tricks for the audience, will set them straight.

*302 BROOME STREET BETWEEN FORSYTH AND ELDRIDGE STREETS IN MANHATTAN. Subway: B, D to Grand Street; J, M, Z to the Bowery. 212-334-9676. www.happyendinglounge.com. For a schedule, visit www.amandastern.com.*

**778.** Although **KGB Bar** is only a decade old, it has already joined the ranks of New York's legendary literary haunts. Having grown from modest beginnings in the heart of the Ukrainian East Village, KGB Bar's mildly Communist theme recalls its origins with propaganda posters and other memorabilia. It has always relied on the quality of its readings and the prestige of its incumbent authors to sustain its reputation and to justify its cheap and powerful drinks. You can catch readings here almost any night of the week, by authors such as Rick Moody, A. M. Homes, Jonathan Lethem, Joyce Carol Oates, and Luc Sante. Even the less-established writers can be counted on to deliver good readings. Sundays are reserved for poetry, and Mondays for fiction; there are mixed readings and debates most weeknights.

*85 EAST 4TH STREET BETWEEN SECOND AND THIRD AVENUES IN MANHATTAN. Subway: F, V to Lower East Side-Second Avenue. 212-505-3360. www.kgbbar.com.*

**779.** If you like your readings big, **Symphony Space** is the place to go. Whereas most venues that host readings (bookstores, bars) tend to be modestly sized, with few professional production amenities, the literary events at Symphony Space are held on the same stages as their concerts, plays, and dance performances, with lighting, a sound system, and ample seating. These events are more "theatrical," so instead of an intimate, informal audience interacting with an author, these feel more like a performance. In addition to "Selected Shorts," the regularly scheduled evening of short stories broadcast on NPR, they also put on readings, discussions, and author Q & A sessions. The events aren't free (or even that cheap), but they're a fun way to see a favorite author among other fans, kind of like seeing them in concert.

*2537 BROADWAY NEAR 95TH STREET IN MANHATTAN. Subway: 1, 2, 3 to 96th Street. 212-864-5400. www.symphonyspace.org.*

**780.** Can't say much for the setting, but we have to include **Barnes & Noble** and **Borders** on our list. Though they don't feel as special as the independents or as carefree as the bars, these mega-stores are able to attract the top literary stars—most any author who's anyone reads here. The real big names (Salman Rushdie, David Sedaris) pack the house, which gives you a warm, fuzzy feeling about the future of the written word. And unless they're *really* eccentric, if authors go on a book tour that includes readings, chances are they'll be at an New York location of one of these chains.

*For schedules and locations, visit www.barnesandnoble.com or www.borders.com.*

## Take a class!

Opportunities for learning in this city are staggering and seemingly limitless, both for the variety in instruction and the available outlets in which to receive it. At major universities, continuing education programs, and informal classes at community and enrichment centers all over the city, you can learn skills and crafts, earn a certification or degree, or simply indulge in the pleasure of learning.

The following is our selection of places, among the many, that we feel are the best sources of enriching courses and activities, taking into account the quality of instruction, facilities, atmosphere, offerings, and cost. In general, degree and certificate programs tend to be the most serious and most expensive, and involve an admission process. Continuing education classes offer serious learners a less-directed, one-off option for study on a particular topic, field, or skill. There are also plenty of places that offer workshops or single-session classes that are good for an afternoon or evening's entertainment. The classes at the community and enrichment centers tend to be the least formal, and are for the most part recreational in focus. Between them all, the possibilities for personal edification are vast, and it is precisely the boundless array of possibility that makes this a best thing to do.

**781. *The 92nd Street Y*** enjoys a reputation as one of New York's premier centers for promoting arts, culture, and education. In addition to lectures, it offers instruction in countless subjects, crafts, skills, and pastimes. They have classes for all ages and levels: parenting classes; children's after-school programs; art, fitness, and language classes; personal development classes in home organization or assertiveness training; instruction in bridge, mah jong, and even juggling and tarot card reading. Though the 92nd Street Y is affiliated with a Jewish organization and some classes have a Jewish theme or focus, you don't have to be Jewish (or even a member) to take classes there. Some classes are held at a facility on the West Side, the Makor/Steinhardt Center.

**Main location:** *1395 LEXINGTON AVENUE AT 92ND STREET IN MANHATTAN. Subway: 6 to 96th Street. 212-415-5500.*

**Makor/Steinhardt Center:** *35 WEST 67TH STREET IN MANHATTAN. Subway: 1 to 66th Street-Lincoln Center; B, C to 72nd Street. 212-601-1000. www.92Y.org.*

**782.** The **Brooklyn Botanic Garden** (for full entry, see page 215) has a great range of classes in all things horticultural, from serious courses that count toward certificates in floral and landscape design, to one-off classes and short series in seasonal gardening activities. There are also classes in flower arranging, bird-watching, candle making, and even watercolor painting. The conservatories, home to the bonsai and tropical collections, are also a great place to learn about unusual plants and exotic creatures like fruit bats.
*1000 WASHINGTON AVENUE IN BROOKLYN. Subway: 2, 3 to Eastern Parkway-Brooklyn Museum; B, Q to Prospect Park. 718-623-7200. www.bbg.org.*

**783. Beads of Paradise**, a jewelry and craft emporium just off Union Square, offers a jewelry-making class on weekends. Participants learn how to use different tools, how to string necklaces and bracelets, and how to make earrings and drop pendants. Also included in the $65 class fee is a set of tools, bead box, and discount card for your next purchase.
*16 EAST 17TH STREET BETWEEN UNION SQUARE WEST AND FIFTH AVENUE IN MANHATTAN. Subway: 4, 5, 6, L, N, Q, R, W to 14th Street-Union Square. 212-620-0642.*

**784. The Center for Book Arts** is a nonprofit arts and education center dedicated to preserving the craft of bookmaking. It holds classes, seminars, and workshops in techniques of traditional and modern bookbinding and printing, including paper marbling, calligraphy, and letterpress. Beginners are welcome. The center also organizes exhibitions and special events.
*28 WEST 27TH STREET BETWEEN SIXTH AVENUE AND BROADWAY, THIRD FLOOR, IN MANHATTAN. Subway: 1 to 28th Street; N, R, W to 28th Street. 212-481-0295. www.centerforbookarts.org.*

**785.** You can eat your way through **a cheese class at Murray's, the Artisanal Premium Cheese Center, or the Institute of Culinary Education**. You can take classes on regional cheeses or cheese and wine pairing, or learn to make your own in a cheese-making class.
**Murray's:** *254 BLEECKER STREET BETWEEN SIXTH AND SEVENTH AVENUES IN MANHATTAN. Subway: 1 to Christopher Street-Sheridan Square. 212-243-3289. www.murrayscheese.com.*
**Artisanal Premium Cheese Center:** *500 WEST 37TH STREET AT TENTH AVENUE, SECOND FLOOR, IN MANHATTAN. Subway: 1, 2, 3, A, C, E to 34th Street-Penn Station. 877-797-1200. www.artisanalcheese.com.*
**ICE:** *50 WEST 23RD STREET BETWEEN FIFTH AND SIXTH AVENUES IN MANHATTAN. Subway: F, V to 23rd Street; N, R, W to 23rd Street/Broadway. 212-847-0700. www.iceculinary.com. For more information, see following page.*

**786. Cooper Union** maintains a small but interesting selection of continuing education classes, including a five-session course on wine tasting, floral design, horticulture and botanical art, and, improbably enough, even a class on selling goods on eBay. *COOPER SQUARE BY ASTOR PLACE AND LAFAYETTE STREET IN MANHATTAN. Subway: 6 to Astor Place. 212-353-4195. www.cooper.edu.*

**787. The French Culinary Institute** offers a small menu of amateur cooking classes focused on technique. It also offers courses in restaurant management, food writing, and wine. *462 BROADWAY AT GRAND STREET IN MANHATTAN. Subway: 6 to Spring Street; 6, N, Q, R, W, J, M, Z to Canal Street. 212-219-8890. www.frenchculinary.com.*

**788. Gotham Writers' Workshop** runs classes and one-session workshops in many genres: fiction and nonfiction, screenplay, memoir, writing for television, travel writing, humor, and more. The instructors are professional writers and teachers. It isn't glamorous, but the egalitarian feel makes it a comfortable environment in which to work on and share your writing. *Classes held at various locations around the city. For more information, class schedules, and locations, call 212-WRI-TERS or visit www.writingclasses.com.*

**789. The recreation division at the Institute of Culinary Education** gives a full range of cooking classes covering everything from basic technique to specific topics, skills, and cuisines, many in one- or two-evening sessions. It also offers diploma programs in culinary arts, pastry and baking arts, and culinary management, and classes for professional development in restaurant and catering, food media, and more. *50 WEST 23RD STREET BETWEEN FIFTH AND SIXTH AVENUES IN MANHATTAN. Subway: ; F, V to 23rd Street; N, R, W to 23rd Street. 212-847-0700. www.iceculinary.com.*

**790. The Jewish Community Center** on the Upper West Side offers classes for all ages in the visual arts, photography, media, sports and exercise, cooking, and subjects of Jewish interest. The facilities are immaculate and state-of-the-art, and include a gymnasium and fitness center, swimming pool, an entire floor of arts and media studios, along with classrooms and auditoriums. Classes are open to members and non-members of any religion, race, or ethnicity. *334 AMSTERDAM AVENUE AT 76TH STREET IN MANHATTAN. Subway: 1, 2, 3 to 72nd Street; B, C to 72nd Street. 646-505-4445. www.jccnyc.org.*

**791. Joe: The Art of Coffee** is considered by many to serve the best coffee in the city. Every year, their perfectly brewed coffee and espresso beverages top local "best of" lists. You can learn how they do it at their coffee classes, which are held sporadically throughout the year at their 13th Street location. There is a class on the basics of coffee preparation and presentation, a tutorial on single-origin coffee, and a hands-on workshop with their espresso machine. To find out more, call, check the Web site, or just pop in—theirs is the friendliest, most mellow staff we've ever encountered in a coffee shop, and it's a good excuse to get a cup of coffee.

*9 EAST 13TH STREET BETWEEN FIFTH AVENUE AND UNIVERSITY PLACE IN MANHATTAN. Classes cost $10 each. Reservations required. Subway: 4, 5, 6, L, N, Q, R, W to 14th Street-Union Square. 212-942-7400. www.joetheartofcoffee.com.*

**792.** The cooking classes at **Miette Culinary Studio** in the West Village feel like a potluck dinner at a good friend's house, except that your host is a chef, and everyone is cooking the same thing at the same time. Housed in a nineteenth-century town-house, the airy studio is more like someone's dream apartment than a cooking school. Paul Vandewoude formerly owned Tartine, the charming BYOB restaurant in the West Village (Tartine still exists, but Paul, who has a young son, moved on to start a more family-friendly venture). The three-hour classes are limited to twelve students and are held on weekday evenings. Each class teaches the preparation of classic but manage-able meals, like marinated salmon in ginger with green beans and roasted potatoes, or a roasted root vegetable salad with pumpkin risotto. The focus is on classic French cooking, but there are also special classes on specific techniques and other cuisines. Afterward, the class sits down together to enjoy the food, and, adding to the homey, convivial atmosphere, participants are encouraged to bring bottles of wine to con-tribute to the meal. Miette also offers classes for kids, wine tastings, and private parties.

*109 MACDOUGAL STREET BETWEEN BLEECKER AND WEST 3RD STREETS IN MANHATTAN. Subway: A, C, E, B, D, F, V to West 4th Street. 212-460-9322. www.mietteculinarystudio.com.*

**793.** The **Manhattan Neighborhood Network**, a local community access channel, offers one of the best deals in the city. In keeping with its mission of promoting free speech through the medium of television, it gives free classes in its studios. Classes include studio production, control-room basics, camera technique and more; stu-dents are also allowed to use their equipment during the term of the class. Classes are first-come, first-served, and you must show proof of residency.

*537 WEST 59TH STREET BETWEEN TENTH AND ELEVENTH AVENUES IN MANHATTAN. Sub-way: 1, A, C, B, D to 59th Street-Columbus Circle. 212-757-2670. www.mnn.org.*

**794.** Proudly proclaiming itself "the leader in adult education," the **New School** is considered the premier institution of continuing education in the country. Most classes at the New School of General Studies, Parsons School of Design, and Mannes College for Music are open to both credit and noncredit students. This means that you can take a regular university class with matriculating students, but because of the university's dedication to continuing education, you won't be made to feel like an anomaly. They also offer certificate programs in several disciplines.

*66 WEST 12TH STREET BETWEEN SIXTH AND SEVENTH AVENUES IN MANHATTAN. Subway: F, V to 14th Street; L to Sixth Avenue. For phone numbers of specific schools and departments, visit www.newschool.edu.*

**795. *The New York Film Academy*** has classes and workshops that range in length and intensity from a few weeks to one year. In addition to traditional filmmaking, it offers classes in digital film, screenwriting, editing, producing, animation, and screen acting.

*100 EAST 17TH STREET AT UNION SQUARE IN MANHATTAN. Subway: 4, 5, 6, L, N, Q, R, W to 14th Street-Union Square. 212-674-4300. www.nyfa.com.*

**796. *The New York Open Center*** is a holistic learning center that offers courses in just about any creative, physical, emotional, psychological, sociological, and spiritual topic you can imagine. From aromatherapy to African-American studies, photography to psychology—you name it, they teach it. (There is an entire section in the catalog devoted to courses in holistic pet care.) A look through the online course catalog is quite an enriching experience in itself.

*83 SPRING STREET BETWEEN CROSBY STREET AND BROADWAY IN MANHATTAN. Subway: 6 to Spring Street. 212-219-2527. www.opencenter.org.*

**797. *New York University's School of Continuing and Professional Studies*** gives adults of any educational background a chance to study pretty much any topic, field, or discipline imaginable. Among the more than 2,500 courses are classes in all the traditional liberal arts (history, literature, social sciences); skills (arts, editing, accounting, languages); professional interests; plus classes in leadership skills, emergency management, and other highly targeted areas of study. There are enough different certificate and degree programs for graduates and professionals to accommodate any educational goal. Whether you are looking to take a college-level literature class for fun, pick up a new skill, get a license to boost your career, or you are considering a graduate degree but not quite ready to invest in a master's program, NYU has a class to meet your needs.

*145 FOURTH AVENUE, ROOM 201, IN MANHATTAN. Subway: 4, 5, 6, L, N, Q, R, W to 14th Street-Union Square. 212-998-7200. www.scps.nyu.edu.*

**798. *PhotoManhattan*** offers photography classes at a fraction of the cost of the ones at other schools and institutes around the city. They have classes in introductory-level photography, darkroom technique, lighting, and more that offer the same level of instruction as the others at half the price. Equipment rentals are similarly affordable. They also have an interesting Artist's Exchange program, through which fashion designers, illustrators, and other artists can have their work photographed for free by students (see Web site for details).

*51 WEST 14TH STREET BETWEEN FIFTH AND SIXTH AVENUES IN MANHATTAN. Subway: F, V to 14th Street; L to Sixth Avenue. 212-929-3302. www.photomanhattan.com.*

**799. *The Pratt Institute*,** one of New York's most celebrated art and architecture schools, offers continuing education and certificate programs in the arts in addition to its undergraduate and graduate degree programs. The Center for Continuing and Professional Studies provides a wide range of classes in fields such as computer skills, technical art skills, fashion design, and feng shui. Classes are held on the main Brooklyn campus, or on the satellite campus in Manhattan.

*Brooklyn: 200 WILLOUGHBY AVENUE NEAR HALL STREET. Subway: G to Clinton-Washington Avenue. 718-636-3600.*

*Manhattan: 144 WEST 14TH STREET BETWEEN SIXTH AND SEVENTH AVENUES. Subway: F, V to 14th Street; L to Sixth Avenue. 212-647-7775. www.pratt.edu.*

**800. *The School of Visual Arts*** runs terrific continuing education programs in advertising, animation, computer arts, film and video, fine arts, graphic design, illustration and cartooning, interior design, and photography, as well as graduate and undergraduate degree courses.

*209 EAST 23RD STREET BETWEEN SECOND AND THIRD AVENUES IN MANHATTAN. Subway: 6 to 23rd Street. 212-592-2000. www.sva.edu.*

**801. *Craigslist.*** It's true that Craigslist exists in many cities here and abroad, but like food, arts, and pretty much everything else in New York, the diversity and ingenuity of our locals really work in your favor. The combination of constant Internet access and the large number of highly skilled but underemployed (or underpaid) New Yorkers makes this city a buyer's market for instruction and tutelage (the excellent public transportation system helps, too—services can often be delivered in under an hour). A quick look at the postings under "classes" reveals offers for lessons in art, dance, languages, music, yoga, computer skills—and that's just one day's listing. The quality of the lessons, of course, is not guaranteed, but if you want to try something out for the hell of it (or you really need to learn HTML *right now*), this is the place to go.

*http://newyork.craigslist.org.*

Another valuable resource for education and enrichment opportunities in New York is **international institutes.** Most have language classes, with some of the major cultural centers offering more comprehensive curriculums in literature, business, and cultural studies, and the classes tend to be less strictly utilitarian than at regular language schools. These institutes also tend to have many other cultural resources, such as film and lecture programs, art exhibits, and libraries. Some of these include:

**802.** *The French Institute/Alliance Française* offers classes in French language for all levels, as well as more advanced classes in writing, literature, film, history, politics, and business.
*22 EAST 60TH STREET AT FIFTH AVENUE IN MANHATTAN. Subway: N, R, W to Fifth Avenue/59th Street. 212-355-6100. www.fiaf.org.*

**803.** *The China Institute* runs fun and informative courses in a range of Chinese cultural pursuits, from calligraphy and languages to painting and taijiquan (tai chi). Most classes are taught in the evening and can be taken on a night-by-night basis or as a full program.
*125 EAST 65TH STREET IN MANHATTAN. Subway: 4, 5, 6 to 59th Street; F to Lexington Avenue/63rd Street; N, R, W to Lexington Avenue/59th Street. 212-744-8181. www.chinainstitute.org.*

**804.** *The Deutsches Haus* holds classes on a quarterly basis in German language, with special courses on reading, business German, and other topics. There is also a language-focused book club for contemporary German literature to help students practice their German in a more relaxed setting. (For an additional fee, the book club is open to non-students who speak German or are in the process of learning.) Another plus is the center's lovely setting by the Washington Mews.
*42 WASHINGTON MEWS BETWEEN UNIVERSITY PLACE AND FIFTH AVENUE IN MANHATTAN. Subway: N, R, W to 8th Street-New York University. 212-998-8660. www.nyu.edu./deutscheshaus.*

**805.** *The Japan Society* maintains a comprehensive program of Japanese language classes for children and adults, from beginner on up. It also offers classes in ESL, business Japanese, and *shodo*, an art form using Japanese calligraphy.
*333 EAST 47TH STREET BETWEEN FIRST AND SECOND AVENUES IN MANHATTAN. Subway: 4, 5, 6, 7, S to Grand Central-42nd Street. 212-832-1155. www.japansociety.org.*

**806.** *The Instituto Cervantes* offers Spanish language classes for adults, from beginner on up. It also runs special classes for children, as well as classes on Spanish culture and history, business Spanish, and classes with a reading or writing focus. Students receive a free six-month membership to the institute's library, and are given access to other educational support.
*211-215 EAST 49TH STREET AT AMSTER YARD IN MANHATTAN. Subway: 6 to 51st Street; E, V to Lexington Avenue/53rd Street. 212-308-7720. www.cervantes.org.*

**807. *Scandinavia House*** offers a wide range of language classes, including a super program for kids. There is also an exhibition space for works by Scandinavian artists, sculptors, and photographers, where lecture and film series are held throughout the year. Get the events calendar and try to make it to one of the parties—Scandinavians know how to have fun.
*58 PARK AVENUE BETWEEN 37TH AND 38TH STREETS IN MANHATTAN. Subway: 4, 5, 6, 7, S to Grand Central-42nd Street. 212-879-9779. www.scandinaviahouse.org.*

## Lectures

As a center for arts, politics, international relations, history, and culture, New York attracts authorities on every field imaginable, a great number of whom will be speaking about something, somewhere, on any given night. If the word lecture is off-putting to you, take note: most bear no resemblance to the stuffy, sleep-inducing assemblies of your school days (some even serve food and drink). Most of the schools and community and cultural centers listed earlier in this chapter also have lecture series, symposia, panel discussions, and other speaking programs that are open to the public. The following are other places around the city that compile interesting programs:

**808. *Museum at the Fashion Institute of Technology***. Most of the lectures and debates that take place in New York's top school of fashion and textile design are open to the public for $10. Topics vary from the history of textiles around the world to more specific elements of contemporary fashion, and they often relate to the current exhibitions at the museum. A little time here can provide an interesting perspective on the hours spent schlepping around boutiques uptown and in SoHo. (See page 128 for more information on visiting the museum.)
*SEVENTH AVENUE AT 27TH STREET IN MANHATTAN. Subway: 1 to 28th Street. 212-217-5800. www.fitnyc.edu.*

**809. *The Interfaith Center*** is a secular organization whose goal is to celebrate New York's religious and cultural diversity through education, entertainment, and enrichment. It hosts a broad range of lectures, seminars, and workshops on topics of local and cultural interest. It also holds exhibitions and performances on-site at the Onisaburo Gallery.
*20 EAST 79TH STREET IN MANHATTAN. Subway: 6 to 77th Street. 212-685-4242. www.interfaithcenter.org.*

**810.** *The Tibet House* holds speaking events related to Tibet and Buddhism and has an on-site gallery for exhibitions of visual art. Classes are offered as part of the Tibetan studies program at the **New York Open Center** (see page 298), and there are weekly meditation sessions.

*22 WEST 15TH STREET BETWEEN FIFTH AND SIXTH AVENUES IN MANHATTAN. Subway: F, V to 14th Street; L to Sixth Avenue. 212-807-0563. www.tibethouse.org.*

### 811. AIA Center for Architecture.

The New York headquarters of the American Institute for Architects is a wonderful and underused resource. The building itself is unique in the city because, by virtue of a deep well that was dug out beneath, it is the only structure in New York with an eco-friendly geothermal heating and cooling system. The library is a nice, quiet place to work; it is well stocked with glossy volumes of contemporary and historic architecture, and allows for eavesdropping on university classes that take place here. Almost all lectures are free, and range from debates on important issues of contemporary urban planning to retrospective talks from renowned architects. The guests are often world-famous, the after-parties are great, and there are always interesting faces in the crowd.

*536 LAGUARDIA PLACE BETWEEN BLEECKER AND WEST 3RD STREETS IN MANHATTAN. Subway: 6 to Bleecker Street; A, C, E, B, D, F, V to West 4th Street. 212-683-0023. www.aiany.org. See AIA President Ric Bell's favorite classic New York buildings on page 54.*

### 812. Attend an organized meditation session.

The focus, relaxation, and calm achieved through meditation are just what every New Yorker needs, right? Meditation sessions are a sure way to nourish a weary psyche, and they are as prevalent as hot dog vendors, if you know where to look. In addition to Tibet House (see above for more information), which offers weekly meditation on Tuesday nights, sessions can be found at yoga studios, wellness centers, and at some of the community centers listed earlier in this chapter. Many places offer instructional sessions, where a leader teaches you how to meditate, so skeptics who scoff at the exercise should give it a go. You may think you don't have time, or that you're too "type A" to go in for this kind of stuff, but isn't the chance of improving your mental well-being worth a try?

*Sessions take place all over the city; check local listings for specific times and venues.*

## 813. Take a meditation walk in **the Greenbelt**.

**The Jacques Marchais Museum of Tibetan Art** (see page 125) organizes walks through the borough's chain of woodlands and parks led by monks from the Staten Island Vihara. By exposing you to the beauty and harmony in the park, the walk is intended to make your spiritual journey as wonderful as your literal one.

*338 LIGHTHOUSE AVENUE IN STATEN ISLAND. Call or visit the museum for dates and details. Ferry to St. George; then S74 bus to Lighthouse Avenue. 718-987-3500. www.tibetanmuseum.org.*

## 814. Learn to focus on the task at hand at a **Japanese tea ceremony**.

Urasenke Chanoyu is one of the most prestigious tea schools in the world. Based in Japan, the school teaches the art of Japanese tea ceremonies at various outposts around world. The New York branch is an uncommonly tranquil spot in the city, hidden on a quiet block on the Upper East Side. A small door in the middle of the block opens onto a peaceful Japanese rock garden courtyard, which is surrounded by kitchens, classrooms, libraries, and storerooms. To be a full-time student here is serious business (training to be a tea master can take years), and there is a long waiting list to be approved for entry. But the center holds monthly tea ceremony demonstrations for the public, which include an introductory lecture on the practice and etiquette of the Japanese tea ceremony, the tea ceremony itself, and a question and answer session. Focusing on the task at hand is an integral part of a tea ceremony, and you are supposed to perform the movements of pouring and serving tea by treating these tasks as the most important in the world. The experience shows how concentration can elevate ordinary-seeming actions into meaningful parts of life—a lesson from which most of us could surely benefit.

*153 EAST 69TH STREET BETWEEN THIRD AND LEXINGTON AVENUES IN MANHATTAN. Subway: 6 to 68th Street-Hunter College. 212-988-6161.*

## 815. Once a year, toward the end of summer, the Four Seasons Chinese tea ceremony demonstration is held at the **Queens Botanical Garden**. A traditional

table is set up in a peaceful part of the gardens, and the scent of nearby plants and flowers mingle with the aromas of the teas being prepared.

*43-50 MAIN STREET IN QUEENS. Subway: 7 to Flushing-Main Street. For details and specific dates, call 718-886-3800 or visit www.queensbotanical.org.*

## 816. Hone your mind against the smartest hustlers in the world at the chess tables in **Washington Square Park**.

It's a different kind of focus, but one that will sharpen your mind (and your reflexes) like none other. Washington Square Park's tables (also known as the "snake pit") are legendary, but remarkably, despite their popularity among sightseers, this technically illegal chess racket hasn't been shut (or watered) down. A mixture of serious amateurs, college chess club dropouts, and the occasional unwitting novices play against seasoned regulars for three dollars and up per game. Look out for "the Lithuanian," an anonymous master in a trench coat—he never loses.

*WASHINGTON SQUARE PARK AT THOMPSON STREET IN MANHATTAN. Subway: A, C, E, B, D, F, V to West 4th Street.*

Also: **Chess Forum** (219 Thompson Street) and the **Village Chess Shop** (230 Thompson Street) are great places to engage in anything from idle games to competitive championships with other would-be grand masters. See page 329 for details.

## 817. Recharge with a **midday nap**.

Going somewhere to conk out in the middle of the day might sound illicit, but if you're lucky enough to be around the Empire State Building or Nassau Street on a weekday, check out MetroNaps. This one-of-a-kind business venture has single-occupancy "pods" that can be rented for twenty-minute naps. The pods are semi-enclosed reclining chairs equipped with a wake-up mechanism that gently vibrates and lights up when naptime is up. The entire experience has been specifically choreographed to maximize the many restorative benefits of a nap, so while the hushed voices and low lights give it a little bit of a speakeasy feel, there's nothing shady about the increase in energy and productivity you'll feel afterward.

*Both locations in Manhattan. EMPIRE STATE BUILDING: 350 FIFTH AVENUE, AT 34TH STREET, SUITE 2410. Subway: B, D, F, V, N, Q, R, W, to 34th Street-Herald Square. 212-239-3344. FINANCIAL DISTRICT: 120 NASSAU STREET BETWEEN ANN STREET AND BEEKMAN PLACE. Subway: 2, 3, 4, 5, J, M, Z to Fulton Street; A, C to Broadway-Nassau Street. Naps cost $14 for twenty minutes, and can be reserved by calling 212-239-3344 or by purchasing NapPasses online at www.metronaps.com.*

## 818. Find **yoga** you like.

It seems like there are as many places to take yoga as there are delis in this city, and if you lump the gyms, community centers, and private teachers in with the studios, there probably are. Some devoted practitioners may lament the mass production of this sanctified ancient practice, and to be sure, there are plenty of untraditional teachers and classes out there. But looked at strictly in terms of accessibility and convenience, this is a great thing.

If you live in the city and you practice yoga, you may have a place that you are loyal to. But if you're visiting, are interested in beginning, or perhaps are an experienced yogi but haven't found a teacher or class that you like, then explore! Many centers offer **free introductory classes** or packages (see page 284). Classes, studios, and teachers vary greatly from one studio to another, from basics like the style of yoga practiced and the size and condition of the facilities to less tangible factors, including the atmosphere, attitude, and clientele. Some studios are very social and hold other, non-yoga gatherings; some are very serious about one form of yoga, and teach classes only in a single style (there are even studios that have created their own signature practices); some are particularly accommodating to people with special interests: beginners, mothers, and pregnant women, or people very pressed for time (even one that offers classes for dogs and their owners). With so many different outlets available, you have the luxury to sample and compare, so don't feel limited by one style, teacher, or studio. Citysearch (http://newyork.citysearch.com) and NYMetro.com (the Web site for *New York* magazine) have comprehensive listings for studios all over the city, and the Yogafinder.com has an international database, where you can search for yoga classes by zip code. You can also find out about new studios and deals on yoga classes in the "Chill Out" section of *Time Out*.

A nice alternative to a regular class in a studio is **outdoor yoga**. Particularly nice if you're suffering from urban claustrophobia, this change of pace lets you escape the confines of the studio and practice in a more ambient environment. Outdoor yoga classes are offered in parks and gardens (we even found one on a rooftop) around the city during the warmer months. We've included listings for some of these in chapter 6, "The Great Outdoors."

## Learn to **dance**.

Taking a dance class is a refreshing (and socially empowering) way to get some exercise, and, not surprisingly, there is no shortage of classes offered around the city. Here are some favorites:

**819. *For beginners:* The Sandra Cameron Dance Center**. Started in 1979 by ballroom dance champion Sandra Cameron, this dance school offers classes in all types of Latin, swing, hip-hop, and, of course, ballroom dancing. Their Basic Six course is a great introduction to ballroom dancing, where you learn the steps of six popular dances (foxtrot, swing, waltz, tango, rhumba, and cha-cha), as well as basic dance principles. The monthlong course, which is given all year round, meets once a week for an hour, and also includes a free review class near the end of the term. After Basic Six, you can go on to more advanced classes in these or other dances, such as salsa, merengue, or break dancing. The center also holds open practice sessions for specific dances, free for enrolled students, where you can work on your steps with an instructor present.

*199 LAFAYETTE STREET BETWEEN BROOME AND KENMARE STREETS IN MANHATTAN. Subway: 6 to Spring Street. 212-431-1825. www.sandracameron.com.*

**820. *African dancing:*** The Djoniba Dancing & Drum Centre offers more than sixty classes each week in different types of ethnic dance, drumming, and martial arts. The African dance classes attract a wide range of students—all ages, sizes, and backgrounds—who come to let loose in the spirited hour-and-a-half lessons accompanied by live percussion. The center has a drop-in policy for adult classes and also offers children's sessions in African dance and ballet.

*37 EAST 18TH STREET BETWEEN PARK AVENUE SOUTH AND BROADWAY, SEVENTH FLOOR, IN MANHATTAN. Subway: 4, 5, 6, L, N, Q, R, W to 14th Street-Union Square. www.djoniba.com.*

**821. *Belly dancing:*** The belly-dancing community in New York is bigger than you might think, and **www.bellydanceny.com** is the best resource for finding classes, teachers, studios, and performances around town. The Web site has regularly updated listings of classes, teachers, and venues, as well as bars and restaurants that feature dancers, and schedules of performances.

**822. *Partner dancing:*** There are many studios that teach partner dancing around the city, and most have comparable offerings like packages for beginners, free introductory classes, wedding packages, and complimentary practice sessions and parties. The biggest dance center in New York is **DanceSport**, near Central Park South, famous for the celebrities and Broadway stars they've worked with. (The center's claim to fame is that its founders choreographed the tango scene in *Scent of a Woman*.) DanceSport offers classes in dozens of types of partner dances at all levels. The Chelsea studios **Dance Manhattan**, **Stepping Out**, and **Sandra Cameron** are also good places for lessons.

*All studios located in Manhattan.* **DANCESPORT:** *1845 BROADWAY AT 60TH STREET. Subway: 1, A, C, B, D to 59th Street-Columbus Circle. 212-307-1111. www.dancesport.com.*
**DANCE MANHATTAN:** *39 WEST 19TH STREET BETWEEN FIFTH AND SIXTH AVENUES. Subway: 4, 5, 6, L, N, Q, R, W to 14th Street-Union Square. 212-807-0802. www.dancemanhattan.com.*
**STEPPING OUT:** *37 WEST 26TH STREET BETWEEN BROADWAY AND SIXTH AVENUE. Subway: N, R, W to 28th Street. 646-742-9400. www.steppingoutstudios.com.*

# Study a **martial art**.

The organized systems of movement and postures that characterize martial arts were developed originally as means of self-defense, but their individual principles, philosophies, and focus techniques provide benefits beyond fighting skills. Like yoga, martial arts can enhance both physical and mental fitness, and though the styles vary in approach and specifics, they are all quite beautiful to watch and perform. Karate, tai chi, and tae kwon do are only some of the many kinds of martial arts practiced in New York, and each of these can found at gyms and studios all around the city. Following are several places that offer less well-known varieties. We've also included listings for **outdoor tai chi classes** on page 226 in chapter 6, "The Great Outdoors."

**823. *The Japanese Swordsmanship Society*** is an organization dedicated to preserving ancient Japanese martial arts. They offer classes in several types of swordsmanship: *iado, naginata*, and *jodo*. They welcome beginners and are eager to introduce anyone to the art of the sword.
*Classes, times, and locations vary; see Web site for details. www.ny-jss.org.*

**824.** Grappling, or Brazilian jujitsu, is a cross-cultural martial art that resembles wrestling. It was developed in Brazil in the early twentieth century by a family that received instruction in traditional Japanese jujitsu from a visiting master. In Manhattan, you can study it at the ***Renzo Gracie Academy*** with a member of the original Brazilian family and an international martial arts champion.
**RENZO GRACIE ACADEMY:** *224 WEST 30TH STREET, SUITE 100, IN MANHATTAN. Subway: 1 to 28th Street. 212-279-6724. www.renzogracie.com.*

**825.** At the ***USA Shaolin Temple***, you can visit the origins of all martial arts and be instructed in various disciplines of ancient Chinese practices. There are classes in various styles of kung fu, tai chi, chi kung, plus teachings in Chan Buddhism and the rich history of the Shaolin Temple.
*678 BROADWAY, THIRD FLOOR, BETWEEN WEST 3RD AND BOND STREETS IN MANHATTAN. Subway: 6 to Bleecker Street; A, C, E, B, D, F, V to West 4th Street. 212-358-7876. www.usashaolintemple.com.*

# 826. Pick a sport at **Chelsea Piers**.

This thirty-acre waterfront sports complex has literally transformed physical activity in New York since it opened ten years ago, and it remains one of the best places in the city for unbridled recreation. Nowhere else can you find this much space for so many different kinds of activities, and some of the facilities are the only ones of their kind.

There's a forty-lane bowling alley; **golf club** (see page 347); an ice-skating rink; a roller rink and skate park; the Field House, with an indoor rock-climbing wall, batting cages, soccer and basketball courts, and gymnastics; a fitness center with a pool; an Origins spa; plus restaurants, shops, studios, and more. (To some New Yorkers, the most exotic amenity, however, might be the on-site parking.) Finally, there are also camps, after-school activities, training programs, and extensive adult sports programs—including the world's largest adult gymnastics program.

*23RD STREET AND THE HUDSON RIVER IN MANHATTAN. Subway: C, E to 23rd Street. For information, hours, prices, and phone numbers of specific facilities, call 212-336-6666 or visit www.chelseapiers.com.*

## Expert Contributor: Pavia Rosati

Pavia Rosati is a journalist who has been living in New York for fifteen years. She is the executive editor of DailyCandy.com, and she writes about food and travel for *Departures*, the *New York Times*, and *Bon Appetit*. She travels extensively for work, but finds special pleasure in her favorite New York escapes.

### MY FIVE FAVORITE RETREATS IN NEW YORK

**827. *Balthazar:*** Everyone is beautiful at Balthazar. The restaurant is New York at its best: buzzy, sceney, cool, and usually insanely (and annoyingly) packed, which is why I only go for breakfast or a late midweek supper. The tables in the back left corner are perfect for hiding out in plain sight.

*80 SPRING STREET BETWEEN BROADWAY AND CROSBY STREET IN MANHATTAN. Subway: 6 to Spring Street. 212-965-1785. www.balthazarny.com. For more information on Balthazar, see page 163.*

**828. *Rose Reading Room at the New York Public Library:*** I love to play hooky from the office and spend the day working here. Soaring ceilings, pink cloud murals, long tables, plus a mishmash of students, tourists, and researchers—easily the most inspiring yet quiet place in town. Plus there's free Internet access, and Wi-Fi right outside in Bryant Park.

*FIFTH AVENUE AND 42ND STREET AT BRYANT PARK IN MANHATTAN. Subway: B, D, F, V to 42nd Street-Bryant Park; 7 to Fifth Avenue-Bryant Park. www.nypl.org. For more information on the New York Public Library, see page 291.*

**829. *Housing Works Used Book Café:*** I work in a creative, noisy office in SoHo. When I can't hear myself think, I head to Housing Works Café, an oasis in an otherwise zoo-like neighborhood. That Crosby is the sexiest, gritty street in the city only adds to the charm.

*126 CROSBY STREET BETWEEN HOUSTON AND PRINCE STREETS IN MANHATTAN. Subway: 6 to Spring Street; B, D, F, V to Broadway-Lafayette; Street N, R, W to Prince Street. 212-334-3324. www.housingworks.org. For full entry, see page 292.*

**830. Juvenex Spa:** Now this is a miracle: a 24-hour spa in the middle of the city. It's women only from 6:00 a.m. until 7:00 p.m.; co-ed thereafter. There's no better chaser to an overly rich dinner than the jade igloo sauna.
*25 WEST 32ND STREET BETWEEN FIFTH AND SIXTH AVENUES IN MANHATTAN. Subway: B, D, F, V, N, Q, R, W to 34th Street-Herald Square. For full entry, see page 326. www.juvenexspa.com.*

**831. Williamsburg Bridge:** As much as I love to travel, I love coming home more. I always tell the driver to take the BQE (Brooklyn-Queens Expressway) from the airport so I can stare at the skyline and cross the Williamsburg Bridge on my way home to the East Village.

# Massages, baths, acupuncture, spas, herbal remedies and other ways to relax

Along with exercising your mind and body with classes, sports, and entertainment, part of improving yourself and your well-being involves taking time to relax and recharge. In New York, there are innumerable ways to do just that, such as spa visits, massages and body treatments, and alternative medicine, to name a few. Here we've listed the particularly notable options for bolstering your inner health.

## 832. Float for an hour in the tanks at La Casa Day Spa.

The mission of this Flatiron spa is to draw on the healing powers of the five earthly elements (earth, water, fire, air, and sky) to draw pesky toxins out of the body, and to restore balance and well-being. So it follows that one of the signature treatments is floatation. Inside a private tank, you rest peacefully in water saturated with 800 pounds of Epsom salts. The salts draw toxins from the body, so they can be washed away. The water is heated to the precise temperature of your skin, which prevents nerve transmissions from skin to brain. What results is a relaxing and purifying experience more profound than a regular massage.
*41 EAST 20TH STREET BETWEEN PARK AVENUE SOUTH AND BROADWAY IN MANHATTAN. One-hour float is $50 or $25 when combined with another treatment. Subway: 6 to 23rd Street; N, R, W to 23rd Street. 212-673-CASA. www.lacasaspa.com.*

## 833. Have someone walk on your back at **Osaka**.

During the famous sixty-minute shiatsu acupressure massage, which has been enjoyed by movie stars, politicians, and plenty of other celebrities not usually found in west Midtown, the therapist walks on your back (while holding on to ropes hanging from the ceiling), expertly releasing hidden tension with her toes. It sounds strange, but it does the trick, and is the perfect way to end a long day, no matter when your days ends (the 46th Street location is open until midnight; 56th Street location is open until 2:00 a.m.).

*Both locations in Manhattan.* **OSAKA 46:** *37 WEST 46TH STREET BETWEEN FIFTH AND SIXTH AVENUES. Subway: B, D, F, V to 47th-50th Streets-Rockefeller Center. 212-575-1303.* **OSAKA 56:** *50 WEST 56TH STREET BETWEEN FIFTH AND SIXTH AVENUES. Subway: F to 57th Street; N, R, W to Fifth Avenue/59th Street. 212-956-3422. www.osakahealthspa.com.*

## 834. Meet a friend and sweat out the toxins after a hard day's work in the "igloo" at **Athena Spa**.

This tri-level Midtown sanctuary combines the services of a spa with the luxuriating amenities of a bathhouse, with one additional special feature: an igloo-shaped sauna made with *hwangto*. Hwangto is a special yellow soil from Korea used in purifying and cleansing treatments; it has special properties that filter out toxins and boost circulation and metabolism. The igloo at Athena also has amethysts and jades embedded in the wall, which, in addition to looking pretty, have restorative properties. The air has a cleaner, lighter feel than most saunas, so despite the heat, you can lie there for quite a while without feeling stifled, as the impurities seep out of your body (really, you can feel them!). Use of the igloo is included in the cost of admission to the wet spa ($35), which also includes use of the steam room, showers, soaking tub, and lounge area for an unlimited time. No appointment is necessary for the wet spa, so instead of unwinding with a drink, grab a friend and spend a couple of hours at Athena letting yourselves really relax. (N.B.: Juvenex Spa, listed on page 326, also has an igloo.)

*32 EAST 31ST STREET BETWEEN PARK AND MADISON AVENUES IN MANHATTAN. Subway: 6 to 33rd Street. 212-683-4484. www.athenaspany31.com.*

## 835. Have a facial at **Sava Spa**.

Why is having a facial at this tiny Washington Heights spa such a treat? Because when owner Joanna Czech works on your face, she's not merely giving a treatment; she's practicing a craft. Her warm demeanor and artistlike dedication to her clients' faces make this often uncomfortable beauty ritual a personal and pleasant experience. If the Washington Heights location makes you balk, consider how rare it is that a famed and highly sought-after craftsperson in New York eschews the limelight in favor of opening her own place, in her neighborhood, where she can work on customers herself, as well as hand-pick and personally train everyone she hires. You'd be hard-pressed to find either the homey, relaxed manner of Joanna and her staff, or the quality of their work, at any other spa closer to home.

*211 PINEHURST AVENUE BETWEEN 186TH AND 187TH STREETS IN MANHATTAN. Subway: A to 181st Street. 212-543-0008. www.savaspa.com.*

---

## 836. Experience reflexology at **Angel Feet**.

Nestled between the brownstones on Perry Street, this tiny West Village reflexology parlor is about as far from a spa as you can get. The sterile, businesslike feel that more chic operations can't quite escape is entirely absent here. In lieu of a high-tech check-in desk and lots of tools and machines, there is a table up front where someone takes appointments by hand, plus overstuffed armchairs, and a staff that *really* knows reflexology. The cozy, off-the-beaten-path setting and the single-minded focus on the treatments offered make a trip to Angel Feet one of the most genuinely therapeutic treatments around—not to mention an unusually pleasurable experience.

*77 PERRY STREET BETWEEN BLEECKER AND WEST 4TH STREETS IN MANHATTAN. Subway: 1 to Christopher Street-Sheridan Square; A, C, E, B, D, F, V to West 4th Street. 212-924-3576. www.angelfeet.com.*

---

## 837. Get all fixed up in an hour at **SimplySpa**.

One problem with spa treatments in New York is that no matter how transporting they are once you're there, fitting in that kind of downtime is sometimes not worth the stress. This user-friendly downtown spa doesn't have a lot of fancy treatments, but its special emphasis on efficiency may be just what you need to unwind. Instead of choosing individual services, you can book a block of time for multiple treatments, up to three in an hour or four in an hour-and-a-half. The technicians are trained in multiple treatments, and the space was designed to accommodate a complete spa experience, so clients experience minimal shuffling around between massages, facials, manicures, and pedicures. You will emerge feeling relaxed and pampered—with plenty of time to make it to your next appointment.

*104 WEST 14TH STREET BETWEEN SIXTH AND SEVENTH AVENUES, SUITE 2C, IN MANHATTAN. Subway: F, V to 14th Street; L to Sixth Avenue. 212-647-8919. www.simplyspanyc.com.*

## 838. Open your mind to a *platza* and salt scrub at the **Russian and Turkish baths** in the East Village . . .

The first is an oddly relaxing thrashing with oak twigs soaked in olive oil, and the second is a natural exfoliation to rid you of excess body weight. For the courageous, there are single-sex days when everyone in the baths can go naked.

*268 EAST 10TH STREET BETWEEN FIRST AVENUE AND AVENUE A IN MANHATTAN. Subway: 6 to Astor Place; L to First Avenue. 212-505-0665.*

## 839. . . . or relax like a Russian at **Sandoony USA**.

If the East Village baths aren't serious enough for you, then go to Sandoony, the largest of Russian Brooklyn's *banya*. Baths here serve the same purpose they do in Russia—as places to clean up, shave, relax, eat, and be social—so the atmosphere is busier and more family-oriented than at other baths in the city. For the complete experience: order a drink and a plate of fresh Mediterranean fruit, try each of the steam rooms, take a dip in the ice water, swim in the pool, ask to be smacked with a soapy besom (a bundle of leaves and branches), and finally get doused with cold water in the hottest sauna.

*1158 MCDONALD AVENUE AT AVENUE I IN BROOKLYN. Subway: F to Avenue I. 718-951-9000. www.sandoonyusa.com.*

## 840. Make like a mafioso at **Spa 88**.

With an interior decked out like a Miami beach club, this is probably the most garish of all the spas in Manhattan. But where else can you lounge by a pool surrounded by fake palm trees with a large cocktail in your hand after your choice of saunas, mud treatments, massages, or ear candling?

*88 FULTON STREET BETWEEN WILLIAM AND GOLD STREETS IN MANHATTAN. Subway: 4, 5, J, M, Z to Fulton Street. 212-766-8600. www.spa88.com.*

## 841. Have your ailment diagnosed and healed with natural remedies at **Kamwo Herb and Tea Shop**, the largest authentic Chinese herbal medicinal store on

the East Coast. No medical knowledge is required on your part—just name your ailment, and the professionals will pull leaves, roots, and powders from the rows of drawers that line the walls, and chop and grind them together into a neat little paper packet for you to take home. There are more than 1,000 items to choose from, from magnolia and ginseng to peppermint leaves and dried seahorses. The traditional remedies purport to cure everything from headaches to stiff joints, from a blocked nose to insomnia, and there are mixtures designed for general relief from stress,

fatigue, or other symptoms of urban malaise.
*211 GRAND STREET BETWEEN MOTT AND ELIZABETH STREETS IN MANHATTAN. Subway: B,*
*D to Grand Street. 212-966-6370.*

Note: Chinatown is full of herbal stores and hidden havens of alternative medicine.
Check out www.nychinatown.com/herbalteabottom.htm for a full and up-to-date list
of stores and treatment centers.

## 842. Try an acupuncture session at **Lin Sisters in Chinatown**.

Acupuncture is the other specialty of Chinese natural medical practitioners, and it is
believed by many to be the ultimate way to relax and, literally, let the pressure out. Of
course you know it's not supposed to hurt, but for those with needle fears, Lin Sisters
is among the quainter, more genuine and reassuring places to be pricked. Adjoining
a respected herb and tea store, Lin Sisters charges $55 per session and treats each
customer with great care and respect; you can sip a bowl of tea until you're relaxed
and ready to begin. N.B.: Chinatown is home to the most authentic and least expensive practitioners of acupuncture in the city, but be careful—check for certification
either by New York State or by the National Certification Commission for Acupuncture and Oriental Medicine. You can find a list of all certified acupuncture practitioners in New York City at www.nccaom.org.
**LIN SISTERS:** *4 BOWERY AT PELL STREET IN MANHATTAN. Subway: N, R, Q, W, J, M, Z, 6 to*
*Canal Street. 212-962-5417.*

CHAPTER 9:

# 24-Hour Fun

**N**ew York is wide awake at all hours of the day, and even if it's 11:00 p.m. on a Sunday or eight o'clock in the morning on Thanksgiving Day, there are more things to do, see, and take advantage of here than in most places on a typical weekday afternoon. In this city of schemers, dreamers, high rollers, and people struggling to get by, one person's bedtime is another's graveyard shift, and the start of someone else's night on the town. Subways, taxis, and even the Staten Island ferry run around the clock, coursing up, down, and around the city, bringing life and activity wherever they go. Traffic lights tick away all through the night, ushering vehicles and pedestrians from rush hour to the break of dawn without missing a beat, while all-night diners, coffee shops, and delis beckon to wanderers with fluorescent lights, coffee, and ATMs.

This chapter celebrates New York's unique, unceasing vibrancy, its inexhaustible spirit that does not discriminate between early birds and night owls; the lunch crowd and the after-hours bunch; morning people and insomniacs. We've found the best of the always-open and odd-hour amenities, as well as plenty of places and activities that offer something special at a time when most people are asleep—not just the kinds of things you want only if you're in a fix. Sure, New York has resources for emergencies of all kinds just like everywhere else, but in our opinion, just because you can get something at a certain hour doesn't necessarily mean that it is a great thing to do. Here you'll find 24-hour diners and restaurants; late-night movies, dance parties, and yoga; early-morning bird-watching and late-night stargazing, and many other wonderful things to do and see that are worth staying up—or rising early—for.

N.B.: Although everything we list here is ostensibly safe, and we don't hesitate to make these recommendations, it should go without saying that if you are out late at night or in the early morning, you should be alert and be extra careful, especially if you are alone.

## 843. Take the **subway anytime** you want . . .

Even if you wouldn't get on the train at 5:00 a.m. in a million years, consider how great it is that you can, and appreciate what it means for a transit system to provide that level of service, when so many others do not.

*For schedules and routes, visit www.mta.info.*

## 844. . . . or hail **a cab** . . .

Cabs also run 24/7, which is helpful if you find yourself out late at night in an unfamiliar place, if you need to make an early-morning plane, train, or bus, or if you just want someone to talk to at a rate of $2.50 plus $.40 for every ⅕ mile.

*Anywhere you can find them!*

## 845. . . . or take **the ferry**.

In addition to being one of the best deals in New York, the **Staten Island Ferry** (see page 68) is also the most reliable form of mass transit. Running every hour or half-hour 24 hours a day, 7 days a week, 365 days a year, the ferry offers free transportation and sightseeing with the highest on-time performance of any form of mass transit in the city—over 96 percent.

*Manhattan: WHITEHALL TERMINAL AT 1 WHITEHALL STREET AND SOUTH STREET. Staten Island: 1 BAY STREET AT RICHMOND TERRACE. For more information on the ferry and ferry service, visit www.nyc.gov/html/dot/html/masstran/ferries/statfery.html#info.*

## 846. Look at the night sky from inside **Grand Central**.

Late at night is the best time to view the incredible painted ceiling in the main hall, a glittering astrological motif by French artist Peter Cesar Helleu. Obscured by dirt and disrepair, Helleu's 1912 masterpiece was revealed after a 1990s renovation. During the day, the constant commotion of the terminal distracts from the ceiling's subtle beauty, but at night, after the shops and restaurants close and the last commuter goes home, the main hall becomes still and eerily quiet, and you can drink in the gold-painted constellations and the ornate decorated windows as peacefully as if you were stargazing in the country—except that the sky is painted backwards, because that's how it looked in the medieval manuscript that the artist relied on (the manuscript presented the sky from the perspective of someone looking down at it instead of gazing upward). You can visit until 1:30 a.m., when the terminal closes, or show up when it reopens at 5:30 a.m., when the commuters begin charging in again. See if you can find the **dark patch** left over from before the renovation (see page 112).

*42ND STREET BETWEEN LEXINGTON AVENUE AND PARK AVENUE IN MANHATTAN. Subway: 4, 5, 6, 7, S to Grand Central-42nd Street. For full entry on Grand Central Terminal, see page 23.*

## 847. Walk the **Great White Way** after dark.

Times Square, and the neighboring stretch of Broadway between 40th and 47th Streets, is one of the signature images of New York, almost as widely recognized as the skyline and its skyscrapers. Named for the city's most famous newspaper—it opened its offices here a little over a century ago—Times Square remains the heart of New York, pumping life into the city with lights, sounds, and crowds twenty-four hours a day, every day of the year. Although its most famous attractions are the tourist stalls, the **Broadway shows** (see page 28) that entertain daytime and evening crowds, and the New Year's Eve festivities, the place is bright and busy all about, all the time. In addition to late-night haunts like the **Virgin Megastore** and **Sephora** (see page 318), and the nightlong pull of the **Broadway City** video arcade (see page 343), there are enough dazzling lights, blazing billboards, and unexpected street entertainment to make a nighttime stroll around the Square exhilarating. The light from storefronts and advertisements is so bright that Times Square never approaches darkness, making it a surreal place to get a cup of coffee and snack in the middle of the night. Amuse yourself with diversions like the Cup of Noodles billboard, whose steam wafts out above the street; the Reuters news ticker that keeps the streets abreast of breaking news; the NYPD station that's lit up like a diner; and the McDonalds on 42nd Street that projects cartoons on the walls of the restaurant all day and all night.

*TIMES SQUARE IN MANHATTAN. Subway: 1, 2, 3, 7, N, Q, R, W to Times Square-42nd Street; A, C, E to 42nd Street-Port Authority Bus Terminal.*

## 848. Watch the lights go out on the **Empire State Building**.

An eerie urban sight if ever there was one, and a good piece of trivia. The lights on the **Empire State Building** (see page 19), often colored to commemorate certain holidays or occasions, go off most of the year precisely at midnight; during the summer they stay lit until 2:00 a.m. Occasionally they are left on a little later for special occasions, and there are five holidays when they stay lit until 3:00 a.m.: Christmas Eve, Christmas Day, New Year's Eve, New Year's Day, and, interestingly, St. Patrick's Day. You can check the lighting schedule on the Web site, which tells what color the building will be and what occasion the lights are honoring, or check the current issue of *Time Out*, which lists the coming week's lighting schedule in their "Around Town" section.

*FIFTH AVENUE AT 34TH STREET IN MANHATTAN. Subway: B, D, F, V, N, Q, R, W to 34th Street-Herald Square. 212-736-3100. www.esbnyc.com.*

## 849. See what happens at **night court in Chinatown**.

The Criminal Courts Building is where New Yorkers under arrest are formally charged with a crime—and since arraignments are required by law to be open to the public, anyone can drop in and watch the proceedings. Show up for the night session, which runs from 5:30 p.m. to past 1:00 a.m., and you'll take in one of the city's most under-appreciated and unlikely forms of entertainment. To watch the cases come and go is to see real-life dramas play out before your eyes. The judges hear the stories of the cases, the attorneys arrive to argue with one another, and a succession of characters step up to the bench—and eventually are released on bail or led away into the sinister hallways behind the courtroom. If you can feel comfortable sitting next to the family of the accused, you can join the few law students, insomniacs, and other curious New Yorkers on the benches in the back. The court officers are aware of their audience, and will even (on occasion) recommend one court over another depending on the drama of the cases that night. (On a recent visit, one officer advised, "You ought to check out AR2. There's a cocaine bust going on in there.") Just around the corner from some of the best restaurants in Chinatown, night court is the perfect (free) after-dinner show. Anyone who can't make it to the gallery in person can keep up with the action at the brilliant Web site www.courttv.com/fluorescent, where an "insomniac observer" reports on each night's happenings.

*100 CENTRE STREET BETWEEN LEONARD AND FRANKLIN STREETS IN MANHATTAN. Subway: 1, 6, A, C, E to Canal Street; 4, 5, 6 to Brooklyn Bridge-City Hall; B to Grand Street. 646-386-4511. www.courts.state.ny.us/courts/nyc/criminal.*

## Go **early-bird** or **night-owl shopping**.

Most retail stores and boutiques in the city have generous hours, and are open seven days a week from around ten or eleven in the morning until seven or eight at night, with slightly shorter hours on Sunday, and sometimes slightly longer hours in the evening one or two days a week. However, a few stores have carved out off-hours niches for themselves by deviating from these unofficial rules. For shoppers, this means less time constraints on an otherwise busy day; for others, it means more places to visit, hang out in, and explore if you happen to be in the neighborhood when everything else is closed up.

**850. _American Apparel:_** The Lower East Side branch is open until midnight on Friday and Saturday, and a still-respectable 10:00 p.m. from Monday through Thursday (it closes at 9:00 p.m. on Sunday). It's a great place to pick up trendy, affordable leisurewear, and browsing the store is a good way to pass the time before a midnight movie at the **Sunshine** (see page 344).

*183 EAST HOUSTON STREET AT ORCHARD STREET IN MANHATTAN. Subway: F, V to Lower East Side-Second Avenue. 212-598-4600. www.americanapparel.net.*

**851. *Lowe's:*** Pick up some lumber on your way to work at the Brooklyn branch of Lowe's, which opens at the extremely go-getter time of 5:00 a.m. *every day.* (Home Depot doesn't open until 7:00 a.m.) Or pop in for a late-night home improvement fix before the store closes at midnight—a good three hours later than HD. (The Staten Island location has slightly more conservative hours: 6:00 a.m. to 11:00 p.m., 8:00 a.m. to 9:00 p.m. on Sunday.)
*Brooklyn: 118 SECOND AVENUE BY 12TH STREET. Subway: F to Smith-9th Streets. 718-249-1151. Staten Island: 2171 FOREST AVENUE NEAR SAMUEL PLACE. 718-682-9027. Ferry to Staten Island; for bus directions, visit www.mta.info. www.lowes.com.*

**852. *Virgin Megastores:*** In addition to shopping, Virgin's two conveniently located behemoths offer refuge and entertainment from the early morning well into the night. The Times Square store claims to be "the largest entertainment store in the world"—a claim that's hard to dispute once you've seen it, despite how vague that sounds—and the Union Square store can't be far behind. You can listen to music, read a book, and have a coffee or a meal long before most rock stars wake up and well after the concerts let out. Both stores open at 9:00 a.m. most days. The Times Square store is open until 1:00 a.m. from Sunday through Thursday, and 2:00 a.m. on Friday and Saturday. The Union Square store stays open until 1:00 a.m. every night except Sunday (when it's open from 10:00 a.m. to midnight). A great resource for the unemployed, or if you've got time on your hands between a Broadway show and a bus from Port Authority, or if you absolutely must have a new CD the minute it comes out. There are also lots of in-store events around the clock, as well as the occasional impromptu performance.
*Both locations in Manhattan. Times Square: 1540 BROADWAY BETWEEN 45TH AND 46TH STREETS. Subway: 1, 2, 3, 7, N, Q, R, W, S to Times Square-42nd Street; A, C, E to 42nd Street-Port Authority Bus Terminal. 212-921-1020. Union Square: 52 EAST 14TH STREET AT BROADWAY. Subway: 4, 5, 6, L, N, Q, R, W to 14th Street-Union Square. 212-598-4666. www.virginmegamagazine.com.*

**853. *Sephora:*** Need to primp before heading out to a club? The Times Square store is open until midnight, with plenty of makeup stations, where you can touch up, try out, get a free consultation, and, of course, buy products.
*1500 BROADWAY BETWEEN 42ND AND 43RD STREETS IN MANHATTAN. Subway: 1, 2, 3, 7, N, Q, R, W, S to Times Square-42nd Street; A, C, E to 42nd Street-Port Authority Bus Terminal. 212-944-6789. www.sephora.com.*

## 854. Shopping in New York around **the holidays**

is, generally speaking, not such a great thing to do, but many stores offer extended holiday hours in the weeks before Christmas, which, when taken advantage of at the extremes, can actually make last-minute shopping kind of fun. These extra hours vary by store, and change from year to year (and day to day): Macy's in Herald Square, for instance, opens at 7:00 a.m. on selected days between Thanksgiving and Christmas, and stays open some nights until midnight. If you get there when the store opens, you'll feel like you have it pretty much to yourself for a good two hours before the craziness begins, at which point you'll be ready to head home for a nap. (This is also a good time to see **Santa**—see page 346).

*151 WEST 34TH STREET BETWEEN BROADWAY AND SEVENTH AVENUE IN MANHATTAN. Subway: 1, 2, 3, A, C, E to 34th Street-Penn Station; B, D, F, V, N, Q, R, W to 34th Street-Herald Square. For information and specific hours, call 212-695-4400 or visit www.macys.com. For other stores with extended holiday hours, check listings during the season.*

## 855. **Wait until the last minute** to mail your Christmas cards/ postcards/college applications.

The **James A. Farley Post Office** is one of only a handful of post offices in the country that is open 24/7. It offers pretty much all postal services—albeit with a more limited staff than usual—at all hours of the day or night. However, we advise that you judge carefully when to take advantage of this resource—a procrastinator's dream can quickly become a sender's nightmare when you spend your New Year's Eve waiting in line to get your kid's college application postmarked along with every other worried parent in the city. (Note: The post office at 90 Church Street is another good late-night bet during the week—it's open until midnight from Monday through Friday.)

*421 EIGHTH AVENUE BETWEEN 31ST AND 33RD STREETS IN MANHATTAN. Subway: 1, 2, 3, A, C, E to 34th Street-Penn Station. 212-330-2902. www.usps.com.*

## 856. Get that **prescription filled** at 4:30 a.m. in Manhattan . . .

Thanks to the many **Duane Reade** drugstores that keep their doors open round the clock, New Yorkers can get all the pharmaceuticals they need at any time of night. Aside from the obvious practical advantages of 24-hour drugstores—besides medicine, they carry snacks, condoms, cigarettes, and many other lifestyle essentials—browsing around the empty, sterile, white stores after dark is oddly compelling. There are forty 24-hour stores in Manhattan alone (only three have round-the-clock pharmacies, listed below), so check online for your nearest all-night savior.

**DUANE READE 24-HOUR PHARMACIES:** *224 WEST 57TH STREET AT BROADWAY, 212-541-9708; 1279 THIRD AVENUE AT EAST 74TH STREET, 212-744-2668; 2522 BROADWAY AT WEST 94TH STREET, 212-663-1580. Call for directions to locations. www.duanereade.com.*

## 857. . . . or in Brooklyn.

Brooklyn residents can be smug about the fact that when they get their late-night prescriptions filled, they do so without resorting to a chain. The family-owned **Neergaard** pharmacies have been serving Brooklynites since 1888. There are two branches, but only the Fifth Avenue location is open 24 hours; they also deliver until 9:00 p.m.

*454 FIFTH AVENUE BETWEEN 9TH AND 10TH STREETS IN BROOKLYN. Subway: F to Fourth Avenue; M, R to 9th Street. 718-768-0938. (The other branch is at 120 SEVENTH AVENUE BETWEEN CARROLL AND PRESIDENT STREETS IN BROOKLYN. Subway: F to Seventh Avenue. 718-857-1600.)*

## 858. Pick up your dry cleaning whenever you want at
## Baby Girl's Bubbles & Cleaners.

In addition to 24-hour laundry facilities, Baby Girl's also offers dry-cleaning services round the clock, so your clean clothes will never be held hostage if you can't make it there during normal business hours. Baby Girl's also delivers (laundry within twenty-four hours; dry cleaning within two days), but if you want to wait around, there's cable TV, a beverage machine, and an ATM.

*2212-14 EIGHTH AVENUE BETWEEN 119TH AND 120TH STREETS IN MANHATTAN. Subway: B, C to 116th Street. 212-662-1080.*

## 859. Find out how to get anything you want at any hour with
## Quintessentially.

An anonymous warehouse building in the Meatpacking District is the suitably clandestine home of Quintessentially, a concierge company so secretive and so effective that it deserves to be referred to in the same hushed breath as James Bond or the CIA. For a hefty annual fee, members can call on Quintessentially any time of the day or night to advise on any problem they might have, wherever they might be in the city. The staff—skilled researchers and publicists with myriad guides, references, and public and private directories at their fingertips—can address clients' needs, and can tell them where to go, whom to see, and what to do. Whether directing you to round-the-clock pet food suppliers in Harlem, locating emergency tailors in the financial district, booking same-day front-row tickets to a hit Broadway show, or getting your name on the guest list at the hottest club of the moment, the people at Quintessentially have

the answers. If the fee doesn't put you off (depending on your level of membership, it's around $2,000), this is a truly great resource for the 24-hour New Yorker.
*25 NINTH AVENUE AT 14TH STREET, SUITE 201, IN MANHATTAN. Subway: A, C, E to 14th Street; L to Eighth Avenue. 212-206-6633. www.quintessentially.com.*

## 860. Find out if the early birds **really do** get the worm.

Birds are busiest in the morning, so instead of sleeping in one Sunday, make your way to Prospect Park for an Early Bird Walk, a monthly guided tour of the park's feathered friends given for free by the Audubon Center. Trekking around the park's nature trails, you'll see some of the 200 species of birds that reside in the park at different points during the year, and learn about different species and migration patterns.
*The Audubon Center is located in Prospect Park; ENTER AT LINCOLN ROAD AND OCEAN AVENUE IN BROOKLYN. First Sunday of every month, from 8:00 a.m. to 10:00 a.m. Meet at the Boathouse. Subway: B, Q, S/Franklin Avenue Shuttle to Prospect Park. 718-287-3400. www.prospectpark.org.*

→ **DID YOU KNOW?** *Prospect Park's Audubon Center is the first urban Audubon Center in the nation. One of the reasons that Prospect Park was chosen as the site was its position along the Atlantic Flyway, a major route for bird migration.*

# New Year's Fun

Every year, three-quarters of a million people migrate to Times Square to watch the ball drop at midnight. To each their own, but standing in a pen in the freezing cold, corralled with hundreds of thousands of people, with no access to food, drink, or restrooms (alcohol, backpacks, and large bags are not permitted; there are no public toilets or food vendors on New Year's; and if you leave, you lose your space) for up to ten hours (space is first-come, first-served, and people usually begin arriving in the early afternoon) doesn't sound like a best thing to do, in our opinion. Instead, here are our favorite New Year's activities:

## 861. Do the **midnight run** in Central Park . . .

Start the New Year off on the right foot, literally and figuratively, with this annual four-mile run through Central Park, sponsored by the New York Road Runners Club. If you don't expect to be in top shape come midnight, there's also a dance party, a costume show for the runners, and a fireworks display at midnight.
*MEET AT THE BANDSHELL, LOCATED ON THE CENTRAL PARK TRANSVERSE NEAR 72ND*

STREET IN MANHATTAN. To participate in the race costs $25 to $30 in advance or $35 on the day of, depending on availability. Dance party begins at 10:00 p.m.; costume parade and contest begins at 11:00 p.m.; race starts at midnight. Subway: 1, 2, 3 to 72nd Street. 212-860-4455.
www.nyrr.org.

## 862. . . . or in Prospect Park.

The Brooklyn Road Runners Club also puts on a midnight run in Prospect Park that is slightly shorter than the Manhattan counterpart (3.3 miles, which is one loop around the park). But the Brooklyn version has everything else—free food and drink, and fireworks at the finish line.
MEET AT GRAND ARMY PLAZA ENTRANCE TO PROSPECT PARK AT FLATBUSH AVENUE IN BROOKLYN. $15 in advance or $20 on the day of. Race starts at 11:15 p.m. Subway: 2, 3 to Grand Army Plaza. 917-238-9447. www.runbrooklyn.com.

## 863. Ring in the New Year in silence at **Jivamukti**. . .

This popular downtown yoga center (see page 284) holds a free annual New Year's Eve "celebration," where they observe *mauna*, the yogic practice of silence. From 9:00 p.m. until midnight, they open the studio to silent individual practice and meditation. At midnight, the silence is broken with chanting led by the center's directors, followed by vegan snacks.
841 BROADWAY AT 13TH STREET IN MANHATTAN. Subway: 4, 5, 6, L, N, Q, R, W to 14th Street-Union Square. 212-353-0214. www.jivamuktiyoga.com.

## 864. . . . or hear the steam whistles **at Pratt** on New Year's Eve.

Brooklyn's **Pratt Institute** (see page 299) maintains one of the world's largest collections of steam whistles—and a power plant and steam engine to blow them. On New Year's Eve, nearly 2,000 whistles of all shapes and sizes—some tiny, some over eight feet tall with flanges more than three inches wide—are brought into the quadrangle, and at midnight, they start the new year with a blast! Arrive early and spend the evening eating and drinking while you check out the whistles (and their unlikely enthusiasts), listen to the legendary steam calliope's jolly piping music, and try in vain to prepare your ears for the cacophony that strikes at midnight—it's one of the strangest, loudest noises you'll ever hear. Pratt also supplies steam and compressed air for energetic spectators who bring their own horns to participate.
200 WILLOUGHBY AVENUE IN BROOKLYN. Subway: G to Clinton-Washington Avenues. 718-636-3600. www.pratt.edu.

## 865. Party on the **Brooklyn Bridge**.

Celebrate the crossing of one year into the next by crossing from one borough to another on the annual "Walk into the New Year." This guided walk starts with a historical talk about the bridge, and then leads you across, when, if the timing is right (and you can bear the cold), you will see fireworks displays from Central Park, Grand Army Plaza, Staten Island, New Jersey, and the Empire State Building light show.

*Meet at Blimpie's Restaurant: 38 PARK ROW BETWEEN SPRUCE AND BEEKMAN STREETS IN MANHATTAN. $35 per person in advance or $40 day of. Children 15 years and under are $20. Registration begins at 10:30 p.m., walks start between 10:30 p.m. and 11:15 p.m. Subway: 4, 5, 6 to Brooklyn Bridge-City Hall. 888-377-4455. www.newyorktalksandwalks.com.*

## 866. **Milonga!**

*Milongas*, or tango socials, are parties where dancers come to hang out and practice their moves. In New York, there are milongas almost every night of the week, held at different places around the city. Each milonga does its own thing, but most start around 9:00 p.m. or 10:00 p.m. and can go until any time between 1:00 a.m. and 5:00 a.m. Some of the more novice-friendly gatherings start with a free lesson. New York milongas are held at dance studios, restaurants, and clubs, and most occur regularly, on the same night each week, and many have live music or DJs. There's also an outdoor milonga that takes place on Sunday night between May and October at the South Street Seaport. A good source for learning more is www.dancetango.com, which has an up-to-date calendar with milonga listings, addresses, and details.

*Various locations. The South Street Seaport milonga is held on the PIER 16 BOARDWALK (BETWEEN THE AMSTERDAM AND THE PEKING) IN MANHATTAN. Subway: 2, 3, 4, J, M, Z to Fulton Street. For more details, visit www.tangoporteno.org.*

## 867. Go **clubbing**.

Nightclubs, bars, and lounges are what most people think of when they say "the city that never sleeps," and no chapter on 24-hour New York would be complete without a mention of nightlife. From the glitzy, star-studded Cotton Club and famous Prohibition-era joints like the **21 Club** (see page 287) and **Chumley's** (see page 50), to the notoriously wild times at Studio 54 in the '80s and the scandalous happenings at Limelight, the Tunnel, and Twilo in the '90s, New York nightlife has long been a potent mix of glamour, scandal, and late-night decadence, and every night promises the potential for excitement. Movies, books, celebrity magazines, and TV shows like *Sex and the City* have mythologized the experience of going out in New York, making names like Lotus, Tao, and Bungalow 8 familiar to people well outside taxi range.

Bars, clubs, and lounges are generally open until 4:00 a.m.; clubs usually don't open until 10:00 p.m. or even 11:00 p.m., but many bars are open all day, and lounges fall somewhere in between. The difference between the three types of venue is a little vague, but as a rule, clubs have a cover (anywhere from $10 to $30) and usually a bouncer; bars for the most part do not have either; and lounges, again, fall somewhere in between. There are also after-hours venues that stay open until 5:00 a.m. and later (or earlier, depending on how you think of it). What constitutes a great club is subjective, and depends on your taste in music, preference for environment, crowd, and décor—and, of course, what's hot at the moment (which, lately, is anything in the Meatpacking District or west Chelsea). There are many, many Web sites devoted to New York bars and clubs, and an equally inexhaustible number of nightlife guides with listings and addresses. *Time Out New York* (www.timeoutny.com), *Citysearch* (http://newyork.citysearch.com), and *Shecky's* (www.sheckys.com) are all thorough sources for finding information on different places, but our recommendation for figuring out where to go is word of mouth, and trial and error. The adventure of winding up somewhere new is part of the fun.

*Every night of the week, all over town.*

---

## Expert Contributor: Wendy Mitchell

Wendy Mitchell is an entertainment journalist, and the author of *New York City's Best Dive Bars.*

### MY FIVE FAVORITE DIVE BARS IN NEW YORK

**868. *Siberia:*** Admire the wall paintings and graffiti at this impossibly cool hangout for media types and rockers. The bathrooms may challenge your hygienic senses, but they're worth a look just for the graffiti. (If you're too shy to even venture into the toilets, you can find one of the graffiti masterpieces hanging above the bar.) In keeping with the cool vibe, you won't see a sign outside—just look for a black door and a red light that marks the entrance to this den of sin.
*356 WEST 40TH STREET AT NINTH AVENUE IN MANHATTAN. Open 3:00 p.m. to 4:00 a.m., seven days a week. Subway: A, C, E to 42nd Street-Port Authority Bus Terminal. 212-333-4141. www.siberiany.com.*

**869. *Nancy Whiskey Pub:*** Avoid the chic Tribeca crowd at this neighborhood pub (established in 1967), a favorite of cops and postal workers. Make sure you try your hand at Manhattan's only bank shuffleboard table. If you don't know the rules, an affa-

ble regular or bartender will be glad to show you the ropes.
*1 LISPENARD STREET AT WEST BROADWAY IN MANHATTAN. Open 9:00 a.m. to 4:00 a.m., Monday through Saturday; noon to 4:00 a.m. on Sunday. Subway: A, C, E to Canal Street. 212-226-9943. www.nancywhiskeypub.com.*

**870. *Mars Bar:*** Even if you are a very tough guy (or gal), you might still be scared to walk into this bar, which is probably the creepiest hole in New York. It long had a reputation as a heroin addict hangout, and even if that's no longer true, there will definitely be some unsavory characters at the bar, some ear-splitting punk blaring from the jukebox, and a cockroach or two crawling around. Explore at your own risk!
*25 EAST 1ST STREET AT SECOND AVENUE IN MANHATTAN. Open noon to 4:00 a.m. daily. Subway: F, V, to Lower East Side-Second Avenue. 212-473-9842.*

**871. *Hogs & Heifers:*** Shed your bra, your necktie, or just your inhibitions at this classic biker bar. Julia Roberts famously took her bra off and danced on the bar here; you may very well be inspired to do the same.
*859 WASHINGTON STREET BETWEEN 13TH AND WASHINGTON STREETS IN MANHATTAN. Open 11:00 a.m. to 4:00 a.m. Monday through Friday; 1:00 p.m. to 4:00 a.m. Saturday; 2:00 p.m. to 4:00 a.m. Sunday. Subway: A, C, E to 14th Street; L to Eighth Avenue. 212-929-0655. www.hogsandheifers.com.*

**872. *Johnny's Famous Reef:*** A daytrip to City Island wouldn't be complete without dining and drinking at this fish shack at the tip of the island. Grab some no-frills fried seafood, a cheap can of beer, and try to avoid the predatory seagulls.
*2 CITY ISLAND AVENUE NEAR BELDON AVENUE IN THE BRONX. Open 11:30 a.m. to 1:00 a.m. (closed December through February). Subway: 6 to Pelham Bay Park; Bx29 bus to City Island. 718-885-2086.*

## 873. Enjoy live music until the **wee hours** of the morning.

At the time of publication, **CBGB**—one of the city's most beloved and celebrated musical institutions, and a significant benchmark in the history of punk and rock music as we know it—has been sentenced to the dismal fate of so many of the city's beloved legendary establishments, as skyrocketing rents are forcing it to shut its doors for good (see page 52 for more info). Hopefully, the spirit of CBGB will live on, in the rest of the city's many live venues, which range from indie rock bars in Williamsburg and hip-hop clubs in Queens to country-and-western pubs in the West Village and the great **jazz havens** of Harlem and Midtown (see page 44). Every big city has its share of bars and clubs with crowded floors and hallowed stages, but New York is a place apart, where names are made and legends are forged, and where one night in a bar can range from a great little party to a date memorialized for a lifetime. As longtime haunts like the Bowery Ballroom, Mercury Lounge, Bitter End, and CBGB are continually surrounded by new venues, the best thing to do is to keep an eye on the listings in magazines like *Time Out New York* and *New York*, then pick the ones you like the sound of, and try them out. But we suggest you pay your respects to CBGB, the father of so many, while it's still alive.

**CBGB:** *315 BOWERY BETWEEN 1ST AND 2ND STREETS IN MANHATTAN. Open 3:00 p.m. to 1:00 a.m., Sunday; 7:00 p.m. to 3:00 a.m., Monday through Thursday; 8:00 p.m. to 4:00 a.m., Friday and Saturday. Subway: 6 to Bleecker Street; F, V to Lower East Side-Second Avenue. 212-982-4052. www.cbgb.com.*

### 874. Forgo sleep in favor of a different kind of nocturnal revitalization at **Juvenex**.

At this midtown oasis, you can enjoy massages, facials, manicures, pedicures, and body treatments any time of day or night. You can also visit the steam room, saunas, showers, and special soaking tubs, which are infused with purifying elements that include seaweed, ginseng, and tea tree oil. During the day (6:00 a.m. to 7:00 p.m.), the spa is women only; but in the evenings, the doors open to couples as well. Who goes to a day spa after midnight, you may ask? Juvenex says that its late-night clientele consists of Broadway stars who come to unwind after a show, people who drop by after a night of clubbing, and couples enjoying an extended romantic evening.

*25 WEST 32ND STREET, FIFTH FLOOR, BETWEEN FIFTH AND SIXTH AVENUES IN MANHATTAN. Subway: B, D, F, V, N, Q, R, W to 34th Street-Herald Square. 646-733-1330. www.juvenexspa.com.*

### 875. Get your nails done first thing in the morning, or have a **ten-minute chair massage** right before bed.

**Clio** would be indistinguishable from the Bloomie's, Pinky's, and their non-chain counterparts except for one small detail—it opens at 9:00 a.m. and stays open until just about midnight. In addition to nail treatments and chair massages, the salon offers waxing, facials, and the other standard quickie spa offerings. It's no-frills, but it's clean, efficient, and even a little bit cheaper than its many competitors, most of whom open at least an hour later, and close between two and four hours earlier.

*270 THIRD AVENUE BETWEEN 21ST AND 22ND STREETS IN MANHATTAN. Subway: 6 to 23rd Street. 212-677-4900.*

# Take advantage of your insomnia and hit the gym.

What would the city that never sleeps be without 24-hour gyms? There are a handful of gyms around the city that are open continuously throughout the week (though most close for a few hours on Friday, Saturday, and/or Sunday nights).

**876.** *24/7 Fitness Club:* This utilitarian gym lacks many of the amenities of other gyms in the city (including, most prominently, multiple locations), but it is the only gym in the city that is open 24/7, as its name suggests.
*47 WEST 14TH STREET BETWEEN FIFTH AND SIXTH AVENUES IN MANHATTAN. Subway: F, V, to 14th Street; L to Sixth Avenue. 212-216-1504.*

**877.** *New York Sports Clubs:* Several NYSC clubs are open twenty-four hours through the week (meaning that they're open continuously from 5:00 a.m. on Monday through 10:00 p.m. on Saturday), and close only from 10:00 p.m. on Saturday through 8:00 a.m. on Sunday and again from 10:00 p.m. Sunday through 5:00 a.m. on Monday. The gym is open to members only, but it offers special night-owl memberships, which give you access to one of these clubs between 11:00 p.m. and 5:00 a.m. for only $39 a month.
*For 24-hour locations, visit www.mysportsclubs.com.*

**878.** *Crunch:* The Lafayette Street location is open continuously between 5:00 a.m. on Monday and 9:00 p.m. on Saturday, for members only (no guests are permitted late at night for security reasons).
*404 LAFAYETTE STREET AT EAST 4TH STREET IN MANHATTAN. Subway: 6 to Astor Place. 212-614-0120. www.crunch.com.*

**879.** *Dolphin Gyms:* This small local chain has five locations in Brooklyn, the Bronx, and Queens that are open twenty-four hours during the week (and from 8:00 a.m. to 8:00 p.m. on Saturday and Sunday). In addition to its flexible and unbelievably cheap memberships, Dolphin offers single-day passes for $10, and will customize temporary membership packages for out-of-town visitors.
*For 24-hour locations, visit www.dolphinfitnessclubs.com.*

## 880. Go on a **moonlight bike ride** . . .

If you're curious about what goes on in the park after dark, or you want to ride without those pesky joggers getting in your way, here's your opportunity. Time's Up! has free late-night group rides in Central and Prospect Parks. (Rollerbladers are welcome, too, but should be very competent to keep up with the bikes.) Cyclists of all levels can join, and the pace is leisurely, with plenty of ride leaders lighting the way.

*FOR CENTRAL PARK RIDE, MEET AT COLUMBUS CIRCLE IN MANHATTAN; FOR PROSPECT PARK RIDE, MEET AT GRAND ARMY PLAZA IN BROOKLYN. Rides are held at 10:00 p.m. on the first Friday of every month and at 9:00 p.m. on the second Saturday of every month. For more information, call 212-802-8222 or visit www.times-up.org.*

### 881. . . . or take an early-morning ride, jog, or roll in the park **before it opens** up to cars.

In both Central and Prospect Parks, the drives are closed to cars from 7:00 p.m. to 7:00 a.m. on weekdays, and from 7:00 p.m. on Friday to 7:00 a.m. on Monday. (Note: the parks are officially closed between 1:00 a.m. and 5:00 a.m.)

*For address information and directions, see entries for Central and Prospect Parks in chapter 6.*

### 882. Get your car washed (or grab a snack) at the **Tenth Avenue Car Wash**.

In a city where people barely have time to find a parking spot, let alone the opportunity to stand outside on a Sunday morning with a hose, bucket, and cloth, this all-night garage and car wash on the edge of the Meatpacking District is a gem. For a little over ten dollars, the people at the Tenth Avenue Car Wash will scrub, buff, and polish your car inside and out, and they'll do a much better job than you could with a sponge and soap. And you don't have to be a driver to appreciate the adjacent 24-hour convenience store—in addition to novelty license plates, fluffy dice, and other automobile essentials, this store sells everything from beer and sandwiches to batteries and magazines.

*70 TENTH AVENUE AT 14TH STREET IN MANHATTAN. Subway: A, C, E to 14th Street; L to Eighth Avenue. 646-486-4550.*

### 883. Pick up some midnight reading at the **Lafayette Smoke Shop**.

In order to remain as fashion-conscious, politically aware, and culturally literate as they are, New Yorkers are insatiable consumers of papers, journals, quarterlies, reviews, and periodicals. How do they fit it all in? While bookstore chains like Barnes & Noble and Borders help out during daylight hours, this small, unassuming store in SoHo has pretty much every magazine from all corners of the world available from 6:00 a.m. to 1:00 a.m. With a surprisingly diverse selection of publications, from European fashion magazines to local papers and political and literary journals, Lafayette Smoke Shop has something for every nighttime reader.

*63 SPRING STREET AT LAFAYETTE STREET IN MANHATTAN. Subway: 6 to Spring Street; B, D, F, V to Broadway-Lafayette Street; N, R, W to Prince Street. 212-226-3475.*

Also worth a mention is **Universal News**, an independent chain of news stores with ten locations south of Central Park that are stuffed full of publications in every genre and in every language. All stores are open from 5:00 a.m. to midnight daily. *Multiple locations. For more information, visit www.universalnewsusa.com.*

## 884. Play pool at **Corner Billiards** . . .

Corner Billiards is the king of the late-night pool circuit. Occupying a cavernous space on Fourth Avenue, this classy pool hall has scores of tables in perfect condition, and the space affords the luxury of ample distance between each table. The jukebox is packed with classic rock and soul, and on weekends, when the hall stays open until 3:00 a.m. (till 2:00 a.m. every other night of the week), there are often live DJs. The café and bar are so comfortable that playing can sometimes seem like an afterthought, and when the pool tables are full, the beer, cocktails, and tasty snacks such as gourmet pizzas and burgers served in **Balthazar** buns (see page 175) can take your mind off the wait.

*110 EAST 11TH STREET BETWEEN THIRD AND FOURTH AVENUES IN MANHATTAN. Subway: 4, 5, 6, L, N, Q, R, W to 14th Street-Union Square. 212-995-1314. www.cornerbiliards.com.*

## 885. . . . or at **Broadway Billiard Café**.

One of the last remaining truly 24-hour pool places in the city, Broadway Billiard Café is everything that an old-school pool hall should be: dark, loud, and crowded. With some of the cheapest tables in the city ($4 per person), a jukebox full of classic rock tunes, and a door that never (ever) closes, it's a dependable friend for any late-night hustler.

*10 EAST 21ST STREET BETWEEN BROADWAY AND FIFTH AVENUE IN MANHATTAN. Subway: N, R, W to 23rd Street. 212-388-1582.*

## 886. Play **chess** at midnight.

The two long-standing rivals of New York's chess capital on Thompson Street—**Chess Forum** and the **Chess Shop**—both stay open until around midnight, hosting games between keen amateurs and sleepless masters alike. On busy nights, each place can fill up, and small crowds have been known to gather to watch the more interesting games. If there's a slow game going on and it's time to close, you'll see players sketching the board so that the following night, they can resume where they left off. Each place supplies all the essentials—boards, pieces, clocks, and cheap coffee—all you have to bring is an impregnable defense.

**CHESS FORUM:** *219 THOMPSON STREET BETWEEN WASHINGTON SQUARE AND WEST 3RD STREET IN MANHATTAN. 212-475-2361.*

**CHESS SHOP:** *230 THOMPSON STREET BETWEEN WASHINGTON SQUARE AND WEST 3RD*

*STREET IN MANHATTAN. 212-475-9580. www.chess-shop.com.*
*Subway (for both): A, C, E, B, D, F, V to West 4th Street.*

## 887. Start your week with a new look from Robert Kree.

Robert Kree is one of the most pleasant hair salons in the city, thanks to perks like a lovely garden where you can relax with a drink (coffee, tea, or wine) during your appointment. On Mondays, however, they start their scissors at 6:30 a.m., so you can pop in for a cut and a color, then peruse the newspaper with a cup of coffee in the backyard, and still be out with time to spare before that 9 o'clock meeting.
*375 BLEECKER STREET BETWEEN CHARLES STREET AND PERRY STREET IN MANHATTAN. Subway: 1 to Christopher Street; A, C, E, B, D, F, V to West 4th Street. 212-989-9547. www.robertkree.com.*

## 888. Ride the night loop and see the city after dark.

While there aren't too many city bus tours that we'd recommend, the Nightline (operated by Grayline Tours) deserves a mention. Following the traditional route of the Manhattan tour, the double-decker Nightline buses whisk passengers around the city, from Midtown on the West Side up around the top of Central Park, then down past the UN building to the East Village, SoHo, and Chinatown, and up through Greenwich Village and Chelsea, then back to Rockefeller Center, the Empire State Building, and Times Square. They offer the same tours during the day, but the difference, of course, is that by night everything is much more exciting! (And you'll move a lot faster.) From the roof of the Nightline bus, you'll see how great the city looks after dark: the luminescent tips of the skyscrapers in Midtown, paths carved through the park with lanterns, skies glowing orange above Harlem and downtown, searchlights illuminating the city's most beautiful buildings, and an endless parade of bright storefronts, and drinkers and diners posing in neon-lit windows. On its route downtown, the bus goes over the Manhattan Bridge for a stop in Brooklyn and a look back across the East River at the Manhattan skyline in full effect. Tours run every half hour from 6:00 p.m. to 9:00 p.m., and last around two and a half hours. Try to sit on the top deck, even (or especially) during the winter; the snow, Christmas trees, and seasonal street decorations only make the ride brighter.
**GRAYLINE VISITORS CENTER:** *777 EIGHTH AVENUE BETWEEN 47TH AND 48TH STREETS IN MANHATTAN. Subway: C, E to 50th Street. 888-609-5665. www.grayline.com.*

## 889. See where the **Meatpacking District** gets its name.

Although its heyday as one of the most thriving markets on the East Coast has passed, there are still enough wholesalers, butchers, and warehouses operating in the Meatpacking District—otherwise known as the Gansevoort Market—to make a nighttime stroll worthwhile. Around four or five in morning—when most bars and clubs in the area are emptying out—the market stirs into action, and the austere warehouses and building fronts that provide the silent backdrop to the trendy neighborhood at night spring into life. Then, if you can stay awake, go to **Florent** (see page 335) or one of the nearby diners for a really fresh bacon breakfast.

*MEATPACKING DISTRICT (BORDERED BY WEST 14TH STREET, HUDSON STREET, GAN-SEVOORT STREET, AND ELEVENTH AVENUE) IN MANHATTAN. Subway: A, C, E to 14th Street; L to Eighth Avenue.*

## 890. Party at the **Guggenheim**.

On the first Friday of most months, the **Guggenheim** (see page 123) throws a dance party from 9:00 p.m. to 1:00 a.m., with DJs, drinks, and, of course, art to view. All galleries are kept open for the evening, although drinks are off-limits outside of the lobby.

*$15 dollars entry; cash bar. 1071 FIFTH AVENUE AT 89TH STREET IN MANHATTAN. Subway: 4, 5, 6 to 86th Street. 212-432-3500. www.guggenheim.org.*

## 891. Get food **delivered to you** ...

When we polled New Yorkers about their absolute favorite things about the city for this book, food delivery was the single most popular answer. At any hour of the day, you can dial up a meal of any shape, size, or cuisine, from basic pizza or Chinese, to exotic ethnic food, to meals from trendy places like **Pastis** (see page 163). Although all restaurants don't deliver 24/7, most neighborhoods have plenty of places that deliver on both the early and late sides, and at least one or two that deliver around the clock, so there's never an hour when you can't get a hot meal brought to your door. *New York* magazine has a great online guide to food delivery in Manhattan and Brooklyn, organized by neighborhood, that lists the hours during which places deliver (**www.newyorkmetro.com/restaurants/articles/delivery/index.htm**). The Web site Menupages.com goes a step further by providing full delivery menus for all the restaurants listed on its site. Go to **www.menupages.com**, and click on "Restaurants with Delivery" at the top right. Choose a neighborhood, and you'll get a list of restaurants in that area that deliver, along with menus, hours, and user reviews.

### 892. . . . or **go out** to grab a bite.

Hankering for a midnight snack but not sure where to go? **Menupages.com** also has a list of 24-hour restaurants (with menus), including delis, cafés, ethnic restaurants, and diners (for our favorite late-night spots, see page 335). With more than 5,000 restaurants (and counting) on the site, you're bound to find something that hits the spot. *Anywhere you are!*

### 893. Do your **grocery shopping** in the middle of the night.

Not the most glamorous of the city's nocturnal activities, to be sure, but when you stop and think about it, there's something extremely intriguing (and romantic) about being able to buy a ripe cantaloupe in the middle of the night. There are many delis and grocery stores in the city that stay open all night—too many to list here, or to single out, although there are more downtown than uptown—that make it possible to live as nourishing a life by night as by day. If you're up late working, if you've just come back from a long night on the town, or if you're simply sleepless and hungry, try stepping out for a snack, and you'll probably feel much better.
*All over the city.*

### 894. Get a hot dog (or two) from **Gray's Papaya**.

For some people, there's never a bad time for a hot dog. For them, there's Gray's Papaya. With locations scattered all over the city and open round the clock, with delicious, crispy dogs for sale, and prices friendly enough for any budget, Gray's Papaya has it sewn up and is king of the Papaya family (although fans of Papaya King would disagree—for more on classic New York food wars, see page 167). You can get one hot dog for under a dollar, or try the "recession special" (see page 283): two dogs and a cup of ice-cold juice for $2.75—the perfect midnight snack.
*All locations in Manhattan. 539 EIGHTH AVENUE AT 37TH STREET. Subway: A, C, E to 34th Street-Penn Station. 212-904-1588. 2090 BROADWAY AT 72ND STREET. Subway: 1, 2, 3 to 72nd Street. 212-799-0243. 402 SIXTH AVENUE AT 8TH STREET. Subway: A, C, E, B, D, F, V to West 4th Street. 212-260-3532.*

### 895. Get a late-night cupcake from **Magnolia**.

The absurd lines and constant crowds keep this popular bakery out of the running for a best thing to do during most hours of the day, but its late-night hours—unusual for a bakery—make it impossible for us to resist. At midnight, when most bakeries are taking a rest before an early morning of baking, Magnolia is still open for business. In the realm of after-hours street treats, the fresh, hand-frosted cupcakes are a big step up from day-old pizza or a bag of chips from a deli. But don't think that you'll beat the lines by coming at night—the dessert crowds are in full force right up until closing. To avoid the rush, your best bet is probably to come right when they open at 9:00 a.m. *Open until 12:30 a.m., Friday and Saturday; 11:30 p.m., Sunday through Thursday. 401 BLEECKER STREET AT 11TH STREET IN MANHATTAN. Subway: A, C, E to 14th Street; L to Eighth Avenue. 212-462-2572.*

## 896. Go ice-skating **off-hours**. . .

A seasonal treat, ice-skating at any of the city's rinks is often frustratingly crowded, especially around Christmas. However, a few rinks have generous night or morning hours, which are the best times to avoid crowds. The **rink in Rockefeller Center** (see page 33) is open until midnight every night of the week during the holiday season (from November through New Year's), and on Friday and Saturday nights during the rest of the season (mid-January through April). On the other end, the **Pond at Bryant Park** opens at 8:00 a.m. every day of the week, so you can squeeze in an hour of ice time before heading to work.

*Both locations in Manhattan. THE ICE RINK IS LOCATED IN THE MIDDLE OF ROCKEFELLER CENTER. Subway: B, D, F, V to 47th-50th Streets-Rockefeller Center. Call 212-332-7654 for information and current schedules. www.therinkatrockcenter.com. THE POND IS LOCATED ON THE LAWN IN BRYANT PARK, 42ND STREET BETWEEN FIFTH AND SIXTH AVENUES. Open late October through January. Subway: B, D, F, V to 42nd Street-Bryant Park; 7 to Fifth Avenue-Bryant Park. 866-221-5157. www.bryantpark.org.*

## 897. . . . or **roller-skating** in the middle of the night.

There are several roller rinks around the five boroughs, but this club puts an authentic New York spin on an activity more commonly associated with suburban malls. On Wednesdays, you can roller-skate (or blade) the night away at the **Roxy**. You can rent skates or bring your own; there is also music, drinks and refreshments, and air conditioning to keep skaters cool until 2:00 a.m. If you're really dedicated, you can sign up for the four-week skating course ($65), taught by teachers from the Lezly Skate School. *515 WEST 18TH STREET BETWEEN TENTH AND ELEVENTH AVENUES IN MANHATTAN. Wednesday nights, 8:00 p.m. to 2:00 a.m.; skate lessons start at 6:45 p.m. All skaters must be at least twenty-one years old, I.D. required. Subway: 1 to 18th Street; A, C, E to 14th Street; L to Eighth Avenue. 212-645-5157. www.roxynyc.com. For information on lessons, call Lezly Skate School at 212-777-3232 or visit www.skateguru.com.*

### 898. Shop with the chefs at the **Union Square Greenmarket**.

The **Greenmarket** (see page 169) isn't just a grocery store alternative for New York residents; it's also the source of many of the ingredients that wind up in dishes at the city's finest restaurants. Any chef worth his or her salt comes to the main Greenmarket in Union Square to pick up specific items from favorite vendors, chat with farmers, and be inspired by seasonal offerings. Wednesday and Friday are the big days for chefs, who usually arrive right when the market opens to beat the crowds and get first pick of the day's bounty. So come early and keep your ears open: you can pick up some tips about what's fresh and the best way to prepare it.

*Opens at 8:00 a.m., Monday, Wednesday, Friday, and Saturday. NORTH AND WEST SIDES OF UNION SQUARE PARK BETWEEN 14TH AND 17TH STREETS IN MANHATTAN. Subway: 4, 5, 6, L, N, Q, R, W to 14th Street-Union Square.*

### 899. Regress on a Sunday night at **Southpaw**.

Since opening in 2002, Southpaw has become one of Brooklyn's best-known music venues, attracting big names and fun crowds. On some Sunday nights, from about six or seven in the evening until well after midnight, the space turns into an after-hours playground for kids of legal drinking age, with games, toys, and a killer jukebox. There's a Ping-Pong table, some classic pinball machines, a basketball hoop affixed to the wall, and usually a skateboard or two rolling around. It's always a terrific place to see a band, but on Sundays, it's a great place to let your inner kid enjoy some low-key fun.

*Contact bar for upcoming dates. 125 FIFTH AVENUE BETWEEN BUTLER STREET AND SAINT JOHN'S PLACE IN BROOKLYN. Subway: 2, 3 to Bergen Street; 4, 5, Q to Atlantic Avenue; F to Fourth Avenue; M, N, R to Union Street. 718-230-0236. www.spsounds.com.*

### 900. Borrow a telescope in **Central Park**.

On clear, mild nights, scores of amateur lunar enthusiasts and more serious astronomers emerge from their homes and labs to set up telescopes of all shapes and sizes in clearings around Central Park. Even in the depths of night, the city is so bright that visible stars are few and far between; but knowledgeable astronomers can train their glass on anything from constellations to shooting stars. Most of the park's nocturnal viewers are amenable to the curious, and will happily trade telescope time for an audience eager to share in the delights of the sky at night. Here's a hint: to guarantee a good turnout of telescopes, look for tips in the newspaper's weather section for good nights for star-gazing before you head out.

*For the best chances of finding a glass, scout Central Park's Great Lawn (enter through the entrances at 72nd Street). Subway: B, C to 72nd Street; 6 to 68th Street-Hunter College. See note on page 328 regarding closing hours of the park. See page 216 for more on Central Park.*

## 901. Get something printed at the **24-hour Village Copier**.

With top-quality equipment and an intelligent and helpful staff, the Village Copier has acquired a legendary status among students, writers, designers, and others frequently in need of late-night printing facilities. The branch by Columbia University stays open twenty-four hours from Monday through Friday (9:00 a.m. to 9:00 p.m. on Saturday and Sunday), and will take care of anything, from a stubborn dissertation that won't print out at home to a thousand color flyers for a birthday party. Besides printing posters, cards, and invitations to order, Village Copier also loans out computers to anyone whose laptop has folded under pressure. On top of the practical advantages, these copy shops also feature an amazing cast of nocturnal New Yorkers: a few hours here and you'll understand where all the posters tacked to streetlamps come from, and why all of those bootleg DVD covers sold on Canal Street look so good. *2872 BROADWAY BETWEEN 111TH AND 112TH STREETS IN MANHATTAN. Subway: 1, B, C to Cathedral Parkway (110th Street). 212-666-0600. For information and addresses of other (not 24-hour) locations, visit www.villagecopier.com.*

# Get a meal anytime you want.

Round-the-clock diners and coffee shops are a great odd-hours thing to do anywhere, and have long been supplying food and coffee to truck drivers, cab drivers, and other night crawlers at hours when no one else will take them in. In New York, we've got plenty, and when you're starving at 4:00 a.m., the best one in the city is whichever is closest. However, not all are created equal, and there's quite a range in type of place and quality of experience. If you can make the trip, here are the places you should seek out for off-hours eating. From authentic Greek coffee shops to French bistros, we've managed to narrow it down to a dozen places, with a greasy spoon or two thrown in for good measure.

## 902. Discover what a French diner is at **Florent**.

Even in the daylight hours, this stylish restaurant is a great place to go for a good meal, so it's a treat to find that it's not just open but packed in the wee hours of the night. A Meatpacking District pioneer from 1985, long before the district was a destination, Florent is like the bastard child of an all-American diner and a chic French brasserie, complete with neon lights, booths, great music, and a menu that mixes cheeseburgers and fries with mussels, blood sausage, herbed chicken with mashed potatoes, rich liver salads, and other savory French dishes. Florent has a full bar and wine list, and an exuberant and good-looking staff, which make it the perfect place to stop for supper (or breakfast) and a drink after a night of dancing at the clubs in the **Meatpacking District** (see page 331).

*69 GANSEVOORT STREET BETWEEN WASHINGTON AND GREENWICH STREETS IN MANHAT-TAN. Subway: A, C, E to 14th Street; L to Eighth Avenue. 212-989-5779.*
*www.restaurantflorent.com.*

### 903. Eat a hearty midnight snack at **Big Nick's**.

One of the best places on the Upper West Side to satisfy nighttime appetites, Big Nick's is a small diner with a huge menu and one of the biggest burgers in New York City. Decorated in classic diner style, with small tables covered by red-and-white checked tablecloths and faded photographs adorning the walls, the space is cozy in a nostalgic sort of way, and the staff does its best to keep patrons amused. If you think you're up to the challenge, discard the weighty menu and order the sumo burger—it's one of the largest, best-cooked, and tastiest sandwiches in the city.

*2175 BROADWAY BETWEEN 75TH AND 76TH STREETS IN MANHATTAN. Subway: 1, 2, 3 to 72nd Street. 212-362-9238. www.bignicksnyc.com.*

### 904. People-watch at **Cafeteria** . . .

Some 24-hour joints are great for winding down after a long night; this is where to come when you want to keep the action going. No matter the hour, this upscale Chelsea eatery is a place to see and be seen, and, as evidenced by the large plaque on the corner warning patrons to keep the noise down and the street clear, it's always a party. And though the cravings satisfied here tend to be more visual and audible than edible, the macaroni and cheese tempts even the most ascetic of New York waifs.

*119 SEVENTH AVENUE AT 17TH STREET IN MANHATTAN. Subway: 1 to 18th Street. 212-414-1717.*

### 905. . . . or at **Diner 24**.

If you haven't gotten your fill of the scene when the clubs close at 4:00 a.m., or you prefer people-watching to paper-reading over breakfast at 7:00 a.m., you can also try Diner 24. Like Cafeteria, Diner 24 offers stylized comfort food to a trendsetting and fashionable crowd. The atmosphere is a tad friendlier than Cafeteria's, although sometimes the lack of attitude is undermined by the restaurant's correlating popularity. The extensive late-night menu mixes classics with more creative after-hours fare; if you're feeling daring, order the fish taco; otherwise, stick to the disco fries topped with Brie fondue, or the grilled cheese sandwich.

*102 EIGHTH AVENUE AT 15TH STREET IN MANHATTAN. Subway: A, C, E to 14th Street; L to Eighth Avenue. 212-242-7773. www.diner24.com.*

## 906. Try to get in to **Chelsea Square**.

Of all the late-night eateries in Chelsea, this one offers the most deliciously incongruous, only-in-New-York type of experience—if you can get in. For years, this classic (in the least polished sense of the word) diner has been located on the corner of 23$^{rd}$ Street and Ninth Avenue, an unremarkable structure with unmemorable food. But when nightclubs started popping up around the neighborhood in the '90s, Chelsea Square acquired a new image: a bustling after-hours spot. By day and into the evening, it still serves a neighborhood crowd, but on weekend nights, it performs a Superman-style quick change, and by the time the kids start leaving the clubs, it's sporting bouncers and a makeshift velvet rope. Waiting in line to get into a Greek coffee shop at 4:00 a.m. may not be everyone's cup of tea, but if you persevere, you will be treated to the unusual sight of made-up and decked-out club kids fighting over well-worn booths, and feasting on plates of shrimp cocktail, Jell-O and cottage cheese salads, and London broil.

*368 WEST 23RD STREET AT NINTH AVENUE IN MANHATTAN. Subway: C, E to 23rd Street. 212-691-5400.*

## 907. Have a snack at the other Empire State Building at the **Empire Diner**.

The west side of Manhattan is something of a haven for America's favorite kind of eatery, and this sparkling 1950s-style diner in Chelsea is the best of the bunch. With comfy booths, a long row of high stools at the bar, and a proud replica of the city's most celebrated skyscraper sitting on top of its chrome roof, the Empire Diner is the perfect blend of classic and kitsch. As its popularity has grown among the young, hip, late-night Chelsea crowd, so its prices have risen and its traditional diner dishes have taken on trendy new twists—you now have to specify if you want American cheese on your tuna melt—but the food is still great, and it's the liveliest and most welcoming place to find breakfast after a night on the tiles.

*210 TENTH AVENUE AT 22ND STREET IN MANHATTAN. Subway: C, E to 23rd Street. 212-924-0011.*

## 908. See the inside of **Tom's Restaurant**.

Anyone who's ever watched an episode of *Seinfeld* will recognize the famous exterior of Tom's. In reality, Tom's looks different on the inside from the restaurant you see on the TV show, but it's a great place to eat, and an institution of the Columbia University area. As a rule, comfort food gets better the farther uptown you go, and the melts, shakes, and fried chicken at Tom's are close to perfect. Always busy and always friendly, a late-night snack or an early breakfast here is worth a trip from just about anywhere in the city. Go at dawn on a summer weekend, and you can watch the market setting up on the street outside the diner.

*2880 BROADWAY AT 112TH STREET IN MANHATTAN. Subway: 1, B, C to Cathedral Parkway (110th Street). 212-864-6137.*

→ **DID YOU KNOW?** *The "other" diner frequented by the characters in* Seinfeld *was actually the Munson Diner. The Munson stood on the corner of Eleventh Avenue and 49th Street for more than half a century, until 2005, when its stainless steel façade was packed up and transferred upstate. A group of investors bought the sixty-year-old diner, and then loaded it—deep fryers, industrial-size refrigerators, and all—on a flatbed truck, and moved it up to the Catskills, where it began its new life as, well, a 1950s diner-themed restaurant. For information on visiting the "new" Munson Diner, visit www.munsondiner.com.*

## 909. Become a regular at **Moondance**.

Many people are familiar with its tacky sparkling sign with the revolving moon, but not-so-well known is that Moondance is three-quarters of a century old. Its silver chrome exterior is wonderfully out-of-place on the murky edges of SoHo, while the interior feels as simple and homey as it looks. Although it might close for an hour or so toward dawn, Moondance is relied upon to be open by an eclectic mix of daylight regulars, late-night downtown diners, and SoHo artists with erratic appetites. It's not the cheapest place in town, but with little touches that enhance the classic menu— the latticed fries that accompany the burger, or the herbed mayonnaise that comes with the roast beef sandwich—it's the perfect old diner for New York City.

*80 SIXTH AVENUE AT GRAND STREET IN MANHATTAN. Subway: A, C, E to Canal Street; C, E to Spring Street. 212-226-1191.*

## 910. Have late-night *lyonnais* at **L'Express** . . .

If you happen to be hungry at 3:00 a.m. in the Union Square area, you are in luck. Just a few blocks north is a restaurant that far and away exceeds the usual expectations of a 24-hour joint. No matter what hour you arrive at L'Express, you'll never feel like you've arrived at an off time: the food is always good, and the atmosphere is never dead. Other pluses include the lighting (or lack thereof), which is just right for hunkering down after a big night on your feet, and the speedy service, which at night is fast even by diner standards (Sunday brunch is a different story). Burgers, salads, croque monsieur, and an excellent French onion soup are all good choices day or night, but if you're in the mood for something more unusual at an odd hour, try one of the *spécialités Lyonnaises*, such as the charcuterie plate *or tripe à l'Ancienne* (tripe in tomato sauce).

*249 PARK AVENUE SOUTH AT 20TH STREET IN MANHATTAN. Subway: 4, 5, 6, L, N, R, Q, W to 14th Street-Union Square; 6 to 23rd Street. 212-254-5858. www.lexpressnyc.com.*

## 911. . . . or borscht for breakfast at **Veselka**.

If hearty Eastern European fare is what you crave come midnight, check out this East Village greasy spoon, where you can feast on pierogis, borscht, and blintzes at any hour of the day or night. The diner-sized menu has something for everyone, including soups, salads, and sandwiches, and plenty of hearty vegetarian options, from the meatless stuffed cabbage to veggie burgers. A sentimental favorite that has been on the same well-traveled corner for fifty years, Veselka may not stand out on today's Second Avenue restaurant row in the light of day. But late at night and in the early morning, the unpretentious food and old-time atmosphere seem mighty appealing, and if you come in the wee hours of the morning, you'll appreciate how the harsh, garish lighting knocks the sleep right out of your eyes.

*144 SECOND AVENUE AT 9TH STREET IN MANHATTAN. Subway: 6 to Astor Place. 212-228-9682. www.veselka.com.*

→ **DID YOU KNOW?** *Veselka means "rainbow" in Ukrainian.*

## 912. Go to a **Greek diner** in Astoria.

If you want an old-fashioned 24-hour Greek diner, plastic-covered booths and all, Astoria is the place to go. The **Neptune** is a local favorite, beloved for its homey atmosphere, retro tableside jukeboxes, and faithful renditions of Greek diner classics, from tuna melts to spinach pie.

*3105 ASTORIA BOULEVARD AT 31ST STREET IN QUEENS. Subway: N to Astoria Boulevard. 718-278-4853.*

## 913. Beat the crowds at the **Carnegie Deli**.

Technically, the **Carnegie Deli** (see page 169) doesn't belong with the eateries above, since it's open only twenty-two hours a day. But discounting the hours between 4:30 a.m. and 6:30 a.m., this historic restaurant is a great place to have a decadent late-night or early-morning meal. Polish off a mountainous Reuben sandwich or triple-decker deli meat combo that you might not be caught dead eating during the day at this tourist trap. Under cover of night, luxuriate in the elbow room, and worry about your arteries in the morning.

*854 SEVENTH AVENUE AT 55TH STREET IN MANHATTAN. Subway: N, Q, R, W to 57th Street. 212-757-2245. www.carnegiedeli.com.*

---

### 914. Buy a bagel at **H&H** . . .

You can top off a midnight stroll or get a head start on the day with breakfast from one of New York's **most beloved bagel purveyors** (see page 168) because, as the nice man who answered the phone when we called said in a weary voice, "We *never* close." *Both locations in Manhattan: 2239 BROADWAY AT 80TH STREET, Subway: 1 to 79th Street, 212-595-8000. 639 WEST 46TH STREET AT TWELFTH AVENUE, Subway: A, C, E to 42nd Street-Port Authority Bus Terminal, 212-595-8000. www.hhbagel.com.*

### 915. . . . or at **Fifth Avenue Bageltique Café,**

Brooklyn's best 24-hour bagelry, and a favorite late-night eatery of both cops and night crawlers. It looks like a deli, but the large selection of cream cheeses shows its true *raison d'être*; or you can have the best of both worlds by ordering a sandwich or burger served on a bagel.

*242 FIFTH AVENUE BETWEEN CARROLL AND PRESIDENT STREETS IN BROOKLYN. Subway: 2, 3, 4, 5, B, Q to Atlantic Avenue; D, M, R to Atlantic Avenue-Pacific Street; N to Pacific Street. 718-638-1866.*

---

### 916. Eat Chinese at **Wo Hop** . . .

Many Chinatown restaurants have surprisingly generous hours, often staying open until four or five in the morning, but Wo Hop marries two New York passions—Chinese food and 24-hour service—in what is one of the neighborhood's only round-the-clock restaurants.

*15 MOTT STREET AT MOSCO STREET IN MANHATTAN. Subway: 6 to Canal Street. 212-566-3841.*

### 917. . . . or an early-morning burger at **Pop Burger**.

It's not open a full twenty-four hours (it closes at 5:00 a.m. on weekends; 2:00 a.m. on weekdays), but Pop Burger still merits a mention among the all-hours eateries because one, in any other city but New York, being open as late as it is would qualify as "after-hours"; two, the burgers and shakes are great, morning, noon, and night; and three with the number of clubs, bars, and other late-night entertainment in the Meatpacking District and west Chelsea, hungry nightcrawlers need all the options they can get. Although the place looks more posh than the average fast-food joint (there's a lounge in back), the menu is simple and crowd pleasing: burgers, fries, milkshakes, and onion rings.

*58-60 NINTH AVENUE AT 15TH STREET IN MANHATTAN. Subway: A, C, E to 14th Street; L to Eighth Avenue. 212-414-8686.*

## 918. Read after dark at **St. Mark's Bookshop**.

This brilliant bookshop in the East Village comes as close as you can get to a late-night bookstore, closing around midnight seven days a week. With so many restaurants, clubs, and watering holes around NoHo and the East Village, there are always plenty of tired revelers wandering the store looking for something good to read on the train home or simply passing time before their night-on-the-town begins. Even if you're not searching for something in particular, the store has an excellent selection, including a lot of new fiction, wonderful art books, an impressive collection of nonfiction titles, and a full stock of American and international magazines, so it's a great place to browse for something to take home and curl up in bed with.

*31 THIRD AVENUE AT EAST 9TH STREET IN MANHATTAN. Subway: 6 to Astor Place; L to Third Avenue. 212-260-7853. www.stmarksbookshop.com.*

## 919. Camp out at the **NYHoS** . . .

Ever take kids to a museum and have to pull them out kicking and screaming at closing time? OK, maybe not every museum captures children's attention quite like that, but the **New York Hall of Science** (see page 123) is one they'll definitely be reluctant to leave. Luckily, the museum has come up with the perfect solution: a sleepover! Starting at 6:00 p.m. and finishing at 9:00 a.m. the next day, the Science Sleepover is an adventure that kids will never forget. For three or four hours, the museum belongs to the sleepover kids, who can explore the entire hall at their own pace and with staff at their disposal. When they're through making giant bubbles, playing games with light, and learning how sound travels through space, they can have a snack, roll out their sleeping bags, and camp out among the exhibits. On summer evenings, kids can play in the outdoor science playground, where swings, slides, and monkey bars all serve to demonstrate different scientific concepts. And maybe, after having breakfast and sewing a NYHoS patch onto their shirt in the morning, the kids will be ready to go home.

*47-01 111TH STREET IN QUEENS. Subway: 7 to 111th Street. 718-699-0005. www.nyhallsci.org. Note: There is usually a minimum of 200 guests required for a sleepover, so check online for available dates and then organize the trip with your kids' school or with other parents in the community.*

## 920. . . . or spend the night at **FAO Schwarz**.

This sounds like something from the mind of Roald Dahl—a child's fantasy come to life in a way that's almost too stupendous to believe. For $25,000, you and/or your child can have a sleepover birthday party at **FAO Schwarz** (see page 25), with up to

fifteen friends. The party starts at 9:00 p.m. with treats and cake at the FAO Schweetz Ice Cream Parlor; for the next eleven hours, you'll have the store to yourselves, and can dance on the famous piano from the movie *Big*, ride on the 3-D motion simulator, and play with any toy that tickles your fancy. Sleep, if it happens, takes place in sleeping bags on the floor. In the morning, there's breakfast and goodie bags before the staff has to wrap up the party before opening the store to regular customers.
*767 FIFTH AVENUE AT 58TH STREET IN MANHATTAN. Subway: F to 57th Street; N, R, W to Fifth Avenue/59th Street. 212-644-9400. www.fao.com.*

## 921. Midnight yoga at **Laughing Lotus.**

As the name suggests, Laughing Lotus takes a playful approach to practicing yoga. It teaches serious yoga, but with a welcoming and enthusiastic attitude, which makes the classes as fun as they are enriching, perfect for beginners and dabblers, as well as experienced yogis. The popular midnight yoga session on Friday nights is a lively practice that runs from 10:00 p.m. to midnight with live music. The late-night class is both relaxing and invigorating, and unlike other, more indulgent Friday nights out, you won't regret it in the morning.
*59 WEST 19TH STREET, THIRD FLOOR, IN MANHATTAN. 212-414-2903. www.laughinglotus.com. For information on Laughing Lotus's seasonal rooftop yoga series, see page 226.*

## 922. Bowl until you fall asleep at **Night Strike** at Bowlmor Lanes . . .

On Monday nights, this popular and historic bowling alley (it's been open in the same location since 1938, making it one of the oldest bowling alleys in the country) offers a $20 all-you-can-bowl deal (including shoe rental) between 10:00 p.m. and 3:00 a.m. Other perks include glow-in-the-dark bowling balls and a live DJ.
*110 UNIVERSITY PLACE BETWEEN 12TH AND 13TH STREETS IN MANHATTAN. Subway: 4, 5, 6, L, N, Q, R, W to 14th Street-Union Square. 212-255-8188. www.bowlmor.com. N.B.: Night Strike is open to those twenty-one and older; ID required.*

## 923. . . . or at Extreme Bowling at **Harlem Lanes.**

On Friday and Saturday nights, Harlem's premier bowling alley stays open until three in the morning as well, and in addition to glow-in-the-dark balls and DJs, they've got a lounge full of comfy couches in case you need to take a snooze mid-game.
*2110-2118 ADAM CLAYTON POWELL BOULEVARD AT 126TH STREET IN MANHATTAN. Subway: 2, 3, A, C, B, D to 125th Street. 212-678-BOWL. www.harlemlanes.com.*

## 924. Hammer joysticks until your fingers bleed at
# Broadway City Video Arcade.

Nothing says midnight like the blinking neon of a video game arcade. Broadway City, an enormous arcade in the heart of the city's own neon wonderland, is far and away the best place to satisfy the late-night yearning for bright lights and constant motion. Every classic arcade attraction is here, from fairground hoops and basketball nets to old-school fighting games and shoot 'em ups, as well as newer editions, with cutting-edge video-game technology. There are Japanese dancing games with dance steps mapped out on flashing disco floors, fake one-armed bandits, and banks of multi-player racing games, so entire teams of friends and strangers can yell at one another in competitive fury. There's a whole level devoted to sports games housed in a mock Yankee Stadium, a fleet of pristine air hockey tables, brand-new pinball machines, and something for pretty much anyone with a taste for gaming. It's so bright in here that you can easily lose track of time—you may be amazed to see dark skies outside when you eventually leave.

*241 WEST 42ND STREET AT TIMES SQUARE IN MANHATTAN. Subway: 1, 2, 3, 7, N, Q, R, W, S to Times Square-42nd Street; A, C, E to 42nd Street-Port Authority Bus Terminal. 212-997-9797.*

## Attend a midnight movie.

For some years the province solely of *Rocky Horror* fans, the midnight movie has again become, if not mainstream, at least a bit more common, and the offerings more diverse. You can catch midnight shows of everything from classics and cult films to special one-night-only engagements to showings of first-run films on occasion. The following theaters have regular midnight shows; other NYC movie theaters also run them from time to time, so check current listings.

### 925. *The Two Boots Pioneer Theater:* There are many unconventional things about the Pioneer, the spin-off independent movie house of the Two Boots pizza chain. One is the programming, which erratically but reliably schedules midnight movies, mostly on Friday and Saturday nights. Some movies are one-shot deals, others stick around, like *Donnie Darko*, which played at midnight for over a year. But be warned—the seats are so comfy, you might start to doze off. N.B.: If you want pizza, you had better get it before you go in—the restaurant closes at midnight. (For more information on the Pioneer, see page 158.)

*155 EAST THIRD STREET BETWEEN AVENUES A AND B IN MANHATTAN. Subway: F, V to Lower East Side-Second Avenue. 212-591-0434. www.twoboots.com/pioneer.*

**926.** *The Sunshine:* The glorious **Landmark Sunshine Cinema** (see page 159) runs series of midnight movies for the hip, indie Lower East Side crowd that congregates around Houston Street. On Friday and Saturday nights, the "Sunshine at Midnight" shows always pull the biggest audiences, and the choices are real crowd pleasers, from cult classics like *Dog Day Afternoon* to nostalgic favorites like *Heathers* and *Clue*. Selections change every week, but if you become a regular, you'll start to see many familiar faces in the crowd.

*143 EAST HOUSTON STREET BETWEEN FIRST AND SECOND AVENUES IN MANHATTAN. Subway: F, V to Lower East Side-Second Avenue. 212-330-8182. www.landmarktheatres.com.*

**927.** *The Paris:* Surprisingly enough, the buttoned-up **Paris** (see page 40) occasionally does midnight screenings of classic films on Saturday nights. Shows are old-fashioned style, one-night-only engagements; selections have included *Rebel Without a Cause, North by Northwest,* and *Pink Floyd—The Wall.*

*4 WEST 58TH STREET BETWEEN FIFTH AND SIXTH AVENUES IN MANHATTAN. Subway: N, R, W to Fifth Avenue/59th Street. 212-688-3800.*

**928.** *IFC Center:* In tribute to its former incarnation as the beloved Waverly, the splendid new **IFC Center's** (see page 158) series of late-night movies, "Waverly Midnights," runs themed programs of independent-flavored modern classics. The theme varies by season—the recent "Midnight Rocks" series revived rockumentaries and pop-influenced films like *A Hard Day's Night, Purple Rain, Sid and Nancy,* and the New York disco epic *The Apple*—but every show is edgy, nostalgic, and ideal for late-night viewing.

*323 SIXTH AVENUE AT WEST 3RD STREET IN MANHATTAN. Subway: A, C, E, B, D, F, V to West 4th Street. 212-924-7771. www.ifccenter.com.*

# CHAPTER 10:

# Only in New York

"**O**nly in New York, kids, only in New York," is the signature sign-off of the *Post*'s famous gossip columnist, Cindy Adams, and a phrase that—whether they read her or not—echoes in New Yorkers' ears each time they see an oven filled with wine bottles; refer without irony to a 650-square-foot-apartment as "palatial"; hear about a members-only luxury social club for babies, a yoga class for dogs, and a recreational juggling team, all in the same neighborhood; or catch themselves nearly getting into fisticuffs over who makes the best bagels or pizza. In this, our final chapter, we celebrate New York's great idiosyncrasies. Here you'll find offbeat activities (learning the secret manufacturing techniques on a tour of the world's finest piano factory; a finishing school for drag queens; and plenty of things to do at the city's favorite hub of eccentricity, Coney Island), unique or signature NYC services, and a handful of oddities that defy categorization (elephants marching through the Midtown Tunnel).

Throughout the book, we've tried to pick out the city's best features—the sites, entertainment, and activities that stand out from the multitude of simply wonderful things here as experiences worth taking a detour for. In this chapter, we hope to convey what makes just being in New York one of the best things to do in and of itself.

## 929. Get a little extra protection from erratic cab drivers at the **Blessing of the Bikes** at the Cathedral of Saint John the Divine.

In May, right around the time when many of them take to the streets for the season, cyclists and their bikes are invited to **Saint John** (see page 21) to receive a blessing for good health and no accidents during the coming year. Cyclists of all religions (and levels) are welcome. If you aren't a hardcore biker, it is still worth the trip to witness this hearty group of weekend warriors in skin suits ringing their bike bells inside the majestic cathedral.

Another blessing event worth checking out is the annual **Blessing of the Animals**, held on the Feast of Saint Francis Assisi in October. During this spectacular occasion, Saint John turns into an unlimited-capacity Noah's Ark, opening its doors to thousands of pets of all shapes and sizes, whose owners bring them to receive a protective blessing and a sprinkling of holy water. After the service, the animals—which include both common house pets as well as snakes, farm animals, and, one year, a camel—proceed down the aisle and out to the cathedral grounds for an animal fair. *1047 AMSTERDAM AVENUE NEAR 110TH STREET IN MANHATTAN. Subway: 1 to 110th Street; B, C to Cathedral Parkway (110th Street). 212-316-7490. www.stjohndivine.org.*

## 930. Visit Santa at Macy's.

This is the only place in the world where you can see the real one—don't you remember *Miracle on 34th Street?* After making the trip down from the North Pole for the **Thanksgiving Day Parade** (see page 89), Santa takes up residence at Santa's Village on the eighth floor of Macy's from the Friday after Thanksgiving through Christmas Eve. There is also a puppet show there, which is fun for kids (as opposed to visiting Santa, which is an imperative activity for all ages). Tip: Depending on when you go, the line of impatient visitors who are corralled around the store and through Santaland can threaten Santa's status as a best thing to do. Macy's has **extended hours** (see page 319) during the holidays, so if you can, try to get there right when the store opens at 7:00 a.m., and you and your little one can move through Santaland at your own pace, and have an audience with Santa while he's fresh.
*Santaland is located on the eighth floor. 151 WEST 34TH STREET BETWEEN BROADWAY AND SEVENTH AVENUE IN MANHATTAN. Subway: 1, 2, 3, A, C, E to 34th Street-Penn Station; B, D, F, V, N, Q, R, W to 34th Street-Herald Square. 212-494-4495. www.macys.com.*

## 931. Excuse me, Mr. Science Man–what's this?

Ever come across a creature in the park and wonder what it is? Ever wonder what the real story is behind some of the treasures in your grandparents' cupboard? For all those with a hunger for knowledge, there's the **American Museum of Natural History's Identification Day**, an annual event during which an expert panel drawn from the museum's staff—including biologists, archaeologists, historians, and paleontologists—is available to the public to examine and explain any natural object or man-made curiosity you care to bring in. Each of the museum's representatives is a specialist in some field or other, so a kid who unearths an antique board game might be referred to one person for an authoritative answer, and a sunbather who stumbles on an unusual rock at the beach might be sent to another. As well as the identifications—which are as fascinating to observe for passersby as it is for the discoverers—there are special lectures, films, and events, and the museum staff is around to answer questions about pretty much anything that's in the museum as well.

*Contact the museum for dates and more information. 79TH STREET AND CENTRAL PARK WEST IN MANHATTAN. Subway: 1 to 79th Street; B, C to 81st Street-Museum of Natural History. 212-769-5100. www.amnh.org. For more information on the museum, see page 118.*

---

## 932. **Watch the elephants** come out of the tunnel on the way to the circus.

Why did the elephants cross the road? For the punch line, join the spectators (and ASPCA protestors) on the night when the circus comes to town. Each year, a night or two before the circus opens, the Queens-Midtown Tunnel closes to traffic to allow the Ringling Brothers' largest performers to march through on their way to Madison Square Garden. This is no publicity gimmick—there's really no other way to get the elephants into the city. The procession usually occurs between 11:00 p.m. and 1:00 a.m., although the start and end time are subject to change due to the unpredictability of the performers. If you're in the area around that time, it's hard to miss them, but the best place to watch is right by the tunnel entrance on First Avenue. You can also try to follow the pachyderms along their journey to MSG—but good luck. They may look like they're moving slowly, but with legs that long, they're not so easy to keep up with.

*March. For exact date of the procession, contact the circus. 34TH STREET AND FIRST AVENUE IN MANHATTAN. Subway: 6 to 33rd Street. www.ringling.com.*

---

## 933. Smack golf balls at **New Jersey**.

With space at a premium in New York City, a golfer can get pretty frustrated. You can release your aggression (without hitting anybody) at the **Chelsea Piers Golf Club**, the only place to putt in Manhattan. The ingenious conversion of disused piers at the Chelsea harbor into an outdoor driving range allows space-deprived city dwellers to practice their swings without fear of breaking windows or injuring passersby. With 200-yard Astroturf fairways, state-of-the-art automated tees that disappear after each drive and then rise again with each new ball, and unobstructed views of glorious sunsets over the neighboring state, the driving range is a fun and surprisingly scenic alternative to a trek out to a course in the country. As well as the outdoor range, the center offers group and individual instruction and other amenities to improve your game, including electronic swing simulators, small picket-fenced greens for putting practice, and indoor sandpits to perfect those vital bunker escapes. And although resolute netting keeps the balls from doing any damage, for city sophisticates, there may be something cathartic about aiming a strong drive at their neighbors across the Hudson.

*PIER 59 AT 23RD STREET AND THE HUDSON RIVER IN MANHATTAN. Subway: C, E to 23rd Street. 212-336-6400. www.chelseapiers.com/gc. For more information on Chelsea Piers, see page 307.*

## 934. Try to catch a glimpse of **Pale Male and Lola**, and their luxury nest.

Of all the beloved **New York characters** (see page 361), one of Gotham's most unique longtime residents is Pale Male, a red-tailed hawk. Since he was first spotted in the mid-'90s, Pale Male has become a familiar sight to bird-watchers and pedestrians, who used to congregate in Central Park and around his posh digs on upper Fifth Avenue hoping for a glimpse. But like so many high-profile New Yorkers, he has also been the subject of controversy—and a victim of the city's strict co-op boards. In 2004, the board of 927 Fifth Avenue voted to dismantle Pale Male's nest, a 200-pound structure anchored by pigeon wire where he had lived for years, and where he and his mate, Lola, had produced several offspring, on the grounds that it was unsafe. Immediately, there was a virulent public outcry protesting the eviction, and a few weeks later, the board acquiesced, and reinstalled the nest, along with a safety rail. Unflappable as ever, Pale Male and Lola moved back in time for the 2005 nesting season. Today, the lovebirds freely roam the neighborhood, and can be seen flying around the park and perched on buildings on the Upper East Side, or at their newly renovated nest on the twelfth-floor ledge of 927 Fifth.

*The nest is located on FIFTH AVENUE BETWEEN 73RD AND 74TH STREETS IN MANHATTAN. Subway: 6 to 77th Street. Best viewing locations are in Central Park, or along Fifth Avenue in the neighborhood. But there's no telling where the birds may be, so don't forget to look up!*

# Coney Island

is the best one-of-a-kind attraction in the city, hands down. Along with a beach, a boardwalk, and an amusement park, it is home to one of the world's oldest and most famous roller coaster, the only circus sideshow still operating in the U.S., a world-famous hot dog–eating competition, and an annual maritime-themed parade (see page 90). With the quaint beachside amusement park replaced by large, centrally managed theme parks, this is a special place that cannot be duplicated or rendered obsolete. Long live Coney!

*SURF AVENUE AND WEST 12TH STREET IN BROOKLYN. Subway: D, F, N, Q to Coney Island-Stillwell Avenue.*

## 935. See the last of the **great sideshows**—and learn the tricks of the trade.

The Amusement Park at Coney Island is home to one of America's last great circus sideshows, a strange theater of outrageous acts, revolting tricks, and feats of unimaginable oddity. With a cast of characters that includes Diamond Donny V (the human pincushion), Heather Holiday (the youngest female sword swallower in the world), and Insectivora (one of the top fire performers in the country), the sideshow's acts

Only in New York

range from freakshow staples, such as fire-breathing and hammering a nail into someone's face, to more postmodern variations and innovative tricks, such as the "bed of nails sandwich" or the "neon sword swallowing." Founded by Yale Drama MFA graduate Dick D. Zigun, the sideshow is one of Coney Island's priceless contributions to New York City culture, and judging from the packed houses it draws every summer weekend, it's not going anywhere anytime soon. If you think you've got what it takes, sign up for a semester at the sideshow school, an acclaimed instructional program run by one of the show's most senior performers, Todd Robbins, that will teach you how to walk on glass, lie on nails, and swallow fire with the best of them.

*1208 SURF AVENUE IN BROOKLYN. 718-372-5159. www.coneyisland.com/sideshow.shtml.*

## 936. Watch the Nathan's Famous July Fourth **hot dog–eating contest**.

Watch the world's top hot dog "gurgitators" (as they are known within the competitive eating circuit) vie for the sport's highest honor, the Mustard Yellow International Belt, at this annual event, which has been held at Nathan's since 1916. Twenty top eaters from around the world go head to head on the beach to see how many hot dogs (and buns) each one can down in twenty minutes (current record: 53½).

*Contest is held every year on July 4, at noon, at NATHAN'S FAMOUS, CORNER OF SURF AND STILLWELL AVENUES IN BROOKLYN. For more information, visit www.nathansfamous.com.*

## 937. Ride the **Cyclone.**

Astroland, the name of the amusement park on Coney Island, bills itself as "NYC's largest amusement park." We don't dispute the claim, but let's face it, there isn't that much competition. The Cyclone, however, is something to brag about. The crown jewel of Astroland, it is probably the only National Historical Landmark that it's okay to throw up on. Though it was built in 1927, the Cyclone is still beloved by New Yorkers and roller-coaster aficionados alike, and for more than just nostalgic reasons. With twelve drops, six 108-degree turns, and sixteen changes of directions at 60 miles per hour during the course of the two-minute ride, the Cyclone holds its own against the newer, sleeker models at more modern amusement parks. (Don't worry—despite the rickety-looking wooden structure, the owners of the park work very hard to maintain it.) Afterward, if you're not feeling too queasy, you can follow the ride with a hot dog and curly fries from the original **Nathan's** (see above) on Surf Avenue, which has been serving them since before the Cyclone was built.

→ **DID YOU KNOW?** *Though the Cyclone has many distinctions, it is not the first rollercoaster. It was, however, built on the site of what is considered to have been the first rollercoaster in the world: LaMarcus A. Thompson's Switchback Railway.*

## 938. See a puppet show at the Swedish Cottage Marionette Theater.

For thirty years, the hands behind the stage at the Swedish Cottage have been making puppets dance around to the delight of children and parents from all over the city. Imported from Sweden in the late nineteenth century and moved to Central Park by Frederick Law Olmsted, the cottage houses what is now the only performing public marionette theater in the country. With charming performances of classic children's stories from *Cinderella* to *Jack and the Beanstalk*, a trip to the cottage is a fairy tale for kids from their very first sight of the charming log cabin to the puppets' last bow.

*CENTRAL PARK NEAR THE 79TH STREET ENTRANCE ON THE WEST SIDE IN MANHATTAN. Subway: 1 to 79th Street; B, C to 81st Street-Museum of Natural History. 212-988-9093. www.centralparknyc.org/virtualpark/thegreatlawn/swedishcottage .*

## 939. See the palm trees at the Winter Garden . . .

If you're sick of snow, and February seems like it's never going to end, one of the best cures for the winter blues is a visit to the sixteen *Washingtonia robusta* palm trees in the World Financial Center's Winter Garden. The trees, which come from the Mojave Desert, stretch an impressive forty feet high. They are a lovely backdrop for the performances and events that regularly take place in the Winter Garden (this is where the final competition took place in the film *Mad Hot Ballroom*), but they're worth a visit on their own. If you look at the trees from the steps on the north side of the atrium, the Hudson River is visible through the glass wall behind them, and if you squint a little, it almost looks like a Caribbean beach scene. (Note: the Winter Garden is one of the **Wi-Fi hotspots** sponsored by the Downtown Alliance. For more information, see page 212.)

*THE WORLD FINANCIAL CENTER IS BORDERED BY WEST STREET, VESEY STREET, LIBERTY STREET, AND THE HUDSON RIVER IN MANHATTAN. Subway: 1 to Rector Street; 2, 3, 4, 5, J, M, Z to Fulton Street; A, C to Broadway-Nassau Street; E to World Trade Center. www.worldfinancialcenter.com.*

## 940. . . . or step into the jungle at the Ford Foundation building.

A well-kept secret in the heart of Midtown, the stunning lobby of the Ford Foundation is one of the city's most pleasant surprises. A three-tier landscaped garden occupies the building's 160-foot atrium, with thousands of colorful exotic plants covering the terraces, vines climbing all over the interiors, and seventeen fully grown trees looming above. Vast glass walls let in an amazing amount of sunlight, and the atmosphere is a warm, moist, and refreshing antidote to the oppressive asphalt world outside. The gardeners in charge of this horticultural microcosm vary the vegetation by season, ensuring vibrant springs of tulips and daffodils and restful autumns of dahlias and chrysanthemums. For those who know it's there, the Ford Foundation is one of the city's most cherished eccentricities.

*320 EAST 43ʳᴅ STREET BETWEEN LEXINGTON AND THIRD AVENUES IN MANHATTAN. Subway: 4, 5, 6, 7, S to Grand Central-42ⁿᵈ Street. 212-573-5000.*

## The best places to go

When we first started to work on this book, one suggestion that came up repeatedly was that we include a list of the city's nicest restrooms. And why not? This is a city of pedestrians and amblers of all kinds, who need amenities while en route or aimlessly exploring on foot, and although it's never difficult to find a public restroom wherever you happen to be in the city (department stores, hotel lobbies, and Starbucks are reliable sources in a pinch), it's true that some are (much) better than others. Whether boasting design elements that make them worth a detour or simply offering clean, convenient facilities that are easy to pop in and use on your way, the following is a list of our favorite restrooms in the city. Note: All of these are technically open to the public, except for the two in restaurants—Cha An and Peep—which can be used only if you are a patron.

**941. *Cha An:*** This quiet, traditional teahouse in Manhattan's **Japanese Village** (see page 196) happens to have some of the most high-tech bathrooms in the city. Built seamlessly into the subtle, dark décor of the ladies' room is an elegant, electronically operated toilet-cum-bidet imported from Japan, which will leave you feeling cleaner and more refreshed than in your own bathroom at home.

*230 EAST 9ᵀᴴ STREET BETWEEN SECOND AND THIRD AVENUES IN MANHATTAN. Subway: 6 to Astor Place. 212-228-8030. www.cha-an.com.*

**942. *Pearl River Mart:*** This recently renovated Asian emporium gives shoppers more than an amazing array of unusual, well-priced clothing, goods, furniture, and miscellany. **Pearl River Mart** (see page 257) has, somewhat surprisingly, the best public bathrooms in SoHo. Painted a cheery yellow, they literally sparkle, and located on the lower level just to the side of the stairs, they are perfectly placed—easy to find on your own, but not so prominent that you won't be able to slip in from the street unnoticed.

*477 BROADWAY BETWEEN BROOME STREET AND GRAND STREET IN MANHATTAN. Subway: 6, J, M, Z, N, Q, R, W to Canal Street. 212-431-4770. www.pearlriver.com.*

**943. Balducci's:** The bathrooms at this gourmet market are a useful and little-known treasure on the Chelsea–West Village–Meatpacking District border, right above the subway station. Located on the upper level by the café, they get their share of visitors but are largely under-trafficked, and are kept in immaculate condition. The interior is stylish, though nothing special, but there is ample stall and sink space, and a genius little ledge above the sink in the women's room, where you can rest a purse or shopping bag while you wash your hands. When you leave, don't forget to stop and look up at the beautiful vaulted ceiling with its ornate architectural details.
*81 EIGHTH AVENUE/314 WEST 14TH STREET (NORTHWEST CORNER OF EIGHTH AVENUE AND 14TH STREET) IN MANHATTAN. Subway: A, C, E to 14th Street; L to Eighth Avenue. 212-741-3700. www.balduccis.com.*

**944. Peep:** This SoHo Thai restaurant's R-rated bathrooms aren't for the shy, but if you're up for a cheap thrill, give them a try. The walls are done in one-way glass, so the occupant (it's a single occupant bathroom) can see out into the restaurant, but the people in the restaurant only see mirrored glass. If that weren't risqué enough, there is a video screen above the sink in the bathroom that plays steamy films like *sex, lies, and videotape* on an ongoing loop. (There are also one-way-glass bathrooms at **Pukk**, an excellent vegetarian Thai restaurant in the East Village.)
**PEEP:** *177 PRINCE STREET BETWEEN SULLIVAN AND PRINCE STREETS IN MANHATTAN. Subway: C, E, to Spring Street. 212-254-7337. www.peepsoho.net.*
**PUKK:** *71 FIRST AVENUE BETWEEN 4TH AND 5TH STREETS IN MANHATTAN. Subway: F, V to Lower East Side-Second Avenue. 212-253-2741. www.pukknyc.com.*

**945. The Royalton Hotel:** The Royalton is Philippe Starck's minimalist masterpiece, a relic of clean lines and smooth surfaces that defined the early '90s. This aesthetic extends to the bathrooms off the lobby bar, where even door handles are considered too clunky. The Royalton's bathrooms were edgy before bathroom design mattered, and with mirrors reflecting your every move, the feeling inside is still a bit disconcerting. Because the stall doors have no handles, it can be difficult to figure out where you're supposed to go (no pun intended), which may not be ideal in some situations, but they are nonetheless pretty cool to look at. The real highlight, though, is the urinal "waterfall" in the men's room (sorry, ladies).
*44 WEST 44TH STREET BETWEEN FIFTH AND SIXTH AVENUES IN MANHATTAN. Subway: B, D, F, V to 42nd Street-Bryant Park; 7 to Fifth Avenue-Bryant Park. 212-869-4400. www.royaltonhotel.com.*

**946.** *The Waldorf-Astoria:* The public restrooms at the **Waldorf** (see page 37) deserve a mention because one, compared to efficient, no-frills, or high-concept modern bathrooms, they are pretty special, in an anachronistic sort of way; and two, there is so much going on in the hotel's lobby, these are really easy to slip in and use (they are across the hall from Sir Harry's Bar, near to the Park Avenue side). The décor is not stylish (some might even call it garish), but neither is it shabby or worn-looking, and there's a cozy lounge area with couches where you can hang out and rest your feet. One anachronism that may not charm everyone: the stalls are considerably narrower than most modern ones, so they can seem slightly cramped.
*301 PARK AVENUE BETWEEN 49TH AND 50TH STREETS IN MANHATTAN. Subway: 6 to 51st Street; E, V to Lexington Avenue/53rd Street. 212-255-3000. www.waldorfastoria.com.*

**947.** *Bryant Park:* Nicely kept bathrooms in city facilities are few and far between, but the public toilets in Bryant Park are among the greatest marvels of Midtown. Housed in a small but majestic stone building behind the New York Public Library, the bathrooms are under constant supervision and are kept wonderfully clean, fresh smelling, and adorned with pretty bouquets. There are simply no better public restrooms in the city.
*42ND STREET AT FIFTH AVENUE IN MANHATTAN. Subway: B, D, F, V to 42nd Street-Bryant Park; 7 to Fifth Avenue-Bryant Park.*

## Famous faces in the bar

Celebrity-owned bars aren't unique to New York—there was the infamous Viper Room in Los Angeles owned by Johnny Depp, the pharmacy-themed Damien Hirst bar in London, and U2 owns a hotel in Dublin. But in New York, where movie shoots are practically as common as street vendors, celeb-cred alone does not a destination make. There have been ventures nominally affiliated with a high-profile name or two, many of which closed once the initial buzz died down (the Fashion Café and the Britney Spears restaurant come to mind); then there are some really great places that just happen to be run or owned by someone of note. Here are the best of the latter, the ones that would be worth going to, no matter whose name was on the door, but whose backstory edges them up a notch or two.

### 948. Risk playing the jukebox at **Jimmy's Corner**,

a dive bar run by an ex-boxing manager of some repute. The walls are covered with photos of Jimmy with Ali, Tyson, and other legends of the ring, past and present, and Jimmy hovers around looking formidable and telling stories to regulars and (pretty) newcomers at the bar. The jukebox is one of the best in the city—but if you put something on that Jimmy doesn't like, he'll let you know.

*140 WEST 44TH STREET BETWEEN SIXTH AVENUE AND BROADWAY IN MANHATTAN. Subway: B, D, F, V to 42nd Street-Bryant Park. 212-221-9510.*

### 949. Commune with writers at the **Half King**.

This casual pub is owned by the writers Sebastian Junger (author of *A Perfect Storm*) and Scott Anderson. The two friends wanted to open a bar that resembled in atmosphere the journalist hangouts the two frequented while covering wars in Chechnya, Bosnia, and Sierra Leone. In 2000, they opened a modest bar in what was then a barren no-man's-land in west Chelsea, attracting both writers and journalists from around the city, as well as people from the galleries that were beginning to crop up in the neighborhood. Today, although the area is no longer considered on the fringe, the Half King remains deliberately unpretentious right down to its understated oak structure (made from a collapsed Mennonite barn in Pennsylvania) and excellent pub grub (try the fish and chips). Exhibits by photojournalists line the walls, and at the Monday night readings, expect to hear excerpts from books about child soldiers in Asia, or an exposé about the self-help industry in America. Other nights, the conversation may not be quite as heavy, but any time you go, you'll be surrounded by a thinking crowd taking refuge from the chaos on the frontlines and the headlines.

*505 WEST 23RD STREET AT TENTH AVENUE IN MANHATTAN. Subway: C, E to 23rd Street. 212-462-4300. www.thehalfking.com.*

### 950. Dance with hip-hop stars at the **40-40 Club**.

Jay-Z is one of the biggest things to have come out of New York in recent years, and 40-40, the dance club he co-owns in Flatiron, is becoming quite a big thing itself. If Mr. Z isn't there in person, you're sure to hear his tunes on every floor, and you won't be starved of other hip-hop celebrities either. The seats are leather, the bar is slate, the plasma screens are enormous, and the block is a landing strip for limos. Look your best.

*6 WEST 25TH STREET BETWEEN BROADWAY AND SIXTH AVENUES IN MANHATTAN. Subway: 1 to 23rd Street; F, V to 23rd Street; N, R, W to 23rd Street. 212-832-4040. www.the4040club.com.*

## 951. Go to **De Niro's neighborhood joints**.

Staunch New York antihero and eternal favorite son Robert De Niro can often be seen introducing friends and fellow celebrities to the delights of Tribeca Grill and **Nobu** (see page 167). Opened in the early 1990s, four years apart, these two restaurants are cornerstones of the Tribeca dining scene, and packed nightly with plenty of patrons who don't even realize whose table they are sitting at.

*Both locations in Manhattan.* TRIBECA GRILL: *375 GREENWICH STREET AT FRANKLIN STREET. Subway: 1 to Franklin Street. 212-941-3900.*

**NOBU:** *105 HUDSON STREET AT FRANKLIN STREET. Subway: 1 to Franklin Street. 212-219-0500. www.myriadrestaurantgroup.com.*

## 952. Catch a band at **Mr. Big's bar**.

Though the goal was to open a bar and live-music/performance venue with an "adult" feel, the Cutting Room still attracts youngsters yearning for a glimpse of "Mr. Big," aka Chris Noth, one of the bar's owners. However, though the former *Sex and the City* star and current *Law and Order* cast member can be spotted there, the Cutting Room is really about the music. From live jazz to vaudeville to the jukebox (Noth's personal passion), the fervor for music is intense, and given the owners' connections, they've got no problem attracting quality performers.

*19 WEST 24TH STREET BETWEEN BROADWAY AND SIXTH AVENUE IN MANHATTAN. Subway: F, V to 23rd Street; N, R, W to 23rd Street. 212-691-1900. www.thecuttingroomnyc.com.*

## 953. Karaoke with one of the great Jews in sports at **Tracey J's**.

Emblazoned across this popular karaoke spot and watering hole is a banner touting the owner, Art Heyman. Duke basketball fans will know him as the player who led the Blue Devils to their first-ever Final Four appearance in 1963; native New Yorkers may know him as a local kid from Long Island who went on to play for the Knicks. Heyman is also the only Jew ever chosen as the NBA's overall number-one draft pick. His bar is a dive of the best kind: dark, with no obvious gesture toward style, and authentically rowdy, especially on Fridays, when happy hour starts at noon. The after-work crowd gives way to the karaoke scene on Thursday, Friday, and Saturday nights, and then it kicks up again in the morning, with sports fans gathering to watch the day's games. During the day, Art often sits on a stool outside the bar reading the papers, so if you're in the neighborhood, wave as you go by.

*106 EAST 19TH STREET BETWEEN IRVING PLACE AND PARK AVENUE SOUTH IN MANHATTAN. Subway: 4, 5, 6, L, N, Q, R, W to 14th Street-Union Square. 212-674-5783. www.tracyjs.com.*

## Have a meal at a **grilled cheese restaurant**, followed by dessert from a **rice pudding restaurant**...

New York is probably the only place on the planet where a restaurant that serves only rice pudding has a better shot at making it than a Wendy's. The city has a bunch of restaurants that focus on one item—and we're not talking about donuts or ice cream. Inspired by tastes, practical concerns, or who knows what, the owners of the following restaurants decided that these particular foodstuffs were exactly what the city needed.

**954. *Say Cheese:*** Say Cheese is a favorite Hell's Kitchen lunch spot, offering a long menu of variations on the American classic, the grilled cheese sandwich. Say Cheese departs from the traditional preparation by offering a variety of imported cheeses such as Gouda and Gruyère, and fancy flavored breads from **Amy's** (see page 175). But you can also get a plain old American cheese and tomato, grilled in butter, just the way Mom used to make.
*649 NINTH AVENUE BETWEEN 44TH AND 45TH STREETS IN MANHATTAN. Subway: A, C, E to 42nd Street-Port Authority Bus Terminal. 212-265-8840.*

**955. *Rice to Riches:*** Who would have thought that a restaurant that serves only— and we mean only—rice pudding would be a hit? But Rice to Riches is a New York darling and the unofficial queen of the city's eccentric specialty restaurants. Just looking at the restaurant will make you smile—with its sleek, pod-shaped exterior, it looks like something out of *The Jetsons*. And apparently in the future, at least according to R-to-R, people have forsaken South Beach and gone back to ingesting all-American staples like cream, white sugar, and carbs. Twenty different flavors are whipped up daily, from basic vanilla and cinnamon to wild concoctions like chocolate hazelnut, maple and blueberry, French toast, and Rocky Road. The puddings can be topped with cocoa, espresso, pound cake, graham crackers, and more, and are served in colorful plastic tubs that look like futuristic Tupperware. Sizes come in solo (one person), sumo (five people), and the Moby, a ten-person pudding vat.
*37 SPRING STREET BETWEEN MOTT AND MULBERRY STREETS IN MANHATTAN. Subway: 6 to Spring Street. 212-274-0008. www.ricetoriches.com.*

**956. *Peanut Butter & Co.:*** Forget mashed potatoes and macaroni and cheese— PB&J is the real American comfort food, at least according to the folks here. Peanut Butter & Co. serves a dozen versions of the lunch-box staple made with freshly ground peanut butter. Classic sandwiches include the Lunchbox Special, with your choice of strawberry or grape jelly, and the Elvis, a grilled sandwich with bananas, honey, and bacon (optional), both served with your choice of chunky or smooth peanut butter. There are also sandwiches made with special flavored peanut butters (spicy, cinnamon raisin, white chocolate, and dark chocolate), plus peanut butter milk-shakes (with jelly or without), a host of peanut butter desserts, and the preschool snack-time favorite, Ants on a Log. Oh, and they'll cut the crusts off for no extra charge.

*240 SULLIVAN STREET BETWEEN BLEECKER AND WEST 3RD STREETS IN MANHATTAN. Sub-way: A, C, E, B, D, F, V to West 4th Street. 212-677-3995. www.IlovePeanutButter.com.*

**957. S'mac:** American or Cheddar? Breadcrumbs or without? Contentious issues among lovers of this comfort food classic, but this cheery East Village hole-in-wall caters to mac-and-cheese enthusiasts from all traditions, then forges ahead with unconventional preparations featuring gruyere, brie, goat cheese, sausage and ground beef, assorted veggies, and even roasted figs. On the sweltering July day that we checked it out, it was standing room only for the steaming skillets of gooey, cheesy mac, and though there's a green salad on the menu, we didn't see anyone eat-ing one.

*345 EAST 12TH STREET BETWEEN FIRST AND SECOND AVENUES IN MANHATTAN. Subway: L to First Avenue. 212-358-7912. www.smacnyc.com.*

**958. The Hummus Place:** The name says it all. At these downtown holes-in-the-wall, the only things you can get are heaping plates of hummus, and pita to sop it up with. But don't let the narrowness of the menu dissuade you: the hummus is so tasty that serious foodies (it was a chef who tipped us off) come from around the city to feast on one of the three preparations: plain with tahini, or topped with whole chickpeas or *foul* (cooked fava beans and soft-boiled egg). You can get it to take go, and they do deliver, but we highly recommend that you eat in—the taste of warm hummus with a sprinkle of fresh paprika on a warm pita is heavenly.

*Both locations in Manhattan. 99 MACDOUGAL STREET AT BLEECKER STREET. Subway: , A, C, E, B, D, F, V to West 4th Street. 212-533-3089; 109 SAINT MARK'S PLACE NEAR FIRST AVENUE. Subway: 6 to Astor Place; L to First Avenue. 212-529-9198.*

**959. Fresh yogurt from the Yoghurt Place II:** Gorge on rich, sinful-tasting Mediterranean yogurt covered in fresh strawberries, nuts, or honey, or get a giant tub to take home. But take our advice and stock up—after this, you'll never again be sat-isfied by the offerings at the supermarket.

*71 SULLIVAN STREET BETWEEN SPRING AND BROOME STREETS IN MANHATTAN. Subway: C, E to Spring Street. 212-219-3500.*

**960. Risotteria:** A true New York original if ever there was one—a place where food-ies, vegetarians, and celiacs can eat together! The Risotteria serves more than fifty kinds of risotto, made with three different kinds of rice. But if that weren't enough to merit an entry in this category, there's more: almost all the dishes are strictly gluten-free, so people with celiac disease (a severe intolerance to gluten that prevents suf-ferers from eating wheat, rye, barley, and most grains) can order most anything off the menu without thinking twice. There are also many vegetarian dishes. (Menu items are clearly marked as gluten-free, vegetarian, or prepared with chicken stock.) In addition to risotto, they also serve lots of gluten-free goodies, such as pizza, panini, breadsticks, and desserts, all made with rice-flour dough.

*270 BLEECKER STREET AT MORTON STREET IN MANHATTAN. Subway: 1 to Christopher Street-Sheridan Square; A, C, E, B, D, F, V to West 4th Street. 212-924-6664. wwwrisotteria.com.*

**961. *Chikalicious:*** Perhaps best not to tell the kids about this one. This East Village restaurant serves dessert, and only dessert, in three-course prix fixe meals, starting with an *amuse bouche*, and finishing with petit fours. For the main course, you choose among the menu's half-dozen gourmet dessert plates (complete with side dishes of ice cream and garnishes like toasted pecans), which change regularly. The meals cost $12 per person; you can also add wine or coffee/tea pairings ($7 and $3.50, respec-tively). But if you want a breadbasket, you'll have to go elsewhere.

*203 EAST 10TH STREET BETWEEN FIRST AND SECOND AVENUES IN MANHATTAN. Subway: L to First Avenue. 212-995-9511. www.chikalicious.com.*

## . . . or try some **one-of-a-kind fusion**.

Jewish comfort food and ceviche may sound like strange meal-fellows, but they are only one of a number of unlikely pairings that have made it onto restaurant menus. Here are several strange-but-true fusions that are worth a try. Who knows, maybe they'll catch on.

**962. *Judeo-Latino dishes at Mo Pitkins:*** Borscht and brisket are served alongside ceviche and Cuban sandwiches at this Lower East Side joint, any combination of which can be washed down with sangria or egg creams. But the diverse offerings don't stop at the menu here: the management also hosts readings, stand-up comedy, variety shows, and other performances in keeping with the offbeat spirit. Mo's is the only place in the city we know where you can hear a klezmer band and order Manis-chevitz at the bar.

*34 AVENUE A BETWEEN EAST 2ND AND 3RD STREETS IN MANHATTAN. Subway: F, V to Lower East Side-Second Avenue. 212-777-5660. www.mopitkins.com.*

**963. *Tuscan-Texan cuisine at Maremma:*** Fans of **Beppe** (see page 174) may remember the Tuscan cowboy–style ribs that chef Cesare Carella serves at his notable Flatiron restaurant, a fusion that he's expanded on at Maremma. Named for a little-traveled region of Tuscany, the restaurant is known for its "Spaghetti Western" dishes, such as the sloppy Giuseppe, Tuscan chili, and penne a la bourbon.
*228 WEST 10TH STREET BETWEEN HUDSON AND BLEECKER STREETS IN MANHATTAN. Subway: A, C, E to 14th Street; L to Eighth Avenue. 212-645-0200. www.maremmanyc.com.*

**964. *Cream puffs and cheese bread at Puff & Pao:*** This West Village snack shop serves bite-size morsels of two foreign specialties: Brazilian *pao de quiejo* (cheese bread) and French *choux* buns, more commonly known as cream puffs. The cream puffs are piped to order with your choice of cream fillings, while the paolitos, as they are called, come in a variety of savory flavors. To add to the multicultural mix, the shop has put a modern, American finish on these two traditional snacks: they offer sugar- and gluten-free options, and you can get an egg-and-paolito breakfast sandwich that's like a spiffed-up Egg McMuffin.
*105 CHRISTOPHER STREET BETWEEN BLEECKER AND HUDSON STREETS IN MANHATTAN. Subway: 1 to Christopher Street-Sheridan Square. 212-633-PUFF (7833). www.puffandpao.com.*

## 965. Race the **rubber duckies** in the East River.

Each September, tens of thousands of rubber ducks race from the Brooklyn Bridge to Pier 17 in this annual benefit for the Special Olympics. For $5, you can "adopt" a ducky to race—the training regimen is up to you.
*For more information and event date, contact the Special Olympics New York Office at 212-661-5217 or visit www.nyso.org.*

## 966. See a professional magic show at **Monday Night Magic**.

Many people think that New York is a magical city, but until fairly recently, there wasn't any place where you could actually see magic performed. Every Monday night, Monday Night Magic puts on a live show at a theater near Broadway—the only regular magic show in town. Each show features a different group of live performers, who pull off mystifying feats of escape, strength, and illusion, as well as card tricks, juggling, and comedy.
*Monday at 8:00 p.m. ST. CLEMENTS THEATER: 423 WEST 46TH STREET BETWEEN NINTH AND TENTH AVENUES IN MANHATTAN. Subway: A, C, E to 42nd Street-Port Authority Bus Terminal. 212-615-6432. www.mondaynightmagic.com.*

## 967. **Race to the top** of the Empire State Building.

High-speed elevators will whisk you up in seconds; but if you feel like you need to climb your monuments to really appreciate them, there's an annual run up the 1,576 steps to the observatory of the **Empire State Building** (see page 19). Current record: 9 minutes and 33 seconds.

*FIFTH AVENUE AT 34TH STREET IN MANHATTAN. Subway: B, D, F, V, N, Q, R, W to 34th Street-Herald Square. Observatory open daily. For more information on hours, ticket prices, and the run, visit www.esbnyc.com.*

## 968. Nominate your favorite street vendor for a **Vendy**.

If you asked us to name New York's single signature cuisine, we would have to say **street food** (see page 111 for some of our favorite offerings). Yet, as many loyal cart-followers would agree, the vendors have largely been the unsung heroes of the city's culinary scene. To remedy this, the Street Vendor Project put on the first annual Vendy Awards in 2005. Four finalists, chosen from hundreds of nominees, competed for the title in a live cook-off, which took place in one of the garages where vendors store their carts. At the event, organized by the Urban Justice Center to raise money for programs for vendors, a panel of judges crowned Rolf "Hallo Berlin" Babiel (and his bratwurst) the winner, edging out the **dosa man** in Washington Square (see page 111), a grilled chicken guy from Midtown, and an all-night Halal meat posse. Outraged by the results? Stay tuned for next year's contest, and make sure to nominate your favorite vendors.

*November. Tickets: $35. For more information on the Vendys and other events, call 646-602-5679 or visit streetvendor.netfirms.com. The Hallo Berlin bratwurst cart is located at 54TH STREET AND FIFTH AVENUE IN MANHATTAN. Subway: E, V to Fifth Avenue/53rd Street.*

## 969. Take a **hybrid**.

Town Car, meet your match. Those familiar black sedans that have long ferried high-powered execs around the city now have a formidable opponent: OZOcar, New York's eco-friendly luxury car service. The fleet is comprised of hybrid vehicles, which produce up to 89 percent less emissions than other cars. But that's not the only way they differ from the lumbering black dinosaurs: each car has satellite radio, a wireless Internet connection, and an iBook in the backseat for passengers' use during the ride. If you're not in a position to ride in them to work each day, you can still enjoy them on your next trip to the airport, or to Westchester, Long Island, or Connecticut.

*For reservations, call 866-OZO-5966 or visit www.ozocar.com.*

## 970. Go **bike jousting** in Brooklyn.

The **Black Label Bicycle Club** is a citywide society devoted to manic, violent fun on bicycles. Held in suitably sparse industrial parts of Brooklyn and Queens, the Black Label club draws masochistic cyclists from all around the country to events that resemble medieval fairs, where anyone can take part in crazy contests from bicycle polo and bike-hurling to the Whiplash, in which two bikers joined at the hip by a long rope pedal in opposite directions until the weaker is thrown from his seat. The king of these games is the joust, which involves two cyclists, armed with giant rubber lances, racing at each other to an obvious and spectacular end. The club, whose members are largely Brooklynites and who vary from city-loving cycling fanatics to *Jackass* fans, also organizes all manner of races, scavenger hunts, and rollicking dance parties. Even if you don't fancy being a competitor, it's worth turning up to an event just to see the amazing fleet of customized, vandalized, and bastardized two-wheelers that roll in.

*For details of upcoming parties, events, and locations, visit www.blacklabelnyc.com.*

## Try to catch a glimpse of an all-time favorite **New York character**.

New York is full of interesting (and interesting-looking) people, but there are a few who stand out from the rest as local celebrities. These are people whose faces or names are not necessarily recognizable outside—or, in some cases, even inside—the city but who, for whatever reason, are well known here, by profession or reputation or distinctive look. We've chosen our five favorites: a legendary hippie activist, a drag queen extraordinaire, a mild-mannered sideshow performer, a photogenic weatherman, and a very striking man with avian delusions. Unlike regular celebrities, these people can regularly be seen walking the streets, so keep your eyes open!

**971. *Adam Purple:*** For years, a man known to all as Adam Purple was a familiar sight on the Lower East Side, riding his bike wearing a purple T-shirt, sunglasses, with his long white beard flapping in the wind like a hippie Santa Claus. This elusive character is one of the most quixotic activists in New York history; legend has it that he squatted in his apartment at 184 Forsyth Street without gas, electricity, or water for almost two decades after the landlord abandoned it, apparently in protest of the city's bureaucracy. Although next to nothing is known about Adam (who has gone by a litany of other names as well), his Garden of Eden, a circular community garden that was razed by the city in 1986, is still an oft-referenced phenomenon in some circles (there is even a small movement to try to recreate it on the World Trade Center site). The garden was an amazing work of horticulture, and included fruit-bearing trees that provided free healthy snacks to people in the area. Adam hasn't been spotted in the neighborhood for quite some time, and according to a 1999 *New York Times* article, he is suspected to have finally left 184 Forsyth—but who knows? It would have been pretty out of character for him to divulge his real whereabouts to such a mainstream institution. He may well be lurking somewhere in our midst, but in the meantime, until he reappears, you can take a trip to 184 Forsyth for a glance into local activist history.

*184 FORSYTH STREET BETWEEN RIVINGTON AND STANTON STREETS IN MANHATTAN. Subway: F to Delancey Street; J, M, Z to Essex Street.*

**972. *Amanda Lepore:*** Explaining it-girl transvestite, party-hopper, and fashion muse Amanda Lepore is kind of like Justice Potter's famous description of pornography: hard to describe, but you'll know her when you see her. With her signature white-face makeup, bulbous breasts, and enormous red lips, she looks like a comic book villainess come to life. She dabbles in many creative and business pursuits—singing, modeling, merchandising—and is a regular on the New York club scene, but she's probably best known for the photographs of her taken by David LaChappelle. When she's not on photo or movie shoots, attending parties, or otherwise indisposed, she resides at the Hotel 17, from which she roams the otherwise sleepy strips of Second and Third Avenues in the teens by day (we once spotted her coming out of a dry cleaner's), and by night, she drops in on one lavish party after another.

*For more on Amanda, visit www.hotel17ny.com.*

**973. *Eak the Geek:*** In a city of unparallel diversity, Eak stands out in a crowd, owing to the constellation of tattoos running all over his body and across his face. Also known as "the painproof man," the **Coney Island sideshow** performer (see page 348) earns his living by showing off his illustrated body and being walked on while lying on a bed of nails. Eak is a fixture in the East Village, where he lives, but his popularity skyrocketed last year, when he appeared in an advertising campaign for HSBC bank, which photographed a series of New York residents to emphasize the city's diversity. If you happen to spot him, try not to stare too long—we've heard it makes him uncomfortable (he's shy).

*To read more about Eak, visit www.coneyisland.com.*

**974. *Sam Champion:*** The golden weather boy of WABC shines like a star among the drab mortals of downtown Manhattan. Living proof that television weathermen can be celebrities, too, Champion can all too often be seen (or his unmistakable broadcaster's voice overheard) in the trendiest bars and restaurants of Chelsea and the Meatpacking District. Unlikely as it is, Sam is a true local icon, a Big Apple Adonis who divines the fates of our days by proclaiming sun or rain. We dare you to ask him for a forecast.

*For more on Sam, visit www.7online.com.*

**975. *The Birdman:*** If you find yourself in Times Square on a busy afternoon and you hear—over the traffic and the crowds—a squawking, twittering, or whistling from an eccentric-looking man with wings tattooed across his chest and feathers in his fedora, don't be alarmed: he is the Birdman of Times Square. This ornithological stranger is a familiar face around the area, and like all rare birds, should be photographed quickly upon sighting.

*TIMES SQUARE, BROADWAY AND 42ND STREET. Subway: 1, 2, 3, 7, N, Q, R, W, S to Times Square-42nd Street.*

## 976. Take the **Steinway factory tour** . . .

For over 150 years, Steinway guarded its manufacturing process with the ferocity of a prize-winning baker. The world-class instruments produced by the legendary family-owned company were crafted in secrecy, and exactly how they got the uprights and baby grands to play so beautifully was a mystery—until now. Recently, the factory in Queens has started giving tours, albeit on a restricted and reservations-only schedule. Steinway makes fewer than 5,000 pianos per year, each one a yearlong endeavor of sawing, sanding, fittings, and stringing. On the two-and-a-half-hour tour, viewers are privy to the exacting and meticulous processes that go into the construction of these precious pieces—they see, for instance, the "Pounder Room," where a machine bangs on all of the keys of each piano 10,000 times to make sure the sound is correct.

*1 STEINWAY PLACE (NINETEENTH AVENUE AND 38TH STREET) IN QUEENS. Reservations required. Subway: N, W to Astoria-Ditmars Boulevard. For reservations, call 718-721-2600 x3164. www.steinway.com.*

## 977. . . . or see the famous fan mail at **Steinway Hall**.

Also of interest to music lovers is Steinway Hall, the lavish, historic piano gallery in Midtown. In addition to three floors displaying some of the finest musical instruments in the world, there is the Rotunda, a dome-topped room filled with art, paintings, and memorabilia from Steinway's illustrious 150-year history, including displays of fan mail from everyone from Rachmaninoff to Thomas Edison. Below ground, there is the famous piano bank, where loaner pianos for traveling concert musicians are kept.

*109 WEST 57TH STREET AT SIXTH AVENUE IN MANHATTAN. Subway: N, Q, R, W to 57th Street. 212-246-1100. www.steinwayhall.com.*

→ **DID YOU KNOW?** *Ninety-eight percent of concert pianists play on Steinway pianos.*

## 978. See the gold at the **Federal Reserve Bank of New York**.

Eighty feet below Liberty Street in the heart of downtown Manhattan, locked in a maximum security vault to which no one individual holds all the keys and codes, sits nearly a third of the world's monetary gold reserves. The Federal Reserve Bank has held the U.S. reserves on these premises for nearly a century, since it was decided in 1924 that the very bedrock of Manhattan, fifty feet below sea level, was the safest place to hide all that bullion (and the strongest, because a vault like this needs a sturdy floor). Call in advance and reserve a place on a tour of the Gold Vault, and you'll come as close as you will ever get to ten billion dollars' worth of solid gold bars—and you'll learn something of the history of the city while you're at it.

*33 LIBERTY STREET BETWEEN BROAD AND WILLIAM STREETS IN MANHATTAN. Subway: J, M, Z to Broad Street. 212-720-5000. www.ny.frb.org.*

## 979. Hang out in the limo at **David Burke & Donatella** . . .

This is a best thing to do only if you're a smoker, although it's quite a sight and a clever gimmick. To attract patrons in the wake of the city's smoking ban in restaurants, this upscale Midtown restaurant has a stretch limo parked outside the restaurant every night during the winter months (except Sundays), so smokers can puff away out of the cold. With seating for eight to ten people, the limo often evolves into its own social scene, as people climb in with their drinks and sit shoulder-to-shoulder with their fellow smokers. Note: The chef David Burke also has a restaurant across the street, on the ground floor of **Bloomingdale's** (see page 241).

*133 EAST 61ST STREET BETWEEN LEXINGTON AND THIRD AVENUES IN MANHATTAN. Subway: 4, 5, 6 to 59th Street; F to Lexington Avenue/63rd Street; N, R, W to Lexington Avenue/59th Street. 212-813-2121. www.dbdrestaurant.com.*

## 980. . . . or drape yourself in **Balthazar furs**.

Diners who take a tobacco break on the wooden benches outside **Balthazar** (see page 163) during the colder months can expect to be followed out by the dutiful waitstaff and draped in luxurious blankets of fur—the perfect way to keep SoHo's most civilized smokers toasty and warm between courses.

*80 SPRING STREET BETWEEN BROADWAY AND CROSBY STREET IN MANHATTAN. Subway: 6 to Spring Street; N, R, W to Prince Street. 212-965-1414. www.balthazarny.com.*

## 981. Learn everything you want to know about living in New York (and then some) through **Manhattan User's Guide**.

Quick, what's the city's largest park? Where were the original Oreos made? And who is Donna Faske? The answers to these questions and countless others can be found on Manhattan User's Guide, or MUG, an unrivaled source of information on every-thing and anything New York. Every weekday, it publishes an informative e-newslet-ter on a subject of particular local interest, from entertainment and goings on (i.e., upcoming sample sales and restaurant reviews) to practical information (instructions on how to register a complaint with the city, for instance), to things you never would have thought to ask (like the number of unsolved murders). The articles are then archived on the site, where you can look them up any time you feel the urge. There is also a monthly quiz of New York trivia (with some questions that stumped even your authors), and photos by **Joseph O. Holmes** (see page 80) of a different New York scene each day. MUG covers everything—arts, dining, sports, shopping—but the most interesting articles are in the "Services" and "Info" categories, where you'll find information on topics like organ donation, how to take your landlord to court, or where to find someone to clean a hat, fix a typewriter, disassemble a sofa, or sharpen knives. P.S.: The answers to the questions above are Pelham Bay Park, the old Nabisco factory (now the Chelsea Market), and Donna Karan.

*Subscription is free. Visit www.manhattanusersguide.com for more information or to subscribe.*

## At our service.

New York is a mecca for those with an entrepreneurial spirit, and thanks to the surplus of creative people looking for a niche, the city supports a bunch of eccentric-sounding services that are geared toward the idiosyncrasies of a Big Apple lifestyle. We've also included one pop-ular service that New Yorkers can use to provide something for others.

**982. *Give your clothes all the comforts of home by sending them to the Ladies Who Launder.*** "Even better than your mom" proclaims this lovely laundry service. When we asked New Yorkers to name their favorite thing about the city, a disproportionate number replied, "Having your laun-dry done and delivered." (Almost as many as those who chose **food deliv-ery**—see page 331.) The combination of childhood nostalgia and the paucity of on-site laundry facilities in apartment buildings makes this posh-sounding service a non-negotiable luxury to many New Yorkers. But not all wash-and-deliver services are of the same caliber, and few do the job with the TLC you remember from your youth. The Ladies Who Launder are like moms with a delivery van: women who wash your clothes with care, and bring them to your doorstep. They do far more than separate the lights from the darks: they are experts at stain removal, know what delicates are and how to treat them, and will follow any special instructions you provide. The basic service is competitive with most other laundries; for an additional fee, they will also hand-wash or iron. They pick up anywhere in Manhattan, whether or not you have a doorman, and bring back items within 48 hours. They also do dry cleaning, something even mom couldn't pull off.

*For more information, schedules, and rates, call 212-828-3800 or visit www.ladieswholaunder.com.*

**983. *Order reflexology from Cloud Nine.*** Masseuses who make house calls? Old news. Cloud Nine can bring reflexology—a healing and relaxation treatment that stimulates organs through pressure points in the hands and feet—directly to you. These practitioners will travel to your home or office, anywhere in Manhattan, and to certain locations in Brooklyn and Queens.

*$100 for sixty minutes. For information and to make an appointment, call 212-714-3921 or visit www.cloudninereflexology.com.*

**984. *Ask and receive with MaxDelivery.*** The ideal service for the downtown idler, MaxDelivery.com is a deli, drugstore, video store, and novelty shop. Customers below 24th Street on the West Side and 26th Street on the East Side can call MaxDelivery and arrange for an immediate delivery of anything from shampoo and soda to fresh food, cigarettes, razor blades, and DVD rentals. Orders are guaranteed to arrive within the hour, and they even carry cards, gifts, and wrapping paper for urgent, last-minute forgotten birthday, holiday, or anniversary presents. They have also put together special packages for different occasions, such as "Sick in Bed," "Exam Cram," and "Date Night." Outside of Max's range? Zip codes are added regularly, so check www.maxdelivery.com.

*Check online for details of stock, delivery rates, and delivery locations.*

**985. *Get your sweaters rewoven at French-American.*** Reweaving—the meticulous process of mending other woven garments by hand—is a dying art. French-American Reweaving is one of the few places in the country where you can get sweaters, jackets, and other clothing items repaired by professional reweavers. French-American has been around since 1930, and has fixed the torn and moth-eaten garments of Leonard Bernstein, Gloria Swanson, and Mrs. Lionel Hampton. Each tear is evaluated and then repaired using one or more of a variety of methods. Because of the labor involved, jobs take much longer than alterations at a local tailor, and can cost anywhere from $50 to $500 (depending on the work needed), but if you're attached to the article, a few days and few extra bucks is a small price to pay for a service that produces such results—and is nearly impossible to find anywhere else.

*119 WEST 57TH STREET, ROOM 1406, BETWEEN SIXTH AND SEVENTH AVENUES IN MANHATTAN. Subway: N, Q, R, W to 57th Street. 212-765-4670.*

**986. *Start your own business at Your Neighborhood Office.*** New York is full of entrepreneurs who spend their lives in line at the post office, freelancers who don't leave their apartments for fear of missing a package, and a whole lot of other people who can't afford the cost of office space. Your Neighborhood Office is a genius niche service that caters to these atypical professionals by making available to them the office services that a business needs to survive in this town. It messengers packages, receives mail, writes and prints brochures, sorts, labels and sends out mailings, sends and receives faxes, provides supplies and legal forms, and performs virtually any other office service you could ever need—so you can toil away on your screenplay/business plan/first novel without a care.
*332 BLEECKER STREET BETWEEN WEST 10TH AND CHRISTOPHER STREETS IN MAN-HATTAN. Subway: 1 to Christopher Street-Sheridan Square. 212-989-8303. www.neighborhoodoffice.com.*

**987. *Get the closet of your dreams from GardeRobe.*** GardeRobe is a luxury clothing storage company that fulfills the number-one wish of New Yorkers: more closet space. Clients can store "racks" of clothing (up to fifty items per rack, which also includes a special storage box for accessories and ten shoe boxes) in the temperature-controlled, air-purified, video-moni-tored GardeRobe loft. The items are photographed, cataloged, and then posted online in the Cyber Closet, where you can search, review, and request items. Items can be requested anytime, as often as you want; they are delivered at no extra charge, within hours, at your convenience, and then get picked up, professionally cleaned with any repairs or alterations needed, and returned to your rack. At $350 per rack, per month, it may sound extravagant to people with a basement or a garage, but consider that it costs over $300 per month for a medium-sized storage cube here, and that doesn't come with delivery! GardeRobe's services aren't just for New Yorkers—frequent travelers can use them as a way of keeping the fash-ion equivalent of a pied-à-terre.
*For more information, and to sign up, call 212-255-3047. www.garderobeonline.com.*

**988. *Help out Santa and the post office on Christmas.*** In the 1920s, inspired by the number of letters they received for Santa, postal workers in New York asked the public to assist them with Operation Santa, inviting them to come to the **General Post Office** (see page 319) to pick out letters and answer the children's wishes. Today, the post office receives more than 150,000 letters each year, from all over the world, mostly from poor, inner-city kids. All you have to do is go to the post office sometime in December, select as many letters as you want, and fill the children's requests by Christmas Day. (If you don't live in New York, you can still participate by requesting letters from the post office here, or by contacting your local post office to see if it runs a similar charity.)

*421 EIGHTH AVENUE AT 33RD STREET IN MANHATTAN. Subway: 1, 2, 3, A, C, E to 34th Street-Penn Station. 212-330-3084. www.operationlettertosanta.com.*

## 989. Decorate like a TV star at **Props for Today**.

Every hit television show filmed on location in New York City needs props, and no one wants the same props twice. Props for Today takes care of the problem. When Carrie Bradshaw is through with her pillows and Conan O'Brien is done with his couches, Props for Today moves in for the kill, picks up the debris, and sells it to their adoring public. Thanks to moderate prices and helpful tags that detail the merchandise's televised life—which episode of *CSI* or *Saturday Night Live* a piece was used on, say, or which celebrity's behind warmed it up for you—you, too, can decorate your home to resemble the set of your favorite TV show.

*330 WEST 34TH STREET BETWEEN EIGHTH AND NINTH AVENUES IN MANHATTAN. Subway: 1, 2, 3, A, C, E to 34th Street-Penn Station. 212-244-9600. www.propsfortoday.com.*

## 990. Enroll in Miss Vera's Finishing School for **Boys Who Want to be Girls**.

The name of this prestigious Manhattan academy says it all. A veteran of the adult entertainment industry and a tireless researcher into the preferences and practices of modern Americans, Miss Vera opened her transvestite's finishing school to boost the confidence of those who feel held back and to polish up the acts of those already living the life. With a faculty of experts to offer individual or group instruction, and with classes that cover everything from walking in heels and applying makeup to focusing a more feminine sexual energy and refining a suitable voice, Miss Vera's school aims to improve every aspect of the "Cinderfella experience." Classes cost between $500 and $4,000 and take place on campus, with occasional field trips around the city.

*For more information, class descriptions, and locations, call 212-242-6449 or visit www.missvera.com.*

## 991. Take the **Great Saunter**.

Once a year in early summer, a group of seasoned amblers meets at the South Street Seaport to begin a daylong walk along the entire perimeter of Manhattan. The **Shorewalkers** (see page 235), a nonprofit organization dedicated to the preservation, improvement, and above all, the appreciation of the city's coastal walkways and vistas, have been holding walks, tours, and other events for likeminded city enthusiasts for twenty-five years, and the annual Great Saunter is their greatest adventure. A thirty-two-mile hike taken at a strolling pace, the walk begins at 7:30 a.m. and usually lasts a full twelve hours, moving from the island's southernmost tip up the West Side, around Inwood Hill Park at the northernmost end, along the Harlem River, down the East Side and back to the Seaport by suppertime. Hardened amblers can make the full tour, while part-timers are welcome to join the walk at any point for any length to enjoy the route's beautiful vistas.

*For more information and updates on events like the Great Saunter, visit*
*www.shorewalkers.org.*

## Citizens: Know your subway entertainers!

New York's rambling and irrepressible subway system is a perpetual stage for the most eclectic and prolific cast of buskers and street entertainers in the world. With each train characterized by the neighborhoods and ethnic enclaves along its route (as well as the amount of tourist spots it runs through), each line has its own brand of entertainment, its own set of characters, and its own trademark sights and sounds. The world of busking is a fickle one: while some performers forge careers that span decades, new acts arrive on the scene almost daily; and though there are some amazingly talented types working the MTA circuit, not everybody would agree that a mariachi band clamoring inside a packed commuter train is a good idea. Look out for these stalwarts of the underground scene and judge for yourself:

**992. *The Brighton Trumpeter:*** An inexhaustible old man with a poor grasp of English, this experienced trumpet player blows traditional, rousing Russian melodies over backing tracks that blare from a CD player strapped to his chest.
*Q train.*

**993. *Hip-Hop Acrobats:*** An impressive duo of athletic kids who get in a subway car, set down a stereo, and perform amazing turns and break

dancing moves in the impossibly narrow walkways between seats—all while the train is moving. Their signature move is a linked somersault, during which they grab each other's ankles to form a ball and roll from one end of the car to the other, swerving unerringly past poles and passengers to the sound of "Thriller."
*A train.*

**994.** *Museum Mile Mariachi:* Targeting tourists as their primary audience, this Mexican three-piece has perfected the art of the two-minute fiesta, striking up as the doors close in one station and reaching a passionate climax as the train draws to a halt at the next. They are a tight outfit, from well-rehearsed performances to the ornately sequined authentic mariachi jumpsuits.
*4, 5, 6 trains.*

**995.** *Midtown Break-dancers:* If you come upon a circle of people congregated in the concourses of Midtown's bigger terminals, it's probably the crowd surrounding one of the city's teams of break-dancers who commandeer corners of the station to perform elaborate choreographed routines, dressed in matching Adidas jackets, accompanied by loud, old-school hip-hop.
*Times Square and Grand Central stations.*

**996.** *Gospel Barbershop Quartet:* A relic, perhaps, of the soulful subways of the '60s and '70s, this group of beautiful and varied voices reworks classic Motown hits in the barbershop quartet style. When they're performing formally (standing together by a doorway), the spectacle is enthralling; but catching them rehearsing on quiet rides, when they sit apart, move around, and don't even look at each other while they sing and work out new harmonies, is a genuine thrill.
*A train.*

# Expert Contributor: A. J. Jacobs

A. J. Jacobs is a writer and New York native. He is the editor-at-large of *Esquire* and the author of several books, including *The Know-It-All: One Man's Humble Quest to be the Smartest Person in the World* (2004), about a year he spent reading the entire *Encyclopædia Britannica*. (You can read more about him at www.ajjacobs.com.)

## MY FIVE FAVORITE THINGS I LEARNED ABOUT NEW YORK FROM THE ENCYCLOPEDIA

**997.** Short story writer **O. Henry** came up with one of the all-time greatest nicknames for New York: "Baghdad on the Subway" (sometimes misquoted as "Baghdad on the Hudson," after another one of his NYC pet names, "Yaptown on the Hudson"). He meant it as a compliment, referring to the magical, cosmopolitan, and culturally rich city of Scheherazade's *1001 Arabian Nights*. Still, we doubt that the Chamber of Commerce will be adopting it anytime soon.
*For more on O. Henry, see entry on Pete's Tavern, page 43.*

**998.** In New York, everyone's got a real-estate horror story. But in 1667, the Dutch engaged in the single worst real-estate deal in history. They traded Manhattan to Britain, in exchange for the South American country of Suriname. However, a bit of the Dutch legacy can still be seen at the **Collegiate School**, an elite secondary school for boys, which is the oldest educational institution in the country (it was founded in 1628). The school mascot is "the Dutchman."
*Collegiate is located at the* **WEST SIDE COLLEGIATE CHURCH:** *260 WEST 78TH STREET AT WEST END AVENUE IN MANHATTAN. Subway: 1 to 79th Street. www.collegiateschool.org.*

**999.** With a street, hotel, parkway, bridge, and 300-mile river named after him, **Henry Hudson** is one of the city's most popular pre-Revolutionary celebrities. Unfortunately, he wasn't so beloved by his crewmembers. In 1611, during a voyage up the waters in Canada, his crew mutinied and sent him off to die in a rowboat.
*For more activities on the Hudson River, see chapter 6, "The Great Outdoors."*

**1000.** We all know the *New York Times*' famous motto: "All the News That's Fit to Print." But I actually prefer the paper's slogan from the early twentieth century: "It will not soil the breakfast cloth."
**THE NEW YORK TIMES BUILDING** *is located at 229 WEST 43RD STREET BETWEEN SEVENTH AND EIGHTH AVENUES IN MANHATTAN. Subway: 1, 2, 3, 7, N, Q, R, W, S to Times Square-42nd Street. 212-556-1234. www.nytimes.com.*

**1001.** The **Empire State Building** shrank eighteen feet in 1985—from 1,472 feet to 1,454—because the old antenna was replaced. That doesn't make the ride—or run—to the top any shorter.

*FIFTH AVENUE AT 34TH STREET IN MANHATTAN. Subway: B, D, F, V, N, R, Q, W to 34th Street-Herald Square. 212-736-3100. www.esbnyc.com. For more information, see full entry on page 19. For Empire State Building lights, see page 316. For Empire State Building Run, see page 360.*

# THE BEST NEW YORK WEBSITES

## General Information:

**www.hopstop.com**
See page 103.

**www.lowermanhattan.info**
An invaluable website devoted to the communities and development of downtown Manhattan, and a great place to find out about new places to go and things to do south of Canal Street.

**www.manhattanusersguide.com**
See page 364.

**www.mta.info**
The website for the Metropolitan Transit Authority, with maps, schedules, and information about subways, buses, Metro-North, and the Long Island Railroad. You can also check for night and weekend services advisories.

**www.nycgovparks.org**
The Department of Parks and Recreation website, with information on events, facilities and programs in parks in all five boroughs.

**www.nymetro.com**
NYMetro.com, the online version of New York magazine, is hands-down the best source on the web for listings (stores, restaurants, services, museums, parks, etc), information, and addresses. It beats comparable sites for its thoroughness, up-to-date and informative content, and straightforward and user-friendly layout.

**www.smalltownbrooklyn.com**
This website has up-to-date street-by-street listings of Brooklyn storefronts. It also marks where the subways are.

**www.timeoutny.com**
The NY annex of the world's most popular what's-on guide. A good place to find out about events around town for the coming week.

## Dining:

**www.menupages.com**
See page 331.

**www.opentable.com**
Free online reservation service with more than 600 area restaurants.

**www.strongbuzz.com**
News, reviews, and articles and restaurants and food-related events around the city by Andrea Strong (see page 173).

# Entertainment:

**www.cityparksfoundation.org**
The website for the foundation that organizes programming in city parks. The website includes information and events on their programs, including concerts and events, sports, and education. Lots of stuff for kids.

**www.freenyc.net**
Everything free in New York: Concerts, parties, museums, film screenings, and other events. Updated daily.

**www.go-brooklyn.com**
An excellent resource for finding out about events in Brooklyn, organized by day. Also has a Brooklyn dining guide.

**www.jimsdeli.com**
Information and listings for hotels, Broadways shows, museums, music and dance, nightlife, sports, and other events.

**www.nycstreetfairs.com**
This is the website for Mardi Gras Productions, the company that puts on most of the street fairs around the city. The website has a calendar of all their fairs for the current or upcoming season.

**www.playbill.com**
The best source for information on theater in New York, and online ticketseller. Discounts on tickets, restaurants and hotels are available to members (membership is free).

# Misellaneous & Fun

**www.barrypopik.com**
Contains information, history, commentary, about New York, edited by Barry Popik, an administrative judge and etymologist credited with discovering the origin of the nickname "the Big Apple".

**www.craiglist.com**
See page 299.

**www.forgotten-ny.com**
See page 98.

**www.movie-locations.com**
This website has a list of movies shot in New York, with places and addresses from them.

**www.songlines.com**
See page 97.

**www.thebathroomdiaries.com**
This site has listings of public restrooms around the world, rated by users. You can search for ones in different neighborhoods in all of the five boroughs.

**www.watsonadvenutres.com/culture**
The website for this walking tour company (see page 104) issues a monthly online newsletter with lots of New York trivia.

# INDEX

## BY NEIGHBORHOOD

## BRONX

## BROOKLYN

CALENDAR OF EVENTS

## FREE ACTIVITIES

## RESTAURANTS, FOOD MARKETS, AND BARS

CAITLIN LEFFEL, a native New Yorker, is a writer and editor who has contributed to *Daily Candy* and *Publishers Weekly*.

JACOB LEHMAN, a recent arrival to the Big Apple, works in the editorial division of a major New York publisher. This is their first book.